CATALOGUE
OF THE
Museum of Archaeology at Sarnath

CATALOGUE
OF THE
Museum of Archaeology at Sarnath

BY

DAYA RAM SAHNI, M.A.

Assistant Superintendent, Archaeological Survey of Inida

WITH AN INTRODUCTION BY

Dr. J. PH. VOGEL, Ph.D.

Superintendent, Archaeological Survey, Northern Circle

GYAN

Published by

Gyan Publishing House
5, Ansari Road
Daryaganj, New Delhi-110002
Phone: 011-47034999, 9811692060
E-mail: books@gyanbooks.com

Distribution Network
gyanbooks.com
India, USA, Canada, UK, Australia, France

ISBN : 978-81-212-2432-1 (HB)
First Published, 1914

2nd Impression 2021

Printed at: Gyan Press, Delhi.

Catalogue
of the
Museum of Archaeology at Sarnath
Author: Daya Ram Sahni

CATALOGUE

OF THE

Museum of Archaeology at Sārnāth

BY

DAYA RAM SAHNI, M.A.

Assistant Superintendent, Archaeological Survey of India

WITH AN INTRODUCTION BY

Dr. J. PH. VOGEL, Ph.D.

Superintendent, Archaeological Survey, Northern Circle

CALCUTTA
SUPERINTENDENT GOVERNMENT PRINTING, INDIA
1914

PREFACE.

THE creation of a local Museum at Sārnāth was due to the initiative of Dr. J. H. Marshall, C.I.E., Director-General of Archæology in India, who during two seasons personally conducted the excavations on this important Buddhist site. The plans were prepared by Mr. James Ransome, late Consulting Architect to the Government of India. As at the end of the cold season of 1908-09, when the building was nearly completed, Dr. Marshall proceeded home on long leave, it fell to my task to take measures for the proper arrangement of the sculptures in the new quarters. The work of arranging and labelling was done in the cold season following under the personal supervision of Lala Daya Ram Sahni, M.A., who had taken an active part in Dr. Marshall's explorations, and was, therefore, well qualified for the task. At the same time he prepared a catalogue of the exhibits which is now offered to the public.

The labels on the objects themselves are, of necessity, very brief, and it has, therefore, been our aim in the present catalogue to embody all information which may be of interest both to the dilettante and to the expert. The order followed in listing the exhibits is chiefly chronological. At the same time it seemed advisable, for practical purposes, to adopt a division into three main sections—images (B), bas-reliefs (C) and architectural pieces (D)—corresponding to the arrangement of the sculptures in the galleries. It will be noticed that the first gallery adjoining the central hall has been reserved for images, whilst the architectural pieces have been arranged in the second gallery which forms the southern wing of the Museum building. The central hall contains mainly large-sized images, besides the Aśōka capital described in the first section of the catalogue. It is true that, with the exception of a very few statues which are in the round, all the images so-called, are carved in relief and that architectural pieces are frequently decorated with figures of Buddha or with scenes of his life. It is, therefore, not always easy to decide to which section a particular sculpture should be relegated. On the whole, however, the method of grouping followed seems to have distinct advantages for the purpose of comparative study.

In assigning the sculptures to certain periods we can in several cases rely on inscriptions which afford a firm chronological basis, even if they are not dated and one has to depend on palæographical evidence alone. In the great majority of cases, however, the only means of dating a sculpture has been the testimony of style. Such evidence is at first sight sometimes deceptive, as, apart from the characteristics of a certain school or of a certain period, there is the element of the skill of the individual artisan to be taken into account. Thus a piece of sculpture, apparently debased and consequently late, may be merely the production of a bad workman. On the whole, however, the sculptures of Maurya, Śuṅga, Kushāṇa, Gupta and Mediæval[1] periods represent very distinct types and within those main divisions, at least, may, in nearly all cases, be classified with confidence.

In an introductory note I have given a brief account of the ancient site of the Deer-park (the modern Sārnāth), of the explorations carried out on this locality for more than a century and of the sculptures which in the course of these explorations have come to light. Those who wish for more detailed information, are referred to the works cited in my bibliographical list.

J. Ph. VOGEL, Ph.D.,

Superintendent, Archæological Survey of India.

---

[1] The Mediæval period we have subdivided in early Mediæval (600—900 A.D.) and late Mediæval (900—1200 A. D.).

CONTENTS.

Introduction.

Catalogue.

B.—Images.

C.—Bas-reliefs.

D.—Architectural pieces and inscribed slabs.

F.—Terracottas.

LIST OF PLATES.

BIBLIOGRAPHY.

A.—Buddhist Texts.

The Vinaya Piṭakam, one of the principal Buddhist holy scriptures in the Pali language. Edited by Hermann Oldenberg. London, 1879-83. Vol. I, pages 7-14 (I, 6).

Vinaya texts, translated from the Pali by T. W. Rhys Davids and Hermann Oldenberg. [Sacred books of the East, Vol. XIII.] Part I, pages 89-102. Mahâvagga I, 6.

The Jātaka together with its commentary, being tales of the anterior births of Gotama Buddha. Edited by V. Fausböll. London, 1877. [Nidāna-kathā] Vol. I, pages 81 f.

Buddhist birth stories or Jātaka tales, being the Jātakatthavaṇṇanā, translated by T. W. Rhys Davids. London, 1880. Vol. I, pp. 112 f.

Lalita Vistara herausgegeben von Dr. S. Lefmann. Halle, 1902. Vol. I, pages 402-438 [Chapter XXVI, Dharmachakra-pravartana-parivarta].

Le Lalita Vistara. Dévelopement des jeux contenant l'histoire du Bouddha Çakya-mouni depuis sa naissance jusqu'à sa prédictation traduit du Sanskrit en Français par Ph. Ed. Foucaux. [Annales du Musée Guimet, Vol. VI.] Paris, 1884. Part I, pages 335-368, Chapter XXVI.

Le Mahāvastu. Texte Sanscrit publié pour la premiere fois et accompagné d'introductions et d'un commentaire par E. Senart. Paris, 1882-97. Vol. III, pages 329 seq.

The Buddha-Carita of Aśvaghosha, edited by E. B. Cowell. [Anecdota Oxoniensia, Aryan Series, Part VII.] Oxford, 1893. XV, 84—XVII, 8 (pages 135-157).

The Buddha Carita of Aśvaghosha, translated by E. B. Cowell. [Buddhist Mahāyāna Texts, Sacred Books of the East, Vol. XLIX.] XV, 84—XVII, 8 (pages 168-192).

B.—Chinese Pilgrims.

A record of Buddhistic kingdoms, being an account by the Chinese Monk Fā-Hien of his travels in India and Ceylon (A. D. 399-414). Translated by James Legge. Oxford, 1886, pages 94-96.

Histoire de la vie de Hiouen-Thsang et de ses voyages dans l'Inde, depuis l'an 629 jusqu'en 645, suivie de documents et d'éclaircissements géographiques tirés de la relation originale de Hiouen-Thsang ; traduite du chinois par Stanislas Julien. Paris, 1853.

Hiouen-Thsang. *Mémoires sur les contrées occidentales,* tradits du Sanscrit en Chinois, en l'an 648, et du Chinois en Français par Stanislas Julien. Paris, 1857-58.

Hwui Li and Yen Tsung. *The life of Hiuen-Tsiang.* With a preface containing an account of the works of Itsing. By Samuel Beal. London, 1888.

Hiuen Tsiang. *Si-yu-ki. Buddhist Records of the Western World.* Translated by Samuel Beal. London, 1884. Vol. II, pages 44-61.

Thomas Watters. *On Yuan Chwang's travels in India, 629-645 A. D.* London, 1904-05. [Oriental Translation Fund. New Series, Vols. XIV-XV.] Vol. II, pages 46-59.

I-tsing. *A record of the Buddhist religion as practised in India and the Malay Archipelago* (*A. D. 671-695*). Translated by J. Takakusu. Oxford, 1896. See index i. v., Deer-park (*Mṛigadāva*).

C.—Exploration and Research.

Jonathan Duncan. *An account of the discovery of two urns in the vicinity of Benares* in Asiatic Researches. Vol. V (1798), pages 131 f.; with copy of inscriptions. (Cf. also Vol. IX, page 203.)

Wilford. *Vicramaditya and Salivahana their respective Eras with an account of the Bala Rayas or Balhar Emperors* in Asiatick Researches. Vol. IX (1807), pp. 203-205. (Cf. also Vol. X (1808), pp. 129-133.)

James Prinsep. *Further particulars of the Sárun and Tirhut Láths, and account of two Buddha inscriptions found, the one at Bakhra, in Tirhut, the other at Sārnāth near Benares* in Journal Asiatic Society of Bengal, Vol. IV (1835), pages 124-138; with plate.

Kittoe's *Drawings,* Vol. I. India Office Library. No. 83. Case 3-5.

E. Thomas. *Note on the present state of the excavations at Sārnāth* in Journal Asiatic Society of Bengal, Vol. XXIII (1854), pages 469-477; with 3 plates.

E. Thomas. *Correspondence relating to the explorations of the ruins of Sārnāth* in Journal Asiatic Society of Bengal. Vol. XXV (1856), page 395.

List of articles dug up at Sārnāth, the ancient Buddhist holy ground near Benares, under the superintendence of Professor F. E. Hall, and left by him on his departure for Ajmere in June 1855 under my charge. Ibidem, page 399.

A. Cunningham. *Archæological Survey of India, Reports.* Vol. I (1871), pages 103-130; Vol. III (1873), pages 121 f.; Vol. VIII (1878), page 16; Vol. XI (1880), page 181 f.

A. Rivett-Carnac. *Figure of Buddha recently found at Sārnāth* in Proceedings Asiatic Society of Bengal for 1878, page 68.

J. Anderson. *Catalogue of the archæological collections in the Indian Museum.* Calcutta, 1883. Part II, pages 1-31.

E. Hultzsch. *The Sārnāth inscription of Mahīpāla* in Indian Antiquary, Vol. XIV (1885), pages 139 f.

J. F. Fleet. [*Corpus Inscriptionum Indicarum*, Vol. III.] *Inscriptions of the early Gupta kings and their successors*, Calcutta, 1888. [Page 281, No. 75, plate XLII *C*. *Sārnāth stone inscription.* Pages 284-286, No. 79 ; plate XLIII *C*. *Sārnāth stone inscription of Prakaṭāditya.*]

J. Ph. Vogel. *Buddhist sculptures from Benares* in Archæological Survey of India, Annual Report, 1903-04. Calcutta, 1906, pages 212-226; plates LXII-LXIV.

F. O. Oertel. *Excavations at Sārnāth in* Archæological Survey of India, Annual Report, 1904-05. Calcutta, 1908, pages 59-104 ; Plates XV-XXXII.

J. Ph. Vogel. *Epigraphical discoveries at Sārnāth* in Epigraphia Indica, Vol. VIII (1905-06), pages 166-179 ; with two plates.

A. Venis. *Some notes on the so-called Mahīpāla inscription at Sārnāth* in Journal and Proceedings of the Asiatic Society of Bengal. New Series, Vol. II, 1906, pages 445-447.

A. Venis. *Some notes on the Maurya inscription at Sārnāth* in Journal and Proceedings, Asiatic Society of Bengal. New Series, Vol. III (1907), pages 1-7.

E. Senart. *Une nouvelle inscription d'Asoka.* Comptes Rendus des séances de l'Académie des Inscriptions et Belles-Lettres (1907), pages 25 ff.

Boyer. *L'inscription de Sārnāth et ses parallèles d'Allahābād et de Sānchi.* Journal Asiatique, 10th Series, Vol. X (1907), pages 119 ff.

F. O. Oertel. *Some remarks on the excavations at Sārnāth carried out in the year 1904-05* in Indian Antiquary. Vol. XXXVII (1908), pages 227-280 ; with plate.

J. H. Marshall. *Archæological exploration in India, 1906-07*, in Journal Royal Asiatic Society for 1907, XXXIII [Sārnāth], pages 995-1000 ; plates II-IV.

J. H. Marshall and Sten Konow. *Sārnāth* in Archæological Survey of India, Annual Report for 1906-07. Calcutta 1909, pages 68-101 ; plates XVII-XXX.

J. H. Marshall. *Archæological Exploration in India, 1907-08*, in Journal Royal Asiatic Society for 1908, XXVII [Sārnāth], pages 1088-1095 ; plates II-IV.

J. H. Marshall and Sten Konow. *Excavations at Sārnāth, 1908,* in Archæological Survey of India, Annual Report for 1907-08. Calcutta, 1911, pages 43-80 ; plates XI-XXI.

Sten Konow. *Two Buddhist inscriptions from Sārnāth* in Epigraphia Indica, Vol. IX (1907-08), No. 43, pages 291-293 ; with two plates.

Sten Konow. *Sārnāth inscription of Kumaradēvī* in Epigraphia Indica, Vol. IX (1907-08), No. 51, pages 319-328, with plate.

T. Bloch. *Ueber einige bildliche Darstellungen altindischer Gottheiten* in Zeitschrift der Deutschen Morgenländischen Gesellschaft. Vol. LXII (1908), pages 653 f.

Vincent A. Smith. *Identification of the Aśoka Pillar north-east of Benares City described by Hiuen Tsiang* in Zeitschrift der Deutschen Morgenländischen Gesellschaft. Vol. LXIII (1909), pages 337-345.

A. Venis. *Note on the Sārnāth inscription of Aśvaghosha* in Journal Royal Asiatic Society for 1912, pages 701-703 [with additional note by Dr. J. F. Fleet, pages 703-707].

D.—Handbooks, Gazetteers and Guidebooks.

Buyers. *Recollections of Northern India with observations.* London, 1848, pages 347 ff.

M. A. Sherring. *The sacred city of the Hindus. An account of Benares in ancient and modern times.* London, 1868. [Chapter XVIII, pages 230-270.]

R. Elliott and Emma Roberts. *Views in India, China and on the shores of the Red Sea.* London [Sarnat, a Boodh monument near Benares, with plate]. Vol. II, pages 7-9.

James Fergusson. *History of Indian and Eastern architecture.* London, 1899, pages 65-68 and 173 f.

James Fergusson. *History of Indian and Eastern architecture.* Revised and edited, with additions by James Burgess and R. Phené Spiers. London, 1910, Vol. I, pages 71-75.

Parker. *Handbook of Benares,* 2nd edition. Trivandrum, 1901, pages 75-78.

E. B. Havell. *Benares, the sacred city. Sketches of Hindu life and religion.* London, 1905. Chapter III, pages 32-58.

H. R. Nevill. *Benares, a gazetteer, being Volume XXVI of the district gazetteers of the United Provinces of Agra and Oudh.* Allahabad, 1909 [Sārnāth], pages 345-362.

R. R. Sen. *The holy city, Benares.* With 58 illustrations and a map. Chittagong, 1912 [Chapter VI, Sarnath, pages 83-115].

D. R. Sahni. *Guide to the Buddhist ruins of Sārnāth.* Calcutta, 1911.

E.—The Sculptures.[1]

A. Cunningham. *Mahabodhi or the great Buddhist temple at Buddha-Gaya.* London, 1892. Plate VIII, 3.

J. Fergusson. *Tree and Serpent worship.* London, 1873. Part I, Plate XXIX, 2. Part II, Plate LXXI, 2.

J. Burgess. *The Buddhist Stūpas of Amarāvatī and Jaggayyapeta.* London, 1887. Plates XII, 1; XXXVIII, 6; XLV, 4; XLVI, 1; XLVIII, 1.

J. Burgess. *The ancient monuments, temples and sculptures of India.* London, 1897. Part I. Plates 65-68, 80 and 96.

J. Burgess. *Journal of Indian Art and Industry.* Vol. VIII (1898), Nos. 62-63. Plate 10, 4 and 5.

C. M. Pleyte. *Die Buddha-Legende in den Skulpturen von Boro-budur.* Amsterdam, 1901-02. Figs. 117-120.

A. Grünwedel. *Buddhist art in India,* revised by J. Burgess. London, 1901, pages 143-146; fig. 96.

A. Foucher. *Etude sur l'iconographie bouddhique de l'Inde d'après des documents nouveaux.* Paris, 1900. [See index i. v. *Mṛgadāva, Benares* and *Sārnāth.*]

A. Foucher. *L'art gréco-bouddhique du Gandhāra.* Tome I, Paris, 1905. Pages 427-435; fig. 209, c. 216-221.

D. B. Spooner. *Handbook to the sculptures in the Peshawar Museum.* Bombay, 1910, pages 20 f.

---

[1] For this section which includes all known sculptural representations of the first sermon I have mainly followed A. Foucher's *Liste indienne des actes du Buddha.* Paris, 1908, page 14, No. 29.

INTRODUCTION.

I.—The Deer-park of Benares.

"Thus the Wheel-of-the-Law of twelve forms has been set in motino and has been understood by Kauṇḍinya, and the three Jewels have sprung up. The Buddha, the Law and the Community, these are the three Jewels; carried from one to the other, the Word has reached the abode of the City of Brahmā. It has been turned—the spotless Wheel-of-the-Law—by the Lord of the World, the Saviour, and there have come forth the three Jewels very hard to attain in this world." *Lalita-vistara* (ed. Lefmann), p. 421.

It is recorded in a sacred text[1] that shortly before his final extinction the Buddha enjoined on his disciples that they should visit the four places connected with the main events of his life—his birth, enlightenment, first preaching and death. This commandment has been faithfully kept by his followers up to the present day, and this accounts for the importance of Sārnāth as one of the four great places of pilgrimage of the Buddhist. For it was here that the third event is believed to have taken place—the preaching of the first sermon by the Buddha or, in the more picturesque language of the ancient scriptures, the "Turning of the Wheel-of-the-Law" (Sanskrit *Dharmachakra-pravartana*).

The well-known *Mahāyāna* book, the *Lalitavistara* in its penultimate chapter, relates at considerable length "the Turning of the Wheel-of-the-Law" whilst this episode in the Master's career is only very briefly referred to in the earlier Pali texts. In the Sanskrit book we read that Buddha, after having attained perfect enlightenment, resolved, first of all, to convert Kauṇḍinya and the four other mendicants (called the five *Bhadravargīyas*, i.e., the five "of the blessed Band") who had previously been the companions of his austerities. With his divine eye he discerned that they tarried in the Deer-park (Sanskrit *Mṛiga-dāva*, Pali *Miga-dāya*) at a locality called *Ṛishipatana*[2] (Pali *Isipatana*) near Benares. Accordingly he went thither and, after having begged his food in that city, betook himself to the Deer-park of Ṛishipatana. On seeing him from far, the five mendicants remembered how he had forsaken the rigid vows of ascetic life, and they resolved not to rise from their seats nor to honour him with a respectful salutation. But as he approached, the five, unable to resist the splendour and majesty of the

---

[1] *The Book of the Great Decease* in *Buddhist Suttas* translated from Pali by T. W Rhys Davids [*Sacred Books of the East*, Vol. XI], Oxford 1881, pages 90 f.

[2] The name is explained by Fa Hien. *Record of Buddhistic kingdoms* (transl. Legge). page 94, and by Hiuen Tsiang, *Buddhist records of the Western World* (transl. Beal), Vol. II, pages 50 f.

Enlightened One, rose to their feet and received him with every mark of veneration. He then announced to them that he had attained the supreme state of a Buddha and during the third watch of the ensuing night he preached to them the Law which had been revealed to him.

The text of this sermon was supplied by "the four noble truths" (Sanskrit *chatvāri ārya-satyāni* ; Pali *chattāri ariya-sachchāni*) about suffering, the origin of suffering, the cessation of suffering, and the way leading to the cessation of suffering.[1] The substance of the Buddha's first sermen may be rendered as follows. Human existence is bound up with suffering which is due to desire and can only be overcome by suppressing desire. The way to this end is "the noble eight-fold path" which consists of a noble and unselfish mode of thought and life, in which the extremes of self-indulgence and mortification are equally to be avoided.

The preaching of the first sermon is believed to have taken place in 528 B.C. [2] when the Buddha was thirty-five years of age. For nearly three centuries after that date nothing is recorded regarding the history of the Deer-park of Benares, though it may be assumed that soon after Buddha's Nirvāṇa it became a place of pilgrimage.

The earliest dateable and at the same time the most important relic hitherto found at Sārnāth is the inscribed pillar erected by Aśōka about 250 B.C. This magnificent monument has alas! suffered irreparable damage, only so much of the shaft being preserved intact as was buried underground at the time of its destruction, though the fragments of the upper portion and the lion capital (Plate IV), which once surmounted it were discovered near by. Although, in consequence, the beginning of the inscription has been almost completely lost, its purport can be established with certainty. It is an edict against schismatics, who are to be expelled from the Community of Friars (*bhikshusaṅgha*) and made to don the white garb of the layman.[3] It may seem somewhat surprising that in the edict, at least in the preserved portion, no reference whatever is made to the great event which was supposed to have taken place on the spot where the column was erected. The pillar is apparently not, as one would expect, a memorial of Buddha's first sermon. Most probably it seemed at the time superfluous to record what was a matter of common knowledge among all who visited the spot and which was not likely to be forgotton.

---

[1] A Pali inscription incised on a fragment of an old stone umbrella, found at Sārnāth in 1907 to the west of the Main Shrine, gives the text of Buddha's first sermon. It is No. D (c) 11 of the Museum Collection. Cf. *A. S. R.* for 1906-07, pages 95 f.

[2] The Buddhists of Ceylon celebrated the 2500th anniversary of the preaching of the first sermon in A.D. 1911.

[3] It is interesting that the Buddhist books speak of a difference in the Community regarding certain questions of discipline which led to the second Council being held at Vaiśālī in the time of Aśōka.

Another monument which most probably goes back to the days of Aśōka or at any rate of the Maurya period is the brick *stūpa* or relic tower situated immediately south of the pillar and of the Main Shrine. Little of it now remains owing to the spoliation of one Jagat Singh, who in 1793-94 almost entirely demolished this venerable monument and utilized its material to build the Jagat Ganj at Benares, named after him. In the published accounts of Sārnāth excavations the *stūpa* in question is usually designated as the 'Jagat Singh *Stūpa*.' Its demolition led to the first recorded discovery of antiquities at Sārnāth and opened the era of archæological explorations as will be related in the next chapter.

A third monument of the same epoch is the monolith stone railing which Mr. Oertel discovered in the foundations of the southern chapel of the Main Shrine and which has been left in the position in which it was found. On account of its wonderful polish and the precision with which it is carved, features that are characteristic of Aśōka's monuments, it can be assigned with practical certainty to the Maurya period. Most probably it was erected to protect some object of unusual sanctity, possibly marking the very spot where the Buddha was supposed to have sat while "turning the Wheel-of-the-Law." But whether at the time of discovery it still stood in its original position, it is impossible to decide.

To a somewhat later period—that of the Śuṅga dynasty—we may assign the railing of which several pillars and rails, partly built into later structures, were found round the Aśōka column and the Main Shrine. Some of the pillars bear votive inscriptions which show that the construction of this railing was due to the co-operation of various persons (to use a modern phrase, the cost was met "by subscription"), each individual contributing one member—either an upright, a cross-bar, coping-stone or plinth-stone. The names of the pious donors, which are recorded on the stones in Brāhmī script, are unknown to history, but apparently some were friars and sisters and others lay-members of the Buddhist community. It is curious that two of these railing pillars, Da 15 and 16 in addition to the original votive inscription of about the 2nd century B.C., bear each a later record of the Gupta period (4th or 5th century A.D.), which indicates that the pillar was re-dedicated at that time as a lamp-post at the "Chief Fane of the Lord Buddha" (Sanskrit *Mūla-gandha-kuṭyāṁ Bhagavatō Buddhasya*).

This "Chief Fane of the Lord" is also mentioned in clay sealings of a somewhat later date (6th or 7th century), which in the excavations of 1907 were found to the west of the Main Shrine.[1] It was evidently the principal temple of the "Convent of the Wheel-of-the-Good-Law" (Sanskrit *Saddharmachakravihāra*). The latter name, which occurs first

[1] *Cf.* F (*d*) 5 below.

on these sealings and is also found in later documents up to the 12th century, was evidently the designation given to the whole Monastery on account of its association with the first "turning of the Wheel-of-the-Law."

The inscriptions also throw some light on the various sects which occupied this important monastic establishment. About the beginning of the Gupta epoch (c. 300 A.D.) the Sarvāstivādins appear to have been the predominant fraternity at Sārnāth, for they are mentioned in three short epigraphs, one incised on the topmost step of the stone stairs on the south side of the Jagat Singh *Stūpa* and two on the monolith stone railing found under the southern chapel of the Main Shrine.[1] Now it is a curious circumstance that one of the two latter inscriptions appears to have been engraved on the place of an earlier record which, in all probability, contained the name of another sect, by which the railing had originally been erected. The Sarvāstivādins are an offshoot of the orthodox Sthaviravāda, and must have been powerful in Northern India, in the days of the Kushāṇa Empire, as appears from inscriptions found at Mathurā (Muttra) and Peshawar.

On the Aśōka column we find beneath the original edict a later inscription—a record of another sect, the Sammitiyas, who were a branch of the Vātsī-putriyas, and, like the Sarvāstivādins, belonged to the Hīnayāna or 'Lesser Vehicle.' This additional inscription appears to belong to the 4th century and is but slightly posterior to the records of the Sarvāstivādins. The Chinese pilgrim Hiuen Tsiang, when visiting the Convent of the Wheel-of-the-Law in the 7th century, found it still in possession of the Sammitiyas, who at that time counted no less than fifteen hundred priests.

This brings us to the period of the Chinese pilgrims who have left us such valuable descriptions of the sacred places of Buddhism in India. That the spot where Buddha set the Wheel-of-the-Law in motion, was one of the chief aims of their pilgrimage goes without saying. I-tsing when starting from his home in distant China, tells us :—"I would sometimes direct my thoughts far away to the Deer Park"; and, after describing the priest's simple outfit—his jar, bowl, clothes and umbrella —he continues :—"At the season of pilgrimage to the Chaityas of Rājagriha, the Bodhi tree, the Vulture Peak, the Deer Park, the holy place where the sāla trees turned white like the wings of a crane (in Kusinagara), and the lonely grove that has been dedicated to a squirrel.

In these seasons travelling priests assemble by thousands in every one of the above places day after day from every quarter, and all travel in the same manner (as described above)."

---

[1] *A. S. R.*, 1907-08, p. 73, No. I, Pl. XXI, I; *ibid.* 1904-05, p. 68 and Pl. XXXII, No. IX, and *ibid.* 1906-07, p. 96, and Pl. XXX.

A detailed account of the convent of the Deer-park is given by the pilgrim Hiuen Tsiang, but it is no easy matter to identify the individual monuments mentioned by him. It is clear that in the six centuries which intervened between the time of his visit and the final destruction of the famous Convent many changes must have occurred. In the first place he describes a grand temple, which contained a life-size brass image showing the Buddha in the act of turning the Wheel-of-the-Law. As this was evidently the principal temple, we may perhaps identify it with the "Chief Fane" (*Mūla-gandhakuṭī*), which, as we saw, is repeatedly mentioned in inscriptions. It is also permissible to assume that it occupied the site of the 'Main Shrine' excavated by Mr. Oertel in 1905. This building, which belongs to a comparatively late period, is raised on the ruins of an earlier edifice.

Hiuen Tsiang next mentions a stone *stūpa* built by Aśōka, to the south-west of the temple first described. It is certainly tempting to identify it with the *stūpa* demolished by Jagat Singh in 1793-94, but it should be noticed that this building is due south of the temple and is built of brick, not of stone. It had not even a stone facing like the Dhamēkh. A way of meeting the difficulty is to assume that it was plastered and that, the material consequently being invisible, Hiuen Tsiang erroneously assumed or was informed that it was built of stone.

"In front of the building [*i.e.*, the Aśōka *Stūpa*]," says the pilgrim,[1] "is a stone pillar about 70 feet high. The stone is altogether as bright as jade. It is glistening, and sparkles like light; and all those who pray fervently before it see from time to time, according to their petitions, figures with good or bad signs. It was here that Tathāgata [*i.e.*, Buddha] having arrived at enlightenment began to turn the Wheel-of-the-Law."

This stone pillar glistening and sparkling like light was probably the Aśōka pillar, though it can hardly have attained the alleged height. It seems also most surprising that the pilgrim mentions neither the edict of Aśōka incised on the shaft nor the crowning lion capital which now excites our admiration. But it should be remembered that Hiuen Tsiang was a pilgrim in search of religious edification and not an antiquarian or artist and that a supposed miracle appealed to him far more than the beauty of a sculpture or the historical value of an ancient record.

Notwithstanding discrepancies, I feel inclined to accept the above identifications which were first proposed by Mr. Oertel. Hiuen Tsiang naturally started his account with the main monuments which marked the spot where Buddha preached his first sermon. To my mind there

---

[1] Beal, *Buddhist Records of the Western World*, Vol. II, page 46.

can be no doubt that this most sacred spot was indeed indicated by the Main Shrine, Jagat Singh's *Stūpa* and the Aśōka Pillar. If we are right in our assumption, it would afford a further warning that the accuracy of the pious palmers from China must not be too closely insisted on and that their accounts must be interpreted *cum grano salis*.

In the course of its existence of nearly one millennium and a half, the great Convent of the Wheel-of-the-Law must have known many vicissitudes. We shall see in the sequel that from the circumstances of a find of sculptures made by General Cunningham it is probable that the Sārnāth buildings were destroyed or at least threatened with destruction at the time of the great Hun invasions in the beginning of the 6th century of our era. More than once, we may assume, the main monuments were wilfully destroyed or fell to decay owing to indifference and neglect. But on each occasion some pious patron came forward and new buildings arose on the ruins of the old.

Of one such restoration we possess a record in an inscription dated *Saṁvat* 1083 (=A.D. 1026), incised on the base of a Buddha statuette [1] which came to light in 1794 in the course of the depredations of Babu Jagat Singh. This important record has been discussed more than once and, in the light of recent discoveries at Sārnāth, its meaning may be considered as well-nigh established. Its purport is that in the reign of Mahīpāla, king of Gauḍa (Bengal), the brothers Sthirapāla and Vasantapāla (perhaps his relatives or governors) restored two buildings named *Dharmarājikā* and *Dharmachakra* and, moreover, raised a new shrine of stone relating to 'the eight great places' (*ashṭa-mahāsthāna-śaila-gandhakuṭīm*). We have seen that Dharmachakra was the general name of the Convent of the Deer-park. It is, however, uncertain whether in the present instance the name applies to the monastery or to the principal temple which, in the days of Hiuen Tsiang, contained an image of Buddha in the attitude of turning the Wheel-of-the-Law. The term *dharmarājikā* denotes a *stūpa*, but we are not in a position to decide which of the many *stūpas* of Sārnāth was the one repaired by the Pāla brothers. We may, perhaps, assume that they selected the *stūpa* which in their eyes must have been most important of all, namely, the one which in after days was demolished by Jagat Singh. In support of this conjecture it may be pointed out that the Buddha image bearing the inscription appears to have been found not far from that monument. Its exact find-place was not recorded at the time of its discovery so that it is hopeless now to attempt to identify the new *gandhakuṭī* built by Sthirapāla and his younger brother. Nor is it clear what is meant by 'the eight great places' (*ashṭa-mahāsthāna*) to which it referred. It may, however, be noted that among the sculp-

[1] No. B (c) 1 of the Museum Collection.

tures discovered at Sārnāth there is a slab with representations of the eight main events of the Buddha's life (Plate XIX, *b*). The places where these events were supposed to have occurred were, as we saw, the principal places of Buddhist pilgrimage and might well be indicated by the word *mahāsthāna*, meaning "a great place." It is, therefore, possible that the *Gandhakuṭī* of the two Pāla brothers contained a sculpture of the eight main scenes, although the slab referred to belongs to a much earlier period. This much, however, is certain, that in A.D. 1026 a restoration of the main monuments of Sārnāth took place, and we may perhaps connect this restoration with the capture of Benares by Maḥmūd of Ghaznī, which occurred in A.D. 1017. It may easily be imagined that the Convent of the Wheel-of-the-Law with its numberless images must have had special attractions for the great idol-breaker.

Sir Alexander Cunningham assumed that Sārnāth was destroyed in A.D. 1033 by Aḥmad Niāltigīn, the general of Mas'ūd. But the very passage [1] quoted by him in support of his assumption seems to contradict it. For it is definitely stated that only "the markets of drapers, perfumers and jewellers" were plundered and that "it was impossible to do more." Moreover, it is evident from a fragmentary inscription [2] of the reign of the Kalachuri king Karṇadēva of Tripurī (the date corresponds to the 4th October 1058) that the "Convent of the Turning of the Wheel-of-the-Law" was then in existence, and it seems unlikely that a second restoration had taken place in the meantime. It is interesting that the devotees mentioned in this document were followers of the *Mahāyāna* or "Greater Vehicle." In fact, the inscription records the copying of the famous Mahāyāna text *Ashṭasāhasrikā*, also called *Prajñapāramitā* or 'Transcendental Wisdom.'

The latest historical record of the famous Monastery of Sārnāth is an extensive eulogy (Sanskrit *praśasti*) [3] carved on a stone slab which was found in the course of Dr. Marshall's excavations of 1908. From it we learn that Kumaradēvī, the Buddhist Queen of King Gōvindachandra of Kānyakubja or Kanauj, restored "[the image of] the Lord of the Wheel-of-the-Law" (*śrī-Dharmachakra-Jina*) as it existed in the days of Aśōka the Righteous, and placed it in a temple or *vihāra* built by her. Evidently the image enshrined in this temple represented the Buddha (also called *Jina*, *i.e.*, 'the Conqueror') in the act of turning the Wheel-of-the-Law. As this idol was supposed (wrongly, no doubt) to have existed in the days of Aśōka, it must have been a thing of great sanctity and was perhaps the main object of worship at Sārnāth. But it should be noted that the inscription was found a long distance from

---

[1] *A. S. R.*, Vol. VIII, page 16.
[2] *A. S. R.* for 1906-07, page 100, No. XIII. No. D (*l*) 8 of the Museum Collection.
[3] *Ep. Ind.*, Vol. IX, pages 319 f. No. D (*l*) 9 of the Museum Collection.

the Main Shrine, namely, to the North of the Dhamēkh *stūpa* just below the raised mound running east and west over the remnants of the old Gupta monasteries.

The queenly donor mentioned in the inscription was, through her mother, related to the Pāla kings of the Gauḍa country (Bengal), where, as we know, Buddhism still lingered on after it had disappeared from Northern India. Her royal husband, Gōvinda-chandra of Kanauj, whose inscriptions range from A.D. 1114 to 1154, though apparently not a Buddhist himself, favoured Buddhism. In 1130, he even made a grant of several villages to the famous Convent of Jētavana, which had been the favourite abode of the Buddha outside the city of Śrāvastī.[1] It is significant that in the Sārnāth eulogy Gōvinda-chandra is described as a heavenly champion deputed by Śiva to protect Benares from the wicked Turushka warriors. Indeed, the Turushkas, *i.e.*, the Turks, had become an imminent peril to the ancient civilization and religion of India. Half a century after Gōvinda-chandra's reign, Muslim sovereignty was triumphantly established in the ancient capitals of Delhi and Kanauj (A.D. 1193). In the same year Jai Chand, the Raja of Benares, was slain in battle, his capital taken and a large number of temples and idols destroyed.

It was, no doubt, this violent overthrow of Hindu rule in Hindūstān which brought about the final destruction and abandonment of the Great Convent of the Turning of the Wheel-of-the-Law. The Muslims must have found here ample room for a display of their iconoclastic zeal, and it would seem that whatsoever still remained of convents and temples were overwhelmed in a general conflagration. The crumbling walls of the ruined sanctuaries were gradually buried under the dust of the ages and only the three large monuments—the Dhamēkh, the Chaukhaṇḍī and the ancient Maurya relic-tower—still bore testimony to the departed glories of the ancient Deer-park.

No doubt, the place where the Buddha preached his first sermon was never quite forgotten by his followers; and pilgrims from Burma, Ceylon and Tibet must have continued to visit Sārnāth. The ancient 'Topes,' no longer glittering with gold, but overgrown with grass and shrubs, still received the homage of the faithful. But there were no orange-robed friars to receive the weary palmer from distant lands and to show him each sacred spot hallowed by the acts of the Master. The life of the Deer-park as a place of worship seemed to have ceased for ever.

There is, it is true, in the centuries of silence which follow, the record of an imperial visit. Humāyūn, the second Mughal ruler of Hindūstān, once visited Sārnāth, and some time after his death in the year 1588 A.D., his son, the great Akbar, deemed the fact sufficiently important

---

[1] *Ep. Ind.*, Vol. XI, pages 20 ff.

to have it recorded in stone. "As Humāyūn, King of the Seven Climes, now residing in Paradise, deigned to come and sit here one day, thereby increasing the splendour of the sun, so Akbar, his son and humble servant, resolved to build on this spot a lofty tower reaching to the blue sky. It was in the year 996 A.H. that this beautiful building was erected.[1]"

The octagonal brick tower erected by Akbar on the top of the Chaukhaṇḍī little deserves the extravagant praise bestowed on it in the Persian inscription. The pity is that the Emperor did not rather choose to record the impression made on his mind by the mysterious memorials of the past. No doubt, his feelings were different from those of the early Muslim invaders, eager to sweep away all signs of idolatry. Dimly perhaps he must have felt the curiosity to penetrate into the secrets of bygone ages, of which these quaint and ragged piles had witnessed the long-vanished life. Was it the Great Sikandar who had built them or Rām Chandar whose deeds the Indians sang?

II.—The Explorations.

Yet another age had to dawn to usher in the true spirit of research which was to bring to light the forgotten history of the ancient Deer-park. It was an accidental discovery which gave the first clue. The most venerable monument of Sārnāth, the ancient Maurya *stūpa*, perhaps founded by the great Aśōka himself, fell a victim to the cupidity of one Jagat Singh, Dīwān of Chait Singh, the Rājā of Benares. Not protected by an imperial tower like the Chaukhaṇḍī nor, defended like the Dhamēkh, by a cuirass of stone slabs riveted together with iron clamps, it afforded too ready a supply of good building material not to be utilized by a sober-minded individual like the Dīwān of Rājā Chait Singh. As a new quarter of Benares, named Jagat Ganj after the spoiler, rose into being, the ancient Dharmarājikā disappeared down to its foundations, but it did not vanish without revealing some of its lost history.

Mr. Jonathan Duncan, the Commissioner of Benares, has left us an account of the incidental discovery made by Jagat Singh, which opened the era of archæological exploration at Sārnāth. It was communicated by him in a meeting of the society instituted in Bengal only a few years before "for inquiring into the history and antiquities, the arts, sciences, and literature of Asia.[2]" His "account of the discovery of two urns in the vicinity of Benares" is interesting enough to be quoted in full.

---

[1] *A. S. R.*, 1904-05, page 74.
[2] *Asiatic Researches*, Vol. V (1798), pages 131 f. and Vol. IX, page 203.

"I herewith beg leave to deliver to the Society, a stone and a marble vessel, found the one within the other, in the month of *January* 1794, by the people employed by *Baboo* Juggut Sing, in digging for stones from the subterraneous materials of some extensive and ancient buildings in the vicinity of a temple called *Sarnauth*, at the distance of about four miles to the northward of the present city of *Benares*.

"In the innermost of these cases (which were discovered after digging to the depth of eighteen *hauts* or cubits under the surface) were found a few human bones, that were committed to the *Ganges*, and some decayed pearls, gold leaves, and other jewels of no value, which cannot be better disposed of than continuing in the receptacle in which they must have so long remained, and been placed upon an occasion on which there are several opinions among the natives in that district; the first, that the bones found along with them may be those of the consort of some former rajah or prince, who having devoted herself to the flames on the death of her husband, or on some other emergency, her relations may have made (as is said to be not unprecedented) this deposit of her remains as a permanent place of lodgment; whilst others have suggested, that the remains of the deceased may have probably only been meant to be thus temporarily disposed of, till a proper time or opportunity should arrive of committing them to the *Ganges*, as is usually observed in respect to these *pushpa* or flowers, a term by which the *Hindus* affect to distinguish those residuary vestiges of their friends dying natural deaths, that are not consumed by the fire, to which their corpses are generally exposed according to the tenets of their religion.

"But I am myself inclined to give the preference to a conclusion, differing from either of the two former, *viz.*, that the bones found in these urns, must belong to one of the worshippers of BUDDHA, a set of *Indian* heretics, who having no reverence for the *Ganges*, used to deposit their remains in the earth, instead of committing them to that river; a surmise that seems strongly corroborated by the circumstance of a statue or idol of Buddha having been found in the same place underground, and on the same occasion with the discovery of the urns in question, on which was an inscription, as per the accompanying copy of the original, ascertaining that a temple had between 700 or 800 years ago been constructed there for the worship of that Deity."

As will be noticed, Mr. Jonathan Duncan rightly rejected the native explanations of the find, and thus the Buddhist character of the Sārnāth ruins was at once established. The stone box, which was not removed until forty years afterwards, may still be seen in the Indian Museum at Calcutta.[1] The more precious casket of green marble with its

[1] Anderson, *Catalogue*, Part II, pages 22 f. A proposal to transfer this object and the inscribed slab found in the Dhamēkh *stūpa* to the Sārnāth Museum was opposed by the Trustees of the Calcutta Museum as being against the letter of the law.

contents of pearls, gold leaves and jewels disappeared from the Asiatic Society's Collection. The inscribed Buddha statuette, referred to by Mr. Duncan, is the same as has been mentioned above (page 6), the inscription thereon being the record of a restoration of certain monuments in A.D. 1026.

The discovery made by Jagat Singh's workmen roused a widespread interest in the ruins of Sārnāth—an interest unfortunately more selfish than scientific. We are told that in 1815 a certain Colonel C. Mackenzie explored Sārnāth, but, as far as I know, no account of his work has seen the light. Miss Emma Roberts refers to the Dhamēkh as "an object of great curiosity and interest to all antiquarian travellers."

"These remains," she says,[1] "some forty or fifty years ago, attracted the attention of several scientific gentlemen at that time residents in the European cantonments of Secrole, and they commenced an active research by digging in many places around. Their labours were rewarded by the discovery of several excavations filled with an immense number of flat tiles, having representations of Boodh modelled upon them in wax. It is said by the writer's authority, a gentleman to whose taste and talents the European world is indebted for information relative to India of the most interesting nature, that there were actually cartloads of these images found in the excavations before mentioned ; many were deposited in the museums, and collections of private individuals, but whether they were ever made the subject of a descriptive account seems doubtful, there being at least no public document of the kind."

Explorations of a more scientific nature were inaugurated by Sir Alexander Cunningham, the great pioneer of Indian archæology and the first Director-General of the Archæological Survey of India. The researches which he carried on at his own expense from December 1834 till January 1836, aimed chiefly at an examination of the three large *stūpas*. The Dhamēkh was opened, but yielded nothing but a stone slab inscribed with the Buddhist Creed which he found at 3 feet from the top and ascribed to the 6th century.[2] He concluded that the monument itself belonged to the same period. Cunningham further rediscovered the stone trough found by Jagat Singh's workmen in January 1794 and left by them on the spot. He was thus able to verify the exact find-spot of the Buddhist relics excavated forty years before. An examination of the Chaukhaṇḍī did not lead to any results, beyond establishing the fact that, in all probability, that monument, like the Dhamēkh, was a simple memorial tower and not a relic *stūpa* like the one exploited by Jagat Singh.

---

[1] R. Elliott. *Views in India*, etc., Vol. II, pages 7 f.

[2] *A. S. R.*, Vol. I, page 111. I feel inclined to assign the epigraph a somewhat later date—the 7th or perhaps the 8th century.

A curious find made by Cunningham consisted of a collection of some sixty statues and bas-reliefs which he found packed together in a small room near a monastery and temple explored by him to the north-west of the Dhamékh. He concluded that the whole of these sculptures had belonged to the neighbouring temple and that they were secreted during a time of persecution when the monks were obliged to abandon their monasteries and take refuge in the mountains. This explanation seems very plausible and we may even hazard a conjecture as to the time when the supposed persecution took place. Some of the collection of sculptures thus discovered bear dedicatory inscriptions in Gupta characters and we may perhaps surmise that they were immured for safety's sake at the time of the Hun invasions which swept over the Gupta empire in the beginning of the 6th century of our era. These sixty sculptures were also presented to the Asiatic Society and are now preserved in the Calcutta Museum. Some forty sculptures which remained behind together with most of the carved stones found by Cunningham, were used by a utilitarian-spirited official of the name of Davidson to strengthen the Barnā bridge. The Reverend Sherring in his well-known book *The sacred city of the Hindus* mentions that, "in the erection of one of the bridges over the Barnā [*viz.*, Duncan's bridge], forty-eight statues and other sculptured stones were removed from Sārnāth and thrown into the river, to serve as a breakwater to the piers; and that in the erection of the second bridge, the iron one, from fifty to sixty cartloads of stones from the Sārnāth buildings were employed."

The next systematic excavations, following those of Cunningham, were carried on in 1851-52 by Major Markham Kittoe, "Archæological Engineer" to the Government, who was then employed in designing and constructing the Queen's College. On his departure for Europe in January 1853, he took with him his notes for the purpose of writing from them an account of his explorations. But, owing to his continued ill-health and early death, the report remained unwritten. The sole information, therefore, which we possess of Kittoe's researches is contained in some brief quotations from a letter to Cunningham, which are embodied in the latter's report. First of all Kittoe excavated a large edifice to the west of the Dhamēkh, which on account of the occurrence of pestles and mortars, the explorer concluded had been a Hospital; but there can be little doubt that it is a monastery of the usual type, consisting of a quadrangle formed by four rows of cells built along the sides of an inner courtyard. In reality, Kittoe excavated only this court, and it was not until 1908 that the excavation of the so-called "Hospital" was continued.

Another large Convent was brought to light in 1852. It is situated to the south of the so-called Jagat Singh *stūpa* and possibly had some connection with this edifice. It should be remembered that usually each large *stūpa* has a monastery attached to it for the accommodation of the monks in charge of the sacred monument.

Kittoe further unearthed a large number of small *stūpas* grouped round the Dhamēkh. "I have laid bare *chaityas* upon *chaityas*," he wrote [1] to Cunningham, "four and five deep built one over the other." Everywhere the explorations left on his mind a most vivid impression of a great final catastrophe by fire which had been the end of the famous Deer-park.

After Major Kittoe's departure in January 1853, his excavations were continued first by Mr. E. Thomas, C.S., a judge and coin collector, and then by Mr. FitzEdward Hall, Professor at Queen's College. Brief accounts of their diggings were published in the Proceedings of the Bengal Asiatic Society. The sculptures and other objects found by them were kept in the compound of Queen's College and now form part of the Sārnāth Museum collection. Owing to long exposure to the weather they have become blackened, except those few which, on account of their inscriptions, were preserved indoors. It seems that Mr. Hall's excavations were again continued by a certain Dr. Butler, but of his work no account is available. About 1865, Mr. C. Horn, C.S., "explored" Sārnāth, and his finds went to the Calcutta Museum. There is also the mention of the discovery of a Buddha image at Sārnāth in December 1877, by Mr. A. Rivett-Carnac,[2] C.S., but it is not known what has become of this find. I may mention here that in 1856 the Government acquired the site of Sārnāth with the ruins from Mr. Fergusson, an indigo planter, but it was not until November 1900 that a custodian was appointed to take care of the ruins.

Thus for more than a century the site of Sārnāth was explored by antiquarians and exploited by contractors, and after all their depredations it might well seem that the mine had been exhausted. This, however, was far from the case; and the greatest discoveries of all were still to come. In fact, it appears now that the excavations hitherto described had mainly served the purpose of removing the upper and latest layers, thus opening the way to strata of greater antiquity and importance.

After an interval of half a century had elapsed since Major Kittoe's exploration, the site of Sārnāth drew the attention of Mr. F. O. Oertel, then Executive Engineer of the Public Works Department at Benares. In the construction of a road connecting the site with the highway to Ghāzīpur, a beautiful and well preserved image of Buddha was

---

[1] *A. S. R.*, Vol. I, page 125.
[2] *Proc. A. S. B.*, 1877, page 68.

found—a sure indication that the sacred soil of the Deer-park had not yet yielded up all its treasures. With the sanction and co-operation of the Archæological Department, Mr. Oertel then started regular excavations which he carried on during the cold season of 1904-05, partly under his personal supervision and partly under that of the District Engineer, Rai Bahadur B. B. Chakravarti. Their labours were rewarded by discoveries of the greatest value.

Immediately to the north of the ill-fated *stūpa* of Jagat Singh, there was a mound which up to that moment had remained unexplored. Fifty years before, it had already attracted the attention of Major Kittoe, who surmised that it concealed a fourth large *stūpa* but who apparently made no attempt to verify his conjecture. It was against this tumulus that Mr. Oertel directed his main attack. It soon became evident that the mysterious mound contained no *stūpa* but the remains of a large temple, probably the main shrine of the whole site. At the back of this temple was found the Aśōka column and its wonderful lion capital in the same position in which it was left by the vandals who threw down this mighty memorial of the great Emperor.

Apparently the explorer had struck the very centre and nucleus of the ancient Deer-park—the actual spot where the Buddha was believed to have sat when he delivered his Sermon on human suffering. It was evident that for many centuries devotees had vied to honour and adorn this most sacred place, for images, bas-reliefs and inscriptions were found heaped up here in remarkable numbers. The total harvest reaped in the course of one season's work consisted of 476 pieces of sculpture and 41 inscriptions.

Owing to Mr. Oertel's transfer to Agra the excavations were not continued in the next cold season. But in 1907 the work was resumed under the personal supervision of Dr. J. H. Marshall, Director-General of Archæology, assisted by Dr. Sten Konow, Mr. W. H. Nicholls, Pandit D. R. Sahni and Mr. Chakravarti. Dr. Marshall's excavations, which covered a larger area than any of the previous explorations, served to convey for the first time a clear idea of the general topography of the site and of the relative positions of the large groups of buildings comprised in it. Whereas former explorers had exposed the numberless *stūpas* and shrines covering the southern half of the site, it now appeared that the northern half was once occupied by a series of monastic buildings separated from the southern group by a heavy wall running east and west. In the ruins of these monasteries finds of sculptures were naturally far less numerous than in the "Stūpa and Temple area." Yet the number of sculptures and inscriptions found in 1907 was by no means small, nor was their artistic and historical value insignificant.

There was, therefore, ample justification for further research in the year following when Drs. Marshall and Konow continued the excavation of the "Monastery area." Here, as in the "Stūpa area," buildings were found in strata of different periods. One convent excelling in carved brickwork was found at the surface and belongs to the period immediately preceding the final destruction of the Deer-park. At a much lower level three more monastic quadrangles were found apparently belonging to the early Gupta or Kushāṇa period. A main point established by Dr. Marshall's researches is that under the Gupta emperors the Convent of the Wheel-of-the-Law must have enjoyed great prosperity and that both Buddhist religion and Buddhist art were still in a very flourishing condition during that period. It is true that "the good Law" enjoyed no longer royal patronage [1] as in the days of Aśōka, the Maurya, or of Kānishka, the Kushāṇa ; but the power and influence of the Buddhist Community must still have been very considerable in those days.

Another interesting fact which was proved by these explorations is that the Convent of the Wheel-of-the-Law still existed in the middle of the 12th century.

As year after year the Sārnāth excavations continued to yield a rich harvest of sculpture, inscriptions and minor antiquities, the question how to preserve these priceless relics of the past seriously engaged the attention of the explorers. An open sculpture hall built by Mr. Oertel in 1905 to shelter his finds, soon proved utterly insufficient. It was then proposed by Dr. Marshall to found at Sārnāth a local Museum which would contain all the treasures unearthed on the spot. The advantages of such an institution for purposes of study and research were evident, and accordingly the proposal was approved by the Government of India and the necessary funds provided from Imperial sources.

The building (Plate II), which was completed in 1910, was designed by Mr. James Ransome, late Consulting Architect to the Government of India. It is to be noted that the building, as it now stands, forms only one-half of the complete design, the intention being to build the other half when further finds demand additional accommodation. The guiding idea of Mr. Ransome's design was to provide a building, simple and suitable, which both in its plan and in its decoration would express to some extent its association with the art treasures it was meant to house. He elected, therefore, to follow the general arrangement of an ancient Buddhist Convent of which Sārnāth has produced several

[1] In the course of the excavations of 1908 the lower half of a Buddha statuette was found which, as appears from the inscription, was dedicated by one Kumāragupta. Dr. Konow mentions the possibility that the Gupta Emperor of that name was the donor, but both the absence of any titles and the insignificant character of the gift seem to militate against such an assumption.

examples. Such buildings, as we saw, consisted of rows of cells grouped along the four sides of an inner courtyard with verandahs in front of the cells. For the purposes of a museum the rows of cells had to become sculpture galleries, but for the rest the main idea of a Buddhist convent is well rendered by Mr. Ransome's Museum in its finished state. It may be remarked that the chapel of the Monastery which is invariably found right opposite the entrance is here represented by the large central hall which enshrines some of the largest and finest sculptures of the collection and which may, therefore, be well regarded as a *sanctum sanctorum*.

Since the explorations at Sārnāth have been resumed on systematic lines and with signal success, the site of the ancient Deer-park attracts again an ever-increasing number of visitors, not only Buddhist pilgrims, but also lovers of art and antiquity from East and West. In the autumn of 1905 Sārnāth was honoured by a visit of Her Royal Highness the Princess of Wales, now the Queen-Empress.

During its short existence the new museum has already won the favour of all visitors. In December 1910, when the work of arranging the sculptures had just been started and only some of the larger pieces had found their places in the central hall, the Museum was inspected by Their Excellencies Lord and Lady Minto, and in February 1912 the collection, which had then been completely arranged, was viewed by the present Viceroy and Lady Hardinge.

III.—The Sculptures.

The oldest and at the same time the finest piece of sculpture found at Sārnāth is the lion-capital (Plate IV), which once crowned the column of Aśōka and now occupies the place of honour in the central hall of the Museum. "The capital," Dr. Marshall writes,[1] "which measures seven feet high, is of the Persepolitan bell-shaped type, surmounted by four magnificent lions sitting back to back with a wheel between them—symbolizing the law of the Buddha which was first promulgated at Sārnāth. Beneath the lion is a drum ornamented with four animals in relief, *viz.*, a lion, an elephant, a bull and a horse, separated from each other by four wheels. The four crowning lions and the reliefs below are wonderfully vigorous and true to nature, and are treated with that simplicity and reserve which is the keynote of all great master-pieces of plastic art. India certainly has produced no other sculpture to equal them."

In my account of the Deer-park (page 3) I have already mentioned the curious monolithic railing found in the southern chapel of the

[1] *Benares Gazetteer.* Allahabad, 1909, pages 354 f.

Main Shrine, and it is not unreasonable to expect that a closer examination of the lower strata of the Sārnāth site will bring to light further relics of the earliest periods of Buddhist art. Besides the remarkable pieces already mentioned, the remains of the Maurya and Śuṅga period, so far recovered, are relatively few. Among the antiquities of a somewhat later date a sculpture of great interest is the finely carved capital No. D (*g*) 4 (Plate V) of the first century B.C. On one side is represented a horseman mounted on a prancing horse and on the other an elephant carrying two men—a *mahaut* and a standard-bearer. An interesting feature are the Perso-Ionic volutes and palmettes carved on the sides. This capital was found in 1907 not far from the north-west corner of the Main Shrine, four feet nine inches below the concrete floor surrounding this building.

I may also mention the posts of an Āndhra railing (Plate VI) found by Dr. Marshall in the following season to the north-east of the Main Shrine. Each pillar is carved on one face (the corner posts on two adjoining faces) with various symbols such as a sacred tree decorated with garlands, and the trident (*triśūla*) which indicates the three jewels (*triratna*), namely, the Buddha, the Buddhist Law (*Dharma*) and the Buddhist Community (*Saṅgha*). We notice the latter symbol also combined with the Wheel-of-the-Law (*Dharma-chakra*) on the top of a pillar of the Persepolitan type. Of special interest are the representations of buildings found on these railing posts. Most common is the *stūpa*, or relic tower, surrounded with a railing and decorated with an umbrella, streamers and garlands. Besides, there are a *chaitya* hall and a hermit's hut to which reference has already been made.

It will be noticed that in these early sculptures the Buddha image is never represented. This fact, which has also been established with regard to contemporaneous monuments in Central India and elsewhere, is not easy to explain. I may refer the reader to M. Foucher's study of the beginnings of Buddhist art.[1] It is evident that the presence of the Buddha was indicated by certain symbols and some of these symbols referred particularly to the main events of his life. The tree indicated his Enlightenment (*bōdhi*), the wheel his first preaching of the Law (*Dharma*) and the *stūpa* his final extinction (*nirvāṇa*). Consequently these symbols were associated in particular with the localities where those three great events had taken place. This explains why Aśōka selected the wheel to crown his great pillar at the Deer-park of Benares.

It is true that in an inscription of the 12th century found at Sārnāth (above page 7) it is said that Queen Kumara-dēvī, the consort of Gōnvinda-chandra of Kanauj, restored an image of Buddha called the Lord of the Wheel-of-the-Law, *as it existed in the days of Aśōka*. The

[1] A. Foucher, *Les débuts de l'art bouddhique* in Journal Asiatique, 1909.

results of archæological research, however, point to the fact that in the days of Aśōka the Buddha image had not yet been called into existence. Created by the Græco-Bactrian sculptors of the ancient Gandhāra country (the Peshāwar district and surrounding territories), it was first introduced in Mathurā (*valgo* Muttra), and thence was carried to the centres of Buddhist worship in the Gangetic plains.

This theory derives strong support from a find made at Sārnāth in 1905 in the course of Mr. Oertel's excavations. It consists of a colossal statue No. B (*a*) 1 (Plate VII) which, as stated in the inscription, represents a Bōdhisattva, in all likelihood *the* Bōdhisattva, in other words Śākyamuni before his attaining Buddhahood. The lion between the feet of the image seems to convey an allusion to his epithet *Śākyasiṁha*. "the Lion of the Śākya race." Apart from a few fragments, this Bōdhisattva is the oldest image found at Sārnāth and the inscription it bears states that it was erected in the third regnal year of the great king Kānishka, who was the most prominent ruler of the Kushāṇa dynasty. There are two circumstances which render it highly probable that the statue in question was carved at Mathurā, which was a great centre of sculptural art during the Kushāṇa rule. The material is not the buff-coloured stone of the Chunār quarries, of which all other Sārnāth sculptures are made, but it is the red sandstone of Mathurā. Besides, the donor of the image, Friar Bala, as the inscription says, is also mentioned in a Buddhist sculpture found at Mathurā.[1] There is, therefore, much reason to suppose that the art of image making was brought to Sārnāth from that city in the days of the Kushāṇa kings.

Now, if we compare with the Bōdhisattava statue of Friar Bala, another similar image (No. B (*a*) 2) made of Chunār sandstone, we recognize in the latter a first attempt of the local artisans to imitate the newly introduced representation of Śākyamuni. It must be admitted that neither the example nor the copy can be said to reach any high degree of artistic merit. The attitude of these Bōdhisattvas is singularly stiff and devoid of grace and expression. That the same sculptors who produced these clumsy figures possessed great skill in purely decorative carving is proved by the grand stone parasol (Plate VIII) which once overshadowed the inscribed Bōdhisattva statue.

From the fact that the Bōdhisattva of Friar Bala and other statues of the same period were sheltered by stone umbrellas we may perhaps conclude that in those days image shrines were little known in India. As has been noticed above, the earliest inscriptions found at Sārnāth, which speak of a temple, belong to the Gupta period (4th or 5th century

---

[1] Friar Bala also dedicated a Bōdhisattva statue at the Jētavana near Śrāvasti. It is also made of red sandstone and is very similar to the Sārnāth image. The ancient city of Śrāvasti and the neighbouring Jētavana are marked by the twin sites of Sahēth Mahēth on the borders of the Bahraich and Gonda districts of the United Provinces.

A.D.).[1] It is true that on one of the railing pillars of about the 1st century B.C. a building is shown which might be called a shrine. But it contains no figure and as it has the type of a "leaf-hut" (*parṇa-śālā*), it is most probably meant for a hermit's hut, unless we may identify it with the famous *Gandhakuṭī* of the Jētavana in which the Buddha used to dwell.

There are two points in which the images of the Kushāṇa period betray their western origin, namely, the indication of the drapery and the halo. The drapery is treated in a very schematic fashion and plainly shows the thorough 'Indianization' of the Græco-Buddhist styles, as found in the sculptures of the North-West. The halo is another feature derived from Hellenistic art. It will be noticed that the examples of the Kushāṇa period are perfectly plain but for a simple scalloped border along the edge. This is especially noticeable on the statuette No. B (*b*)1. It is, of course, possible that these haloes were originally decorated in colours, for it is still plainly apparent that the Bōdhisattva of Friar Bala was originally painted, the robe red or orange-coloured like the actual *Kāshāya* robes worn by Buddhist monks, and the body gilt in accordance with the texts which extol the splendour emanating from the Buddha. But the halo, of which only a few fragments were recovered, retains no trace of having originally been painted.

The Gupta period (c. 300-600 A.D.) marks a revival of purely Indian civilisation. Under the mighty patronage of indigenous rulers the arts of the country flourished. Though none of the Gupta emperors is known to have embraced Buddhism, their strong rule must have greatly benefited that religion also. The Convent of the Wheel-of-the-Law enjoyed great prosperity in those days, as is evident from the exuberance of sculptural remains dating back to that epoch. Indeed, the great majority of the sculptures preserved in the Sārnāth Museum belong to Gupta times.

The Buddha figure of this period, though undoubtedly a direct descendant of the Kushāṇa image, shows a new and purely national development and, indeed, represents a new type which in artistic merit is infinitely superior to its predecessor. Some of the Buddha statues of this period, by their wonderful expression of calm repose and mild serenity, give a beautiful rendering of the Buddhist ideal. The indication of the drapery having been almost wholly discarded, the monastic robes are merely marked in outline. On the contrary, the halo encircling the head of the Master becomes lavishly ornamented with floral and foliated ornament. Evidently the real significance of this "circle of light" (Sanskrit *prabhā-maṇḍala*) was completely forgotten. The Gupta sculptors thus went far to eliminate or modify those features

[1] See page 3 above.

which in the Kushāṇa period still indicated the foreign origin of the Buddha image.

The most splendid example which the Sārnāth Museum possesses is undoubtedly the seated Buddha image (Plate X) which was the first sculpture discovered by Mr. Oertel in the course of his excavations and which through numerous reproductions has become known to all lovers of Indian art. It shows the Buddha in the act of preaching his famous sermon of Benares. This is indicated by the peculiar position of the hands (known as that of turning the Wheel-of-the-Law or *dharmachakra-mudrā*) and more particularly by the wheel and the two deer carved on the pedestal.

We have seen that, from the beginning, the Wheel was the symbol of the Buddhist Law and that, consequently, it was used particularly to indicate the first turning of the Wheel-of-the-Law or, in other words, the Buddha's first sermon at Benares. In order to indicate the sermon in the Deer-park more precisely two lying deer or antelopes were placed one on either side of the wheel symbol.

After the Buddha image had been called into existence, it became possible to give a still more direct rendering of the first sermon. Yet the symbolism so dear to the Indian mind was not wholly discarded, not even by the Græco-Bactrian sculptors of Gandhāra, however classically inspired. They show us, indeed, the Buddha seated cross-legged under a tree attended by his first five converts (Kauṇḍinya and the others) seated in like manner and surrounded by numerous deities who witnessed the scene.[1] But in front of the Buddha we discern the ancient wheel symbol placed on a little pillar between two miniature antelopes. The Buddha is shown either in the act of "turning the wheel" or raising his right hand in the attitude which in Gupta and mediæval iconography indicates the granting of protection (Sanskrit *abhayamudrā*).

The sculptors of Mathurā closely followed their brethren of Gandhāra. It is only in the Gupta period that we find the preaching Buddha portrayed in that peculiar attitude or *mudrā* which is regularly found in the Sārnāth sculptures. This *mudrā* (called the *dharmachakra-mudrā*) was known in Gandhāra, but there it appears to be exclusively associated with the great Miracle of Śrāvastī.

It will not be out of place to say a few words about these *mudrās* which play such a prominent part in Buddhist iconography.[2] In sculptures of the Gupta period, when apparently they had become definitely fixed, we find the following represented :—

(*a*) The *abhaya-mudrā* or attitude of granting protection (lit. 'absence of fear or danger') is expressed by the right

---

[1] *Cf.* E. B. Havell, *Indian sculpture and painting*. London, 1908. Plate IX.
[2] *Cf.* A. Foucher, *Iconographie bouddhique*. Paris, 1900, pages 68 f.

hand being raised at the level of the right shoulder with the palm of the hand turned outwards. The left hand usually clasps the end of the upper robe turned round the left arm so as to form a kind of sleeve. This *mudrā* is found both in standing and seated images. It is particularly common in the Kushāṇa period.

(*b*) The *varada-mudrā* or 'gift-bestowing' attitude consists of the right arm being stretched out downwards with the open palm of the hand turned to front. This *mudrā* is only associated with standing figures.

(*c*) The *dhyāna-mudrā* or attitude of 'meditation' is rendered by the two hands being placed in the lap one over the other. It occurs only in seated images.

(*d*) The *bhūmisparśa-mudrā* or 'earth-touching attitude' marks the moment when the Buddha, assailed by Māra the Evil One, called on the Earth to bear testimony to his pious acts in his previous existences. It is, therefore, used in particular to indicate the *bōdhi* or enlightenment which immediately followed the 'temptation,' as Māra's assault is commonly called. The image in the Great Temple of Bōdh Gayā is shown in this position of "touching the earth." The Buddha is invariably seated and sometimes the foliage of the Bōdhi tree (Ficus religiosa) is shown over his head. I may add that very often the miniature figure of the Earth goddess holding up a treasure vase (in Sanskrit she is called *Vasundharā* or 'wealth-carrier') is shown under the Buddha's outstretched right hand. (Plates IX and XII, *a*.)

(*e*) The *dharmachakra-mudrā* or attitude of '[turning] the Wheel-of-the-Law.' The two hands are held in front of the breast, the thumb and fore-finger of the right hand being joined while touching the middle finger of the left hand. The Buddha is invariably seated. The attitude in question, as we have said, indicates the act of preaching and is particularly associated with the first sermon in the Deer-park (at least in Sārnāth sculpture) and with the Great Miracle of Śrāvastī when Buddha was seen preaching in different places simultaneously.

We have seen that the first sermon in the Deer-park is further denoted by the wheel-and-deer symbol which usually occupies the centre of the pedestal. The five converts also are no longer shown on the same level with the preaching Buddha as was the case in Gandhāra; but, together with the wheel and the deer, they have been relegated to the pedestal. Often a sixth figure is added, either to represent the donor of the sculpture or simply for the sake of symmetry.

Thus the Buddha image becomes all-important and such additional figures as once formed an essential part of some scene of his life have become so much reduced in size and subordinated in position, that they are nothing more than a cognizance indicating to which particular event in the Buddha's career the sculpture refers.

Whatever reasons the earlier Buddhists may have had for not portraying the founder of their religion, so much is certain that, as soon as the Buddha image had been created by the Indo-Bactrian sculptors of the North-West, it was received enthusiastically and multiplied in endless numbers through the piety of the faithful. The monks had to yield their cells to the images of the Master. Special chapels were attached to the monasteries and grand temples were built on the spots once hallowed by his presence. Not only did the sanctum contain his effigy, often of gigantic size, but images were placed in the outer niches both of temples and relic towers. The Buddha image, more and more stereotyped, was degraded to a mere decorative device.

Among the Græco-Buddhist sculptures of Gandhāra we find, side by side with statues of the Buddha in his plain monk's robe, princely figures elegantly draped and decked with ornaments. These have been generally described as Bôdhisattva images, but it is an open question whether they represent *the* Bōdhisattva (namely, Śākyamuni before his attaining Enlightenment), or some of the numerous Bōdhisattvas whose cult had become more and more prominent among the Buddhists. However this may be, there is no question that in the princely figure holding an alabastron in his left hand we may recognize Maitrēya, the future Saviour of Buddhism.

In the Gupta period to which most of our Sārnāth sculptures belong, the cult of the Bōdhisattvas is very pronounced. Besides Maitrēya, it is in particular Avalōkitēśvara, "the Lord of Compassion," who is represented by many an image. In his head-dress he wears a miniature effigy of his spiritual father Amitābha, 'the Buddha of boundless light,' seated in the pose of meditation. Avalōkitēśvara usually holds a lotus-flower (*padma*) in his left hand whilst his right is stretched out in the 'gift-bestowing' attitude. Sometimes beneath his outstretched hand we notice the emaciated figure of the *prēta* (Tantalized Spirit) Sūchīmukha (or, 'Needle-mouth') who intercepts the drops of nectar flowing from the fingers of the Great Compassionate (Plates XII, *b*, and XIII, *b*.)

A still further development in the history of Buddhism is illustrated by the numerous images of deities, of which the Sārnāth excavations have yielded so many specimens. The worship of these gods and goddesses, no doubt, formed a part of the popular religion of India at an early stage, in fact it may in many cases go back to pre-Buddhist times. But only at a comparatively late date were they admitted to the Buddhist Pantheon and received their place side by side with the Buddhas and Bōdhisattvas. Several of these godlings, with the weird and terrific shapes with which popular taste has endowed them, seem out of place at the side of the placid Buddha. Their introduction, no doubt, marks a process of degeneration which we find continued and more pronounced in Tibet.

The images of this type found at Sārnāth belong mostly to the mediæval period. They often have many arms, sometimes also many faces, including those of animals. One of the most popular deities of Indian Buddhism is the god of wealth, Vaiśravaṇa or Jambhala, whose image is regularly found in Buddhist monasteries, strange and incongruous though it may seem in the abode of Friars vowed to poverty. Side by side with the god of wealth we find a goddess of fertility, *e.g.*, in the curious group No. B (*e*) 1 (Plate XV, *a*) excavated by Dr. Marshall in 1908. The god with his protruding eyes and tusks, in his stark nakedness exhibiting his corpulent deformity, wearing cobras instead of ornaments and trampling on a prostrate figure, is a worthy prototype of those demoniacal nightmares which are so favourite a subject in the Lamaist art of Tibet.

His female companion, no doubt Vasudhārā, the goddess of plenty, bears a less repulsive aspect. We find her also portrayed separately in a headless statuette No. B (*f*) 19 (Plate XV, *b*) excavated by Mr. Oertel. The most popular of goddesses is, certainly, Tārā, who like Avalōkitēśvara shows her gracious disposition towards mankind by her right hand being stretched out in the 'gift-bestowing' gesture. In her left hand she holds a flowering stem of the blue lotus (*utpala*). A typical example of mediæval sculpture is the standing Tārā, No. B (*f*) 2 (Plate XIII, *a*), who with her luxurious form and elaborate ornaments closely corresponds to the ideal of female beauty extolled in the erotic poetry of mediæval India. The figurine of a Dhyāni-Buddha (apparently Akshōbhya) introduced in her head-dress indicates her connection with Buddhism. A more pleasing effigy of Tārā is found in the well preserved statuette, No. B (*f*) 7 (Plate XVII, *a*), which shows the goddess seated on a lotus flower in the 'graceful pose' (*lalitāsana*). A female attendant is leaning against her left knee and an adoring figure with a censer projects from the base. I may note that in Buddhist, as in Christian plastic art, we often find the donor or donors represented in miniature size at the feet of the deity.

A deity of a less pleasing appearance is the goddess of Dawn, Mārīchī or Vajra-varāhī, 'the she-boar of the thunderbolt.' She has three faces, one of which is a boar's head, and a corresponding number of hands in which she wields various weapons. She stands in the archer's attitude on a chariot drawn by seven boars. The last-mentioned feature reminds us of Sūrya, the Sun-god, whose chariot is drawn by seven horses, evidently an allusion to the seven days of the week. In Tibet the goddess Vajra-varāhī is still worshipped as *r Dorje Phagmo*, a literal translation of her Indian name. (Plate XVII, *b.*)

As the Buddhist pantheon increases and the divine images multiply, we notice a constant decrease in sculptures relating to the life of the Buddha. The Græco-Buddhist school of Gandhāra produced an infinite number of scenes illustrating almost every incident in the Master's career. But already in Mathurā we find these scenes reduced to a very restricted number, and from the Gupta period onwards there are hardly any, except the four great and four minor events of the Buddha's life which become more and more stereotyped. Many of the larger Buddha images relate in reality to one or other of the eight main scenes, as is indicated both by the peculiar position of the hands and by some attendant figures or symbols. We have already pointed out that the latter have usually become very subordinate, both in size and position, with regard to the image of the Buddha.

Among the sculptures of the Gupta period we find high slabs divided into four panels of equal size placed one over the other, which represent the four great scenes of the Buddha's life, his birth, his enlightenment, his first sermon and his death (Plate XIX, *a*). The birth scene invariably occupies the lowermost panel and the death the one at the top, the slab being crowned by a little *chaitya*, an evident reference to the worship of the Buddha's relics. In the beginning of this introduction we have pointed out that the places where the four main events were supposed to have taken place have from early times been the great places of Buddhist pilgrimage.

Already in the Gupta period the representations of the four great scenes are treated in a very stereotyped fashion, but the slabs still show a considerable amount of detail. Sometimes we find each main scene combined with some closely allied events which are placed in the same panel. It is very curious how in this manner the Indian sculptors, after having adopted from their Græco-Bactrian brethren a division of various scenes in clearly partitioned panels, gradually reverted to the primitive method of the earliest school, namely, that of crowding a number of consecutive scenes in one panel. The fragment No. C (*a*) 2 (Plate XX), for instance, shows in the lowermost panel not only the Nativity, but also the Conception (Māyā's dream) with the elephant descending, and the first bath of the future Buddha by the Nāgas or snake-gods, Nanda and Upananda. The second panel contains scenes relating to the Great Renunciation and in the third panel we find both the scenes of the Enlightenment and of the First Sermon shown side by side.

A sculpture of special interest is No. C (*a*) 3 shown in Plate XIX *b*. It will be noticed that it consists of eight panels arranged in two vertical rows of four each. The four great events are shown in the two bottom and two top panels whilst the inner panels portray the four minor scenes, namely, the descent of Buddha from heaven, the great miracle of Śrāvastī, the presentation of a bowl of honey by a monkey and the subduing of the wild elephant, Nālāgiri. For a detailed description of this unique sculpture I may refer the reader to M. Foucher's excellent study which has appeared in the *Journal Asiatique* for 1909.

One of the eight scenes on this slab could be proved to represent the great miracle of Śrāvastī, which enabled M. Foucher to recognize the same subject on a number of other bas-reliefs. The Sārnāth Museum contains several specimens, one of which [No. C (*a*) 6] is shown in Plate XXI. The Buddhist scriptures relate how Buddha in order to confound the heretical teachers, gave a great exhibition of his miraculous powers in the presence of King Prasēnajit of Śrāvastī. His main feat, that of showing himself simultaneously in different places, is rendered by the repetition of Buddha figures in the sculpture whilst a corpulent personage shown beneath seated on a little stool and supported from behind by an attendant appears to be one of the rival teachers. Sometimes King Prasēnajit is also shown, his royal rank being denoted by an umbrella-bearer and by an elephant.

Another of the minor scenes, of which the Sārnāth collection possesses several replicas, is the Buddha's descent from the Trāyastriṁśa Heaven, where he had preached the Law to his mother. According to the texts, the Buddha alighted at Sāṅkāśya (modern Sankisa in the Farrukhābād district of the United Provinces). While descending by a triple ladder, he was accompanied by the gods Brahmā and Indra (or Śakra). Both in Buddhist art and literature we notice the tendency to make the gods of the Brahmanical Pantheon subservient to the Buddha. In the Sārnāth sculptures representing this scene the triple ladder has disappeared [1]; we find Buddha standing in the 'gift-bestowing' attitude between Brahmā and Indra, the former carrying a fly-whisk or *chowrie* (Sanskrit *chāmara*), and the latter a parasol held over the head of the Buddha. The sculptors could, indeed, in no way render the subordination of the great Hindu gods to the Buddha more obvious than by placing them at his sides as his satellites carrying the two chief emblems of sovereignty.

The two remaining minor scenes, the feeding of the Buddha by the monkey and his subduing the wild elephant, seem to have appealed little to the sculptors of Sārnāth, whereas in the later school of Magadha (Southern Bihār) these two scenes are by no means uncommon.[2] The

---

[1] The only sculpture in the Sārnāth Museum, which retains a remnant of the ladder, is C (*a*) 18 where the Buddha stands on the top of a stair of five steps.

[2] There is one sculpture [C (*a*) 8], found at Sārnāth, which represents the offering of a bowl of honey by the monkey. But it is made of Gayā stone and probably was brought from that place.

reason of such local predilections it is difficult to explain. Nor would it be easy to say why a scene like Indra's visit to Buddha in the Indraśaila Cave, one of the most favourite subjects of the sculptors both of Gandhāra and Mathurā, is totally absent at Sārnāth.

In this connection I wish to draw attention to the two capitals, Nos. D (*g*) 5-6, which were found by Mr. Oertel at the entrance of the Main Shrine. Each is carved with four scenes among which we notice some well-known subjects such as the Buddha's Nirvāṇa. The subjects of these carvings are not, however, the four main and the four minor scenes, as we might have expected. On one side of one capital we find Buddha seated in meditation in front of a huge cobra whose expanded hood forms a canopy over the Master's head. It is, no doubt, the Nāga king Muchilinda, who sheltered him during a thunder-storm shortly after his having attained Buddhahood. Considering the scarcity of legendary scenes at Sārnāth, it is not a little curious to meet here with a subject which, as far as I know, is not treated anywhere else in the Buddhist art of India proper.

On the other capital we meet with a curious scene which I am unable to identify. It shows some wild animal on a prostrate human figure which it seems to be in the act of devouring, while behind a low wall three female spectators are partly visible. The figure in the foreground would suggest the Jātaka of the tigress (Sanskrit *vyāghrī-jātaka*), *i.e.*, the story of the future Buddha, born as a Brahmanical ascetic, giving his body to feed a hungry tigress. But on this assumption the three females in the background would remain unexplained. Besides, among scenes of the life of the Buddha as Śākyamuni, such a story of one of his previous existences would have been rather out of place.

Here let me observe that the *jātakas* which were such a favourite subject of the earliest school are almost totally absent among the sculptures of the Gupta period found at Sārnāth. A very noticeable exception to this rule is afforded by the beautiful door lintel (No. D (*d*) 1 ; Plates XXIII, *a*, and XXIV-XXIX) excavated by Dr. Marshall in 1908, on which we find four bas-reliefs relating to the story of *Kshāntivādin*, 'the preacher of forbearance.'[1] The ascetic of this name—in reality the future Buddha—bore with the greatest patience the most cruel treatment inflicted on him by Kalābu, the king of Benares, who, annoyed at the holy man preaching to his dancing girls, caused his limbs to be cut off one after the other. This is clearly shown in one of the four bas-reliefs, whilst in another the saint is apparently portrayed in his divine state as a Bōdhisattva adored by five worshippers. The remaining two

---

[1] The *Khantivād-jātaka* is No. 313 of the Pali collection. *Cf. The Jataka* (ed. Fausböll), Vol. III, pages 39-43 (transl. ed. Cowell); Vol. III, pages 26-29. In its Sanskrit version the story occurs in the *Jātaka-mālā* (ed. Kern) as *Kshānti-jātaka*, pages 181-192 (transl. Speyer).

evidently represent the king's dancing girls, whose regard for the old ascetic was the cause of their royal master's wrath. At either end of the lintel we notice an effigy of the god of wealth recognisable from his corpulence and from his attribute—the money-bag. His presence in Buddhist sculpture has already been commented on above (page 23).

It would be impossible in a short treatise like the present to discuss the various decorative designs of which the Sārnāth excavations have yielded so rich a harvest. They deserve a special study. Here I wish only to draw attention to a few pieces such as the lintel fragment No. C (*b*) 9 (Plate XXIII, *b*) of the Kushāṇa period, which shows a remarkable variety of ornament. It is, moreover, interesting on account of the bas-relief showing a *stūpa* worshipped by an elephant and by a fabulous being—half man, half bird—in which we may recognize a *kinnara*. It will be noticed that the dome of the sacred monument is encircled by a string of three-headed cobras. This makes it highly probable that we have here a representation of the Stūpa of Rāmagrāma, the only one of the eight original relic-towers which remained undisturbed by Aśōka, on account of its being guarded by the Nāgas or snake-gods.

A very frequent decorative device is the leogryph, originally a lion used as a bracket to support the projecting ends of the bar in the back of a throne. Gradually the animal becomes more and more phantastical, as will be evident from some very fine examples of the Gupta period in the Sārnāth Museum, Nos. C (*b*) 1-2 (Plate XXII). The animal is sometimes provided with horns, wings and a tail which give it a dragon-like appearance. Not unfrequently it is mounted by a youthful rider who gradually develops into a warrior armed with sword and shield. The leogryph is then raised on the back of an elephant and sometimes we find both the animals mounted by two warriors who seem to be in the act of fighting each other. It has been supposed that the lion standing on the elephant has some symbolical meaning such as the triumph of Buddhism over Brahmanism. But more probably it is simply a production of Indian phantasy which has produced a still more luxuriant growth of the leogryph ornament in the Dravidian art of Southern India and in the Lamaistic art of Tibet.

J. Ph. VOGEL.

Catalogue of the Museum of Archaeology at Sārnāth.

A.—THE LION CAPITAL OF AŚŌKA.

A 1.—Capital [1] of Aśōka Column (ht. 7′; width across the abacus 2′ 10″). The lower portion, 2′ in height, has, as usual, the shape of a bell decorated with conventional petals in Persepolitan style. They are sixteen in number. The necking above the bell is circular in horizontal section and has a torus moulding with plain surface. The middle portion, which is fashioned into a circular abacus resembling a common drum, 1′ 1½″ high, is decorated with four wheels, of twenty-four spokes each, in high relief. The ends of the axles are left rough, from which it may be surmised that they were originally covered with caps probably of precious metal. This is proved by the existence of three fine holes pierced into the rim of each axle, into which metal pins were evidently inserted to keep the caps in position. The spaces between the wheels are occupied by the figures of an elephant, a bull, a horse and a lion,[2] following each other from right to left in the direction of the *pradakshiṇa*. Three of these animals are represented as walking, the horse as running at full gallop. These figures are all more or less damaged, but they are wonderfully life-like and their pose graceful.

The abacus is surmounted with figures of four life-sized lions placed back to back, so that only the fore-parts are shown. They are each 3′ 9″ high. Two of them are in perfect preservation. The heads of the other two were found detached and have been refixed. The upper jaw of one and the lower jaw of the other were not recovered. In place of eye-balls some sort of precious stones were originally inserted into the sockets, as is clearly shown by the existence of very fine holes in the upper and lower lids, which received thin iron pins to keep the jewels in position. One such pin still remains in the upper lid of the left eye of one of the lions.

The capital was carved out of a single block of sandstone but is now broken across just above the bell. It was originally surmounted by a wheel (*chakra*), the symbol of the Buddhist Law, supported on a short

---

[1] *A. S. R.* for 1904-05, p. 69 and Pl. XX.

[2] The late Dr. Bloch in *Z. D. M. G.*, Vol. LXII (1908), pp. 653 f., conjectured that these four animals symbolize the gods Indra, Śiva, Sūrya and (perhaps) the goddess Durgā, whose *vāhanas* they are and that, consequently, they are meant to indicate the subordination of these Brahmanical gods to Buddha and his Law. This theory, however ingenious, has little to support it, and it seems much more probable that these animals—the four "noble beasts" (*mahājānēya*) of the Buddhists—are merely decorative. They occur also on moon-stones in Ceylon. [Ed.]

stone shaft.[1] The latter was not discovered, but its thickness can be estimated from the mortice hole, 8" in diameter, drilled into the stone between the lions' heads. Of the wheel itself, four small fragments were found. The ends of thirteen spokes remain on these pieces. Their total number was presumably thirty-two.

The capital is one of the most magnificent specimens of art that have yet been discovered in the country. The accuracy of delineation and the feeling of symmetry which pervade every part of the sculpture are not met with except in the few sculptures on the other pillars of Aśōka, which have come down to us.

The material of which the capital is made is a black-spotted buff-coloured sandstone from Chunār, but of a much finer grain than the Chunār stone used in the construction of houses in Benares and its neighbourhood.

Of the shaft on which this capital originally rested four large fragments were discovered. In addition to these there is the lower portion, about 15′ in height, which is standing *in situ* and bears three inscriptions. The earliest one which is a record of Aśōka himself is an edict against schismatic monks and nuns who are threatened with expulsion from the Saṅgha or Buddhist Church. This epigraph originally consisted of eleven lines, but the first three have disappeared with the exception of the first two syllables of the first and second lines and the major portion of the third, which were recovered on three small detached fragments of the shaft. The remaining portion is in excellent preservation. The epigraph runs as follows[2] :—

1. *Dēvā[naṁ-piyē Piyadasi lājā*]*
2. *ēla* ....
3. *Pāṭa[liputē*]......yē kēna-pi*[3] *saṁghē bhētavē ē chuṁ khō*
4. *[bhikhū vā bhikhu]ni vā saṁghaṁ bhākhati*[4] *sē ōdātāni dus[ā]ni saṁnaṁdhāpayiyā ānāvāsasi*
5. *āvāsayiyē* [I*] *Hēvaṁ iyaṁ sāsanē bhikhu-saṁghasi cha bhikhuni-saṁghasi cha viṁnapayitaviyē* [I*]
6. *Hēvaṁ dēvānaṁ-piyē āhā* [I*]. *Hēdisā cha ikā lipī tuphākaṁtikaṁ huvā ti saṁsalanasi nikhitā* [I*]
7. *Ikaṁ cha lipiṁ hēdisaṁ=ēva upāsakānaṁtikaṁ nikhipātha* [I*] *Tē pi cha upāsakā anupōsathaṁ yāvu*

---

[1] Lions carrying a wheel also occur at Sanchi.

[2] *Vide* Vogel, *Ep. Ind.*, VIII, p. 168 *et seq.* and facsimile ; Venis, *J. A. S. B.*, *N. S.*, Vol. III, 1907, p. 1 *et seq.* ; E. Senart, *Comptes rendus des séances de l'Académie des Inscriptions et Belles Lettres*, 1907, p. 25 *et seq.*; A. M. Boyer, *J. A.*, 10th Series, Vol. X (1907), p. 119 *et seq.*

[3] The syllables *yē kēna* occur partly on one fragment and partly on another. Both the pieces, however, fit together precisely and the reading in the transcript is quite certain.

[4] The *ā* stroke of *bhā* is quite distinct.

8. *ētam=ēva sāsanaṁ visvaṁsayitavē* [I*] *Anupōsathaṁ cha dhuvāyē ikikē mahāmātē pōsathāyē*
9. *yāti ētam=eva sāsanaṁ visvaṁsayitavē ājānitavē cha* [I*] *Āvatakē cha tuphākaṁ āhālē*
10. *savata vivāsayātha tuphē ētēna viyaṁjanēna* [I*] *Hēmēva savēsu kōṭa-visavēsu ētēna*
11. *viyaṁjanēna vivāsāpayāthā* [II*]

Translation.

"His sacred Majesty King Piyadasi .... at Pāṭa[liputta] ....The Church is [not] by any one to be divided. But whosoever, monk or nun, shall break up the Church, shall be made to don white robes [1] and made to dwell in another dwelling.[2] Thus should this command be brought to notice in the Order of monks and in the Order of nuns.

"Thus saith his sacred Majesty. One such edict hath been inscribed at the place of assembly in order that it may be near you. And even such an edict ye must inscribe for the laity. And the laity also should come on the Sabbath-days in order to be inspired with faith in this edict. On every Sabbath-day regularly shall each superintendent (of the Law) come to the Sabbath service to be inspired with faith in this Order and to learn it.

"And as far as your district [extendeth] ye must everywhere make [the edict] known according to the letter thereof. So, too, in all fortified towns and provinces, ye must cause it to be made known according to the letter thereof."

The second inscription, which consists of a single line, 4′ 8″ in length, is of the Kushāṇa period and reads [3]

............*rpārigēyhē rajña Aśvaghōshasya chatariśē savachharē hēmata-pakhē prathamē divasē dasamē*..[4]........"In the fortieth year of *Rājan Aśvaghōsha*,[5] in the first fortnight of winter, on the tenth day............"

The third inscription also consists of a single line, 1′ 9″ long, but it is inscribed in characters of the early Gupta period.[6] It reads as follows :—

Ā[chā]ryyanaṁ Sa[mmi]tiyānaṁ parigraha Vātsīputrikānāṁ.

---

[1] *Viz.*, he will become a layman. The Buddhist clergy up to the present day wears orange-coloured (*kāshāya*) robes.

[2] *Viz.*, in a place which is not a residence for the clergy.

[3] Vogel, *Ep. Ind.*, VIII, p. 171 and facsimile.

[4] For readings of the additional words at the end of this epigraph, which were not included in the estampages prepared for Dr. Vogel, and which were afterwards brought to notice by Professor Venis, see *J. R. A. S.*, 1912, pp. 701-707.

[5] It is not known who this ruler was. It is noteworthy, however, that his name with the title of *rājan* also occurs on an inscribed fragmentary slab, D (*l*) 1 of the same period, which came to light some 70′ to the east-north-east of the Main Shrine. It will be noted that the spiritual teacher of Kānishka was also called Aśvaghōsha.

[6] *Ep. Ind.*, VIII, p. 172 and facsimile.

"Homage of the masters of the Sammitiya (?) sect (and) of the Vātsīputrika school." This epigraph is of interest as it shows that the Vātsīputrikas were a branch of the Sammitiya school. The Sarvāstivādins,[1] whose name is met with on the railing in the southern chapel of the Main Shrine, must have flourished side by side with the Sammitiyas at Sārnāth in the early Gupta period. In the time of Hiuen Thsang, the great convent at Sārnāth was entirely in the possession of the Sammitiya sect.

The identification of this column is still an open question.[2] It is tempting to identify it with the column seen by Hiuen Thsang in front of the *stūpa* built by Aśōka. It is highly polished and conforms well with the following description left by that traveller: "The stone is altogether as bright as jade. It is glistening, and sparkles like light."[3] The fact of its being situated in what was undoubtedly the most important portion of the ancient *saṅghārāma* of Sārnāth also points in the same direction. The main objections to this identification were summed up in 1907 by Dr. Marshall[4] in the following words: "But even here we are not absolutely sure of our ground, for the Chinese traveller says that the column was 70 feet or thereabouts in height, while the one discovered could not have been more than 50, and, on the other hand, he says nothing of Aśōka in connexion with it, nor does he mention either the inscription or the magnificent lion capital, which must have been an exceptionally striking feature. Again, if this is the column referred to by Hiuen Thsang, where is the stone *stūpa* 'in front of' which it stood?" In the present state of our knowledge about Sārnāth it is impossible to answer these objections. It may be hoped that future excavations will throw light on the problem.

The column was exposed by Mr. Oertel in 1904-05. The capital and the broken pieces of the shaft were found lying on the concrete terrace around the Main Shrine between the stump *in situ*, and the western chapel. It follows, therefore, that the column was overthrown about the 10th, 11th or 12th century A.D. That this ruthless act was perpetrated by a determined iconoclast is shown by the fact that the column was destroyed right down to the floor which surrounded it at that time. The lower seven lines of the Aśōka edict escaped this fate because they were then not visible. Pl. IV.

---

[1] *A. S. R.* for 1906-07, pp. 96-97.

[2] *Cf.* Introduction, p. 5.

[3] Beal, *Buddhist Records of the Western World*, II, p. 46.

[4] H. R. Nevill, *Benares, a gazetteer, being Vol. XXVI of the district gazetteers of the United Provinces of Agra and Oudh*, pp. 345-362.

B.—IMAGES.

Śuṅga Period.

B 1.—Two fragments of a male head, which fit together (ht. 8″; width 6¼″), carved in the round. Of the face, only a portion of the left cheek and the outer angle of the left eye remain. The right ear is broken off, but the left one is perfect. There are no ear-ornaments. On the crown of the skull is a tuft of hair fastened into a knot in the fashion still followed by the Hindus of the present day, the only difference being that the tuft is not quite in the centre of the head. The rest of the head is represented as shaven. To what kind of image this head belonged is not apparent, but it is of particular interest as being probably of the late Maurya or Śuṅga period. This conclusion follows from the fact that the head is made of the same kind of sandstone as the Aśōka capital (A 1) and has, like it, been highly polished. It was discovered in the year 1906-07 in the area to the north-west of the Main Shrine about the level of the concrete terrace around it.

The material is the buff-coloured sandstone of Chunār, from which it may be inferred that the head was carved at Benares. It was found by Mr. Oertel somewhere in the vicinity of the Main Shrine.

B (*a*).—Kushāṇa Period.

*B (*a*) 1.[1]—Standing statue of a Bōdhisattva,[2] similar in all respects to the Bōdhisattva statue [3] unearthed at Śrāvastī by General Cunningham and now preserved in the Indian Museum, Calcutta. The width of the image across the shoulders is 2′ 10″, the height [4] 8′ 1⅛″ or 9′ 5″ including the tenon by which it was fixed in the ground. The statue is broken into three pieces, namely, the base with the feet, the torso and the head. The right arm is broken off, but four fragments which came to light close to the statue clearly show that it was bent at the elbow and the hand raised to the shoulder in the well-known posture of imparting security (*abhayamudrā*). The palm of the hand is carved with a wheel and the finger-tips each with a mystic cross or *svastika*. These are two of the thirty-two chief signs of a great man (*mahā-purusha-lakshaṇa*) which characterize a Buddha.[5] The stone between the right hand and the shoulder has not been cut away but is decorated with a foliated pattern. This is a device common to all Kushāṇa Buddha and Bōdhisattva images of Mathurā in this attitude [6] and was presumably resorted to by those sculptors to protect the fingers of the right hand from injury. The left hand is, as usual, clenched into a fist resting on the left hip. The lower portion of the body is clad in an under-garment (*antaravāsaka*). The upper garment, which is a broad robe, is thrown over the left shoulder so that its two ends hang down in long folds along the left thigh.[7] The girdle, which holds the lower garment in position, is wound twice round the waist and then tied into a knot, its ends falling on the right thigh. The head seems to have been wilfully damaged; for the chin, nose, eyebrows and ear-lobes are all badly disfigured. The *ūrṇā* mark is absent. The head is treated like the shaven head of a monk.[8] A deep irregular break in the crown of the head suggests that it was originally provided

---

[1] Inscribed sculptures are marked with an asterisk.

[2] *A. S. R.* for 1904-05, pp. 78 sq. and Pl. XXVI, *a*, *b*.

[3] *A. S. R.*, Vol. I, pp. 338 ff. ; Anderson, *Catalogue and hand-book of the archæological collections in the Indian Museum*, Part I, pp. 194-195 ; *J. A. S. B.*, Vol. XLVII, part I, 1898, p. 278 ; *Ep. Ind.*, VIII, pp. 180 ff. and Pl.

[4] The traditional height of Gautama Buddha was 12 cubits according to some and 18 according to others. *Cf.* Kern, *Manual of Buddhism*, p. 62.

[5] Kern, *Manual of Buddhism*, p. 62.

[6] Vogel, *Mathurā Catalogue*, p. 36.

[7] As the two upper garments, the *uttarāsaṅga* and the *saṅghāṭī*, are worn in the same fashion, it is impossible to say whether the statue is meant to be clad in both or in only one upper garment. In neither case, however, would the girdle (*kāyabandhana*) be visible.

[8] This treatment is common enough in the Kushāṇa images of Mathurā, and is only replaced by the conventional schematic curls in the Gupta period. The only known Buddha image of the latter period with the shaven head is that of Kumāragupta's time at Mankuār near Bhiṭā in the Allahabad district. A photo of this image has been published by Smith, *Fine Art in India and Ceylon*, fig. 119. For the inscription on it *cf.* Fleet, *Gupta Inscriptions*, pp. 45 sq.

with a protuberance (*ushṇīsha*).[1] Round the head was a circular halo with a plain scalloped border on both sides such as we find in Mathurā images of the Kushāṇa period. A small portion of the halo still remains behind the shoulders and two other fragments were found close by.

Between the feet of the Bōdhisattva we find a small figure of a lion *sejant*, 14½″ in height. Dr. Vogel is of opinion that this figure is meant for a cognizance of Gautama Buddha,[2] and as the inscription incised on this statue clearly states that it was set up on the " Promenade of the Holy One " (*Bhagavatō chaṁkamē*), he concludes that this image represents Gautama as a Bōdhisattva. In support of Dr. Vogel's first argument it is interesting to note that the lion's head in a circular niche or cave is carved on the pedestals of several Sārnāth images of the Gupta and later periods, which represent Gautama Buddha at the moment of his enlightenment (*bōdhi*).[3]

This statue was originally protected by a stone umbrella [4] (Pl. VIII), which was found broken into ten pieces. Eight of these have been rejoined with copper dowels. The other two are too much worn to be restored. The umbrella is 10′ in diameter and adorned with concentric circular bands of decoration. The pierced projecting portion in the centre assumes the shape of a lotus flower, the fruit being distinct from the enclosing petals. Of the bands around the central portion, the innermost one shows a lotus petal design. The next ring contains a row of twelve fabulous animals in rectangular panels which alternate with lotus rosettes enclosed in squares. The animals have four paws and a pair of wings, and have the heads of a buffalo, a goose, an elephant, a lion (?), a crocodile (?), a leogryph, a goat, a camel, etc. The next band contains twelve mystic symbols which are the three jewels (*triratna*), a pair of fishes (*matsya-yugmam*)[5] with a noose hanging between them, a symbol resembling a *fleur-de-lis*, a vase with foliage. a kind of honeysuckle, one missing, a conch (*śaṅkha*), another honeysuckle, a *svastika*, a pot full of fruit or sweetmeats, a cup of leaves containing a garland and a third honeysuckle. It will be noticed that the honeysuckle ornament occurs three

---

[1] We know of five standing Bōdhisattva images of this type, namely, three (B (*a*) 1-3) from Sārnāth, the colossal image from Śrāvastī and one image from Mathurā now in the Lucknow Museum. None of these has a perfect head, and it is impossible to say whether they had the *ushṇīsha*.

[2] *Śākyasiṁha* or " Lion among the Śākyas " was a common appellation of Gautama Buddha. *Cf.* Kern, *Manual of Buddhism*, p. 63.

[3] *Cf.* B (*b*) 173-175 below. It is, however, possible that the lion in the cave is only meant to indicate the wilderness. Animals in caves are regularly found on Gandhāra and Mathurā sculptures representing Gautama Buddha visited by Indra in the Indraśaila cave near Rājagṛha. *Cf.* Vogel, *Mathurā Catalogue*, H 11, and Pl. VI, *b*.

[4] A plan and a section of this umbrella are published in *A. S. R.* for 1904-05, Pl. XXVII.

[5] This symbol is also sacred with the Jainas, being one of their eight *maṅgalas*.

times. The outermost band, which forms a lotus-petal border around the whole umbrella, is separated from the one just described by a double garland of conventional design relieved with lotus-rosettes at equal distances from one another. On the outside of the rim of the umbrella, are small narrow holes cut at distances of 1′ 7″ from one another from which probably streamers, flower-garlands or other similar objects were suspended by the Buddhist votaries in past days. Such holes occur also in other umbrellas and the back-slabs of images both here and at Mathurā.

Of the stone post which supported the umbrella two fragments, measuring 10′ 5″ altogether in height, were recovered. This portion is octagonal in the lower part, sixteen-sided in the middle and round at the top. The base of the post, which has been lost, was square.[1]

Near the lower end of the octagonal portion on three faces is carved an inscription in mixed Sanskrit and Prakrit. It consists of ten lines and runs as follows[2]:—

1. *Mahārajasya Kaṇishkasya saṁ 3 hē 3 di 22*
2. *ētayē purvayē bhikshusya Pushyavuddhisya saddhyēvi-*
3. *hārisya bhikshusya Balasya trēpiṭakasya*
4. *Bōdhisatvō chhatrayashṭi cha pratishṭhāpitō*
5. *Bārāṇasiyē Bhagavatō chaṁkamē sahā māt[ā]*
6. *pitihi sahā upaddhyāyāchērēhi saddhyēvihāri-*
7. *hi aṁtēvāsikēhi cha sahā Buddhamitrayē trēpiṭika-*
8. *yē sahā kshatrapēna Vanasparēṇa Kharapallā-*
9. *nēna cha sahā cha cha[tu]hi parishāhi sarvasatvanaṁ*
10. *hitasukhārtthaṁ.*

Translation.

"In the third year of Mahārāja Kaṇishka, the third [month] of winter, the 22nd day, on this date [specified as] above, was [this gift] of Friar Bala, a master of the Tripiṭaka and fellow of Friar Pushyavuddhi [namely an image of] the Bōdhisattva and an umbrella with a post, erected at Benares, at the place where the Lord used to walk, together with [his] parents, with [his] masters and teachers, [his] fellows and pupils and with [the nun] Buddhamitrā versed in the Tripiṭaka, together with the satrap Vanaspara and Kharapallāna, and together with the four classes,[3] for the welfare and happiness of all creatures."

In addition to this, there are two short epigraphs carved on the statue itself. One of them is cut on the front of the base and consists

---

[1] This I infer from the fact that the umbrella post of B (a) 2 below, which was obviously copied from this, is square at the lower end.

[2] Vogel, *Ep. Ind.*, VIII, p. 176, and facsimile.

[3] The four classes referred to are monks, nuns, laymen and laywomen.

of two lines, measuring about 2′ 5″ each, including the semi-circular groove cut down the middle of the base. It runs as follows [1] :—

Text.

1. *Bhikshusya Balasya trēpiṭakasya Bōdhisatvō pratishṭhāpitō* [*sahā*] [2]
2. *mahākshatrapēna Kharapallānēna sahā kshatrapēna Vanashparēna.*

Translation.

"This [image of] the Bōdhisattva, [a gift] of Friar Bala, a master of the Tripiṭaka, has been erected together with the great satrap Kharapallāna together with the satrap Vanashpara."

The other inscription, which is carved on the back of the image, begins 17″ above the base. It consists of three lines and runs [3] :—

Text.

1. *Mahārajasya Kaṇi*[*shkasya*] *saṁ 3 hē 3 di 2* [2]
2. *ētayē purvayē bhikshusya Balasya trēpiṭa*[*kasya*]
3. *Bōdhisatvō chhatrayashṭi cha* [*pratishṭhāpitō*].

Translation.

"In the third year of Mahārāja Kaṇishka, the third [month] of winter, the 22nd day, on this [date specified as] above has [this gift] of Friar Bala, a master of the Tripiṭaka, [namely an image of] the Bōdhisattva and an umbrella with a post [been erected]."

Dr. Vogel holds that this statue is called a gift of Bala, because it was carved under the supervision of this monk and that this Bala is identical with the donor of the Śrāvastī Bōdhisattva. who was in all probability a resident of Mathurā, for his name occurs also in another Kushāṇa inscription discovered at Mathurā.[4] This fact is interesting, for it proves that the statue was carved at Mathurā, from where it was brought and set up at Sārnāth. Further evidence is afforded by the material, which is deep red sandstone of Sikrī, of which all Mathurā sculptures are made, and by the style which is that of the Mathurā school. It deserves special mention that this statue is the earliest Buddhist image yet found at Sārnāth.

Mr. Oertel excavated the statue in the area between the Main Shrine and the Jagat Singh Stūpa, on the level of the concrete terrace

---

[1] Vogel, *Ep. Ind.*, VIII, p. 179 and facsimile.
[2] This word is lost but the left loop of *sa* is still traceable.
[3] Vogel, *Ep. Ind.*, VIII, p. 179 and facsimile.
[4] Growse, *Ind. Ant.*, Vol. VI, p. 217, No. 2 and plate; and Lüders, *ibid.*, Vol. XXXII, p. 39 and No. 9. The image is now in the Lucknow Provincial Museum.

around the former structure. This terrace dates from the 10th or 11th century A.D., and it is manifest that the statue must originally have stood on a much lower level and must have been taken down and re-erected as the level gradually rose. The fragments of the umbrella were found lying on the *stūpas* to the south of the Main Shrine. Pl. VII-VIII.

B (*a*) 2.—Image of a Bōdhisattva [1] carved in the round (ht. 6′; width across the shoulders 2′ 5″) which was found standing, facing to the east, on the west side of the cloistered passage to the north-east of the Main Shrine. The right hand which was raised against the shoulder in the attitude of imparting security (*abhayamudrā*) is broken off and the head is wanting. The left hand is clenched into a fist and rests on the left hip. The dress consists of the same garments as in B (*a*) 1, but the drapery is only indicated by very shallow irregular lines incised in the same plane. The girdle is also of the same kind with a similar large loop and with ends dropping on the right thigh. Between the legs of the image is a miniature figure crouching. It is much defaced and difficult to recognize but was perhaps meant for a dwarf or *yaksha*.

The material is buff-coloured Chunār sandstone and as the style of workmanship is similar to that of the statue described above, B (*a*) 1, I conclude that this image was prepared by a sculptor of Benares in imitation of the Mathurā image referred to.

Standing behind the statue was found the lower portion of a stone shaft which originally supported an umbrella of the same material for the protection of the statue from rain and bad weather. The extant portion is 3′ 9″ high, square below and octagonal above. The missing portion, to judge from the analogy of the umbrella post of B (*a*) 1, must have been sixteen-sided and round at the top.

B (*a*) 3.—Standing image of a Bōdhisattva, presumably Gautama Buddha before his enlightenment, 7′ 6½″ high or 10′ 6″ including the tenon at the base. The head is wanting, and the image was fractured at the ankles but has been re-fixed. The right hand is raised against the shoulder in the same way as in B (*a*) 1. The left hand rests not on the hip but lower down on the thigh. In dress and style, the image is similar to B (*a*) 2, but the drapery which in the preceding image had deteriorated into irregular shallow lines, is totally absent on the front of this image except over the left hand. In this respect, therefore, this image clearly marks a transition to the Gupta period when in the Sārnāth sculptures drapery well-nigh disappears.

The figure between the feet is much defaced, but the outline which is still traceable suggests that it was a lion *sejant* as in B (*a*) 1. On both sides of the feet on the flat top of the base are the lower portions

---

[1] *A. S. R.*, 1904-05, p. 79 and Pl. XXVI, *c*.

of two kneeling figures evidently meant for the donors of the image.[1] The head was encircled with a halo which has completely disappeared, but must have been circular. There are traces of red paint on the feet and above the ankles.

The statue was discovered by Mr. Oertel on a mediæval *stūpa* (No. 25 on plan) to the south-east of the Main Shrine. The stone umbrella which originally sheltered this image was not found, but its staff was found lying flat on the ground close by. It has lost the lower part, which was probably square. The existing portion is 11′ high and is mostly octagonal, sixteen-sided for next 22″ and round at the top. The material of the image and the post is buff-coloured sandstone from Chunār.

B (*a*) 4.—Fragment from the halo of an image presumably of the Kushāṇa period. It measures 10″ along the curved edge. It is plain on the reverse with the exception of the scalloped ornament which occurs along the margin. The obverse shows the foliage of the *pīpal* tree (Skt. *aśvattha*) which proclaims the fragment to be a portion of an image of Gautama Buddha shortly before or after his enlightenment under the Bōdhi tree.[2] Since the fragment is made of the red sandstone of Sīkrī, the image, to which it belonged, must have been carved at Mathurā. The style is also typical of that school. It was probably unearthed at Sārnāth by Mr. Oertel, but the exact find-place is not known.

B (*a*) 5.—Fragment (ht. 5″; width 1′ 1½″) of an image which was seated cross-legged, representing the left leg with the major part of the right foot resting on it. On the sole of the foot are carved the wheel (*chakra*) and three-jewel (*triratna*) symbols from which it may be inferred that the fragment belonged to an image of a Buddha or a Bōdhisattva. The material of the fragment is the red sandstone of Sīkrī of which Mathurā sculptures are made, and in style it is similar to the Kushāṇa images of that school. It is, therefore, manifest that the image to which this fragment belonged came from Mathurā. Possibly this and the fragment B (*a*) 4 belonged to the same image.

It was unearthed at Sārnāth in the area to the north of the Main Shrine in 1907-08.

B (*a*) 6.—Crossed legs (ht. 11½″) of a Buddha or Bōdhisattva image. The edges of the upper and lower garments are visible above the ankles. A lotus flower is marked on either sole. Probably Kushāṇa. Chunār sandstone of dark buff colour.

---

[1] Similar figures occur on Kushāṇa and Gupta images of Mathurā (*cf.* Vogel, *Catalogue*, Nos. A 40, A 5, A 6, etc.), and several Gupta images of Sārnāth (*cf.* Nos. B (*b*) 66, 79 and 108 below).

[2] Cf. *Mathurā Catalogue*; plates VI, *a*; VII and VIII.

B (*a*) 7.—Head (ht. 10½″) of an image of Buddha of life-size. Nose, lips, chin and ear-lobes broken. The gap in the crown is presumably due to the loss of the protuberance (*ushṇīsha*). The circular dot between the eyebrows is meant for the *ūrṇā*. This mark does not appear in any of the Gupta images of Sārnāth and Mathurā. The eyebrows are indicated by raised curved lines and the face is square. All these peculiarities seem to show that the head is a work of the Kushāṇa period. Made of Chunār sandstone. Unearthed by Mr. Oertel.[1]

B (*a*) 8.—Head (ht. 7½″) presumably of Buddha. The mark between the eyebrows (*ūrṇā*) is not indicated, nor the folds on the neck. The hair is arranged in schematic curls but the projection of the skull (*ushṇīsha*) is absent. The modelling of the face displays a remarkable affinity to that obtaining in Mathurā in the Kushāṇa period. Reddish Chunār sandstone. Discovered by Dr. Marshall and Dr. Konow to the south of structure No. 37 about 6′ below the surface.[2]

B (*a*) 9.—Hand (length 8″), presumably of a Buddha image in the attitude of protection. Bears traces of red paint. The style seems to be of the Kushāṇa period. Chunār sandstone.

---

[1] *A. S. R.*, 1904-05, p. 92, No. 41.
[2] *Ibid.*, 1906-07, p. 80 and Pl. XXIII, 3

B (*b*).—Buddha Images of the Gupta Period.

B (*b*) 1.—Image of Buddha[1] standing. Height 3′ 5″ up to the top of the halo, width across the shoulders 1′ 2″. The feet and the left hand are missing. Of the three garments (*trichīvara*) prescribed for the use of a monk, the image shows the lower garment (*antaravāsaka*) and an upper cloak (probably the *saṅghāṭī*) which covers the whole body including both shoulders and reaches down to a little above the ankles. The lower garment is bound to the loins by a plain girdle (*kāyabandhana*), the ends of which fall on the left thigh.[2] The drapery of the cloak (*saṅghāṭī*) is not indicated and its existence is only to be guessed from its edges which are shown as hanging from the arms. The right hand is raised against the shoulder, with the palm turned to the front in the posture of granting protection (*abhayamudrā*). The left hand holds up the cloak at the level of the thigh. The hair is arranged in short wavy curls turned to the right (*dakshiṇāvartta*). The protuberance of the skull (*ushṇīsha*) is indicated. The forehead-mark (*ūrṇā*) is absent. The back of the image has been left uncarved except for the general indication of the robe.

Behind the head is a circular halo, 1′ 7″ in diameter, decorated on the front with a plain scalloped border, but rough and undressed on the reverse. From this I conclude that the image marks a transition from the Kushāṇa to the Gupta style.[3] The position of the right hand lends support to this view.

The image is made of buff-coloured sandstone from the Chunār quarries and was discovered in 1906-07, to the west of the Jagat Singh Stūpa.

* B (*b*) 2.—Image of Buddha, standing, 3′ 6″ high, excluding the tenon at the base, and 1′ 2″ wide across the shoulders. The head and the right hand are wanting. The latter was raised with the palm turned to the front, so that the fore-arm assumed a position nearly at right-angles to the upper arm.[4] The left hand holds the hem of the upper garment at the height of the left thigh. The lower garment (*antaravāsaka*) is worn tightly round the loins. There is no girdle, but the edge of the lower garment is marked. The upper robe (*saṅghāṭī*), which covers both shoulders and the entire body down to a little above the ankles, clings, as it were, closely to the limbs thus bringing out their

---

[1] *A. S. R.*, 1906-07, and Pl. XXVIII, 2.

[2] The middle robe (*uttarāsaṅga*) which is worn by the monks under the *saṅghāṭī*, sometimes actually folded with it, is, of course, not visible.

[3] In addition to many fragmentary halos of the Gupta period, the Sārnāth Museum possesses a complete specimen in B (*b*) 4. They are all elaborately carved with concentric bands of ornament. This remark applies also to the Gupta halo of the Mathurā school (cf. *Mathurā Catalogue*, p. 36).

[4] In Kushāṇa images in the attitude of protection, the right hand is placed right against the shoulder (*cf.* B (*a*) 1-3). In Gupta images the position of the forearm is nearly horizontal or at right angles to the upper arm.

outline with perfect distinctness. As in B (*b*) 1, the back of the image is dressed with care, but no attempt has been made at carving beyond the general indication of the robe. There are remains of a circular halo behind the head. It is plain on the reverse, and was apparently also undecorated on the front. The base of the image with the feet was found detached but has been refixed. On it is carved in two lines a Sanskrit inscription in characters of about the fifth century A.D. The epigraph is much abraded, but seems to be the ordinary formula of a votive inscription of that period.

This image is of considerable interest for it helps in determining the age of many other images of the same type in the Sārnāth Museum.[1] It is made of pale buff sandstone of Chunār and was discovered in 1904-05 to the north-west of the Main Shrine.[2] The detached base with the feet came to light in 1906-07 in the same area.

* B (*b*) 3.—Image of Buddha standing, 2′ 6¾″ high including tenon at base and 11″ wide across the shoulders, similar in all respects to B (*b*) 2. The head is broken and both hands are slightly injured. The right hand is raised with the palm turned to the front, in the posture of granting security (*abhayamudrā*). The stone between the back of this hand and the upper portion of the arm has not been cut away.[3] The left hand holds the hem of the upper robe (*saṅghāṭī*). The lower garment (*antaravāsaka*) which covers the legs is visible above the ankles. The upper garment (*saṅghāṭī*) fits closely to the body and covers both shoulders. The back of the image is treated after the fashion of the preceding image. The base of the image which is detached is inscribed with a single line of writing in characters of the 4th or 5th century A.D. The middle portion of the inscription has peeled off. The remaining portion has been read by Dr. Vogel as follows[4] :—

D[ē]yadha[r]mmō=yaṁ vi .... *svāmi-*
Skandava[r]ṇṇa[sya].
" This is the pious gift of............master Skandavarṇṇa."

This image is one of the thirteen Sārnāth sculptures which in 1903, together with eight Magadha images, were presented by the Principal of the Queen's College, Benares, to the Lucknow Provincial Museum[5] and have now been transferred by the Government to the Sārnāth Museum at the instance of Dr. Vogel.

---

1 This type of Buddha in the *abhayamudrā* seems to have been a favourite subject with the Sārnāth sculptors. There are many replicas in this museum and several others including two inscribed specimens of the Gupta period in the Indian Museum.

2 *A. S. R.*, 1904-05, p. 94, No. 115.

3 Such a cushion also occurs in the Kushāṇa images (*cf.* B (*a*) 1-2), but higher up right against the shoulder.

4 *A. S. R.*, 1903-04, p. 214 and facsimile on Pl. LXIV, 1.

5 *Cf.* Vogel, *Buddhist sculptures from Benares* in the *A. S. R.* for 1903-04, pp. 213-214 and Pl. LXII, 1.

B (*b*) 4.—Image of Buddha standing (ht. 8′ 1″ to the top of the halo; width across the shoulders 2′ 4″). The head and both hands were broken off and have been refixed. The halo, which was found broken into four pieces, has also been restored. Eyes, nose, lips, chin and ear-lobes slightly damaged. The hair is arranged in schematic curls turned to the right (*dakshiṇāvartta*) and the protuberance of the skull (*ushṇīsha*) is nearly hemispheric in shape. The right hand is raised in the attitude of imparting protection, the left holds the skirt of the upper robe (*saṅghāṭī*). The lower garment (*antaravāsaka*) is bound tightly to the waist. The girdle is not marked. The back of the image only shows the indication of the robe. There is no writing on the image, but the style and attitude which are identical with those of the two inscribed images B (*b*) 2 and 3 leave no doubt that this image also belongs to the Gupta period.

The halo which is 3′ ½″ in diameter is valuable as a complete specimen of the Gupta period.[1] It is richly sculptured except the central portion. The decoration consists of several concentric bands of ornament. The innermost, which is the broadest, consists of an intricate floral and foliated pattern, the leaves assuming the appearance of scrolls. This is enclosed by a conventional garland in which five rosettes have been introduced. The next pattern is the bead and reel ornament and last of all we find a narrow scalloped border which occurs already on the halo of the Kushāṇa period, but there without any further ornament.

The image is made of buff-coloured sandstone from Chunār and was unearthed in 1904-05 [2] to the south of the Main Shrine.

B (*b*) 5.—Image of Buddha standing (ht. 4′ 5½″; width across the shoulders 1′ 6″). The base with the feet is broken off and the right eye, nose, chin, and ear-lobes are slightly injured. The arms were broken into many pieces and have been restored. The right hand is raised in the attitude of granting security. The left hand which held the hem of the robe is missing. There is no indication of the girdle, but the edge of lower garment (*antaravāsaka*) is clearly marked. The right leg is slightly bent and the halo which is broken into several fragments is circular (2′ 2″ in diameter) and has the same decoration as B (*b*) 4, but much more finely executed.

The image is made of a fine-grained greyish sandstone from Chunār. The style is similar to that of the inscribed Gupta images B (*b*) 2 and 3 and I have no hesitation in assigning this image to the same period. It was found in 1906-07 [3] to the south of Jagat Singh Stūpa.

---

[1] Another Gupta image of Buddha with a well preserved halo, which originates from Sārnāth, is preserved in the Indian Museum, Calcutta (*cf.* Anderson, *Catalogue and handbook of archæological collections in the Indian Museum*, Pt. II, p. 11, No. S. 14).

[2] *A. S. R.* for 1904-05, p. 83 and Pl. XXIX, *d*.

[3] *Ibid.*, 1906-07, p. 91, No. 16 and Pl. XXIX, *a*.

B (*b*) 6.—Image of Buddha, finely carved, of about life-size (ht. 5′ 1½″; width across shoulders 1′ 8″). The right hand is raised in the attitude of protection (*abhayamudrā*); the left holds the robe at the height of the left thigh. From the close similarity of its style to that of the preceding statues this sculpture may also be assigned to the time of the Imperial Guptas.

The image projects from a back-slab which is oval at the top. There is no separate halo, but the margin of the back-slab is decorated with a narrow scalloped border which is combined on the inside with a line of bead and reel. This obviously marks the first stage in the development of the plain scalloped border of the Kushāṇa period.

The head with the slab behind it, and both hands were detached and have been refixed. The right hand was found in 1904-05 to the south-west of the Aśoka column. It is not recorded where the head and the left hand were found. The remaining portion of the image was found standing on a low brick pedestal in the southern chapel of the Main Shrine.[1]

B (*b*) 7.—Torso of a standing Buddha image (ht. 4′ 4″; width across the shoulders 1′ 10″). The head, feet and hands are missing, but the right hand must have been in the posture of imparting protection (*abhayamudrā*). The drapery is of the usual fashion. There is no back-slab, but the torso retains remnants of a circular halo similar in decoration to that of B (*b*) 4. The style of the image points to about the 5th century as its date. The material is pale buff stone of Chunār. Unearthed in 1904-05 to the north of Jagat Singh Stūpa.[2]

B (*b*) 8.—Figure of standing Buddha (ht. 4′ 3″ excluding tenon at base; width across shoulders 1′ 3″), projecting from a back-slab. The top of the back-slab which is broken off must have been oval, like that of B (*b*) 6. The hands are missing. The right hand was evidently raised in the attitude of granting protection (*abhayamudrā*). Chin, lips and nose slightly damaged. The style is that of the Gupta period. The image was fractured at the ankles and has been repaired.

Made of buff-coloured sandstone from Chunār and discovered in 1904-05 to the south-east of Jagat Singh Stūpa.[3]

B (*b*) 9.—Standing figure of Buddha in alto-relievo. The back slab which is 4′ 3″ high and 1′ 9½″ broad in the middle is of the same shape and has the same decoration as that of B (*b*) 6. The right hand is raised in the attitude of imparting protection and the dress is of the usual fashion. Both hands and head were found broken from the image and have been re-set. The upper portion of the back-slab has five holes pierced into the edge, which were probably meant to hold flower-

---

[1] *A. S. R.* for 1904-05, p. 68.
[2] *Ibid.*, p. 91, No. 10.
[3] *Ibid.*, 1904-05, p. 91, No. 36.

sticks or other similar offerings. On account of its style the image is referable to the Gupta period.

Made of Chunār sandstone with fine black spots. Discovered in 1904-05 to the north-west of the Main Shrine.[1]

B (*b*) 10.—Image of Buddha standing in the attitude of protection (ht. 4′ 6″ up to the protuberance of the skull). No back-slab. The hands and the lower portion of the legs are wanting. The face has been disfigured. The dress is of the usual fashion. Behind the head was a circular halo (2′ 6″ in diameter), nearly half of which is extant. The carving on the halo is of the same type as on B (*b*) 4, but much defaced. Gupta period. Made of reddish Chunār sandstone. Unearthed in 1904-05.

* B (*b*) 10 *a*.—Image (ht. 1′ 6¾″; width 6¼″) of Buddha standing in the attitude of imparting security. On the base of the image is a short dedicatory inscription in Gupta characters which reads *Dēyadharmmō=yaṁ Dhanadēvasya*, which means, "this [is] the pious gift of Dhanadēva."

The sculpture was found in 1904-05 built into a niche of a *stūpa* to the west of the Jagat Singh *stūpa*.[2]

B (*b*) 11.—Image of Buddha standing, without back-slab (ht. 4′ 1″; width across shoulders 1′ 7″). The right hand which was raised in the attitude of imparting security is lost. The left hand and the feet are also missing. The face has been cut away right through and the skull protuberance (*ushṇīsha*) is damaged. Behind head, remnants of circular halo with concentric circular rings of decoration similar to those of B (*b*) 5.

The image was formerly preserved in the Queen's College, Benares, but the material and style of carving leave no doubt that it is from Sārnāth.

B (*b*) 12.—Image of Buddha standing in the attitude of protection (ht. 4′ 10″; width across shoulders 1′ 7″). Hands and feet missing. The face has disappeared but the section thus exposed reveals three holes from which it may be concluded that it had already been repaired. This is confirmed by the presence of grooves on each side, which held the metal cramps. There is no back-slab. Behind the head is a portion of a circular halo with a broad band of foliated and floral device and a line of bead and reel ornament.

The material is a dark variety of Chunār sandstone which has weathered owing to exposure. The image was formerly preserved in the Queen's College.

B (*b*) 13.—Headless image of Buddha standing (ht. 4′ ½″; width across shoulders 1′ 6″). The hands are broken off, so also a portion of the base with a part of the feet. The attitude was that of protection.

---

[1] *A. S. R.* for 1904-05, p. 91, No. 32.
[2] *Ibid.*, 1906-07, p. 99, VII.

Traces of circular halo. The style is of the Gupta period. Made of sandstone. The image is one of the Queen's College collection.

B (*b*) 14.—Image of Buddha standing (ht. 3′ 5¼″). The hands are wanting, but the right hand was evidently raised in the posture of granting security. The girdle (*kāyabandhana*) is indicated below the edge of the lower garment, its ends falling on the left hip. Robe indicated on the back of the image. On grounds of style this image can be attributed to the 5th century A.D. The image retains vestiges of red paint. It belonged to the Queen's College collection, but undoubtedly originates from Sārnāth.

B (*b*) 15.—Torso of Buddha, without back-slab (ht. 3′; width across shoulders 1′ 1½″). Head, hands and feet missing. The right hand was apparently raised in the attitude of protection. The girdle is indicated; its ends fall on the left hip. Traces of halo behind head. The image is one of the Queen's College collection, but must have been found at Sārnāth.

B (*b*) 16.—Torso of Buddha (ht. 3′ 2″; width across shoulders 1′ 3½″), without back-slab. Head, hands and feet wanting. Right leg slightly bent at the knee. The attitude of the image was that of imparting security. Girdle not indicated, but edge of lower garment visible through upper robe. Gupta period. Made of buff-coloured sandstone from Chunār and unearthed in 1904-05 to the south-west of the Main Shrine.[1]

B (*b*) 17.—Image of Buddha standing (ht. 3′ 5″; width across shoulders 1′ 2½″) without head and hands. The right hand was in the posture of protection. The base is partly broken off with portions of the feet, and a large piece has peeled off the breast. The halo has entirely disappeared. *Circa* 5th century A.D.

The material is buff-coloured sandstone from Chunār. The image was found in 1904-05 [2] to the south of the Main Shrine.

B (*b*) 18.—A much weather-worn standing image (ht. 4′ 2″; width across shoulders 1′ 6″) of Buddha similar in all respects to B (*b*) 17. Head and hands wanting and toes partly broken off.

Made of Chunār sandstone of a dark colour. Found in 1904-05 to the north-west of Jagat Singh Stūpa.

B (*b*) 19.—Torso of Buddha standing (ht. 3′ 8″; width across shoulders 1′ 5″). The head, arms, right leg and feet are broken off. A square hole in the stone at the proper right end suggests that the right arm was a separate piece. The halo was circular, but only the beginning of it is now left behind the shoulders. The style points to the Gupta period as the date of the image.

---

[1] *A. S. R.*, 1904-05, p. 93, No. 52.

[2] *Ibid.*, p. 92, No. 40.

The material is dark sandstone of Chunār. The image was noticed lying near a temporary culvert to the west of the site of Sārnāth by Dr. Venis in 1907-08.

B (*b*) 20.—Image of Buddha (ht. 3′ 5½″; width across shoulders 1′ ½″) standing in alto-relievo against a back-slab, the upper portion of which is broken off. The decoration on its margin is similar to that on B (*b*) 6. The hands and the feet of the image are wanting. On grounds of style the image is attributable to the Gupta period.

The material is Chunār sandstone. The image was formerly preserved in the Queen's College.

B (*b*) 21.—Image of Buddha standing (ht. 3′ 3″; width across shoulders 1′ 6″) without back-slab. The right hand, which was raised in the attitude of granting security (*abhayamudrā*), is lost; the left hand is all but gone. The lower portion of the image from the knees downwards is also missing. The hair is arranged in spiral curls. The treatment of the dress is similar to that in the preceding images. The girdle takes the form of a plain belt tied into a knot on the left hip. Traces of an elaborately carved halo remain behind the head. Gupta period.

Made of dark-coloured Chunār sandstone. The image belonged to the Queen's College collection.

B (*b*) 22.—Image of Buddha standing (ht. 3′ 8″; width across shoulders 1′) with a plain back-slab which was oval at top. The latter is broken off on the left side and below the level of the elbow on the right. The attitude of the image was that of granting protection. The hands and feet are broken off. The surface of the image is peeling off everywhere. The nose is slightly injured. The style of carving is that of the Gupta period.

The material of the image is the sandstone of Chunār. It was formerly preserved in the Queen's College.

B (*b*) 23.—Image of Buddha standing (ht. 2′ 9″; width across shoulders 10″) in alto-relievo, the back-slab all but gone. The head and the right arm are missing. The remainder is broken into three pieces. The left hand lifts the hem of the upper robe (*saṅghāṭī*) to a little below the shoulder. But as this position of the left hand is invariably associated in the Sārnāth sculptures with the gift-bestowing attitude (*varadamudrā*),[1] we may assume that the right hand was stretched out at the level of the thigh with the palm turned to the front. At the feet of the image we notice traces of a kneeling figurine, probably the donor of the sculpture. The back-slab is decorated with a line of bead and reel. Gupta period.

The image is made of reddish sandstone of Chunār and shows traces of red colouring. Found in 1904-05, the base with the feet to the

[1] In a Mathurā sculpture this position of the left hand is found in the *abhayamudrā*, *Cf.* Vogel, *Mathurā Catalogue*, Pl. XV, *a*.

south of Main Shrine; the legs to north-east of Main Shrine and the upper portion to the west of Jagat Singh Stūpa.[1]

B (*b*) 24.—Torso (ht. 10″; width 7″) of Buddha standing in the attitude of granting security (*abhayamudrā*). Head, hands and legs from knees downwards wanting. Traces of circular halo. Dress indicated on back. Gupta work. Chunār sandstone. Unearthed in 1904-05 south of Main Shrine.[2]

B (*b*) 25.—Two fragments representing the trunk and head of an image of Buddha which was evidently standing in the attitude of granting security (ht. 2′ 2″; width across the shoulders 1′ 4″). The left forearm and the thumb of the right hand are broken off. The features are slightly damaged. Portions of circular halo behind head. Four other small pieces obviously belong to this halo. The decoration on them and the style of the image are distinctly Gupta.

Made of fine-grained sandstone of Chunār. The head was unearthed in 1904-05 [3] to the south-west of Main Shrine. The trunk [4] and the pieces of the halo were discovered in 1907-08 in the area north of the Main Shrine.

B (*b*) 26.—Bust of image of Buddha which must have been standing in the attitude of protection (ht. 1′ 5½″; width across shoulders 8½″). Chin, nose and ear-lobes slightly injured. Traces of halo behind head.

Unearthed in 1904-05. The exact find-spot was not recorded. The head is detached from the trunk and has been refixed.

B (*b*) 27.—Image of Buddha of Gupta period standing (2′ 6″ high, 10″ wide across the shoulders) in the attitude of protection. The face has been cut away and the surface is flaking everywhere. Both forearms and the toes are missing. Behind head, plain circular halo of which about a third now remains. No back-slab.

Made of buff-coloured Chunār sandstone. It was formerly preserved in the Queen's College.

B (*b*) 28.—Image (ht. 1′ 8″; width across shoulders 7″) of Buddha of the Gupta period standing in the attitude of protection. It is broken into four pieces. The head, right arm and left upper arm are wanting. Traces of red colour.

Made of Chunār sandstone and unearthed in 1907-08 in the area to the north of the Main Shrine.

B (*b*) 29.—Torso of standing image of Buddha (ht. 1′ 6½″; width across shoulders 10″) in Gupta style, without head, right arm and feet.

---

[1] *A. S. R.*, 1904-05, p. 93, No. 51; p. 97, No. 235; and p. 98, No. 270.
[2] *Ibid.*, 1904-05, p. 94, No. 109.
[3] *Ibid.*, 1904-05, p. 97, No. 197.
[4] *Ibid.*, 1907-08, p. 72, β 24.

The position of the left hand shows that the attitude of the right hand was that of protection. Traces of halo.

Made of dark buff sandstone of Chunār and found in 1906-07 in the area to the east of the Main Shrine.

B (*b*) 30.—Torso of image of Buddha standing (ht. 2′ 2½″; width across shoulders 1′). The image projects from a back-slab, but the latter is much mutilated. Of the image itself, the head, left fore-arm and feet are missing. It is obvious, however, that the left hand lifted the hem of the upper robe (*saṅghāṭī*) to the height of the shoulder. The right hand is held at the level of the right thigh with the palm turned to the front in the gift-bestowing posture (*varada-mudrā*). Below this hand on the back-slab there remain traces of the upper portion of a miniature human figure which may have been meant for the donor of the image.

Made of Chunār sandstone. Discovered in 1906-07 in the first courtyard to the east of the mediæval monastery I, 3′ below the surface.

B (*b*) 31.—Torso of Buddha figure standing (ht. 1′ 11″; width across shoulders 9½″) in the attitude of protection. Head, both hands and feet missing, and back-slab mutilated. The latter is decorated along the margin with a line of bead and reel and a scalloped border. The style is of the Gupta period.

Made of Chunār sandstone and found in 1904-05 to the north of the Aśōka column.[1]

B (*b*) 32.—Figure of Buddha standing (ht. 1′ 7″; width across shoulders 8″) in the gift-bestowing attitude (*varada-mudrā*). The right hand is in the usual position; but the left hand is placed on the thigh. In all the other Sārnāth images which show Buddha in this attitude, the left hand grasps the hem of the robe at the level of the shoulder. The lower portion below the thighs is missing and the face and both hands have suffered from flaking. The style seems to be of the Gupta period. The back-slab is quite plain.

Made of a very rough kind of Chunār sandstone. Unearthed in 1904-05 to the north-west of the Main Shrine.[2]

B (*b*) 33.—Torso of Buddha standing (ht. 12½″; width across shoulders 7″) in the posture of imparting security. The head, right hand and legs below the knees are broken off. The back-slab which must, as usual, have been oval at the top, is much mutilated. The style is of the Gupta period.

The material is Chunār sandstone. The figure was painted red and was found in 1904-05 in the neighbourhood of the Jagat Singh Stūpa.

---

[1] *A. S. R.* for 1904-05, p. 93, No. 63.
[2] *Ibid.*, 1904-05, p. 94, No. 111.

B (*b*) 34.—**Fragment showing a figure of Budda, in alto-relievo, from the neck to the thighs** (ht. 9½″; width across shoulders 8″). The hands are both lost, but the attitude was undoubtedly that of protection. From the elbows of the arms issue stalks, possibly of lotus-flowers, to support miniature replicas of the main figure. Probably Gupta.

Chunār sandstone. Vestiges of red paint. Found in 1906-07 in the area to the east of the Main Shrine.

B (*b*) 35.—**Torso of Buddha image standing** (ht. 1′ 3″; width across shoulders 8″) of the Gupta period. Head, legs and hands wanting. The attitude was that of protection. No back-slab. Traces of circular halo behind head. The tassels of the girdle (*kāyabandhana*) fall over the left hip.

Chunār sandstone. Discovered in 1904-05 [1] to the west of *stūpa* No. 35 on the east of the Main Shrine.

B (*b*) 36.—**Torso of Buddha standing** (ht. 1′ 3″; width across shoulders 6″). Head, feet and hands broken off. The upper robe (*saṅghāṭī*), as usual, covers both shoulders. The image is in the attitude of protection and, to judge from its style, of the Gupta period.

Made of Chunār sandstone. Discovered in 1906-07 in the area to the north-west of Main Shrine.

B (*b*) 37.—**Torso of Buddha standing** (ht. 1′ 5″; width across shoulders 7″) in the posture of protection. Head, hands and feet missing. Traces of back-slab. Late Gupta period. Made of Chunār sandstone and found in 1904-05 to the south of Main Shrine.[2]

B (*b*) 38.—**Figure of Buddha standing** (ht. 1′; width across shoulders 5″) in the attitude of protection. Head and feet broken off. The back-slab is decorated with a line of bead and reel. The scalloped border is absent. The figure is assignable to the late Gupta period.

Made of Chunār sandstone. Discovered in 1904-05 to the south of the Aśōka Column.[3]

B (*b*) 39.—**Figure of Buddha standing** (ht. 8½″; width across shoulders 3″) in the posture of granting security. The upper portion of the back-slab and the head of the image are broken off. The girdle is indicated. Near the right foot of Buddha is a kneeling female figure obviously meant for the donor. Gupta style.

Made of Chunār sandstone and discovered in 1904-05 to the south of the Main Shrine.[4]

B (*b*) 40.—**Torso of Buddha (?) standing in the attitude of protection** (ht. 12½″ including the remnant of the halo; width across shoulders 5″). Head, hands and feet missing. The upper robe which is

---

[1] *A. S. R.*, 1904-05, p. 94, No. 107.
[2] *Ibid.*, 1904-05, p. 93, No. 54.
[3] *Ibid.*, No. 70.
[4] *Ibid.*, No. 77.

E

draped with care leaves the right shoulder bare. The style is of the Gupta period.

Made of Chunār sandstone and unearthed in 1906-07 in the first court to the east of the mediæval monastery I some 4′ below the surface.

* B (*b*) 41.—Figure of Buddha standing (ht. 8″; width across shoulders 5″) from the throat to the knees. The back-slab which is much mutilated had only a plain incised line around the border. The hands are broken; enough, however, remains to show that the right one was stretched out in the gift-bestowing attitude (*varada-mudrā*) while the left lifted the hem of the upper robe (*saṅghāṭī*) to the shoulder. The back of the sculpture was incised with a Prakrit version of the Buddhist creed in characters of the Gupta period. The only portion that is now legible is *prabhavā tēsaṁ hētuṁ.*

The material is Chunār sandstone and the figure is one of the thirteen Sārnāth sculptures which were returned to this Museum from the Lucknow Provincial Museum.[1]

B (*b*) 42.—Torso of Buddha standing (ht. 8¾″; width across shoulders 5″). The head, hands and the lower portion below the knees are wanting. The right hand was raised at the elbow in the attitude of granting protection. Beginning of circular halo behind shoulders and faint traces of red colour. To judge from the style the image must date from the Gupta period.

Made of Chunār sandstone. The image is one of the thirteen Sārnāth sculptures which have come back from the Lucknow Provincial Museum.[2]

B (*b*) 43.—Image of Buddha standing (ht. 1′ 4½″; width across shoulders 5″) in the attitude of protection. The face has flaked away and the hands and feet are broken off. The upper robe (*saṅghāṭī*), as usual, covers both shoulders. Around the head is a circular halo with bead and reel ornament and scalloped border, of which the top portion is missing. Gupta style.

Made of Chunār sandstone and unearthed in 1904-05 near the Aśōka Column.[3]

B (*b*) 44.—Torso of Buddha figure standing (ht. 11″; width across shoulders 7″) from throat to knees. The right hand which is missing was raised in the attitude of protection. The left fore-arm is wanting. The upper robe covers both shoulders. The style is of the Gupta period.

---

[1] This figure has been described by Dr. Vogel in his article on Buddhist Sculptures from Benares in the *A. S. R.* for 1903-04, p. 225, No. 14.

[2] This image is noticed by Dr. Vogel in the *A. S. R.* for 1903-04, p. 225, as No. 16, ht. 23 cm.

[3] *A. S. R.*, 1904-05, p. 92, No. 34.

Made of Chunār sandstone and unearthed in 1904-05 to the south-west of the Main Shrine.[1] The left upper arm which is detached was discovered in 1906-07 in the area to the east of the Main Shrine.

B (*b*) 45.—Torso of standing Buddha figure (ht. 11½" ; width across shoulders 4½") of the Gupta period. The attitude is that of protection. The head, hands and feet are broken off.

Made of Chunār sandstone and discovered in 1904-05[2] to the south of the Main Shrine.

B (*b*) 46.—Figure of Buddha standing (ht. 1' ; width across shoulders 4") in the attitude of protection. The right hand and feet are wanting. Decadent Gupta style.

The material is Chunār sandstone. The figure was discovered in 1904-05.[3]

B (*b*) 47.—Torso (ht. 6½" ; width 5") of Buddha in the attitude of granting security. Gupta style. Chunār sandstone. Unearthed in 1906-07 in the so-called Hospital (really a monastery) 5½' below the surface.

B (*b*) 48.—Figure of Buddha (ht. 11" ; width across shoulders 4½") standing in gift-bestowing attitude (*varada-mudrā*). Head and feet missing. To judge from the style the image probably dates from the late Gupta period.

Chunār sandstone. Unearthed in 1904-05.[4]

B (*b*) 49.—Figure of Buddha standing (ht. 11½" ; width across shoulders 4") in the gift-bestowing attitude. Feet and upper portion of back-slab missing. Style similar to that of B (*b*) 48. Chunār sandstone. Found in 1906-07 to the west of Jagat Singh Stūpa immediately below the present surface.

B (*b*) 50.—Figure of Buddha standing in the gift-bestowing attitude (ht. 1' 4" ; width across shoulders 6"). The face has been cut away and the feet are missing. The hands are also broken off. The style seems to be of the late Gupta period.

Made of Chunār sandstone and excavated in 1906-07 in the area to the west of the Main Shrine 3' below the surface of the ground.

B (*b*) 51.—Image (ht. 1' 8" ; width 1') of Buddha standing in the gift-bestowing attitude (*varada-mudrā*). The left hand, which raised the hem of the upper robe to the shoulder, and feet are missing. Head detached from body but re-fixed with copper dowel. Gupta style. Chunār sandstone. Excavated in 1904-05.[5]

---

[1] *A. S. R.*, 1904-05, p. 93, No. 64.
[2] *Ibid.*, p. 94, No. 108.
[3] *Ibid.*, p. 94, No. 109.
[4] *Ibid.*, p. 92, No. 39.
[5] *Ibid.*, p. 94, No. 96.

B (*b*) 52.—Image (ht. 1′ 3½″ ; width 9″) of Buddha in the same attitude as B (*b*) 51. Face, left hand and feet broken off. Rest much defaced. Upper robe covers both shoulders. No girdle. Gupta style. Chunār sandstone. Unearthed in 1906-07 in first court on east of mediæval monastery I, north of its entrance, 5′ below surface.

B (*b*) 53.—Bust without head and fore-arms (ht. 5″ ; width 7½″) of Buddha. The attitude cannot be made out. Robe indicated on back. Traces of red paint. Gupta work. Chunār sandstone. Find-spot not known.

B (*b*) 54.—Fragment (ht. 5½″ ; width 7″) with the bust of a worshipper and hem of a standing Buddha image. The hands of the worshipper, which were joined before the chest, are broken off. Gupta style. Chunār sandstone. Unearthed in 1907-08 on the approach to the Main Shrine from the east, 7′ below the surface.

B (*b*) 55.—Fragment of a standing image of Buddha (ht. 9″ ; width across shoulders 8½″) in late Gupta style, from the throat to the thighs. Right fore-arm broken off. The position of the left fore-arm which is detached shows that the attitude of the image was that of granting protection.

Made of Chunār sandstone and unearthed in 1904-05 in Chaukhaṇḍī Stūpa.

B (*b*) 56.—Torso of a standing Buddha image (ht. 1′ 4½″ ; width across shoulders 6″). Head, both arms and lower portions of legs missing. The back of the fragment has been cut away from top to bottom.

Chunār sandstone with traces of red colour. Found in 1904-05 to the south of the Main Shrine.[1]

B (*b*) 57.—Figure of Buddha standing in the gift-bestowing attitude (*varada-mudrā*). Ht. 1′ 2″ excluding tenon at base ; width across shoulders 4½″. Head missing and fore-arms and feet damaged. Traces of kneeling figure on the proper right of the right foot. Late Gupta style.

Chunār sandstone. Found in 1904-05 ; but the exact spot is not known.

B (*b*) 58.—Trunk of a standing Buddha figure (ht. 6½″ ; width across shoulders 5″). The left hand lifted the hem of the upper robe to the shoulder. The right arm is broken off but must have been in the attitude of bestowing a gift (*varada-mudrā*). Gupta style.

Chunār sandstone. Found in 1907-08.

---

[1] *A. S. R.*, 1904-05, p. 97, No. 230.

* B (*b*) 59.—Base of a standing image of Buddha (?) [1] of which only the feet remain (width 14½"). The latter are executed with admirable skill, and exhibit a very close likeness to the feet of the images of the early Gupta period. On the front of the base is incised a dedicatory Sanskrit epigraph in characters of the 4th or 5th century A.D. It consists of two lines measuring (13" and 7½" respectively) and runs as follows [2] :—

1. *Dēyadharmmō=yaṁ śākyabhikshō[r]=Buddhapṛi(ri)yasya yad =attra puṇyaṁ*
2. *tad=bhavatu anuttara-jñānāvātma(pta)yē.*

"This [is] the pious gift of the Buddhist friar Buddhapriya. Whatever merit [there is] in this [gift] let it be for the attainment of supreme wisdom."

Made of Chunār sandstone and unearthed in 1904-05 to the south-east of the Main Shrine.[3]

* B (*b*) 60.—Base with the feet only remaining of an image of Buddha (ht. 1' 3½" including tenon ; width 1' 8¼"). The image must have been life-size and painted red. On the front of the base, there is a Sanskrit inscription of four lines in characters of the 5th century A.D. About a third of the epigraph at the proper left end has altogether disappeared. The remaining portion has also suffered considerably from the peeling off of the surface. I propose to read the inscription as follows :—

1. *[Saṁ*] va [tsara śa] tē... saptat.... asy[āṁ] diva* [4] *pūrvvāyā[ṁ] mārgaśira [mā] sē .... [dēyadharmmō]=*
2. *yaṁ śyā(śā)kya[bhikshōḥ] ..... pratim=ēyaṁ* [5] *nmunē* [6] *śailā bhava—[paṁ] ....*
3. *kārayitv=ā[tma] .... [ya]n=may=ōpārjjitaṁ śubhaṁ[||*] tēna lōkō nirālōkō ...... jñāna ...... [mātā]*
4. *pitrō[r=upādhyāyāch] āryāṇāṁ sarvva-satvānāṁ chāna(u) ttara-jñānā[vāptayē].*

." In the year one hundred ....
... On this day [as specified] above. In the month of Mārgaśiras
This the pious gift of the Buddhist monk ......
.... This stone image of the Sage

---

[1] This may have as well belonged to a Bōdhisattva image. It is, however, more probably a part of a Buddha image. This remark applies to the bases of images which follow.

[2] Published by Dr. Vogel in *A. S. R.*, 1904-05, p. 90, No. XVII and Pl. XXXII, XVII.

[3] *A. S. R.*, 1904-05, p. 92, No. 50.

[4] Read *divasa.*

[5] The following portion seems to be in verse in *Anushṭubh* metre. A similar wish is expressed in an inscription discovered in 1907-08 in monastery I. Cf. *A. S. R.*, 1907-08, p. 75, No. VI and D (*f*) 59 of this catalogue.

[6] Read *munēḥ.*

...... Having caused [it] to be made ....,
What merit I have accumulated ....
By it the benighted world ....
... For the attainment of unsurpassed wisdom by [his parents, preceptors and] teachers and of all sentient beings.''

It is a pity that the beginning portion of the first line which contained the date is so much damaged. The year, which is uncertain, must obviously be referred to the Gupta era.

The material of the sculpture is a reddish kind of Chunār sandstone. Found in 1907-08 in the area to the north of the Main Shrine.[1]

* B (*b*) 61.—Two fragments representing the fore-part of the right foot of a standing image of a Buddha or a Bōdhisattva (width 7″). On the front of it there is a Gupta inscription of three lines which are incomplete at both ends. It runs[2] :—

1. ....*m=aṁgē nāśam=adhiyā*........
2. .... *u[d*]diśyaṁ cha pitā [ta]* ....
3. .... *[pa]nēyaḥ śā* ....

The inscription seems to have contained pious advice. Its fragmentary condition precludes a connected translation.

Chunār sandstone. Found near Jagat Singh Stūpa in 1907-08.

B (*b*) 62.—Base (ht. 1′ 1″; width 1′ 1½″) with the feet of a Gupta standing image of Buddha or Bōdhisattva. Chunār sandstone. Found in 1904-05, but as the number has been washed away by the rain the exact spot cannot be ascertained.

B (*b*) 63.—Base (ht. 6½″; width 1′ 1″) with portions of the feet of a Buddha or Bōdhisattva image. Gupta work. Chunār sandstone. Excavated in 1906-07 to the north-west of the Main Shrine.

B (*b*) 64.—Part of right foot with fragment of base (ht. 4½″; width 6″) of a Buddha or Bōdhisattva image. Chunār sandstone of reddish tint. Find-spot not known.

* B (*b*) 65.—Base with the feet of a standing image of Buddha (?) (ht. 10½″ with tenon; width 1′ 2½″) which has been coloured red. On the front of it was an inscription of three lines in Gupta characters. The epigraph has disappeared with the exception of a small detached fragment from the proper left end. The fragment was discovered in 1904-05.[3] The inscription was not noticed.

I read it as follows :—

1. .... *[datta]-ku[mā]rā(rē)śasya*
2. .... *[yad=atra pu*] ṇyaṁ tad=bhavatuḥ(tu)*.

---

[1] *A. S. R.*, 1907-08, p. 72, No. β 48.

[2] *Cf.* Dr. Konow's reading in the *A. S. R.*, 1907-08, p. 74, No. III and Pl. XXI. My reading differs from Dr. Konow's in one or two points.

[3] *A. S. R.*, 1904-05, p. 97, No. 241.

"Of ...... the heir-apparent ...... [whatever] merit [there is in this gift] it may be ...."

B (*b*) 66.—Base (ht. 1′ 1″ including tenon ; width 1′ 8½″) of a standing image of Buddha (?) of which only the feet remain. On either side of the feet is a votary of which only the lower portion survives. The one on the proper right faced to the front. The face of the base is broken off. Gupta style.

Found in 1907-08. The number has been washed away and the exact find-spot cannot be determined.

B (*b*) 67.—Base (ht. including tenon 11½″ ; width 1′ 5″) of a standing Buddha (?) image of which only the feet remain. A large piece has chipped off the proper right side. Traces of red colour. The style is of the Gupta period.

Made of Chunār sandstone. Discovered in 1907-08 in the trench which crosses the south boundary wall of monastery I on north of Main Shrine.

B (*b*) 68.—Base with imperfect feet of a standing image of Buddha (?) (ht. including tenon 1′ 4¼″; width 1′ 4¼″). Retains remnants of red paint. Gupta period.

Chunār sandstone of reddish tint. Found in 1906-07 in the area around the mediæval monastery I.

B (*b*) 69.—Base of a standing image of Buddha of which the feet only remain (ht. including tenon 10″ ; width 12½″). The lower edge of the lower garment (*antaravāsaka*) is visible over the right foot. Near the latter foot is a much defaced kneeling figure whose hands were clasped before the breast. This figure was probably meant for the donor. Traces of red colour. Gupta period.

Chunār sandstone. Found in one of the recent excavations.

B (*b*) 70.—Lower portion of standing image of Buddha from the shins downwards (ht. including tenon 1′ 6½″ ; width same). The face of the base with the major portion of the feet is broken off. The lower edge and folds of the lower garment (*antaravāsaka*) are intact. Retains vestiges of red colour. Gupta style.

Chunār sandstone. Find-spot not known.

B (*b*) 71.—Base of standing image of Buddha of which only the feet remain (ht. 1′ 6½″ including tenon; width 1′ 5″). Folds of lower garment above right foot. Traces of red colour. Gupta period.

Chunār sandstone. Excavated in 1904-05.

B (*b*) 72.—Base of a standing image of Buddha of which only the feet remain (ht. including tenon 1′ 1″ ; width 1′ 6″). The toes of the right foot are broken off. The fragment retains vestiges of red colour and is probably of the Gupta period.

Chunār sandstone. Unearthed during the recent excavations, but the exact spot is not ascertained.

B (*b*) 73.—Feet of a standing image of Buddha with the base and tenon (ht. 10½″; width 1′ 3″). No trace of colouring. Gupta period.

Chunār sandstone. Found in 1906-07 in the area to the north-west of the Main Shrine.

B (*b*) 74.—Imperfect base with the right foot of a standing image of Buddha (ht. including tenon 11″; width 10¾″). To the right of the foot we notice a miniature figure with hands joined before the breast and hair arranged in plaits which fall on the sides. It is probably the donor. The style is of the Gupta period.

Chunār sandstone. Excavated in 1904-05 on the south of the Main Shrine[1].

B (*b*) 75.—Much weather-worn base of a standing Buddha image of the Gupta period (ht. including tenon 11½″; width 1′ 2¾″). The fragment belonged to the Queen's College collection.

B (*b*) 76.—Lower portion of a standing Buddha image (ht. 1′ 10″; width 1′ 8½″). The feet are broken off. The fragment is much worn. It was probably unearthed during one of the recent excavations.

B (*b*) 77.—Base of standing image of Buddha (ht. 1′ 1″ including tenon; width 1′ 1″). Gupta period. Vestiges of red colour. Chunār sandstone. Unearthed in 1904-05.[2] The exact spot was not recorded.

B (*b*) 78.—Base with the feet and lower portion of the legs of a standing Buddha image (ht. including tenon 9″; width 10″). Edge of lower garment above feet. Found in 1907-08 in the area around the Jagat Singh Stūpa.

B (*b*) 79.—Base (ht. including tenon 8½″; width 11″) with a pair of feet which presumably belonged to a standing image of Buddha. To the right of the feet is a headless figure kneeling with hands joined before the breast. It presumably represents the donor. Another small figure in the same attitude occurs beneath the right foot. The remaining surface of the base is carved in the fashion of a rock as in Buddha images in the earth-touching (*bhūmisparśa*) attitude. The fragment probably dates from the Gupta period.

Unearthed in 1904-05.

B (*b*) 80.—Base with imperfect feet of standing Buddha image (ht. 5½″; width 10″). Slight traces of red colour. Probably Gupta. Chunār sandstone. Discovered in one of the recent excavations at Sārnāth.

B (*b*) 81.—Fragment (ht. 6″; width 9″) with left foot of a standing Buddha (?) image. Gupta work. The number has been lost and the exact find-spot cannot be determined.

---

[1] *A. S. R.*, 1904-05, p. 93, No. 59.
[2] *Ibid.*, p. 92, No. 48.

B (*b*) 82.—Fragment (ht. 5¼″ ; width 8½″) with fore-part of left foot of standing Buddha (?) image. The style is of the Gupta period. Found in the area to the east of the Main Shrine.

B (*b*) 83.—Fragment (ht. 4″ ; width 6½″) with portion of right foot of standing Buddha (?) image. Late Gupta period. Chunār sandstone. Found in 1906-07 in the first court to the east of the mediæval monastery I close to the enclosure wall, 5′ below the surface.

B (*b*) 84.—Fragment of base (ht. 4½″ ; width 7″) with toes of left foot of Buddha (?) image. Late Gupta. Chunār sandstone. Unearthed in 1907-08.

B (*b*) 85.—Fragment of base (ht. including tenon 6½″ ; width 8½″) with the feet of a standing Buddha (?) image. Faint vestiges of red colour. Seems to be of the Gupta period. Found in 1907-08 on south of monastery II.

B (*b*) 86.—Lower portion (ht. including tenon 7½″ ; width 8½″) of standing Buddha figure below knees. On right side of feet, kneeling figure much mutilated. Gupta style. Chunār sandstone. Unearthed in 1904-05.[1]

B (*b*) 87.—Legs (ht. 9″ ; width 9″) between knees and ankles of standing Buddha figure. Much defaced but edges of the lower and upper garments quite distinct. Chunār sandstone. Unearthed in 1906-07 to the west of the Aśōka Column.

B (*b*) 88.—Lower portion (ht. including tenon 9½″ ; width 6½″) of standing Buddha image below knees. Lower garment (*antaravāsaka*) and upper robe (*saṅghāṭī*) as in other Gupta images. Found in 1906-07 in the area to the west of the Main Shrine.

B (*b*) 89.—Base (ht. with tenon 6″ ; width 7½″) with feet of standing Buddha figure. Chunār sandstone. Probably Gupta. Unearthed in 1904-05.[2]

B (*b*) 90.—Legs and feet (ht. with tenon 6″ ; width 5½″) of standing Buddha figure. Remnant of figure to right. Chunār sandstone. Decadent Gupta style. Found in 1906-07.

B (*b*) 91.—Base with feet (ht. with tenon 9″ ; width 8″) of standing Buddha figure. On proper right, kneeling figure with hands joined before breast, probably donor. Decadent Gupta style. Found in 1906-07 in Monastery I, 5′ below the surface.

B (*b*) 92.—Base with feet (ht. with tenon 5½″ ; width 10″) probably of standing Buddha image. Red colour. Decadent Gupta style. Chunār sandstone. Found in 1906-07 in monastery I.

B (*b*) 93.—Fragment of base with portion of right foot (ht. 4¾″ ; width 9½″) of standing Buddha (?). Red colour. Gupta work. Chunār

---

[1] *A. S. R.*, 1904-05, p. 93, No. 61.
[2] *Ibid.*, No. 60.

sandstone. Unearthed in 1904-05 near the north-east corner of Jagat Singh Stūpa.[1]

B (*b*) 94.—Fragment (ht. with tenon 5″; width 6½″) with toes of standing Buddha (?) figure. Late Gupta style. Chunār sandstone. Found in 1906-07 in the area to the east of the Main Shrine.

B (*b*) 95.—Fragment (ht. 3″; width 6¼″) similar to B (*b*) 94. Found in 1906-07, 2′ below surface.

B (*b*) 96.—Fragment (ht. with tenon 6″; width 5″) with portion of right foot of standing image of Buddha. Gupta work. Chunār sandstone. Unearthed in 1904-05.

B (*b*) 97.—Fragment with imperfect left foot of standing Buddha image (ht. 3″; width 4½″). Probably Gupta. Traces of red colour. Chunār sandstone. Found in 1906-07 to the east of Main Shrine.

B (*b*) 98.—Fragment (ht. 5½″; width 5″) with portion of left foot of standing Buddha image. Probably part of the same image as B (*b*) 93.

B (*b*) 99.—Fragment (ht. 4½″ with tenon; width 4″) with toes of right foot of standing Buddha image. Gupta work. Chunār sandstone. Discovered in 1906-07 to west of *stūpa* No. 12 4′ below surface.

B (*b*) 100.—Fragment (ht. 1½″; width 4½″) with feet of standing Buddha figure. To right of feet, lower portion of a kneeling figure, probably donor. Chunār sandstone. Late Gupta work. Unearthed in 1906-07 to the east of Main Shrine.

B (*b*) 101.—Fragmentary right foot (ht. 2″; length 4½″) which seems to have belonged to a standing Buddha image. Red colour. Gupta style. Unearthed in 1907-08 in the western precinct of monastery I.

B (*b*) 102.—Imperfect left foot (ht. 3″; length 6½″) presumably of a standing Buddha image. Gupta style. Chunār sandstone. Unearthed in 1907-08.

* B (*b*) 103.—Right hand and fore-arm (ht. 7½″; length 7″) which belonged to a colossal standing image of Buddha in the attitude of imparting security (*abhayamudrā*). The hand was raised as usual at right angles to the fore-arm. The fleshy portions of the fingers and the lines on the palm are delineated with admirable delicacy. The cushion-shaped portion, which connected the back of the hand to the upper arm behind it, gives it the appearance of a web which according to the texts joined the fingers of Gautama Buddha (*jālāvanaddhāṅgu lipāṇi*). On this stone is cut the Buddhist creed in four lines in characters of the Gupta period which runs as follows :—

1. *Yē-dharmmā-hētuprabhā*(*bhavā*) *tēshaṁ hētuṁ*
2. *Tathāgatō avā*(*ō*)*cha tēshaṁ cha*

[1] *A. S. R.*, 1904-05, p. 97, No. 254.

3. *yō tirōdha*[1] *tōrē*[2] *ēvaṁvādī*
4. *Mahāśrama*[*ṇaḥ*].

This is the earliest instance of the Buddhist creed found at Sārnāth. The specimen on the stele (C (*a*) 1) below is somewhat later. The formula may be rendered into English as follows :—

"Whatever things spring from a cause, their cause the Tathāgata (Buddha) has explained. The great mendicant has, likewise, revealed their suppression."

The fragment was unearthed in 1904-05.[3]

B (*b*) 104.—Right hand and part of fore-arm (ht. 6½"; length 5½") similar to B (*b*) 103. Little finger missing and the other fingers and the thumb slightly injured. Gupta style.

Chunār sandstone. Unearthed in 1904-05 to the south of the Main Shrine.

B (*b*) 105.—Right hand (ht. 9"; length 4½") of a large-sized standing Buddha image in attitude of granting protection. The little finger has disappeared and the ring-finger and the thumb are damaged.

Made of Chunār sandstone. Unearthed in 1904-05.

B (*b*) 106.—Right hand with part of fore-arm (ht. 8½"; length 4½") of a standing Buddha image of the Gupta period. The hand was in the attitude of protection. Traces of red colour.

Made of Chunār sandstone. Unearthed in 1904-05.

B (*b*) 107.—Right hand (ht. 7"; length 4") of similar Buddha image. The fingers are damaged. Vestiges of red paint. Chunār sandstone. Found in 1907-08 on approach to Main Shrine from east 7′ 8" below surface.

B (*b*) 108.—Right hand (ht. of palm 7"; length 6½") in attitude of protection, which formed part of a standing Buddha image of the Gupta period. Beneath it, edge of upper robe (*saṅghāṭī*). Red colour. Chunār sandstone. Unearthed in 1904-05.

B (*b*) 109.—Fragment (ht. 1′) from the right elbow of a standing Buddha image in attitude of protection. Gupta style. Chunār sandstone. Unearthed in 1906-07 to the east of the Main Shrine.

B (*b*) 110.—Right hand (ht. of palm 7") of image of Buddha standing in the attitude of protection. Probably Gupta. Chunār sandstone. Unearthed in 1906-07 in the supposed Hospital (monastery) 4′ below the surface.

B (*b*) 111.—Right hand with fore-arm (ht. of palm 5"; length 5") of a standing Buddha image of the Gupta period. The attitude was

---

[1] The syllable *ti* is inscribed below the line. The correct reading is *nirōdha*.
[2] These two syllables are superfluous. They do not occur in the authentic Pāli version of the *ślōka* and interfere with the metre.
[3] *A. S. R.*, 1904-05, p. 90 and p. 97, No. 265; also p. 103, No. XXI. For a facsimile of the inscription see Pl. XXXII, XXI.

that of protection. Red colour. Found in 1906-07 to the west of the Main Shrine.

B (*b*) 112.—Right hand (ht. of palm 6") of standing Buddha image in the attitude of protection. The lines of the palm and the joints of the fingers are marked with clearness. Gupta work. Red colour. Excavated in 1904-05 in the vicinity of the Main Shrine.

B (*b*) 113.—Right hand (ht. of palm 5") similar to B (*b*) 112. Unearthed to east of *stūpa* No. 22, 2′ below surface.

B (*b*) 114.—Right hand and wrist (ht. of palm 5½") of standing Buddha image in Gupta style. The attitude was that of protection. Chunār sandstone. Found in 1907-08 on south of monastery II.

B (*b*) 115.—Right hand (ht. of palm 6") of similar image. Traces of red colour. Unearthed in 1907-08 on approach to Main Shrine from east 7′ below surface.

B (*b*) 116.—Right hand (ht. of palm 6") in attitude of protection. Gupta work. Red colour. Unearthed in the area around Main Shrine.

B (*b*) 117.—Right hand (ht. of palm 5") with edge of upper robe hanging from it. Red colour. Discovered in 1906-07 to the east of the Main Shrine.

B (*b*) 118.—Right hand (ht. of palm 5½") in attitude of protection, of standing Buddha image. Gupta work. Traces of red colour. The exact find-spot is not known.

B (*b*) 119.—Right hand (ht. of palm 4½") of similar image. Fine Gupta work. Chunār sandstone. Discovered in 1907-08 on eastern approach to Main Shrine 8′ below surface.

B (*b*) 120.—Right hand (ht. of palm 3½") similar to B (*b*) 119. Discovered in 1904-05 in the area around Main Shrine.

B (*b*) 121.—Fragment (ht. 6") of right hand which was held in the attitude of protection. Chunār sandstone. Find-spot not known.

B (*b*) 122.—Right hand broken across the palm (ht. 5½") which evidently belonged to a standing Buddha image in the attitude of protection. The fingers are long and their joints clearly marked. Red colour. Gupta work. Unearthed during the recent excavations.

B (*b*) 123.—Right hand (ht. of palm 5½") similar to B (*b*) 122. Discovered in 1904-05 in the precincts of the Main Shrine.

B (*b*) 124.—Fragment representing right hand (ht. of palm 3") of a Buddha image in the attitude of protection with edge of upper robe below it. Find-spot same.

B (*b*) 125.—Right hand (ht. of palm 3") of similar image. Late Gupta style. Discovered in 1906-07 in mediæval monastery I.

B (*b*) 126.—Right hand (ht. of palm 3") of a Buddha image in the attitude of granting protection. Buff-coloured sandstone. Late Gupta style. Unearthed in 1907-08 in western precinct of monastery I, 3′ below surface.

B (*b*) 127.—Fragment (ht. of palm 3") similar to B (*b*) 126. Chunār sandstone. Found in 1904-05 in the vicinity of the Main Shrine.

B (*b*) 128.—Right hand (ht. of palm 3") of standing Buddha in attitude of protection. Chunār sandstone. Late Gupta style. Found west of *stūpa* No. 13, 3' below surface.

B (*b*) 129.—Fragmentary right hand (ht. of palm 3") of small standing Buddha in the attitude of protection. Typical Gupta style. Chunār sandstone. Discovered in 1907-08 in area around Jagat Singh Stūpa.

B (*b*) 130.—Right hand (ht. of palm 2¾") of small standing Buddha in the attitude of protection. Vestiges of red colour. Unearthed in 1906-07 in *stūpa* No. 17 to north-west of Main Shrine 3' below surface.

B (*b*) 131.—Fragment (ht. of palm 3") similar to B (*b*) 130. Late Gupta work. Find-spot not known.

B (*b*) 132.—Right hand (ht. of palm 4") of small Buddha image in the attitude of protection. Faint traces of red colour. Late Gupta style. Discovered in 1906-07 west of *stūpa* No. 12 to south-west of Main Shrine.

B (*b*) 133.—Right hand (length 5") which must have belonged to a standing Buddha image in the attitude of imparting security. Execution very fine. Evidently carved by the same artist who made B (*d*) 2. Chunār stone of fine grain. Find-spot not ascertainable.

B (*b*) 134.—Fragment of left fore-arm (length 9") of standing Buddha in the attitude of protection. The wrist is crossed by the edge of the upper robe (*saṅghāṭī*). Probably Gupta. Chunār sandstone. Discovered in 1906-07 in the area to the east of the Main Shrine.

B (*b*) 134 (*a*).—Right hand of Buddha image in the attitude of protection. Gupta period. Traces of red paint. Discovered in one of the recent excavations.

B (*b*) 135.—Left hand (ht. 7") holding gathered hem of the upper robe (*saṅghāṭī*) which manifestly belonged to a standing Buddha in the attitude of protection. The fingers are long and tapering and connected by a web (*jālāvanaddha*). From its close resemblance to the left hand of B (*b*) 2 I have no hesitation in assigning it to the time of the Imperial Guptas. Red colour. Chunār sandstone. Unearthed in 1906-07 in the area to the west of the Main Shrine near the surface.

B (*b*) 136.—Left hand (ht. 9") of standing Buddha in the attitude of protection. Hem of monk's upper robe between thumb and fingers. Web between the fingers clearly indicated. Typical Gupta style. Chunār sandstone. Unearthed in 1904-05 in the neighbourhood of the Main Shrine.

B (*b*) 137.—Fragment (ht. 7¼") representing left hand with hem of upper robe of a standing Buddha image in the attitude of protection. Gupta style. Chunār sandstone. Probably discovered in 1906-07 in the area to the west of the Main Shrine.

B (*b*) 138.—Imperfect left hand (ht. 5⅝″) of standing Buddha in the attitude of protection. Little finger missing, the rest damaged. The style is similar to that of B (*b*) 137. Buff-coloured sandstone of Chunār. Discovered in 1904-05 in the vicinity of the Main Shrine.

B (*b*) 139.—Left hand (length 7″) of life-sized standing Buddha image in the attitude of granting protection. The fingers which were closed over the hem of the robe are considerably injured. Reddish sandstone from Chunār. Unearthed in 1906-07, east of *stūpa* No. 22, 4′ below surface.

B (*b*) 140.—Left hand and part of fore-arm (length 11½″) of a similar image. The fingers are broken off, the thumb remains in part. The style is of the Gupta period. Chunār sandstone. It was brought to light during the recent excavations.

B (*b*) 141.—Left hand (length 6½″) of a standing Buddha image in the attitude of granting protection. The fingers are, as usual, closed over the hem of the robe. The little finger and fore-finger are missing. Gupta style. Unearthed in 1904-05 in the area around the Main Shrine.

B (*b*) 142.—Fragment (length 6″) representing the left hand of a standing Buddha image in the attitude of protection. It holds, as usual, the hem of the upper robe. The fingers are injured. Red colour. Chunār sandstone. Discovered in 1907-08 on approach of Main Shrine from east, 6′ below surface.

B (*b*) 143.—Left hand of standing Buddha image in the attitude of imparting protection (length 8″; width 2½″). Gupta style. Unearthed in 1904-05 in the area around the Main Shrine.

B (*b*) 144.—Left hand (length 4″; width 3″) holding hem of upper robe. It belonged to a Buddha standing in the attitude of protection. Gupta style. Remains of red colour. Discovered in 1904-05 in the area around the Main Shrine.

B (*b*) 145.—Left hand (ht. of palm 4″; width 3½″) of the same type as B (*b*) 144. Chunār sandstone. Unearthed in one of the recent excavations.

B (*b*) 146.—Left hand of the same form as the preceding ones (length including part of fore-arm 6½″; width of palm 3″). The fingers have disappeared. There are remains of red colour on the palm. Unearthed in 1907-08 in the area around the Jagat Singh Stūpa.

B (*b*) 147.—Much defaced left hand (length 5″; width 3″) of the form peculiar to standing Buddhas in the attitude of protection. The hem of the upper robe is well preserved. Red colour. Gupta style. Discovered in 1906-07 in the area to the east of the Main Shrine.

B (*b*) 148.—Fragment (length 5½″; width 2″) representing the left hand and fore-arm of a Buddha image in protection. Chunār sandstone. Gupta work. Unearthed in 1907-08 in the area around the Jagat Singh Stūpa.

B (*b*) 149.—Left hand with wrist (length 4″; width 3½″) as in standing Buddha images in the attitude of protection. Remains of red colour. Probably Gupta. Found in the same area as B (*b*) 148.

B (*b*) 150.—Left hand (length 4″; width 3″) of the same type as B (*b*) 149. Thumb and little finger broken off. Unearthed in one of the recent excavations.

B (*b*) 151.—Fragment representing left hand in the attitude of protection (length 4″; width 3″). Fingers slightly damaged. Unearthed in 1904-05 in the area around the Main Shrine.

B (*b*) 152.—Left hand (length 5″; width 3½″) of a standing Buddha image in the attitude of imparting protection. Gupta period. Little finger broken off. Discovered in 1907-08 in the area around the Main Shrine.

B (*b*) 153.—Left hand and wrist (length 5¼″; width 3¼″) of similar image. The palm with tips of fingers has been cut away. Find-spot not ascertainable.

B (*b*) 154.—Fragment (length 3½″; width 3″) of right hand in the attitude of protection which must have belonged to a standing Buddha image. Gupta style. The find-spot cannot be determined.

B (*b*) 155.—Fragment (ht. 7″; width 2½″) carved with drapery from the left side of a standing Buddha image in the attitude of granting protection. Unearthed in 1906-07 in the area to the east of the Main Shrine.

B (*b*) 156.—Right hand with fore-arm (length 7″; width 3″) of an image of Buddha standing in the gift-bestowing (*varada*) attitude. The thumb is missing and the fingers are slightly damaged. The style is presumably of the late Gupta period. Chunār sandstone. Discovered in 1907-08 in the area to the north-east of the Dhamēkh Stūpa.

B (*b*) 157.—Fragment (length 5¼″; width 2½″) similar to B (*b*) 156. Unearthed in 1904-05 in the vicinity of the Main Shrine.

B (*b*) 158.—Right hand with fore-arm (length 5″; width 1½″) such as we find in Buddha images in the gift-bestowing attitude. Probably Gupta. Found in the same year and in the same area as B (*b*) 157.

B (*b*) 159.—Fragment (length 4½″; width 2″) of the same type as B (*b*) 158. Unearthed in 1906-07 in the area to the east of the Main Shrine.

B (*b*) 160.—Fragment (length 4″; width 1½″) similar to the preceding ones. Late Gupta style. Find-spot not ascertainable.

B (*b*) 161.—Mutilated right hand (length 3½″; width 2½″) in gift-bestowing attitude. It belonged to a standing Buddha. Unearthed in 1907-08 on approach to Main Shrine from east 4′ below surface.

B (*b*) 162.—Left arm (length 14″) of image of Buddha which must have been standing in the gift-bestowing attitude (*varadamudrā*). This is evidenced by the position of the hand which lifted the hem of the upper robe (*saṅghāṭī*) to the level of the left shoulder. The style of execution is exceedingly graceful and I feel no hesitation in assigning the fragment to the Gupta period. Chunār sandstone. Unearthed in 1904-05 in the area around the Main Shrine.

B (*b*) 163.—Left arm (ht. 7″) similar to B (*b*) 162 and discovered in the same area with it.

B (*b*) 164.—Left hand and part of fore-arm of the same type (length 6½″). Excavated in 1906-07 in the mediæval monastery I, 3′ 4″ below the surface.

B (*b*) 165.—Left hand (length 6½″) holding hem of Buddha in gift-bestowing attitude (*varadamudrā*). Chunār sandstone. Found in area west of Main Shrine.

B (*b*) 165 (*a*).—Left hand (length 5″) of Buddha as in gift-bestowing attitude. Gupta style. Traces of red paint. Excavated in one of the recent diggings.

B (*b*) 166.—Fragment (length 2½″; width 1½″) of left hand with hem of robe probably from a Buddha image in gift-bestowing attitude. Chunār sandstone. Find-spot not known.

B (*b*) 166 (*a*).—Left hand (length 2¾″) holding hem of robe. It must have belonged to a Buddha image in the gift-bestowing posture. Gupta period. Excavated in one of the recent diggings.

B (*b*) 167.—Hem of robe (ht. 2½″; width 2½″) which was held in the left hand of an image of Buddha standing in the gift-bestowing attitude. Chunār sandstone. Found in 1906-07 near the Old Sculpture Shed.

B (*b*) 168.—Left hand (length 3½″; width 3″) holding hem of upper robe from an image of Buddha in the gift-bestowing attitude (*varadamudrā*). Find-spot unknown.

B (*b*) 169.—Fragment of drapery (ht. 3″; width 2″) from the left side of a standing Buddha image. Found in 1906-07 in area on east of Main Shrine.

B (*b*) 170.—Left hand which held the hem of the upper robe (length 3″; width 1″) of a Buddha image probably in gift-bestowing attitude (*varadamudrā*). Unearthed in the same area as B (*b*) 169.

B (*b*) 171.—Right ear (ht. 5″; width 3″) of a Buddha image. Chunār stone. Found in the same area as B (*b*) 170.

* B (*b*) 172.—Figure (ht. 1′ 7½″; width at base 1′ 1¾″), in relief, representing Gautama Buddha seated in the attitude of touching the earth (*bhūmisparśamudrā*) which in Buddhist art symbolizes his temptation by the Evil One (Pāli *Mārō pāpīyān*), and his subsequent enlightenment at Gayā. The sculpture is broken into three fragments and the face has disappeared with the exception of the right ear. A large piece 7½″ high by 5½″ broad is broken off the proper left side just

above the level of the left shoulder, a smaller piece having vanished at the same level from the other side. The sculpture was quite intact, with the exception of the piece lost from the proper right side, when it was seen by Major Kittoe, who has left us an accurate sketch of it in his "Drawings"[1] in the possession of the India Office.

The base of the image is carved in imitation of a rock or stone platform to indicate the *bōdhimaṇḍa*, seated on which the Buddha reached supreme wisdom. This seat is supported at each end by a dwarfish figure or atlante. The dress of the Buddha consists of a lower garment (*antaravāsaka*), the folds of which appear on the top of the seat, and an upper robe (*saṅghāṭī*) which leaves the right shoulder bare.[2] Around the head is an oval-shaped halo surrounded by a line of bead and reel. Above the Teacher's head is the foliage of a *pīpal* tree (*Ficus religiosa*) which is the tree of wisdom (*bōdhi-vṛiksha*) of Gautama Buddha. To his right, stands the Evil One (Māra) with a large bow in his left hand and an arrow (now defaced) in the other. The female figure standing to the left of the Buddha is one of the three daughters of the Tempter. Her right hand is raised behind her head, while the left is applied to her breasts. Most of this figure is now defaced. Of the army of the Evil One, four warriors of terrific appearance were represented, namely, two on either side of the halo, one above the other. The upper one on the proper right has the head of a lion and is in the act of hurling a rock (*parvata*) on the Buddha. The other demon on this side has disappeared, but the cobra which encircled his body is still visible. The demons on the other side are missing. In Major Kittoe's sketch, alluded to above, the upper one has a bull's head and a face with two tushes on his belly. The lower figure, which has a thick-set dwarfish body, holds a hatchet (*kuṭhāra*) in its left hand.

Beneath the right hand of the Buddha, which is pointing to the earth, is a female figure of which the lower body was presumably not indicated. She holds a vase between her hands which she seems to be presenting to the Buddha. Dr. Vogel has identified this figure as the Earth-goddess (Pṛithivī or Vasundharā) who is rising from the earth to bear testimony to the good works of the Buddha.[3] In the centre of the base is a figure with long dishevelled hair which is apparently fleeing away. This is presumably the Evil One after his defeat, or his daughter if it was a female figure.

---

[1] Vol. 1, No. 164, Pl. 2. In my description I have followed Major Kittoe's drawing.

[2] This is the case in all Buddha images in this attitude in the Sārnāth Museum.

[3] Dr. Vogel was led to this identification by a representation of the Buddha's temptation in Cave No. 11 at Ellura, and a terra-cotta plaque preserved in the Sārnāth Museum (F (a) 4). *Cf.* also C (a) 2. In Burma, Vasundharā is represented in the scene in question as squeezing out water from her hair with which she is said to have inundated the earth on this occasion.

On the front of the base is an inscription of two lines in characters of about the 6th century A.D. I read it as follows :—

1. *Dēyadharmō=ya*[*ṁ**] *Śākyabhikshō*[*ḥ**] *Śrīvinaya*...*bu*...

2. .. *sasya vi ta ja* ....

"This (is) the pious gift of the Buddhist monk........"

The material of the sculpture is Chunār sandstone. That it originates from Sārnāth is apparent from the title attached to Major Kittoe's drawing referred to. But whether he discovered it himself or some one else before him is not known. Major Kittoe does not say that it was recovered by him.

*B (*b*) 173.—Lower part (ht. 7½" ; width at base 13") of figure of Gautama Buddha seated cross-legged in the earth-touching attitude (*bhūmisparśamudrā*). The front of the base is moulded in the fashion of a rock. Beneath the right hand of the Buddha is the Earth-goddess (Mahāpṛithivī or Vasundharā) holding up a vase, and in the centre, in a niche, the head of a lion resting on his fore-paws meant apparently to symbolize the forest of Uruvilva where the Buddha reached supreme wisdom. At the proper left end, we notice two miniature figures fleeing away. One of these is a female and represents, no doubt, one of the three daughters of the Evil One (Māra), who tempted the Buddha and were themselves changed into old hags by his miraculous power. The male figure before her is probably her father Māra who has also been vanquished. On the sole of each foot of the Buddha is a wheel (*chakra*), one of the personal characteristics of a great man (*mahāpurusha*).

On the upper rim of the base is incised a short Sanskrit epigraph in characters of the 5th century A.D., which runs :—

Dē[*ya**]*dharmō=yaṁ Kumāraguptasya.*

"This [is] the pious gift of Kumāragupta." Dr. Konow [1] expressed the opinion that the donor was possibly the emperor Kumāragupta I himself, but the identification is open to serious objections.[2]

Reddish sandstone of Chunār. Unearthed in 1906-07 in the mound of spoil earth which existed to the south of the Jagat Singh Stūpa, at the level of the small *stūpas* surrounding it.

B (*b*) 174.—Figure (ht. 1' 8" ; width 1' ½") of Gautama Buddha, in high relief, at the moment of his enlightenment (*bōdhi*). The face has flaked away. The right hand points towards the earth (*bhūmisparśamudrā*) ; the left rests on the lap. Around the head is an oval-shaped halo, and the foliage of a *pīpal* tree above it. To the right of the Buddha is a daughter of the Evil One, her left hand on her breast, the right holding an uncertain object. To his left we notice a male

[1] *A. S. R.*, 1906-07, pp. 89 and 91, No. 19 and fig. 9 ; also p. 99, inscription No. VIII and facsimile on Pl. XXX.

[2] *Cf.* above p. 15 f. n. 1.

figure, manifestly Māra himself, though he does not hold a bow in this case.[1] On either side of the Buddha's halo is a demon (*rākshasa*). The base is carved in the shape of a rock and is occupied at the proper right end by the Earth-goddess (Pṛithivī) with the usual vase, and in the centre, by the lion resting with its head on its paws. The figures shown at the other end as fleeing away are Māra's daughter and the Evil One himself respectively after their defeat.

The style of the sculpture displays a close affinity to that of B (*b*) 172 for which reason I assign it to about the 6th century A.D. We have a sketch of this sculpture in Major Kittoe's 'Drawings,' where he notes Sārnāth as its provenance.[2]

* B (*b*) 175.—Image of Gautama Buddha seated cross-legged (*paryaṅkanishaṇṇa*) in the earth-touching attitude (*bhūmisparśamudrā*). It is carved in alto-relievo and projects from a stout back-slab 5′ 1″ high, 2′ 7″ broad and 1′ thick at base. The upper portion of the back-slab from the shoulders of the Buddha upwards was broken into several pieces, three of which were recovered.[3] The head of the Buddha is missing as well as most of the arms. Around the head, carved in relief on the back-slab, is a circular halo (1′ 8¾″ in diameter) which is nearly complete, and decorated round the border with two circular bands of rosettes and beads respectively. Over the halo the foliage of the Bōdhi tree was shown, but it is now only visible on the top of the stone. The flying figures on both sides of the halo are celestials (*dēva*) who showered down flowers on the Buddha after he had conquered the Tempter. The folds of the dress are scarcely indicated, so that the edge of the upper robe across the breast is apt to be mistaken for the Brahmanical thread.

The base of the image has broad projecting rims above and beneath and is carved after the fashion of a rock. In the centre of the sunken portion in a circular niche, is a lion in a cave, resting its head on its paws. The Earth-goddess appears beneath the right hand of the Buddha, but she is not shown here as emerging from the earth. Her vase is broken off. In front of her is a male figure kneeling in reverence, perhaps the donor of the image. On the other side of the niche corresponding to the Earth-goddess is a daughter of Māra running away. The miniature figure in front of her is perhaps to be identified as the Evil One in flight.

On the back of the sculpture are sketched the outlines of eight *stūpas* in two vertical rows.

The approximate date of the sculpture is furnished by a Sanskrit epigraph in ornamental characters of the 6th or 7th century A.D. It

[1] It is to be noted that here Māra and his daughter have halos around their heads.
[2] Vol. 1, No. 153, Pl. I.
[3] Only two of these pieces could be re-fixed and may be seen in the photograph.

is the only pre-Moslem inscription known in which the letters are raised. Dr. Vogel reads it as follows[1] :—

Dēyadharmmō=yaṁ Śākyabhikshō[ḥ*] *sthavira=Bandhuguptasya.*

" This [is] the pious gift of the Buddhist friar, the senior monk, Bandhugupta."

The image is made of Chunār sandstone and was discovered by Mr. Oertel in 1904-05 to the south-east of the Main Shrine. Pl. IX.

B (*b*) 176.—Bust of massive image of Buddha which, to judge from its appearance, must have been sitting in the earth-touching attitude (*bhūmisparśamudrā*). Ht. up to top of halo 3′ 4¾″; width across shoulders 1′ 11″. Both arms from the elbows downwards are missing. The upper portion of the face has been cut off and the ear-lobes and the protuberance of the skull destroyed. The hair is arranged as usual in spiral curls.

The right shoulder is bare and as no attempt has been made at marking the drapery, the edge of the upper robe produces the impression of the Brahmanical sacred thread (*yajñōpavīta*). Behind the head is the major portion of an oval halo with a foliated ornament around the margin. This decoration is defaced in the upper part of the halo. A small fragment (ht. 1′ ½″) belonging to the proper left side of the halo was found in a trench south of monastery II. It shows a headless celestial (*dēva*) flying in a cloud.

The material is the sandstone of Chunār. It is said locally that this image was lying near the Dhamēkh Stūpa until 1903 when it was placed in a temporary sculpture shed along with the Queen's College collection.

B (*b*) 177.—Figure of Gautama Buddha sitting cross-legged in the earth-touching attitude (*bhūmisparśamudrā*). Ht. 1′ 5½″ up to the top of the back-slab ; width at base 11″. Above the Buddha's head the foliage of the *pīpal* tree is shown, and to his right, a miniature kneeling figure, presumably the donor. The trunk of the figure has suffered considerably from the action of saltpetre. The back-slab is broken on the proper left side. Judging from the style I attribute the sculpture to the late Gupta period.

Unearthed in 1904-05 to the north of the Jagat Singh Stūpa.

B (*b*) 178.—Lower portion (ht. 8″ ; width 10″), below the waist, of a figure of Gautama Buddha which was seated cross-legged in the earth-touching attitude. The right hand is missing and the figure is much defaced. The front of the base was treated after the fashion of B (*b*) 172-174. Late Gupta style. Discovered in 1906-07 in the mediæval monastery I.

---

[1] *A. S. R.*, 1904-05, pp. 80-81, Pl. XXVIII, *a*, and facsimile on Pl. XXXII, No XXII ; and p. 92, No. 28.

B (*b*) 178 (*a*).—Fragment (ht. 1′ 3¼″) from the proper left side of an image of Gautama Buddha at the moment of enlightenment (*bōdhi*). Below, rock pattern as in other representations of this scene (*e.g.*, B (*b*) 178). Above, two daughters of the Evil One standing side by side in amorous attitude. The head of the figure on the proper right side is wanting. The style seems to be Gupta. Chunār sandstone. Discovered in 1907-08 in the trench crossing the south boundary wall of monastery I, 1′ 6″ below surface.

* B (*b*) 179.—Figure (ht. 1′; width 9½″) of Gautama Buddha seated cross-legged in the preaching attitude on a fully-expanded lotus raised on a vertical stem surrounded with foliage. The hands are disposed in front of the breast in such a way that the thumb and the fore-finger of the right hand just touch the fore-finger of the left hand, the palm of the former remaining turned outward. The treatment of the dress is similar to that in the standing images of Buddha described above, both shoulders being wrapped in the upper robe and not merely the left one as we noticed in the representations of Buddha's enlightenment (*bōdhi*). The upper portion of the back-slab with the Buddha's head is broken off. Beneath the lotus-throne on either side is a miniature replica of the main figure in the same posture. The two lotus-stalks which rise from the base, one on each side, probably also supported similar figures. In all probability the sculpture represents the great miracle of Śrāvastī. (*Cf.* C (*a*) 3, 4, 6 and 7.)

The base of the image contains a Sanskrit inscription in characters of the 4th or 5th century A.D. which runs :—

Dēyadharmmō=yaṁ Śākyabhikshō[*r**]*Dhanadēvasya.*[1] "This (is) the pious gift of the Buddhist monk Dhanadēva."

It is worth noticing that the sculpture under description exhibits a striking affinity in style to the sculptures of the Gandhāra school. This will become apparent when we compare it with a relief found at Muḥammad Nāri in Yusufzai, now at Lahore, and a model shrine from Loriyan Tangai, now deposited in the Indian Museum, Calcutta.[2] We find the same lotus-throne (*padmāsana*) in both cases with this difference that while it is carved in the round in the Gandhāra sculptures mentioned above, it is cut in relief in the Sārnāth specimen. The position of the hands is also nearly the same.

The figure is made of a reddish kind of sandstone from Chunār and was unearthed in 1906-07 in stūpa No. 40 to the north-east of the Main Shrine.[3]

---

[1] The same inscription occurs on a sculpture showing Buddha's descent from heaven, which was enshrined in a niche of a *stūpa* to the west of Jagat Singh Stūpa and is now in the museum (B (*b*) 10*a*). It was read by Dr. Konow (*A. S. R.*, 1906-07, p. 99, inscription No. VII).

[2] Grünwedel-Burgess, *Buddhist Art in India*, figs. 82 and 152. *Cf.* also fig. 121.

[3] *A. S. R.*, 1906-07, p. 80 and p. 90, No. 10 and Pl. XXIII, 6. Also Pl. XXX, VI.

B (*b*) 180.—Image (ht. up to the top of back-slab 3′ 7½″; width at base 1′ 5½″) of Buddha in alto-relievo in the teaching attitude (*dharmachakramudrā*). The image is seated cross-legged on a thick cushion which rests on a full-blown lotus with an erect stalk, partly enveloped in foliage. The head of the image as well as the upper part of the back-slab is missing. The hands are also broken off, but it is evident from the traces of them which remain on the breast that they were held in the same position as those of the preceding image. The upper robe covers both shoulders, but its existence is only indicated along the edges. The folds of this garment are also shown on the cushion.

The delineation of the lotus is particularly artistic and compares favourably with the lotus-throne of Buddhas in Gandhāra sculpture. The two male figures on both sides of the lotus-stalk seated in a devotional attitude on cushions are probably human devotees.

The border of the back-slab is ornamented with a scalloped ornament to which is added on the interior a line of bead and reel and a well-carved garland pattern similar to that on B (*b*) 4. The image is one of the best sculptures of the Gupta period. It was deposited in the Queen's College up to the year 1903, but it is not known who excavated it.

B (*b*) 181.—Image (ht. 5′ 3″ up to the top of the halo; width at base 2′ 7″) of Gautama Buddha seated cross-legged, preaching the first sermon at Sārnāth, on a thick cushion supported on a seat with moulded legs. The position of the hands in front of the breast conforms to that in other images representing this scene with the only difference that in this case it is the middle-finger (*madhyamikā*) of the left hand and not the fore-finger which is touched by the thumb and fore-finger of the right hand. The robe covers both shoulders, but the drapery is only indicated along the edges of the garment and on the top of the cushion. The hair, in accordance with the canon, is treated in short conventional curls turned to the right (*dakshiṇāvartta*) and the protuberance of the skull is nearly hemispheric in shape. The lobes of the ears, which are prolonged as far down as the shoulders, are slightly injured. In the centre of the relief carved between the legs of the seat is a wheel on a throne with couchant deer on either side. The wheel symbolizes the "wheel of the Buddhist law" which Gautama Buddha set going at Sārnāth and the animals indicate the Deer-park (Mṛigadāva) in which his first sermon was preached. The remaining space is taken up by seven kneeling figures with hands joined before the breast. Of these the five figures with shaven heads and in monk's dress are the five comrades (*Pañcha bhadravargīya*) of the Buddha who deserted him at Gayā and afterwards became the first recipients of his doctrine. The two remaining figures, a woman kneeling and a child (?) standing behind her with a garland (?), are possibly the donors of the sculpture.

The back-slab up to the shoulders of the main image is adorned with a pattern simulating the back of a throne. Two crocodile (*makara*) heads emerging from foliage surmount the ends of the horizontal bar which are supported by rampart leogryphs with long wavy tails. Dr. Vogel[1] in tracing the origin of these leogryphs has shown how from an ornamental bracket, such as we find in Sāñchī, essentially an architectural member, this motif has gradually developed into a merely decorative device for the embellishment of pillars, back-slabs of images, etc. The throne itself was possibly derived from the Gandhāra sculptures[2].

The upper portion of the back-slab is fashioned into a beautifully sculptured circular halo (diam. 2′ 8″), the concentric bands of ornament around it being partly similar to those on B (*b*) 4. On either side of the halo is a flying celestial (*dēva*) holding a tray of flowers in the left hand. The figure to the proper right holds in its right hand what looks like a fly-whisk (Skt. *chāmara*) but more probably is meant for a flower.

It is to be noted that the sculpture is characterized by a peculiarly serene expression of repose which, as well as the supple and lithe limbs of the figure, calls to mind Mr. Havell's[3] remarks about the superhuman, spiritualized conception of the Buddha's person, which in his opinion was the guiding principle of the Indian Buddhist sculptor.

The sculpture is made of Chunār sandstone and retains traces of red colouring. It was discovered by Mr. Oertel in 1904-05 to the south of the Jagat Singh Stūpa.[4] Pl. X.

B (*b*) 182.—Image (ht. 3′ 2″ up to top of back-slab; width at base 1′ 7½″) of Gautama Buddha seated cross-legged in the attitude of expounding the law (*dharmachakramudrā*), on the flat top of the base which projects 5¼″ from the back-slab. The position of the hands is the same as in the preceding image. In the centre of the base was the wheel-and-deer symbol which is nearly effaced, but is enough to show that the scene represented is the first sermon at Sārnāth. At both ends are two kneeling figures perhaps the donor and his wife. The five monks are not indicated. The back-slab is oval at top and quite plain. On account of style, I assign this image to the Gupta period. Chunār sandstone. No traces of colouring. Unearthed in 1904-05 at the Chaukhaṇḍī Stūpa.[5]

B (*b*) 183.—Image (ht. 2′ 3¼″; width 1′ 3½″) of Gautama Buddha seated in the attitude of expounding the law. Upper portion of back-

---

[1] *A. S. R.*, 1903-04, p. 216.
[2] *Cf.* sculpture from Swat, Grünwedel-Burgess, *Buddhist art in India*, p. 28, fig. 7.
[3] *Indian Sculpture and Painting*, p. 39.
[4] *A. S. R.*, 1904-05, p. 83, and Pl. XXIX, *c*, also p. 92, No. 23.
[5] *Ibid.*, p. 101, No. 473.

slab with the head of Buddha missing. Behind each shoulder, a crocodile (*makara*) head, as in B (*b*) 181.

On front of the base is a relief consisting of a wheel supported on an expanded lotus with a couchant deer on either side, exterior to which sit the five monks, the first converts of Buddha, namely, two to the proper right and three to the left. This group indicates that the sculpture refers to Buddha's first sermon in the Deer-park of Benares, the modern Sārnāth. The rough sides of the image show that it was meant to be enshrined in a niche perhaps of a *stūpa*. The style is of the Gupta period and the material Chunār sandstone which was coloured red. Unearthed in 1904-05 to the north-west of the Jagat Singh Stūpa.

B (*b*) 184.—Figure (ht. up to top of back-slab 3′ 5″ ; width 1′ 9″) in alto-relievo of Gautama Buddha seated in European fashion in the attitude of expounding the law (*dharmachakramudrā*). The lower portion below the waist is damaged by saltpetre and both hands and right leg are lost. The feet presumably rested on a full-blown lotus. Below it is a wheel between a pair of deer, with two monks in devotional attitude on proper right and traces of the remaining three on the other side. The dress is of the usual type but the right shoulder is bare.[1] Around head, circular halo in relief surrounded by concentric bands of beads and scallops. The corpulent figures on the sides of the halo are garland-carrying celestials.

Style decadent Gupta. Chunār sandstone of reddish tint. Unearthed in 1906-07 to the north-west of Main Shrine, 3½′ below surface.

B (*b*) 185.—Figure (ht. 3′ ; width 1½′) of Gautama Buddha seated cross-legged in the attitude of expounding the law (*dharmachakramudrā*) on a cushion which rests on the flat top of the base. The lower portion of the sculpture is much chipped and the upper part of the back-slab broken off. On front of the base, outlines of the wheel and the five mendicants are traceable, which shows that the scene indicated is the first sermon. The sixth human figure must be the donor. The deer are entirely effaced. The back-slab is ornamented as in B (*b*) 181 with which the image must be approximately coeval. Beginning of halo behind head.

Chunār sandstone. Unearthed in 1904-05 south of Jagat Singh Stūpa.[2]

B (*b*) 186.—Figure (ht. 1′ 3″ ; width 11½″), in alto-relievo, of Gautama Buddha seated in European fashion in the attitude of expound-

[1] It is interesting to note that in this image as well as in B (*b*) 186 the upper robe or *saṅghāṭi* leaves the right shoulder bare. In all the other sculptures illustrating the first sermon both shoulders are covered in accordance with the Buddhist tenets. We also observe that in the same two sculptures the Buddha is shown as sitting in the European fashion. The only other examples in the Museum occur on a lintel (D (*d*) 3), B (*b*) 196 and 245.

[2] *A. S. R.*, 1904-05, p. 92, No. 33.

ing the law (*dharmachakramudrā*) between two Bōdhisattvas. The feet of the main figure are broken off and the right shoulder is bare. Plain circular halo round head. On either side of it is a celestial being (*dēva*) carrying a garland. To the right of Buddha, we find the Bōdhisattva Maitrēya standing, with an antelope hide thrown over his left shoulder. The Bōdhisattva holds his usual emblems, *i.e.*, a rosary, (*japamālā*) in the right hand and an ointment vessel (*amṛita-ghaṭa*) in the left. The figure standing to the left of Buddha is Avalōkitēśvara, or Padmapāṇi, his right hand held forward in the gift-bestowing attitude (*varadamudrā*) and the left holding a lotus stalk. The faces of both the Bōdhisattvas have peeled off.

The base of the sculpture is much worn, but figures of two worshippers are clearly distinguishable. Late Gupta period. Chunâr sandstone. Discovered in 1906-07 in the mediæval monastery I.

B (*b*) 187.—Figure (ht. 1′ 5″; width 1′ 5¼″) of Buddha seated cross-legged on an expanded lotus. The head with upper part of the back-slab is broken off. Lower portion of sculpture much damaged. The attitude of the hands was that of expounding the law (*dharmachakramudrā*). To right and left of Buddha, traces of two standing Buddhas as we find in representations of the Śrâvastī miracle.[1] Remnants of lotus-stalks rising from behind the back of the central figure show that two more miniature Buddha figures were shown in the upper corners of the slab. The treatment of drapery in conventional folds must be due to the influence of the Mathurā sculptures of the Gupta period.[2]

The sculpture is made of the reddish sandstone of Chunār and dates from the Gupta period. It was found in 1906-07 to south of monastery I, 2½′ below the surface.

B (*b*) 188.—Lower portion (ht. 11″; width 1′ 2″) of sculpture representing crossed legs of a figure of Gautama Buddha on a fully expanded lotus flower. Beneath the lotus seat, the wheel-and-deer symbol with six seated figures, three on either side. Five of these are the first converts of Buddha (*pañcha bhadravargīya*) and the sixth has apparently been added for the sake of symmetry, unless it represents the donor of the sculpture. To right and left of Buddha, are the lower parts of two figures standing on lotuses which spring from the same root as his lotus seat. They are presumably the Bōdhisattvas Maitrēya and Avalōkitēśvara. Late Gupta period. Found in 1904-05.

B (*b*) 189.—Trunk (ht. 10″; width 5″) of image of Buddha which must have been seated in the attitude of expounding the law (*dharmachakramudrā*). The back has disappeared. The hands remain on the

---

[1] *Cf.* C (*a*) 3, 4, 6 and 7.
[2] *Cf.* Vogel, *Mathurā Catalogue*, Pl. IX.

breast. To judge from its style the image must be a product of the Gupta period. Chunār sandstone. Discovered in 1904-05. The exact find-spot is unknown.

B (*b*) 190.—Trunk (ht. 7½″; width 10¼″) of figure of Buddha in the attitude of expounding the law (*dharmachakramudrā*). Traces of red colour. Decadent Gupta style. Discovered in 1906-07 in area to west of Main Shrine.

B (*b*) 191.—Trunk (ht. 5″; width 6½″) of Buddha in the same attitude as B (*b*) 190. Right fore-arm broken off. Red colour. Late Gupta work. Excavated in 1907-08 on south of monastery I, 2′ below surface.

B (*b*) 192.—Bust (ht. 8½″; width 1′ 1″) of Buddha without head and fore-arms. Folds of upper robe (*saṅghāṭī*) which covers both shoulders are marked by shallow lines on both sides of the throat. Gupta style. Chunār sandstone. Excavated in 1906-07 in eastern row of cells of mediæval monastery I, 1′ below surface.

B (*b*) 193.—Figure (ht. 1′ 1½″; width 8″) of Gautama Buddha seated cross-legged in the attitude of expounding the law (*dharmachakramudrā*). Below seat, the usual relief consisting of the wheel-and-deer symbol and six human figures of whom five are the first disciples of Buddha and the sixth the donor of the sculpture. The sculpture refers to the first sermon at Sārnāth. To right and left of main figure are two standing attendants, one holding a fly-whisk, presumably Maitrēya and Avalōkitēśvara. Late Gupta style. Traces of red colour.

Chunār sandstone. Excavated in 1904-05 to the north of Jagat Singh Stūpa.

* B (*b*) 194.—Figure (ht. 1′ ½″; width 9½″) of Gautama Buddha seated on inverted lotus preaching first sermon. Badly chipped. On base, wheel-and-deer and the five monks (*Pañchavargīya*). Head and upper part of slab missing. On back, Buddhist creed in two lines in characters of the Gupta period of the western variety. Unearthed inside Jagat Singh Stūpa.[1]

B (*b*) 195.—Figure (ht. 1′ 3″; width 10″) of Gautama Buddha seated preaching his first sermon. Upper part of back-slab broken. Hands damaged. On base, usual relief. The kneeling female at the proper left end is probably the donor. 5th or 6th century A.D. Chunār stone. Discovered in one of the recent excavations.

B (*b*) 196.—Middle portion (ht. 7¾″; width across shoulders 7″) of an image of Buddha seated in European fashion in the attitude of expounding the law (*dharmachakramudrā*). The hands which were held in front of the breast are broken off. The back shows no carving beyond the general indication of the robe. The style is of the Gupta

---

[1] *A. S. R.*, 1904-05, p. 94, No. 114, and p. 103, inscription No. XX.

period. Unearthed in 1906-07 in the area to the west of the Main Shrine.

B (*b*) 197.—Figure (ht. including tenon at base 2′ 2″; width at base 1′ 4″) in alto-relievo, of Gautama Buddha seated cross-legged in the posture of expounding the law (*dharmachakramudrā*). The head is broken off and the right knee damaged. The relief on the front of the base is entirely worn away. Chunār sandstone. On grounds of style, I assign the sculpture to the Gupta period.

B (*b*) 198.—Head (ht. 1′ 1½″) of a life-sized image of Buddha. Forehead, nose, ears and chin damaged. The hair is arranged in schematic curls turned to the right (*dakshiṇāvarta*). In Gandhāra images of Buddha the hair is generally merely brushed back, but the arrangement in curls presumably also began in the same region in the Kushāṇa period. It reached Mathurā probably in the late Kushāṇa period [1] and was used at Sārnāth from the early Gupta period down to about the 10th century A.D. when it seems to have gone out of use and been replaced by the ordinary treatment.[2]

The protuberance on the skull (*ushṇīsha*) is nearly hemispherical in the Gupta heads. It becomes more and more pointed in later images. Other characteristic features of a Gupta head, as pointed out by Dr. Marshall, are round cheeks, full lips, broad nostrils and the three folds on the neck.

Made of Chunār sandstone and unearthed in 1904-05. Exact find-spot not known.

B (*b*) 199.—Head (ht. 1′ 2½″) of image of Buddha of colossal size which dates from the Gupta period. The front portion of the face is wanting, but the existence of two holes with iron nails remaining in them shows that the missing portion had formed part of a repair. The lobes of the ears are slightly damaged.

Presumably unearthed in 1904-05, but as the number given to it has disappeared the exact find-spot cannot be determined.

B (*b*) 200.—Head (ht. 1′ 1½″) of colossal image of Buddha. Eyes, nose, lips, chin and ears injured. Forehead-mark (*ūrṇā*) not indicated. The style of face and treatment of hair proclaim it to be a product of the Gupta age.

Made of Chunār sandstone and discovered in 1904-05 to south of Main Shrine.[3]

B (*b*) 201.—Head (ht. 1′ 1½″) of life-sized image of Buddha in typical Gupta style. Forehead, eyes, nose, chin and ears damaged. Chunār sandstone. Unearthed in 1907-08 in Gupta monastery III.

---

[1] *Cf.* Vogel, *Mathurā Catalogue*, Pl. XVI and figure of Buddha from Sahēṭh-Mahēṭh, *J. R. A. S.*, 1909, Pl.

[2] *Cf.* B (*c*) 31 and 46.

[3] *A. S. R.*, 1904-05, p. 97, No. 210.

B (*b*) 202.—Head (ht. 1′ 2″) of nearly life-sized image of Buddha. Forehead chipped and features of face including ears injured. The head shows all the peculiarities of the Gupta type : round face, broad nostrils, thick lips, etc. The hair is arranged as usual in formal wavy curls. Chunār sandstone. Discovered in 1904-05 to north-east of Jagat Singh Stūpa.

B (*b*) 203.—Head (ht. 1′ 3″) of a nearly life-sized image of Buddha with a fragment of halo remaining behind it. The face is totally destroyed. The decoration on the halo consists of a band of foliated scroll-work and a line of bead and reel ornament. The head undoubtedly belonged to a Gupta image.

Chunār sandstone. Excavated in 1904-05.[1]

B (*b*) 204.—Head (ht. 1′) of image of Buddha. The protuberance of the skull (*ushṇīsha*) is broken in part. The hair is arranged in spiral curls. A fragment of the back-slab is preserved. It is ornamented along the margin with a scalloped border and a line of bead and reel. The style is of the Gupta period.

Chunār sandstone. Found in 1904-05.

B (*b*) 205.—Head (ht. 11″) of image of Buddha in typical Gupta style, characterized by high cheek bones and full lips. Nose and ears injured. Chunār sandstone. Discovered in 1904-05.

B (*b*) 206.—Head (ht. 9″) of Buddha. Eyes, nose and chin damaged. The projection on skull (*ushṇīsha*) and folds on neck clearly marked. Round face, full lips, etc., as in Gupta images.

Greyish sandstone from Chunār. Found at the village of Akthā near Sārnāth, which is situated on a mass of ancient remains.

B (*b*) 207.—Head (ht. 10″) of Buddha of which the back has been cut off across the ears. Nostrils and chin slightly injured. The modelling of the face follows the Gupta type.

Buff-coloured stone from Chunār. Excavated in 1904-05 to north of Jagat Singh Stūpa.[2]

B (*b*) 208.—Head (ht. 1′) of image of Buddha in Gupta style. Nose, lower lip and left ear slightly damaged. For the rest, the head is in an excellent state of preservation.

Chunār sandstone. Unearthed in 1904-05 to the south of the Main Shrine.[3]

B (*b*) 209.—Head (ht. 11¼″) of image of Buddha of nearly life-size. The back half including ears is missing and the forehead is chipped. Late Gupta.

Chunār sandstone. Unearthed in 1906-07 near the south boundary wall of the mediæval monastery I, 2′ below the surface.

---

[1] *A. S. R.*, 1904-05, p. 97, No. 207.
[2] *Ibid.*, No. 215.
[3] *Ibid.*, No. 210.

B (*b*) 210.—Front half of head (ht. 8″) of a Buddha image. Protuberance on skull (*ushṇīsha*) is lost and nose and chin broken. The style is of the Gupta period.

Chunār sandstone. Discovered in 1906-07 in the area to the west of the Main Shrine.

B (*b*) 211.—Head (ht. 8″) of Buddha image with round cheeks, broad nostrils and other characteristics of the Gupta style. Hair arranged in schematic curls. Ears elongated.

Chunār sandstone. Discovered in 1906-07 in the relic-chamber of *stūpa* No. 43 to the south of mediæval monastery I.

B (*b*) 212.—Head and neck (ht. 8″) of Buddha image of the Gupta period. The features are mutilated and the projection on the skull (*ushṇīsha*) broken.

Chunār sandstone. Unearthed in 1904-05 north-west of the site of the umbrella post of the red Bōdhisattva of Kāṇishka's time.[1]

B (*b*) 213.—Head (ht. 7″) of image of Buddha. Nose, lips and chin disfigured. Gupta work. Made of Chunār sandstone. Discovered in 1906-07 in the entrance chamber of the mediæval monastery I, 2′ 2″ below the surface.

B (*b*) 214.—Head (ht. 7½″) of image of Buddha of Gupta period. Nose, lips and chin mutilated. Protuberance of skull (*ushṇīsha*) well-defined but no mark (*ūrṇā*) between the eye-brows. Hair arranged as usual in formal curls which turn to the right. Three folds on neck. Chunār sandstone. Excavated in 1904-05 in the area around Main Shrine.

B (*b*) 215.—Head (ht. 6½″) of Buddha image of small size. The projection of skull (*ushṇīsha*), nose, chin and ear-lobes slightly injured. Hair arranged in schematic curls. Gupta work.

Chunār stone. Excavated in 1906-07.

B (*b*) 216.—Head (ht. 7″) of Buddha of Gupta period. Excavated in 1906-07.

B (*b*) 217.—Head (ht. 6½″) of Buddha image in Gupta style. Lower portion below eyes broken off and protuberance of skull (*ushṇīsha*) damaged. Treatment of hair of the usual type. Fine-grained Chunār stone. Excavated in 1904-05.

B (*b*) 218.—Head (ht. 7½″) of small-sized Buddha image. Nose and ear-lobes slightly injured. Hair arranged in usual curls.

Chunār sandstone. Discovered in 1906-07 on *stūpa* No. 44 to south of Gupta monastery III.

B (*b*) 219.—Head (ht. 6½″) of small image of Buddha of the usual type. Features disfigured. Chunār stone. Found in 1907-08 in monastery IV.

---

[1] *A. S. R.*, 1904-05, p. 97, No. 201.

B (*b*) 220.—Head (ht. 6½") of Buddha of small size. Chin and ear-lobes slightly injured. Rest in excellent preservation. Hair arranged in short curls of the usual style. Gupta period. Chunār stone. Excavated in 1907-08 in area south of monastery II, 3′ below surface.

B (*b*) 221.—Head (ht. 5½") of image of Buddha split into two. Features damaged. Arrangement of hair of usual fashion. Chunār stone. Discovered in 1907-08 on the paved approach to east of Main Shrine, 6′ and 7′ below surface.

B (*b*) 222.—Head (ht. 6½") of small image of Buddha similar to B (*b*) 221. Left ear-lobe slightly injured.

Chunār stone. Found in 1906-07 in area to east of Main Shrine.

B (*b*) 223.—Head with fragment of back-slab (ht. 8") of small-sized figure of Buddha, of Gupta period. The ear-lobes are elongated in accordance with the canon. The projection of the crown (*ushṇīsha*) is prominent. Traces of red colour.

Chunār stone. Discovered in 1904-05.

B (*b*) 224.—Face and throat (ht. 7") of image of Buddha. Hair arranged in schematic curls. Projection of skull (*ushṇīsha*) and folds on neck, but no forehead mark (*ūrṇā*). Chunār sandstone. Excavated in 1906-07 in area to west of Main Shrine.

B (*b*) 225.—Face (ht. 5½") of image of Buddha of miniature size. Hair treated as usual in schematic curls. Chin damaged. Gupta style.

Chunār stone. Discovered in 1904-05.

B (*b*) 226.—Head (ht. 6") of miniature image of Buddha. Neck marked with the usual three folds. Elongated ears and projection of skull (*ushṇīsha*) in perfect condition. Nose mutilated. Gupta work. Chunār stone. Found in 1906-07 in the area to north-west of Main Shrine.

B (*b*) 227.—Head (ht. 5½") of small-sized image of Buddha of Gupta date. Face cut away. Hair arranged in usual fashion. Chunār stone. Discovered in 1906-07 near the south-east corner of mediæval monastery I, 6′ below surface.

B (*b*) 228.—Middle portion of head (ht. 8") of image of Buddha with the face and back half broken off. To judge from treatment of hair, Gupta. Chunār sandstone. Excavated in area to north of Dhamēkh Stūpa.

B (*b*) 229.—Mutilated face (ht. 6") of small image of Buddha. Hair arranged in curls of usual style. Reddish sandstone from Chunār. Discovered in 1906-07 in area to west of Main Shrine, 1½′ below concrete terrace around it.

B (*b*) 230.—Head and throat (ht. 4½") of miniature image of Buddha. Nose broken. Hair arranged in schematic curls; ears elongated in accordance with canon. Folds on neck defaced. Gupta work. Chunār sandstone. Found in 1906-07 in area to north-west of Main Shrine, 4½′ below surface.

B (*b*) 231.—Head and throat (ht. 7") of image of Buddha. Face cut off. Fragment of back-slab behind it. Long ear-lobes and well-defined protuberance of skull (*ushṇīsha*). Folds on throat clearly marked. Gupta style. Chunār sandstone. Unearthed in 1907-08 in area between Dhamēkh Stūpa and easternmost entrance of mediæval monastery I.

B (*b*) 232.—Head and throat (ht. 5") of miniature Buddha image. Protuberance of skull, eyes, nose and chin slightly injured. Hair treated in short curls of usual form. Fragment of back-slab behind head. To judge from style, Gupta. Chunār stone. Discovered in 1907-08 among the group of *stūpas* in trench crossing south boundary wall of monastery I on north of Main Shrine 3' below surface.

B (*b*) 233.—Head with fragment of back-slab behind it (ht. 6½") in decadent Gupta style. Chunār sandstone. Excavated in 1904-05.

B (*b*) 234.—Head (ht. 4⅛") of miniature Buddha image. Nose, ear-lobes and protuberance of skull (*ushṇīsha*) damaged. Hair arranged in schematic curls. Chunār sandstone. Unearthed in 1904-05.

B (*b*) 235.—Head with halo (ht. 5"; width 7½") of Buddha. Late Gupta style. Chunār sandstone of greyish tint. Discovered in 1907-08 in western precinct of mediæval monastery I, 7' below surface.[1]

B (*b*) 236.—Head (ht. 11"; width 6") of Buddha without face. Left ear intact. Protuberance of skull damaged. Hair in usual style. Excavated in 1906-07 near *stūpa* No. 22 to west of Main Shrine, 4' below surface.

B (*b*) 237.—Head (ht. 7"; width 5") of Buddha lacking protuberance of skull (*ushṇīsha*). Features and ears damaged. Presumably Gupta. Chunār sandstone. Excavated in the same year near *stūpa* No. 20 to west of Main Shrine.

B (*b*) 238.—Head with part of back-slab (ht. 5"; width 6½"). Hair arranged in schematic curls. Face cut away. Back-slab adorned along border with bands of beads and scallops. Typical Gupta work. Chunār sandstone. Unearthed in 1906-07 in first cell in north row of mediæval monastery I, some 7' below surface.

B (*b*) 239.—Fragment of head (ht. 5½"; width 3½" from cheek to cheek), face and back both cut away. Hair arranged in formal curls. Gupta style. Chunār sandstone. Excavated in 1906-07 to north-west of Main Shrine 5' below surface.

B (*b*) 240.—Head (ht. 3½"; width 2¼") of Buddha without face. Hair arranged in schematic curls. Chunār sandstone. Gupta style. Excavated in the same year in the area east of Main Shrine.

B (*b*) 241.—Trunk (ht. 9½"; width 1' 1½") of image of Buddha which must have been seated cross-legged in the earth-touching attitude

---

[1] *A. S. R.*, 1907-08, p. 47, *a* 17.

(*bhūmisparśamudrā*). Both fore-arms missing. Right shoulder nude. Drapery indicated by shallow lines. Probably Gupta. Chunār sandstone. Find-spot not known.

B (*b*) 242.—Figure (ht. 1′ 2½″ excluding tenon; width 9½″) of Gautama Buddha much defaced. To judge from the position of the elbows it may have been seated in the attitude of preaching. Umbrella overhead. Late Gupta period. Chunār sandstone. Excavated in a niche of a small *stūpa* north-east of Main Shrine.[1]

B (*b*) 243.—Image (ht. 1′ 1½″; width 11½″) in alto-relievo, of Gautama Buddha seated cross-legged in the attitude of preaching. Head missing. Knees damaged. On base, wheel (*dharmachakra*) between deer and the five monks. To judge from style, Gupta work. Vestiges of red colour. Chunār sandstone. Excavated to west of Main Shrine.[2]

B (*b*) 244.—Figure (ht. 10¾″; width 7″) of Gautama Buddha seated cross-legged preaching the first sermon. Circular halo. Face cut away and hands and right knee damaged. On base, usual relief. Late Gupta period. Chunār sandstone. Excavated in 1906-07 in area to west of Main Shrine.

B (*b*) 245.—Figure (ht. 11″; width 9½″) of Gautama Buddha seated on couch in European style preaching first sermon. Right shoulder bare. Head missing. Rest much defaced. Traces of attendant Bōdhisattvas on right and left. On base, remains of relief as on B (*b*) 243. Late Gupta period. Chunār sandstone. Excavated in 1904-05.[3]

B (*b*) 246.—Trunk (ht. 5½″; width 6″) of image of Gautama Buddha, which to judge from traces of fingers on breast must have been seated in the attitude of preaching. Gupta work. Chunār sandstone. Unearthed in 1904-05.

B (*b*) 247.—Trunk (ht. 7″; width 7″) similar to B (*b*) 246. Probably Gupta. Excavated in 1904-05.[4]

B (*b*) 248.—Fragment (ht. 7″; width 7½″) similar to B (*b*) 247. Probably excavated in 1904-05.

B (*b*) 249.—Figure (ht. 11″; width 10″) of Gautama Buddha delivering first sermon. Head lost. Relief on base much defaced. Possibly late Gupta period. Chunār sandstone. Excavated in 1907-08 in trench crossing south boundary wall of monastery I, north of Main Shrine, 3′ below surface.[5]

B (*b*) 250.—Lower half (ht. 4¾″; width 4¾″) of image in same attitude. On base, wheel and deer and the five mendicants. Late Gupta.

---

[1] *A. S. R.*, 1907-08, p. 71, No. β 82.
[2] *Ibid.*, 1904-05, p. 93, No. 87.
[3] *Ibid.*, 1904-05, p. 93, No. 78.
[4] *Ibid.*, p. 92, No. 43.
[5] *Ibid.*, 1907-08, p. 71, No. β 38.

Chunār sandstone. Excavated in 1906-07 between first outer court of mediæval monastery I and *stūpa* No. 44, 5½′ below surface.

B (*b*) 251.—Trunk with arms (ht. 5″; width 5″) of Gautama Buddha in attitude of preaching. Late Gupta style. Chunār sandstone. Unearthed in 1907-08 in débris above Gupta monastery III.

B (*b*) 252.—Fragment (ht. 4½″; width 4½″) similar to B (*b*) 251. Unearthed in 1904-05 between Jagat Singh Stūpa and Main Shrine.

B (*b*) 253.—Fragment of drapery (ht. 5½″; width 2¾″) presumably from left side of a Buddha image of Gupta date. Chunār sandstone. Excavated in the same year, in area east of Main Shrine.

B (*b*) 254.[1]—Fragment (ht. 3′; width 1′ 7″) of a large circular halo adorned along the border with concentric circular bands of ornament similar to those on B (*b*) 4. The carving is deeply cut and particularly fine. Gupta period.

The material of the fragment is Chunār sandstone though much weather-stained. It was discovered in 1906-07 in structure No. 23 to north-west of Main Shrine, 5′ below the surface.

B (*b*) 255.—Two fragments making up major portion of a halo (diameter about 2′ 8″) of Gupta date which probably belonged to a large-sized image of Buddha. Decoration along margin similar to that in B (*b*) 254; the outermost band consists of small scallops. Chunār sandstone. Excavated in 1904-05 on south of Main Shrine.[2]

B (*b*) 256.—Two fragments which fit together (ht. 10″; width 2′ 1″) of circular halo elaborately carved in Gupta style, the bands of decoration being identical with those on B (*b*) 255 and arranged in the same order. Chunār sandstone. Unearthed in area on north of Dhamēkh Stūpa.

B (*b*) 257.—Fragment (ht. 10½″; width 1′ 3″) of circular halo with the same margin ornamentation as on B (*b*) 255 and in the same order of succession. Typical Gupta style. Chunār sandstone. Excavated in 1904-05.

B (*b*) 258.—Fragment (ht. 11″; width 1′ 4½″) of circular halo. Carving along border exceptionally fine and analogous to that on B (*b*) 255. Chunār sandstone. Excavated in 1904-05.

B (*b*) 259.—Fragment (ht. 8½″; width 1′ 1½″) of circular halo with same ornamentation as on B (*b*) 255. Gupta period. In edge, holes to receive flower-sticks, etc. Chunār sandstone. Excavated in 1906-07 in area east of Main Shrine.

---

[1] The Sārnāth Museum contains a large number of Gupta haloes which might belong to Buddha or Bōdhisattva images. As, however, the number of Gupta Bōdhisattvas unearthed at Sārnāth is comparatively very small, I am disposed to think that most of these halos must have belonged to Buddha images.

[2] *A. S. R.*, 1904-05, p. 91, No. 13.

B (*b*) 260.—Fragment (ht. 7½″; width 10½″) of circular halo adorned with concentric rings of foliated design with beads and scallops outside it. Gupta work. Chunār sandstone. Find-spot not known.

B (*b*) 261.—Fragment (ht. 6″; width 7″) of circular halo which must have been ornamented after the style of B (*b*) 254. Gupta work. Chunār sandstone. Find-spot not ascertainable.

B (*b*) 262.—Fragment (ht. 5″; width 8″) of cirular halo carved in Gupta style. Chunār sandstone. Find-spot not known.

B (*b*) 263.—Fragment (ht. 4″; width 6″) of circular halo adorned with scalloped band with bands of beads and foliated scroll on the inside. Gupta style. Chunār sandstone. Excavated in 1906-07 in so-called Hospital west of Dhamēkh Stūpa, 5′ below surface.

B (*b*) 264.—Upper part (ht. 1′ 1″; width 1′ 6″) of back-slab which is mainly taken up by a circular halo with beaded and scalloped border. Flying celestial (*dēva*) in relief carrying garland on either side. At spring of halo on proper left side, crocodile (*makara*) head. In centre of fragment, traces of head of main image. Gupta style. Chunār sandstone. Excavated in 1904-05.[1]

B (*b*) 265.—Upper part (ht. 8″; width 11″) of back-slab of image adorned along margin like B (*b*) 264. Traces of Buddha head in middle. Gupta work. Chunār sandstone. Find-spot not known.

B (*b*) 266.—Circular halo which was elaborately carved in Gupta style. Much defaced but traces of two outermost bands visible. Chunār sandstone. Traces of red paint. Excavated in 1904-05 at Chaukhaṇḍī Stūpa on north side.[2]

B (*b*) 267.—Fragment (ht. 5″; width 9½″) with traces of three heads surrounded by halos, perhaps Buddha with attendant Bōdhisattvas. Foliage between halos. Halo of central head beaded and scalloped along margin. Gupta style. Chunār sandstone. Unearthed in 1907-08 in area on north of Dhamēkh Stūpa.

B (*b*) 268.—Fragment (ht. 9″; width 4½″), from proper right upper corner of image, with part of plain circular halo and celestial carrying garland, in flight. His head is damaged; he wears a necklace of beads, and a *dhōtī* and has a fat body. Beneath him, foliage and bust of fabulous beast. Gupta style. Chunār stone of pale buff tint. Excavated in 1904-05 south of Main Shrine.[3]

B (*b*) 269.—Fragment (ht. 4¾″; width 5″) from proper left upper corner of the same image as B (*b*) 268 and with analogous celestial figure. Excavated in the same year on west of Jagat Singh Stūpa.[4]

---

[1] *A. S. R.*, 1904-05, p. 91, No. 12, where the height stated is wrong.
[2] *Ibid.*, p. 101, No. 476.
[3] *Ibid.*, p. 98, No. 308.
[4] *Ibid.*, 1904-05, p. 98, No. 293.

B (*b*) 270.—Figure of celestial (*dēva*) (ht. 5" ; width 4") flying towards proper left and similar in style to B (*b*) 268. Gupta work. Chunār sandstone of buff colour. Discovered in 1907-08 in trench crossing south boundary wall of monastery I on north of Main Shrine, 2' below surface.[1]

B (*b*) 271.—Fragment (ht. 5" ; width 4½") from proper right upper corner of an image. Bears figure of celestial (*dēva*) carrying garland, in Gupta style. Defaced but large ear-rings and necklace distinct. His hair hangs back on shoulders. Chunār sandstone. Unearthed in 1906-07 in mediæval monastery I, 2' below surface.

B (*b*) 272.—Fragment (ht. 7½" ; width 3") with a figure of celestial of Gupta type, broken from proper left upper corner of a bigger image. Chunār sandstone. Found in 1904-05 close to B (*b*) 269.

B (*b*) 273.—Fragment (ht. 7½" ; width 7") with part of scalloped and beaded border and headless celestial with garland. From proper left upper corner of bigger image. Gupta style. Chunār sandstone. Excavated in 1904-05.[2]

B (*b*) 274.—Fragment (ht. 8" ; width 6½") from proper right upper corner of image. Contains figure of celestial with usual garland in Gupta style. Chunār sandstone. Discovered in 1906-07 in area north-west of Main Shrine, 1' below level of concrete terrace around it.

B (*b*) 275.—Fragment (ht. 7½" ; width 5½") from proper right upper corner of bigger image. Contains part of circular halo with beaded and scalloped border, and much chipped flying celestial with garland, in Gupta style. The celestial wears a *dhōtī* and is nude as usual in upper body. Chunār sandstone. Excavated in 1904-05.

B (*b*) 276.—Figure of celestial (ht. 4" ; width 3") from proper right upper corner of bigger image. Legs in usual position. Gupta style. Chunār sandstone. Excavated in 1906-07 in mediæval monastery I.

B (*b*) 277.—Two fragments which fit together (ht. 9½" ; width 1' 2") constituting top of an image, and bearing a pair of celestial figures one at each end. They are represented as flying in opposite directions, but instead of garlands they carry bowls of sweets. In this respect, as well as the style, they simulate the celestials on B (*b*) 175 and B (*b*) 181 and must be contemporaneous with them.

Chunār sandstone. Both fragments were found in area east of Main Shrine, one in 1904-05, other in 1906-07.

B (*b*) 278.—Fragment (ht. 5" ; width 10½") of halo which was probably circular, elaborately carved in Gupta style. Chunār sandstone. Excavated in 1906-07 in mediæval monastery I, near well, 6' below surface.

---

[1] *A. S. R.*, 1907-08, p. 72, No. 18.
[2] *Ibid.*, 1904-05, p. 96, No. 169.

B (*b*) 279.—Fragment (ht. 9½″; width 5½″) of halo of similar style and date. Excavated, in same year, in area on east of Main Shrine.

B (*b*) 280.—Fragment (ht. 4½″; width 5″) of halo with same ornamentation as on B (*b*) 255. Gupta work. Chunār sandstone. Unearthed in one of the recent excavations.

B (*b*) 281.—Fragment (ht. 5″; width 4″) of halo with several concentric bands of ornament some of which have been noticed in connection with other Gupta halos. Carving very fine. Chunār sandstone. Find-spot not known.

B (*b*) 282.—Fragment (ht. 4″; width 5″) of halo with garland pattern. Probably Gupta. Chunār sandstone. Unearthed in 1906-07 west of Main Shrine.

B (*b*) 283.—Fragment (ht. 7¾″; width 5″) with figure of celestial (*dēva*) flying in cloud with garland. His hair tied on top of head. Late Gupta. Chunār sandstone. Discovered in 1907-08 in first court on east of mediæval monastery I.[1]

B (*b*) 284.—Fragment (ht. 4¼″; width 5¾″) of halo elaborately carved in Gupta style with concentric bands of ornament. Chunār sandstone. Excavated in 1906-07 in mediæval monastery I, 8′ below surface.

B (*b*) 285.—Fragment (ht. 3½″) of halo similar to B (*b*) 284. Excavated in the same area.

B (*b*) 286.—Fragment (ht. 6″; width 2″) with celestial flying in cloud in relief. Garland between his hands. Gupta style. Chunār sandstone of reddish tint. Discovered in 1904-05 east of Main Shrine.[2]

B (*b*) 287.—Fragment (ht. 4½″; width 4½″) of back-slab of image with portion of halo in relief. Gupta work. Chunār sandstone. Discovered in 1906-07 in south-east corner of court of mediæval monastery I, 5¼′ below surface.

B (*b*) 288.—Fragment (ht. 7½″; width 2½″) similar to B (*b*) 287. Traces of red paint. Unearthed in 1907-08 in area west of mediæval monastery I, 6½′ below surface.

B (*b*) 289.—Fragment (ht. 4″; width 3½″) with finely carved scalloped and beaded margin. From back-slab of an image. Gupta work. Chunār sandstone. Find-spot not ascertainable.

B (*b*) 290.—Pedestal (ht. 11½″; width 1′ 8½″) supported at either end by a couchant lion facing to the front. The head of the lion at the proper right end is broken off. The centre of the pedestal is occupied by a wheel placed on a throne. The pedestal cannot have belonged to an image of Buddha expounding the law (*dharmachakramudrā*) at Sārnāth as the pair of deer symbolizing the Deer-Park

---

[1] *A. S. R.*, 1907-08, p. 49, No. η 27.

[2] *Ibid.*, 1904-05, p. 99, No. 370.

is absent. In the top of the pedestal are two deep mortices which held the tenons of two images. Front portion of top broken.

On grounds of style, I assign the pedestal to the early Gupta period.

* B (*b*) 291.—Pedestal (ht. 7″; width 1′ 7½″) decorated on three sides with a rim at the top and another at the base. On the upper rim is cut in neatly engraved letters of the 5th century A.D. a Sanskrit inscription of a single line 1′ 6¼″ in length. It was first deciphered by Dr. Vogel[1] and runs as follows :—

Ōṁ[2] *Ādityabandhōr=Buddhasya pratim=āpratimadyutēḥ kāritā Śīlayaśasā kāṅkshatā padam=uttamam.*

"[This] image of the Sun's kinsman, the Buddha of matchless splendour, was caused to be made by Śīlayaśas striving after the highest state of bliss."

It is evident that this pedestal must have belonged to an image of Gautama Buddha. It is interesting to find the subject indicated in the epigraph.[3] The material is buff-coloured sandstone from Chunār. The pedestal was discovered in 1904-05 to west of Main Shrine.[4]

*B (*b*) 292.—Pedestal (ht. 6″; width 1′ 3″) similar in form to B (*b*) 291. In top, mortice 4½″ square, to receive tenon of image. On upper rim on front is a Sanskrit inscription of two lines in Gupta characters of the eastern variety. The latter half of the first line and a few syllables in the beginning of the second are somewhat defaced. Mr. Oertel who excavated this pedestal in 1904-05 has published a facsimile of this epigraph along with his paper.[5] I read it from the original stone as follows :—

l. 1. *Dēyadharmmō=yaṁ Dharmmashēṇasya yad=attra puṇyaṁ tad =bha[va*] tu mā tāpi[trōḥ] sarvva—*

l. 2. *[sattvā]nāṅ=cha anuttara=jñānāvāptayē.*

" This [is] the pious gift of Dharmmashēṇa. Whatever merit there is in it, may it be for the attainment of supreme knowledge of [his] parents and of all sentient beings."

* B (*b*) 293.—Pedestal (ht. 8¼″; width 1′ 11½″) similar in shape to B (*b*) 291. The upper rim on front bears a Sanskrit inscription of two lines in characters of the 5th century A.D. of which only the beginning portions remain. It was first read by Dr. Vogel[6] and runs as follows :—

l. 1. *Dēyadharmmō=yaṁ Śākyabhi[kshōḥ........yad=atra puṇyaṁ tad=bhavatv=āchāryōpādhyāyānāṁ]*

---

[1] *A. S. R.*, 1904-05, p. 89 and facsimile on Pl. XXXII, No. XIII.

[2] Expressed by a symbol.

[3] A Kushāna image of Dīpaṅkara Buddha in the Lucknow Museum has a similar inscription.

[4] *A. S. R.*, 1904-05, p. 92, No. 30.

[5] *Ibid.*, pp. 89-90, inscription No. XV and Pl. XXXII.

[6] *Ibid.*, 1904-05, Inscription No. XIV and Pl. XXXII.

l. 2. *pūrvvaṁgamaṁ kṛitvā mātāpitrō........ [sarvvasattvānām=anuttarajñānāvāptayē*]* [1]

"This [is] the pious gift of the Buddhist friar......[Whatever merit there is in it, may it be for the attainment of supreme knowledge of all sentient beings] beginning with [his teachers, preceptors and parents ....]"

Unearthed in 1904-05.[2]

* B (*b*) 294.—Pedestal (ht. 6″; width 1′ 6¾″) similar to B (*b*) 291. On upper rim on front side, epigraph of a single line of which the greater portion is totally effaced. It does not seem to have been noticed before. The characters belong to the Gupta epoch. The extant portion I read as follows :—

Dēyadharmō=yaṁ Śākya[bhikshōḥ stha]vira.....

"This [is] the pious gift of the Buddhist monk the priest......"

The number of the sculpture having been rubbed off there is no means of ascertaining its find-spot.

* B (*b*) 295.—Pedestal (ht. 8″; width 1′ 9″) with a projecting rim at top and another at base running along the front and flanks. The lower rim contains a votive inscription in Sanskrit consisting of a single line in characters of the Gupta period. The inscription does not appear to have been noticed before. The middle portion is much defaced. The rest runs as below :—

=Dēyadharmō=yaṁ Śākyabhikshō=[Rā]madattasya .... yad=attra

puṇyaṁ tad=bhavatu sarvvasattvā[nāṁ]=anuttara jñānāvāpta[yē].

"This [is] the pious gift of the Buddhist monk [Rā]madatta ......Whatever merit there [is] herein, let it be for the attainment of supreme knowledge for all sentient beings."

The number of the sculpture has disappeared and the exact building in which it was found cannot be determined.

* B (*b*) 296.—Pedestal (ht. 7″; width 1′ 6½″) of the same shape as B (*b*) 295. The mortice in the top which received the tenon of the image is 6½″ square by 3½″ in depth. On the rim on the front and the proper left flank was carved a dedicatory epigraph which has flaked away or been rubbed off. A very small portion which survives on the upper rim on the proper left side in a much defaced state is in characters of about the 5th century A.D. and may be read as......

........*Dēvaputrasya* [3] *Śākyamunēḥ........*

---

[1] The missing portions have been supplied according to a 7th or 8th century votive inscription (*A. S. R.*, 1907-08, p. 75, No. V).

[2] *A. S. R.*, 1904-05, p. 92, No. 21.

[3] This epithet has nothing to do with the following Śākyamuni which must be construed with some word in the missing portion of the inscription.

The pedestal was discovered in 1904-05.[1] The inscription seems to have escaped notice.

*B (*b*) 297.—Pedestal (ht. 8″; width 2′ 2″) of an image. Projecting rims on front and sides. On front in sunken panel was cut a Gupta Sanskrit inscription of presumably four lines, but the surface has entirely peeled off and nothing remains with the exception of a few syllables in the beginning of the last line, which I read *satyānanasya*.

The pedestal has been coloured red. Chunār sandstone. Exact find-spot cannot be determined.

* B (*b*) 298.—Pedestal (ht. 4¼″; width 1′ 7″) of an image with a mortice cut through it. The upper rim on the front side is inscribed with a line of writing in Gupta characters, which is much defaced. The portion that can be deciphered reads *sarvvasatvānāṁ chānuttara.*

The pedestal must have been excavated in one of the recent diggings but the precise locality in which it was found cannot be ascertained.

* B (*b*) 299.—Pedestal (ht. 2⅛″; width 9″) with a double rim, the flanks being rough. In the top, there are two square sockets which would show that it was the common pedestal of two statuettes presented by two different parties. In confirmation of this it is interesting to note that the flat top of the pedestal contains two distinct votive epigraphs one in front of each socket and separated from each other by an incised line. The pedestal was excavated in 1907-08 in the area around Jagat Singh Stūpa.[2] The inscription on the proper right side reads :—

Dēyaṁ dharmmō=yaḥ upāskaṁ bhapatōlē. The beginning of the epigraph as pointed out by Dr. Konow must have been *Dēyadharmmō =yaṁ*. The next word is probably meant for *upāsaka*. The remaining four syllables perhaps represent the name of the donor.

The other epigraph runs :—

l. 1. *Dēyaṁ dharmmō=yaḥ*

l. 2. *upāskikula*, which Dr. Konow translates. " This is the pious gift in the collection of laywomen."

* B (*b*) 300.—Pedestal (ht. 2⅜″; width 6″) of a small image. Square socket in top ,in front of which a votive epigraph of two lines in Gupta characters. A facsimile of it was published by Mr. Oertel, who found the pedestal to the north-west of Main Shrine.[3] I read the inscription from the original stone as follows :—

l. 1. *Dēyadharmō=yaṁ Śākya* [4]—

l. 2. *bhichhuṇa-[Nā]gadēvasya.*

" This [is] the pious gift of the Buddhist friar [Nā]gadēva."

---

[1] *A. S. R.*, 1904-05, p. 98. No. 272.
[2] *Ibid.*, 1907-08, p. 74, No. IV and facsimile on Pl. XXI.
[3] *Ibid.*, 1904-05, p. 98, No. 281 and Pl. XXXII, XVI.
[4] This syllable is repeated above the line.

B (c).—Buddha Images of the Mediæval Period.—(Cir. 600—1200 A.D.)

* B (c) 1.—Pedestal (ht. 1′ 7½″; width 2′ 5½″) with the lower portion of a cross-legged image of Buddha preaching his first sermon at Sārnāth. Both knees and right foot are badly damaged. Lotus-flower in relief on sole of left foot. Folds of the lower garment (*antaravāsaka*) gathered on top of pedestal, and edges of both the upper and lower garments visible above the ankles.

The face of the pedestal is divided into seven sunken panels arranged in a row. The wheel and pair of deer which occupy the middle three divisions indicate that the sculpture refers to Buddha's first sermon. The two erect thunderbolts (*vajra*) on both sides of the wheel symbolize the throne on which Gautama Buddha reached supreme wisdom (*bōdhi*). On the other sides of the deer we notice two lions, couchant, each placed on a conventional lotus flower with its face turned to the front and one fore-paw raised. These figures were only introduced by the sculptor as an indication of the lion-throne (*siṁhāsana*) on which great men (*mahāpurusha*) sit. The ends of the throne are supported on fat dwarfish figures or atlantes which resemble the Erotes of classical art and are indeed indicated by the name of Māra (=Cupid).

The lower rim of the pedestal contains a Sanskrit version of the Buddhist creed in two lines in characters of the 11th century A.D. The inscription cut on the upper rim which consists of three lines of writing in excellent preservation is of exceptional value.

Transcript.

l. 1.—*Ōṁ namō Buddhāya* || *Vārāṇaśī(sī)-sarasyāṁ Gurava-Śrī-Vāmarāśi-pādābjam* |
ārādhya namita-bhūpati-śirōruhaiḥ śaival-ādhiśam ||
Īśāna-Chitraghaṇṭādi-kīrtti-ratna-śatāni yau |
Gauḍādhipō Mahīpālaḥ Kāśyāṁ śrīmān=akāra [*yat* ||].

l. 2.—*Saphalīkṛita-pāṇḍityau bōdhāv=avinivarttinau* |
tau Dharmarājikāṁ sāṅgaṁ Dharmmachakraṁ punar=navaṁ ||
Kṛitavantau cha navīnām=ashṭamahāsthāna-śaila-gandhakuṭīṁ |
ētām-Śrī Sthirapālō Vasantapālōś nujaḥ śrīmān[||*].

l. 3.—*Saṁvat 1083-Pausha-dinē* 11 [||*]

Translation.

"Ōṁ. Adoration to the Buddha! The illustrious Sthirapāla [and his] younger brother, the illustrious Vasantapāla, whom the lord of Gauḍa (Bengal), the illustrious Mahīpāla, caused to establish in Kāśī [the temples of] Īśāna (Siva) and Chitraghaṇṭā (Durgā) and other precious monuments of his glory in hundreds—after he had worshipped the foot of Gurava Śrī-Vāmarāśi, which is like a lotus in the lake of Vārāṇasī surrounded, as it were, by *śaivala* plants through the hair of bowing kings; they who have made learning fruitful and who do not turn back [on their way] to supreme knowledge, restored the *stūpa* and [the shrine or the Convent of] the wheel of law completely, and built this new shrine (*gandhakuṭī*) of stone relating to the eight great places. Saṁvat 1083, on the 11th day of Pausha."

This inscription has already been published[1] four times and is of considerable interest as a record of the restoration of two of the principal monuments of the Deer-park and the construction of a new one in the 11th century A.D. For further remarks about this inscription the reader is referred to the Introduction to this catalogue.[2] The sculpture is made of buff-coloured sandstone of Chunār and was most probably excavated by Babu Jagat Singh, Diwan of Raja Chet Singh of Benares, in 1793-94 at or near the Jagat Singh *stūpa* which he demolished for building materials.[3] Pl. XI.

* B (c) 2.—Figure of Gautama Buddha in bold relief against a back-slab (ht. 3′ 8″; width 2′ 5″) which is rounded at top. The attitude is that of touching the earth (*bhūmisparśamudrā*) on the occasion of enlightenment (*bōdhi*) at Gayā. The right hand which is stretched downward, and the left which rests in the lap are both damaged, so also the features of the face. Hair arranged, as usual, in short conventional curls, but protuberance on skull (*ushṇīsha*) more pronounced than in Gupta images. Right shoulder and breast bare; edge of upper robe falls on left breast. Around head oval-shaped halo, enclosed by a garland and a flaming border. Behind shoulders, in relief, ornamental rail resting on small pilasters and supported at both ends by rampant leogryphs. We find on either side of the Buddha's head a celestial being (*dēva*) with elaborate head-dress seated on the rail, and holding a garland between his hands. Base moulded in off-sets and rims. On it, figure of earth-goddess (Vasundharā) with usual vase in left hand. On upper rim, Buddhist creed in Sanskrit characters of about the 9th century A.D.

It will be noted that the sculpture exhibits a remarkable resemblance to images from Magadha and particularly to a Kurkihār relief in the Lucknow Museum.[4] This is especially evidenced by the form of the

---

[1] Wilford, *Asiatick Researches*, Vol. IX (1807), pp. 203-205, and Vol. X (1808), pp. 129-133; Cunningham, *A. S. R.*, Vol. III, p. 114 *sq.*, and Vol. XI, p. 182; Hultzsch, *Ind. Ant.*, Vol. XIV, p. 139 *sq.*, and Vogel, *A. S. R.*, 1903-04, p. 221 *sq.*, and Pl. LXIV, 4.

[2] See p. 6.

[3] Cunnigham, *A. S. R.*, Vol. I, p. 113, and *Mahabodhi*, p. 65. For a sketch of the sculpture see Kittoe, *Drawings*, Vol. I, No. 120, who notes that he recovered the sculpture in 1849. A photograph of the image was published by Vogel in *A. S. R.*, 1903-04, Pl. LXIII, 3.

[4] *A. S. R.*, 1903-04, pp. 215-216 and Pl. LXII, 3.

halo, the celestial attendants and the lotus throne. I am inclined to think that the sculpture under description was carved by a sculptor of Gayā at Sārnāth. Two other reliefs (Nos. B (*c*) 35 and B (*d*) 8) were presumably also prepared by the same workman.

The material is Chunār sandstone. Unearthed in 1907-08 in the second stratum of buildings to north of Dhamēkh Stūpa.[1] Pl. XII, *a*.

B (*c*) 3.—Figure (ht. 1′ 3¾″; width 9¼″) of Gautama Buddha in the attitude of touching the earth (*bhūmisparśamudrā*) at the moment of his enlightenment. The face of the lower portion of the slab has suffered from weather and the hands of the image are lost. Behind the back of Buddha, a cushion—a purely Indian motif. The upper robe (*saṅghāṭi*) leaves right shoulder bare. Hair arranged in formal curls; protuberance of skull (*ushṇīsha*) higher than in Gupta images. Circular halo with beaded border. Above head, foliage of *pīpal* tree (Skt. *aśvattha*), though the leaves have little resemblance to those of that tree. Above, to proper right a demon, his right hand lifted up in menace. The demon on opposite side is in act of flinging a rock.

In respect of workmanship the sculpture is decidedly inferior to those of the Gupta period, and I have no hesitation in assigning it to the mediæval period.

The number on the image having disappeared, the exact find-place cannot be made out. The sculpture was probably excavated in 1906-07 in area to north-west of Main Shrine.[2]

B (*c*) 4.—Figure (ht. 1′ 3″; width 10½″) of Gautama Buddha similar in all details to B (*c*) 3 and possibly carved by the same sculptor. The lower portion and the demons at the upper corners of the slab are effaced.

Traces of red colour. Chunār sandstone. Discovered in 1906-07 in area to east of Main Shrine.

B (*c*) 5.—Fragmentary slab (ht. 1′; width 1′ ½″) with figure of Gautama Buddha in the attitude of touching the earth (*bhūmisparśamudrā*) at the moment of his enlightenment. Upper portion of slab with head of Buddha missing and the rest totally effaced.

Chunār sandstone. Unearthed in 1904-05 to south of Jagat Singh Stūpa.[3]

B (*c*) 6.—Lower half below waist (ht. 9″; width 1′ ¾″) of figure of Gautama Buddha seated cross-legged in earth-touching attitude (*bhūmisparśamudrā*). Both hands and left knee injured. The surface of the figure is defaced but the style evidently mediæval.

---

[1] *A. S. R.*, 1907-08, p. 60 and Pl. XVII, *b*.

[2] It is probably identical with *A. S. R.*, 1906-07, p. 91, No. 20, though the height does not agree.

[3] *Ibid.*, 1904-05, p. 92, No. 38, where the attitude is stated as that of meditation.

Reddish sandstone from Chunār. Discovered in 1907-08 in 2nd outer court of monastery I, 4′ below surface of mound.

B (*c*) 7.—Lower portion below waist (ht. 9½″; width 1′) of statuette of Gautama Buddha seated cross-legged in the attitude of touching the earth (*bhūmisparśamudrā*) at the moment of his enlightenment. The figure as well as the semi-circular double-lotus throne on which it is seated is carved in the round. The left hand which rests in the lap is marked with a lotus symbol but is damaged. Drapery indicated after the fashion of Magadha sculptures. On top of throne in front of Buddha's crossed legs is a thunderbolt (*vajra*) evidently meant to indicate the adamantine pose (*vajrāsana*), seated in which the Buddha obtained supreme wisdom. This symbol was probably borrowed from Magadha.

Chunār sandstone. Excavated in 1904-05 to south of Main Shrine.[1]

B (*c*) 8.—Trunk (ht. 2′) of image of Gautama Buddha. Left shoulder broken. The right shoulder is uncovered and the border of the upper robe falls on front from which it may be concluded that the attitude of the image was that of touching the earth (*bhūmisparśamudrā*).

Drapery is well marked in the style of Magadha sculpture.

Chunār sandstone. The exact find-spot of the image is not known. It was probably unearthed in 1904-05.

*B (*c*) 9.—Figure (ht. 9¾″; width 6¼″) of Gautama Buddha seated cross-legged on double lotus in the earth-touching posture (*bhūmisparśamudrā*) at the moment of his enlightenment (*bōdhi*). Wears dress of a monk but ornaments of a prince, namely, a jewelled necklace, ear-rings and three-peaked crown (*makuṭa*). Right shoulder bare. Lotus-throne supported on a pair of couchant lions with one fore-paw raised. Between them in square niche, figure of earth-goddess (Vasundharā) holding up vase with left hand. Above the head of the Bōdhisattva, foliage of *pīpal* tree. Around head, oval-shaped halo with beaded border. Below it, design of back of throne in relief. On either side of Bōdhisattva, an attendant Bōdhisattya standing on lotus with hair arranged in conventional curls. The Bōdhisattva at the right side holds his right hand against shoulder in the attitude of protection. The figure on the left has its right hand stretched out in gift-bestowing attitude (*varadamudrā*) while its left holds a lotus flower with a long stalk. On either side of halo of Gautama Buddha a miniature *stūpa* with elaborate *hti*.

On back of sculpture, Buddhist creed in two lines in mixed Sanskrit in characters of the 9th century A.D.

---

[1] *A. S. R.*, 1904-05, p. 92, No. 57.

The sculpture is made of blue stone, and must therefore have been carved in Magadha. Discovered in 1907-08 on approach to Main Shrine from east 6′ below surface.[1]

* B (c) 10.—Figure (ht. 10″ ; width 7″) of Gaumata Buddha seated cross-legged in the pose of touching the earth (*bhūmisparśamudrā*). On either side, standing demon with a weapon in right hand. Above head of Buddha, branch of *pīpal* tree and around it halo of irregular shape. Base defaced., Traces of red colour.

Workmanship very inartistic. On back, Buddhist creed in four lines in characters of 9th century A.D.

Chunār sandstone. Excavated in 1904-05 east of shrine to south of Main Shrine.[2]

B (c) 11.—Figure (ht. 11″ ; width 6¾″) of Gautama Buddha seated in earth-touching attitude. Much defaced. Hair arranged in curls. Around head, circular halo adorned with lotus pattern. On either side, a twig which is meant for the *pīpal* tree. Style very poor. *Cir.* 10th century A.D.

Chunār sandstone. Unearthed in 1904-05 south of Aśōka Column.[3]

* B (c) 12.—Figure (ht. 7″ ; width 5½″) of Gautama Buddha seated cross-legged in earth-touching attitude. Badly defaced. On back, Buddhist creed in corrupt Sanskrit in characters of 9th or 10th century A.D.

Chunār sandstone. Unearthed in 1907-08 in débris above Gupta monastery III.

B (c) 13.—Figure (ht. 10″ ; width 7″) of Gautama Buddha in the posture of touching the earth. Hair arranged in conventional curls. The protuberance on skull (*ushṇīsha*) is pointed. Circular dot between eyebrows meant for *ūrṇā*. Body much defaced. Elliptical halo around head. Late mediæval. Chunār sandstone. Discovered in 1904-05 south-east of Main Shrine.[4]

* B (c) 14.—Lower half (ht. 4¾″ ; width 9″) of statuette of Gautama Buddha seated cross-legged on a double lotus. The figure was carved in the round like B (c) 7. The right leg is chipped, but a remnant of the right hand on its knee shows that the posture was that of touching the earth. On either side of throne, a kneeling worshipper. Workmanship very poor. On front of base, remains of an inscription, possibly the Buddhist creed in characters of 11th century A.D.

Chunār sandstone. Unearthed in 1907-08 in débris on courtyard of mediæval monastery I, 4¼′ below surface of mound.

---

[1] *A. S. R.*, 1907-08, p. 67, γ 30, and Pl. XIX, *a*.
[2] *Ibid.*, 1904-05, p. 93, No. 80.
[3] *Ibid.*, No. 69.
[4] *Ibid.*, p. 93, No. 74.

B (*c*) 15.—Lower half (ht. 5¼″; width 8¾″) of figure of Gautama Buddha seated cross-legged on conventional double-lotus in the earth-touching attitude at the moment of enlightenment. On either side, pair of feet on lotus with stalk. Probably Maitrēya and Avalōkitēśvara. To judge from style, late mediæval.

Chunār sandstone. Unearthed in 1904-05.[1]

B (*c*) 16.—Figure (ht. 10¼″; width 5¾″) of Gautama Buddha seated in the same posture as B (*c*) 15. Broken across above the shoulders. Much defaced. 9th or 10th century A.D.

Chunār sandstone. Discovered in 1906-07 to north-west of *stūpa* No. 21 to north-west of Main Shrine 3′ below surface.

B (*c*) 17.—Figure (ht. 9¾″; width 7½″) of Gautama Buddha in earth-touching attitude (*bhūmisparśamudrā*) on a double lotus. Nose and mouth broken. Oval halo and design as on B (*c*) 19. Style exceedingly rough.

Chunār sandstone. Discovered in 1904-05 south of Main Shrine.[2]

B (*c*) 18.—Figure (ht. 10″; width 6¾″) of Gautama Buddha as Bōdhisattva at the moment of his enlightenment. Base much defaced and proper left side of back-slab broken off. Feet of standing Buddha to proper left. Shows close conformity in style to B (*c*) 9. Perhaps in the 9th or 10th century, Gayā masons were employed at Sārnāth.

Chunār sandstone. Excavated in 1906-07 to east of Main Shrine.

B (*c*) 19.—Trunk (ht. 9½″; width 10½″) of figure of Gautama Buddha which must have been seated cross-legged in the earth-touching posture (*bhūmisparśamudrā*). Left hand and right fore-arm missing. Right shoulder bare. Miniature *stūpa* near left arm. Late mediæval.

Chunār sandstone. Unearthed on eastern approach to Main Shrine, 7′ below surface.

B (*c*) 20.—Fragment (ht. 5¼″; width 7½″) similar to B (*c*) 19, but probably later in date. Execution exceedingly crude. Chunār sandstone. Discovered in 1904-05 between Jagat Singh Stūpa and Main Shrine.

B (*c*) 21.—Fragment (ht. 5″; width 7½″) showing lower portion of figure of Gautama Buddha seated cross-legged on inverted lotus in the attitude of touching the earth. Late mediæval.

Chunār sandstone. Unearthed in 1907-08 in area to south of monastery II, 3′ below surface.

B (*c*) 22.—Figure (ht. 6″; width 5½″) of Gautama Buddha seated cross-legged on double lotus in earth-touching posture. Head and right hand wanting. Workmanship very inartistic. Chunār stone.

---

[1] *A. S. R.*, 1904-05, p. 92, No. 49.
[2] *Ibid.*, p. 93, No. 71.

Unearthed in 1904-05.[1]

B (*c*) 23.—Fragment (ht. 4½″; width 4¼″) representing Gautama Buddha in same attitude as B (*c*) 22. Much defaced. Head missing. Late mediæval. Chunār sandstone. Unearthed in 1907-08 south of monastery I, 2′ below surface.

B (*c*) 24.—Fragment (ht. 4″; width 7″) with right leg of image of Gautama Buddha on inverted lotus. The attitude must have been that of touching the earth (*bhūmisparśamudrā*). This is evident from the figure of the earth-goddess carved on front as emerging from the earth. She holds a vase filled with foliage between her hands. Mediæval period.

Chunār sandstone. Discovered in 1907-08 in débris above Gupta monastery IV, 9′ below surface.

B (*c*) 25.—Fragment (ht. 4″; width 4¼″) with lower half of miniature figure of Gautama Buddha seated cross-legged in the earth-touching attitude (*bhūmisparśamudrā*) on a double conventional lotus. Flame pattern along border showing Magadha influence. *Cir.* 9th century. Chunār stone of greenish colour. Unearthed in 1907-08, 6′ below surface in trench crossing the south boundary wall of monastery I.

B (*c*) 26.—Fragment (ht. 3½″; width 4¼″) with lower half of similar figure. Much defaced. Modelling exceedingly rough. Chunār stone.

B (*c*) 27.—Fragment (ht. 3¼″; width 5″) showing the crossed legs and left hand of a figure of Gautama Buddha at the moment of enlightenment. Early mediæval.

Chunār sandstone. Discovered in 1907-08, 2′ below surface on south of monastery I.

B (*c*) 28.—Fragment (ht. 2″; width 3″) with lower half of figure similar to B (*c*) 27. Blue stone. Hence presumably brought from Magadha for presentation at Sārnāth. *Cir.* 9th century A.D. Exact find-spot not known.

B (*c*) 29.—Fragment (ht. 5″; width 6½″) showing head of Gautama Buddha under the foliage of a *pīpal* tree which symbolizes his enlightenment at Gayā. Execution very crude.

Chunār sandstone. Excavated in 1906-07 on site of mediæval monastery I, 1½′ below surface.

B (*c*) 30.—Fragment (ht. 5″; width 7″) similar to B (*c*) 29 and evidently of the same date. Chunār sandstone. Unearthed in 1906-07 in area to east of Main Shrine.

B (*c*) 31.—Fragment (ht. 10″; width 5½″) with head of Gautama Buddha under large branch of *pīpal* tree. The posture must consequently have been that of touching the earth (*bhūmisparśamudrā*).

---

[1] *Ibid.*, p. 92, No. 46.

Unlike other images of Buddha, the hair in this instance is arranged in long curls on the sides.[1] This marks the latest development in the treatment of Buddha's hair. Badly chipped. Late mediæval.

Chunār stone. Unearthed in 1906-07 in area to east of Main Shrine.

B (*c*) 32.—Fragment (ht. 4″; width 5½″) consisting of right portion of crossed legs and right hand hanging low which manifestly belonged to a figure of Gautama Buddha in the earth-touching posture. Drapery well-marked on right leg. To judge from style, early mediæval.

Chunār stone. Discovered in 1907-08 in débris above Gupta monastery IV, 9′ below surface of mound.

B (*c*) 33.—Trunk (ht. 10½″; width 7″) which to judge from the position of the upper robe (*saṅghāṭī*) must have belonged to an image of Gautama Buddha seated cross-legged in the earth-touching attitude. Back broken off. On grounds of style I assign the fragment to the late mediæval period.

Chunār sandstone. The number of the sculpture has disappeared and the exact find-spot cannot be determined.

B (*c*) 34.—Fragment (ht. 6″; width 6½″) similar to B (*c*) 33 and of the same date. Unearthed in 1906-07 in area to east of Main Shrine.

*B (*c*) 35.—Image (ht. 3′ 10″; width 2′ 5″) in alto-relievo of Gautama Buddha seated cross-legged on a conventional double lotus flower, delivering his first sermon at Sārnāth. Hands and fore-arms broken off and nose and chin damaged. For the rest, the relief is in excellent preservation. Halo and ornamentation of back-slab as in B (*c*) 2. On either side of halo, a garland-carrying celestial figure in flight, projecting from a cloud. On base, relief consisting of wheel (*dharmachakra*) between two deer and six human figures in devotional attitude. Five of these are the mendicant friars (*Pañcha-vargīya*) while the sixth at proper right end holding a garland is probably the donor of the image.

On upper rim of base, Buddhist creed in Sanskrit in characters of about the 9th century A.D. From the close similarity of its style to that of B (*c*) 2 and B (*d*) 8, Dr. Marshall, who discovered all three, has expressed the opinion that they were all carved by the same artist.[2] Chunār sandstone. Excavated in 1907-08 among *stūpas* to north-west of Dhamēkh Stūpa.

*B (*c*) 36.—Image (ht. 2′ 3″; width 1′ 11″), in high relief, of Gautama Buddha seated in the same attitude and on a similar throne as B (*c*) 35. Upper part of back-slab with Buddha's head missing. Hands and fore-arms badly injured. Part of oval halo surrounded by garland and

---

[1] *Cf.* B (*c*) 46.

[2] *A. S. R.*, 1907-08, p. 60 and Pl. XVII, *a*, *b*, and *c*.

flames. On base, wheel and deer and the five monks. On petals of lotus on which Buddha is seated is the Buddhist creed in characters of 11th century A.D.

Chunār sandstone. Unearthed in 1906-07 to east of stūpa No. 19 to west of Main Shrine.[1]

B (c) 37.—Image (ht. 1′ 10″; width 1′ 7½″) of Gautama Buddha carved in the round, seated cross-legged in posture of preaching. Head, left arm and right fore-arm wanting. Broken across waist, and right upper arm detached. Left foot slightly injured. Ornamental hem of dress around neck and above ankles. Relief on base consisting of wheel with pair of deer on either side. The two additional antelopes were perhaps suggested by the lions which sometimes support the throne. On lower rim of base, fragmentary kneeling figure, presumably the donor. Late mediæval.

Chunār sandstone. Discovered in 1904-05 south-west of Main Shrine.[2]

B (c) 38.—Figure (ht. 1′ 9″; width 1′ 1″) of Gautama Buddha seated cross-legged expounding the law at Sārnāth, on a full-blown lotus. Lower portion of slab below legs chipped and upper portion of back-slab above shoulders broken off. Behind the back of Buddha, pillow and pattern of throne; above it, halo adorned with scallops and other devices. Margin of back-slab ornamented with pattern resembling flames. The image is clad in a lower garment (*antaravāsaka*) and a robe (*saṅghāṭī*) which covers both shoulders. Arrangement of hair and protuberance on skull (*ushṇīsha*) as in Gupta images; but workmanship decidedly inferior to Gupta work. The sculpture may be attributed to the 7th or 8th century A.D.

Traces of red colour. Chunār sandstone. Discovered in 1906-07 in area east of Main Shrine.[3]

B (c) 39.—Figure (ht. 1′ 9″; width 1′ 1″) in alto-relievo similar to B (c) 38. The seat in this case is a cushion and not a lotus. Base damaged by saltpetre but traces of the wheel of the law (*dharmachakra*) and the monks who listened to the first sermon still traceable.

Vestiges of red paint. Chunār sandstone. Excavated in 1907-08 in western precinct of mediæval monastery I, 2′ 4″ below surface.[4]

B (c) 40.—Image (ht. 1′ 5½″; width 1′) in alto-relievo of Gautama Buddha seated cross-legged on a cushion which rests on a throne with moulded legs, preaching the first sermon. Head missing. Hands slightly injured. Behind the neck of Buddha, pillow and design of back of throne. Traces of halo with scalloped and beaded border around

---

1 *A. S. R.*, 1906-07, p. 74, Pl. XX, 6, and p. 90, No. 5.
2 *A. S. R.*, 1904-05, p. 94, No. 110.
3 *Ibid.*, 1906-07, p. 90, No. 6.
4 *Ibid.*, 1907-08, p. 47, No. *a* 3 and Pl. XIII, *a*.

head. The halo was probably round. On front of base, wheel on throne between deer and five monks (*pañcha-bhadravargīya*). Owing to style the sculpture may be ascribed to about the early mediaeval period.

Chunār sandstone. Excavated in 1904-05 north-east of Jagat Singh Stūpa.[1]

B (*c*) 41.—Figure (ht. 11½″; width 7¼″) of Gautama Buddha in the same attitude and style as B (*c*) 40. On front of base, however, only four monks are represented, the fifth was probably omitted for the sake of symmetry. Head detached and upper portion of back-slab broken off. Early mediaeval. Traces of red paint. Chunār stone. Unearthed in 1904-05 between Main Shrine and chapel to south of it.[2]

B (*c*) 42.—Figure (ht. 1′ 1¼″; width 8½″) in alto-relievo of Gautama Buddha preaching first sermon. Fingers disposed in the prescribed manner before the chest. On base, relief consisting of wheel-and-deer symbol and five friars, the first disciples of Buddha, and the donor. To Buddha's right, portion of standing figure holding a rosary (*akshamālā*) in left hand, presumably Maitrēya. To left, Avalōkitēśvara, holding a lotus with stalk in left hand and a fly-whisk (*chāmara*) in right.

To judge from style nearly coeval with B (*c*) 41. Chunār sandstone. Unearthed in 1904-05 south-west of Aśōka Column.[3]

B (*c*) 43.—Figure (ht. 11¼″; width 9¾″) of Gautama Buddha seated in European fashion on couch, his feet resting on fully expanded lotus. Head and upper portion of back-slab missing and hands and knees damaged. To his right, standing Maitrēya without head, dressed like a prince, with a fly-whisk (*chāmara*) in right hand and the ointment vessel (?) in left. To left, Avalōkitēśvara holding a fly-whisk in right hand and a lotus with stalk in left. Outside the lotus on which Buddha's feet rest, six figures in reverential attitude. Five of these are evidently the first disciples and the sixth the donor.

Early mediaeval. Chunār sandstone. Discovered in 1906-07 in entrance chamber of mediaeval monastery I, 3′ 6″ below surface.

B (*c*) 44.—Figure (ht. 1′ 6½″ excluding tenon at base; width 1′ 2″) of Gautama Buddha seated in usual fashion preaching first sermon. Upper portion of back-slab, and the right knee and hands missing. Rest broken across above waist. Behind the back of Buddha, pattern of throne. On base, usual symbol and monks.. Hair arranged in formal curls turned to right. Style of carving very much conventionalized. Probably late mediaeval.

Traces of red colour. Excavated in 1904-05 south of Aśōka Column.[4]

---

[1] *A. S. R.*, 1904-05, p. 94, No. 113.
[2] *Ibid.*, p. 93, No. 90.
[3] *Ibid.*, p. 93, No. 75.
[4] *Ibid.*, p. 93, No. 85.

B (c) 45.—Image (ht. 2′ 1″; width 1′ 6¼″) of Gautama Buddha in alto-relievo, seated on conventional double lotus in same attitude as B (c) 44. Broken into two across waist. Upper portion of back-slab broken off. Rest ornamented with design of throne, its ends supported on leogryphs raised in air. On either side of Buddha, is a figure seated in Indian style on a lotus; probably Maitrēya and Avalōkitēśvara. The identity of the left figure is confirmed by Amitābha in his headdress. Below them, also on lotus-flowers, two figures perhaps two of the five friars. Wheel-and-deer symbol traceable on base. Workmanship exceedingly inartistic. *Cir.* 10th century A.D.

Red paint. Chunār sandstone. Lower portion unearthed in 1904-05 [1]; upper in 1906-07, north-west of Main Shrine.[2]

*B (c) 46.—Figure (ht. 1′ 8½″; width 1′ 1″) in alto-relievo. of Gautama Buddha seated on a lotus-flower, preaching the first sermon. Proper left upper, and right lower, corners of slab broken off. Edges of upper robe (*saṅghāṭī*) visible round the neck and ankles. Nose and lips slightly injured. Hair arranged in long twisted curls as in B (c) 31 and protuberance on skull marked with a spiral pattern. Around the head is an oval halo adorned with lotus pattern. To proper right of halo, a celestial in air carrying a garland. On base, wheel (*dharmachakra*) and one deer, behind which female donor kneeling.

Execution very rough. On sides, Buddhist creed in three vertical lines in characters of 9th century A.D. Chunār sandstone. Excavated in 1904-05 north-west of Jagat Singh Stūpa.[3]

*B (c) 47.—Figure (ht. 1′ 4¾″; width 9½″) in high relief, of Gautama Buddha in same posture as B (c) 46. The fingers meet in prescribed manner before the chest and the hair is arranged in conventional curls. Circular halo with beaded border. Behind back, pillow and throne pattern. On either side of halo, blue lotus (*utpala*). Legs of couch broken off. Between them, wheel and pair of deer. On base, two lines in characters of 9th century A. D. consisting of Buddist creed.

Traces of red paint. Chunār sandstone. Discovered in *stūpa* No. 40 to north-east of Main Shrine.[4]

B (c) 48.—Figure (ht. 1′ 9″; width 10″) similar to B (c) 47. Badly defaced. Chunār sandstone. Unearthed in 1904-05 west of Jagat Singh Stūpa.[5]

B (c) 49.—Figure (ht. 1′ 2½″; width 1′ 1″) in alto-relievo of Gautama Buddha in same attitude and of same date as B (c) 48. Head missing.

---

[1] *A. S. R.*, 1904-05 p. 94, No. 91.
[2] *Ibid.*, 1906-07, p. 71, Pl. XIX, 7 and p. 90, No. 1.
[3] *Ibid.*, 1904-05, p. 93, No. 88 and p. 103, inscription XXVIII.
[4] *Ibid.*, 1906-07, p. 81, Pl. XXIII, 9 and p. 91, No. 11.
[5] *Ibid.*, 1904-05, p. 94, No. 99.

Behind back, crude sketches of pillow and leogryphs supporting crocodile heads.

Chunār sandstone. Discovered between south boundary wall of mediaeval monastery I and *stūpa* No. 21, 2′ below surface.

B (*c*) 50.—Figure (ht. 1′ 1½″; width 1′ 2¼″) of Gautama Buddha in same attitude as B (*c*) 49. Head lost. To right and left, roughly carved figures, holding lotuses, presumably meant for Maitrēya and Avalōkitēśvara. On front of base, wheel between deer exterior to which the first five disciples. The third figure on proper right holding a garland must be the donor.

Style exceedingly inartistic. Late mediaeval. Chunār sandstone. Unearthed in 1904-05 east of the chapel to the south of Main Shrine.[1]

B (*c*) 51.—Figure (ht. 1′ 2″; width 10″) in high relief, of Gautama Buddha seated preaching his first sermon. Head missing, surface much defaced. Find-spot not known.

B (*c*) 52.—Figure (ht. 1′ 3½″; width 9¾″) of Gautama Buddha in same posture as B (*c*) 51 and nearly co-eval with it. Broken across waist, and proper left upper corner of slab wanting. Circular halo with beaded border. To its right, celestial (*dēva*) with garland. Relief on base as on B (*c*) 51. Traces of red paint. Chunār sandstone. Unearthed in 1906-07 in area to east of Main Shrine.

B (*c*) 53.—Figure (ht. 1′ 5¼″; width 1′) in high relief similar to B (*c*) 52. Head detached and upper part of back-slab broken. *Cir.* 9th century A.D. Chunār sandstone. Excavated in 1904-05 south of Jagat Singh Stūpa.[2]

B (*c*) 54.—Figure (ht. 1′ 1½″; width 10½″) of Gautama Buddha seated in preaching attitude on inverted lotus with vertical stalk. Head and hands and sides of slab broken off. Below lotus, relief much defaced but wheel between deer and three friars distinctly traceable. Late mediaeval. Chunār sandstone. Discovered in 1907-08 among the remains to north-west of Dhamēkh Stūpa.

B (*c*) 55.—Figure (ht. 10¾″; width 9½″) in high relief, of Gautama Buddha in same attitude as B (*c*) 54. Head and upper part of slab lost. Relief on base effaced but heads of three monks traceable. Late mediæval. Red paint. Chunār sandstone. Found in relic-chamber of stūpa No. 45 to north-east of Main Shrine.

B (*c*) 56.—Figure (ht. 11″; width 11″) of Gautama Buddha preaching his first sermon. Head lost. Rest much defaced. Late mediaeval. Chunār sandstone. Excavated in 1906-07 in area to west of Main Shrine.

---

[1] *A. S. R.*, 1904-05 p. 93, No. 79.
[2] *Ibid.*, p. 94, No. 93.

B (*c*) 57.—Lower half (ht. 9″; width 1′) of figure of Gautama Buddha seated cross-legged preaching the first sermon. Portions of standing figures to right and left: probably Maitrēya and Avalōkitēśvara. On base, wheel and pair of deer with five friars (*pañcha-bhadravargīya*) to proper right, and two men and two women with presents on other side. Late mediaeval. Chunār sandstone. Found in 1906-07 in *stūpa* No. 40 to north-east of Main Shrine.[1]

B (*c*) 58.—Statuette (ht. 1′ 1½″; width 1′ 1½″) of Gautama Buddha in same posture as B (c) 57. Head and hands missing. On base, usual relief with wheel and deer and five disciples. Late mediæval. Traces of red paint. Chunār stone. Excavated in 1904-05 south-east of Aśōka Column.[2]

B (*c*) 59.—Figure (ht. 1′ ½″; width 9″) in alto-relievo, of Gautama Buddha seated on cushion preaching first sermon. Head and sides of back-slab broken off. On base, relief as in B (*c*) 58. On account of style the image may be assigned to about the 7th century A.D.

Chunār sandstone. The image is one of the thirteen Sārnāth sculptures which were presented by Principal, Queen's College, to Lucknow Provincial Museum in 1903 and have now been transferred to Sārnāth Museum at Dr. Vogel's instance.[3]

B (*c*) 60.—Figure (ht. 11″; width 6¾″) of Gautama Buddha seated delivering his first sermon. Broken across waist. Sides of back-slab broken off. Hair arranged in schematic curls. On base, usual relief. Early mediaeval. Chunār stone. Upper part found in 1906-07 in area east of Main Shrine; lower portion in 1907-08 in area north of it.

*B (*c*) 61.—Figure (ht. 10½″; width 6¾″) of Gautama Buddha seated on coventional double lotus preaching his first sermon. The circular line around the neck is obviously meant to indicate the edge of the upper robe (*saṅghāṭī*). On base, wheel in elevation between pair of deer. Along border, Buddhist creed in Sanskrit in characters of 9th century A.D.

Vestiges of red paint. Chunār stone. Unearthed in 1904-05, south-west of Main Shrine.[4]

*B (*c*) 62.—Figure (ht. 11″; width 7½″) of Gautama Buddha in same attitude as B (*c*) 61; execution even rougher. Broken across waist. Sides of back-slab damaged. Behind the back of Buddha, pattern consisting of throne, its horizontal bar supported on rampant leogryphs. On back, Sanskrit version of Buddhist creed in six lines. The

---

[1] *A. S. R.*, 1906-07, p. 81, Pl. XXIII, 5 and p. 91, No. 12.

[2] *Ibid.*, 1904-05, p. 93, No. 76.

[3] Dr. Vogel has identified this image with Kittoe, *Drawings*, Vol. I, Pl. 4, No. 95, (not 59). *Vide* A. S. R. 1903-04, p. 225 and figure 4. The head is shown detached in Kittoe's drawing. It must be in the Lucknow Museum.

[4] *A. S. R.*, 1904-05, p. 93, No. 72.

characters belong to the 10th century A.D. Chunār sandstone. Discovered in 1904-05 south of Jagat Singh Stūpa.[1]

B (*c*) 63.—Figure (ht. 9″; width 8½″) in alto-relievo, of Gautama Buddha seated cross-legged on full-blown lotus delivering his first sermon. Head and upper part of back-slab missing. To right and left, traces of figures on lotuses. Base effaced but kneeling worshipper traceable at proper left end. Chunār sandstone. Early mediaeval. Unearthed in 1904-05.[2]

B (*c*) 64.—Figure (ht. 10¼″ including tenon at base; width 8½″) of Gautama Buddha preaching. Head and hands broken off. Traces of wheel and deer on base. Too much chipped to allow of dating. Chunār sandstone. Excavated in 1904-05.

B (*c*) 65.—Figure (ht. 10½″; width 8″) of Gautama Buddha in same posture as B (*c*) 64. Head and part of circular halo missing. Behind back, pattern of throne with crocodile heads on its ends. On base, besides wheel and deer, two mendicants and two worshippers. Late mediaeval. Chunār sandstone. Found in 1904-05 north-west of Main Shrine.[3]

B (*c*) 66.—Upper half (ht. 7½″; width 8″) of similar figure. Circular halo with beads and scallops. Drapery marked by undulating lines. In background, pattern of throne with its ends supported on leogryphs. Traces of red colour. Late mediaeval. Excavated in 1904-05.[4]

B (*c*) 67.—Upper half (ht. 9″; width 10½″) of image of Gautama Buddha, without head, in same posture. Traces of red paint. Late mediaeval. Chunār sandstone. Unearthed in 1904-05 north-west of Main Shrine.[5]

B (*c*) 68.—Fragment (ht. 8½″; width 9¼″) with upper half of similar image. Much effaced. Chunār sandstone. Unearthed in 1907-08 north of Main Shrine, 1′ below surface.

B (*c*) 69.—Figure (ht. 9½″; width 6″) of Gautama Buddha preaching his first sermon. Head broken off. Style exceedingly rough. Much defaced. *Cir.* 1000 A. D. Excavated in 1904-05.[6]

B (*c*) 70.—Figure (ht. 1′ ¼″; width 8¾″) of Gautama Buddha in same posture. Chipped and otherwise damaged. Chunār sandstone. Discovered in 1906-07 in area to west of Main Shrine.

B (*c*) 71.—Figure (ht. 7½″; width 6″) of Gautama Buddha seated cross-legged preaching the first sermon. Horse-shoe-shaped halo with

---

[1] *A. S. R.*, 1904-05, p. 98, No. 288 which only answers for the upper portion.
[2] *Ibid.* p. 93, No. 86.
[3] *Ibid.*, p. 92, No. 44.
[4] *Ibid.*, p. 93, No. 82.
[5] *Ibid.*, p. 94, No. 103.
[6] *Ibid.*, p. 92, No. 35.

beaded border. On either side is a rose. Behind back, pillow and throne pattern. On base, wheel and deer and only four mendicants. Late mediaeval. Excavated in 1907-08 in trench crossing south boundary wall of monastery I, 3′ below surface.[1]

B (*c*) 72.—Figure (ht. 7″; width 5½″) similar to B (*c*) 71. Much defaced. Head lost. Traces of leogryphs on sides. Wheel between pair of deer and a mendicant and a worshipper. *Circa*. 8th or 9th century A.D. Chunār stone. Excavated in 1907-08 in area to north-west of Main Shrine.

B (*c*) 73.—Figure (ht. 10¾″; width 6½″) of Gautama Buddha in same posture as B (*c*) 72. Too much chipped to allow of dating. Chunār sandstone. Unearthed in 1904-05 south-west of Main Shrine.

B (*c*) 74.—Image (ht. 8″; width 7″) of Gautama Buddha in same posture. Head lost. Parts of figures on sides. Base effaced. Chunār stone. Unearthed in 1904-05 west of Main Shrine.[2]

B (*c*) 75.—Figure (ht. 8¼″; width 5¼″) of Gautama Buddha seated delivering his first sermon. Defaced. Unearthed in 1904-05 south-west of Main Shrine.[3]

B (*c*) 76.—Figure (ht. 6¾″; width 4¾″) similar to B (*c*) 75 and same material. Excavated in 1906-07 west of Jagat Singh Stūpa.

B (*c*) 77.—Headless figure (ht. 7½″; width 5″) of Gautama Buddha seated on inverted lotus in the same attitude. Excavated in 1907-08 in area north of Main Shrine, 5½′ below surface.

B (*c*) 78.—Figure (ht. 6″; width 5¼″) of same type as B (*c*) 77. Badly chipped. Head lost. Excavated in 1904-05 between Main Shrine and Jagat Singh Stūpa.

B (*c*) 79.—Fragment (ht. 5¼″; width 5″) similar to B (*c*) 78. Chunār sandstone. Discovered in 1907-08 to north of Main Shrine, 4′ below surface.[4]

B (*c*) 80.—Trunk and arms (ht. 3″; width 4½″) of Gautama Buddha preaching his first sermon. Hands injured. Chunār stone. Unearthed in 1907-08 among *stūpas* to west of passage north of Main Shrine, 4′ below surface.

B (*c*) 81.—Fragment (ht. 4½″; width 3½″) of lower half of figure of Gautama Buddha seated cross-legged preaching his first sermon. On base, two friars, other monks and wheel and deer missing. Chunār sandstone. Exact find-spot cannot be determined.

B (*c*) 82.—Fragment (ht. 4″; width 3½″) similar to B (*c*) 81. On base, only one deer. Excavated in 1907-08 in débris above Gupta monastery IV, 1½′ below surface.

---

1. *A. S. R.*, 1907-08, p. 71, No. β-39.
2. *Ibid.*, 1904-05, p. 94, No. 102.
3. *Ibid.*, 1904-05, p. 93, No. 73.
4. *Ibid.*, 1907-08, p. 68, No. γ 22.

B (*c*) 83.—Trunk (ht. 5½″; width 4″) of image of Gautama Buddha which to judge from traces of fingers on the chest was seated in the attitude of preaching. Back split off. Chunār sandstone. Unearthed in 1906-07 in area to east of Main Shrine.

B (*c*) 84.—Miniature figure (ht. 3½″; width 2″) of Gautama Buddha seated preaching the first sermon. Much defaced. On base, roughly sketched wheel between pair of deer. Latest epoch. Excavated in 1904-05 between Jagat Singh Stūpa and Main Shrine.

B (*c*) 85.—Lower half (ht. 3″; width 4½″) of figure of Gautama Buddha on double lotus which must have been in the same posture as B (*c*) 84. Chunār stone. Excavated in 1904-05 between Jagat Singh Stūpa and Main Shrine.

B (*c*) 86.—Fragment (ht. 2½″; width 4¼″) similar to B (*c*) 85. Presumably unearthed in 1904-05.

B (*c*) 87.—Figure (ht. 10″; width 8″) of Gautama Buddha seated cross-legged on throne supported on very roughly sketched lions. Between the latter, wheel and pair of deer. Head of Buddha missing. The workmanship is of the crudest type conceivable. Excavated in 1904-05 south of Main Shrine.[1]

B (*c*) 88.—Image (ht. 11¼″; width 7¾″) of Gautama Buddha seated cross-legged preaching the first sermon. On front of base, rudely sketched wheel and pair of deer. The Buddha wears three-peaked coronet (*makuṭa*) and ear-rings, which is uncanonical. This image as well as B (*c*) 87 is a typical example of the extreme deterioration to which Sārnāth sculpture had been reduced in 10th or 11th century A.D. Chunār sandstone. Unearthed in 1904-05.[2]

B (*c*) 89.—Trunk and head (ht. 10″; width 6″) possibly of Gautama Buddha preaching the first sermon. High headdress. *Cir.* 11th century A.D. Trunk unearthed in 1906-07 and head in 1907-08 on approach to Main Shrine from east 6′ below surface.

B (*c*) 90.—Figure (ht. 7½″; width 6½″) of Buddha seated preaching the first sermon. Head missing. Found lying outside the Śvētāmbara Jaina temple near Sārnāth Railway Station.

B (*c*) 91.—Figure (ht. 7″; width 6¼″) of Gautama Buddha seated in meditation (*dhyānamudrā*). Much defaced. Unearthed in 1907-08 in area to north of Main Shrine 5′ below surface.[3]

B (*c*) 92.—Fragment (ht. 5½″; width 5″) with figure of Buddha or Jaina Tīrthaṅkara seated cross-legged on lotus in the attitude of contemplation (*dhyānamudrā*). Head wanting. 10th or 11th century A.D. Discovered in 1907-08 in 2nd outer court of monastery I, 6′ below surface of mound.

---

[1] *A. S. R.*, 1904-05, p. 97, No. 242.
[2] *Ibid.*, p. 93, No. 83.
[3] *Ibid.*, 1907-08, p. 71, No. β-33.

B (*c*) 93.—Upper part (ht. 6″; width 6½″) of relief showing Gautama Buddha's enlightenment (*bōdhi*). Portion of circular halo with a demon on either side, and above it, foliage of *pīpal* tree. *Cir.* 7th century. Chunār sandstone. Excavated in 1907-08.

B (*c*) 94.—Fragment (ht. 9″; width 9″) with portion of crossed legs of Buddha. Reddish sandstone. Unearthed in 1907-08 in 2nd court on east of monastery I, 1½′ below surface of mound.

B (*c*) 95.—Fragment (ht. 9¾″; width 10½″) showing the left leg of an image of Buddha which was seated cross-legged on conventional double lotus. *Cir.* 8th or 9th century A.D. The style shows Magadha influence. Greenish stone perhaps from Chunār. Excavated in 1904-05 south-east of Main Shrine.

B (*c*) 96.—Fragment (ht. 8½″; width 10″) with crossed legs of figure of Buddha. Much defaced. Chunār stone. Excavated in 1907-08 in area to north of Dhamēkh Stūpa.

B (*c*) 98[1].—Upper half (ht. 6½″; width 4½″) of figure of Buddha. Face defaced and arms wanting. Chunār sandstone. Excavated in 1904-05.

B (*c*) 99.—Portion of crossed legs (ht. 2″; width 5″) presumably of Buddha. Chunār sandstone. Find-spot not known.

B (*c*) 100.—Fragment (ht. 2¼″; width 5½″) similar to B (*c*) 99. Excavated in 1906-07 in area to east of Main Shrine.

B (*c*) 101.—Fragment (ht. 3″; width 5½″) similar to B (*c*) 99. Chunār sandstone. Unearthed in 1906-07 in area to east of Main Shrine.

B (*c*) 102.—Fragment (ht. 2½″; width 5½″) showing the crossed legs of a miniature Buddha image. Traces of red colour. Chunār sandstone. Find-spot not known.

B (*c*) 103.—Fragment (ht. 3″; width 4½″) from the crossed legs of a Buddha image. Chunār sandstone. Red paint. Unearthed in 1906-07 between *stūpas* 16 and 17 to north-west of Main Shrine, 3′ below surface.

B (*c*) 104.—Piece (ht. 2″; width 3½″) split from well-draped and crossed left leg of Buddha figure. Chunār stone. Excavated in 1907-08 in second court east of monastery I, 9′ below surface of mound.

B (*c*) 105.—Fragment (ht. 3″; width 7½″) showing chest and part of right arm of a small figure of Buddha and a remnant of a circular halo with beaded margin. Chunār sandstone. Unearthed in 1907-08 on eastern approach of Main Shrine, 6′ below surface.

*B (c) 106.—Lower part (ht. 1′ 4½″; width 1′ 6½″) of image of Buddha consisting of his crossed legs on double lotus which is placed on a throne

---

[1] The fragment which was numbered as B (*c*) 97, is found on closer examination to be a part of stele No. C (*a*) 9.

supported by a couchant lion at each end. On upper rim of throne, Buddhist creed in characters of about 10th century A.D.

The material is blue stone. It is evident from the style that the image was carved in Magadha. Find-spot not known.

B (c) 107.—Trunk with upper arms (ht. 7"; width 8") of Buddha which on account of vestiges of fingers on chest must have been in the attitude of preaching. Chunār sandstone. Excavated in 1904-05.

B (c) 108.—Image in alto-relievo (ht. up to top of back-slab 3′ 2½" with tenon; width 1′) of Buddha standing in the attitude of imparting protection (*abhayamudrā*). Head wanting and left forearm detached but re-fixed. The Buddha is, as usual, clad in a lower garment (*antaravāsaka*) and an upper robe (*saṅghāṭī*) which fits close to his person. Folds beneath left arm well indicated. To judge from style, late Gupta.

Chunār sandstone. Traces of red paint. Unearthed in 1904-05 north-west of Jagat Singh Stūpa.[1]

B (c) 109.—Image (ht. 2′ 9"; width 2′), in high relief, of Buddha in the attitude of granting security (*abhayamudrā*). Head lost. Rest dressed in usual fashion. Right hand raised against shoulder and marked with lotus in relief; left grasps hem of robe at level of thigh. Red colour. Left hip protrudes outwards. On account of style, I ascribe the image to about the 8th century A.D.

Chunār sandstone. Excavated in 1904-05 north-west of Jagat Singh Stūpa.[2]

B (c) 110.—Image (ht. 2′ 2"; width 1′ 4"), in alto-relievo, of Buddha standing in the posture of granting protection (*abhayamudrā*). The upper part of back-slab which has no margin decoration and right hand and feet of Buddha are broken off. To his right, standing figure of Maitrēya with oval halo behind head, fly-whisk in right hand and rosary in left. To left, Avalōkitēśvara with similar halo, but lotus with stalk in left hand. The hair of the two Bōdhisattvas is arranged in plaits, that of Buddha in usual short curls. The style appears to be of about the late Gupta period. Traces of red paint.

Chunār stone. Unearthed in 1904-05 north of Jagat Singh Stūpa.[3]

B (c) 111.—Torso (ht. 1′ 6"; width 1′), in high relief, of Buddha standing in the attitude of granting security. Head and feet lost. The dress consists of usual garments. The margin decoration of back-slab consists of beads and reels and curves which must have been developed from the scallops of the Gupta period. Defaced in part.

Chunār stone. Excavated in 1906-07 in area to north-west of Main Shrine, 5′ below surface.

---

1 *A. S. R.*, 1904-05, p. 94, No. 117.
2 *Ibid.*, No. 60.
3 *Ibid.*, 1904-05, p. 94, No. 94.

B (*c*) 112.—Image (ht. 1′ 9½″; width 10½″) in high relief, of Buddha standing in the attitude of protection (*abhayamudrā*). Hands in the usual position. Face damaged and rest badly defaced.

Chunār sandstone. Excavated in 1906-07 in a *stūpa* to north-west of Main Shrine, 2½′ below surface.

B (*c*) 113.—Image (ht. 1′ 7½″ with tenon; width 6¾″), in alto-relievo, of Buddha standing in same posture as B (*c*) 112. Hands damaged. Back-slab adorned along margin with bead and reel and roughly drawn scallops. Near left foot, kneeling female figure. Late Gupta. Chunār sandstone. Find-spot not known.

B (*c*) 114.—Image of Buddha (ht. 1′ 10″; width 9″) in attitude of protection (*abhayamudrā*) without feet. Hands damaged. The face had split off and has been re-fixed. The back-slab is oval at top and adorned along the border with lines of beads and scallops.

Chunār sandstone. Excavated in 1904-05 south of Aśōka Column.[1]

B (*c*) 115.—Image (ht. 1′ 3″; width 6½″) similar to B (*c*) 114. Traces of red paint. Upper part of back-slab broken. Chunār sandstone. Unearthed in 1904-05 west of Jagat Singh Stūpa[2].

B (*c*) 116.—Image in high relief (ht. 1′ 2″; width 7½″) of Buddha in the attitude of imparting security. The feet of the image and top of back-slab missing. Right hand injured. Hair in conventional curls, protuberance of skull (*ushṇīsha*) low and pointed. Girdle (*kāya-bandhana*) visible through upper robe. Margin decoration as in B (*c*) 115. Mediaeval.

Chunār sandstone. Excavated in the same year as B (*c*) 115 north of Main Shrine.[3]

B (*c*) 117.—Torso (ht. 1′ 4″; width 8″), in two pieces, of standing Buddha which to judge from the position of the left arm must have been in the attitude of protection (*abhayamudrā*). Head, right arm and legs below knees missing. Right shoulder bare. Chunār sandstone. Excavated in 1906-07 west of *stūpa* No. 20 to west of Main Shrine, 4′ below surface.

B (*c*) 118.—Torso (ht. 11½″; width 7″) of Buddha in the attitude of granting security. Head, feet, and hands missing. Early mediaeval.

Reddish Chunār sandstone. Excavated in 1907-08 in area north of Main Shrine, 4½′ below surface.[4]

B (*c*) 119.—Fragment (ht. 10¼″; width 8″) of Buddha image which must have been standing in the same posture as B(*c*) 118. Upper part of body above loins, right arms, and feet missing. Chunār sandstone.

---

[1] *A. S. R.* 1904-05, p. 93, No. 68.
[2] *Ibid.*, p. 94, No. 98.
[3] *Ibid.*, p. 93, No. 84.
[4] *Ibid.*, 1907-08, p. 68, *f. n.* 3.

Unearthed in 1906-07 in first court on east of mediaeval monastery I, 4′ 4″ below surface.

B (*c*) 120.—Torso (ht. 10″; width 9½″) of standing Buddha in reassuring attitude (*abhayamudrā*). Head, hands and legs broken off. The upper robe (*saṅghāṭī*) leaves right shoulder bare. Lower garment bound to loins by girdle (*kāyabandhana*). Chunār sandstone. Weather-stained. Excavated in 1906-07 in area to east of Main Shrine.

B (*c*) 121.—Torso (ht. 8½″; width 7″) of standing Buddha in reassuring posture (*abhayamudrā*). Much defaced. Head and legs below knees wanting. Chunār stone. Unearthed in the same year and same area as B(*c*) 120.

B (*c*) 122.—Torso (ht. 1′; width 9″) similar to B (*c*) 121 but totally effaced. Chunār stone. Excavated in trench crossing the south boundary wall of monastery I to north of Main Shrine, 1′ below surface.[1]

B (*c*) 123.—Figure (ht. 8½″; width 8″) of Buddha standing in reassuring attitude (*abhayamudrā*). Head and right hand missing. Upper robe (*saṅghāṭī*) covers both shoulders. Sides of back-slab broken. To left of Buddha standing Bōdhisattva, fly-whisk in right hand, left hand on hip. Feet of another Bōdhisattva attendant to right of Buddha. Perhaps Avalōkitēśvara and Maitrēya.

To judge from style, early mediaeval. Chunār sandstone. Traces of red paint. Unearthed in relic-chamber of *stūpa* No. 45 to south of first court east of mediaeval monastery I.

B (*c*) 124.—Fragment (ht. 8″; width 7″) of image of Buddha which must have been standing in reassuring attitude (*abhayamudrā*). Upper part above loins and feet missing. To right, portion of standing attendant, fly-whisk in right hand, perhaps Maitrēya.

Chunār sandstone. Early mediaeval. Excavated in 1907-08 on approach to Main Shrine from east, 7′ 8″ below surface.

B (*c*) 125.—Figure (ht. 10″ with tenon; width 4″) of Buddha standing in reassuring attitude (*abhayamudrā*). Head and hands lost. Chest cut off. Chunār stone. Excavated in 1906-07 in area west of Main Shrine.

B (*c*) 126.—Torso (ht. 8″; width 5″) of Buddha standing in reassuring attitude (*abhayamudrā*). Head, hands and legs below knees wanting. Upper robe covers both shoulders. Late Gupta, or perhaps earlier. Chunār sandstone. Excavated in 1904-05 between Jagat Singh Stūpa and Main Shrine.[2]

B (*c*) 127.—Figure (ht. 7½″; width 4½″) of Buddha standing in reassuring attitude (*abhayamudrā*). Feet missing. Face split away.

---

[1] *A. S. R.* 1907-08, p. 72, No. β-31.
[2] *Ibid.* 1904-05, p. 90, No. 310.

Dress of usual fashion, and workmanship rough. *Cir.* 900 A.D. Chunār sandstone. Excavated in 1904-05 north of Jagat Singh Stūpa.[1]

B (*c*) 128.—Torso (ht. 7¼"; width 3½") of Buddha in the same attitude. Head, hands and feet wanting. Late Gupta. Chunār sandstone. Excavated in 1904-05 in the same area.[2]

B (*c*) 129.—Torso (ht. 1' 3"; width 1' ½") of Buddha in gift-bestowing attitude (*varadamudrā*). Head, left hand and legs below knees missing. The upper robe after the usual style covers both shoulders. The decoration on the back-slab consists of a line of beads and another of scallops outside it. Chunār stone. Excavated in 1904-05 north of Jagat Singh Stūpa.[3]

B (*c*) 130.—Image (ht. 1' 9¼"; width 1' 1½") of Buddha in the same position. Face split away. Hands and feet missing. Weather-stained. Chunār stone.

B (*c*) 131.—Image (ht. 1' 7"; width 6"), in alto-relievo, of Buddha standing in the gift-bestowing attitude, in excellent preservation. Right hand stretched out with the palm facing to the front. The left hand lifts hem of robe to the level of shoulder. Base of image somewhat defaced. On it, near right foot of Buddha, defaced kneeling figure presumably the donor of the image. Back-slab plain and round at top. Traces of red colour. Late Gupta. Chunār sandstone. Unearthed in 1904-05 north-west of Main Shrine.[4]

B (*c*) 132.—Image (ht. 1' 1½"; width 9") of Buddha in the same posture as B (*c*) 131. Right hand, feet and upper part of back-slab broken off and left thigh damaged. Back-slab decorated along border with bead and reel and roughly incised curves. Style decidedly later than Gupta period. Excavated in 1906-07 in area to west of Main Shrine.

B (*c*) 133.—Fragment (ht. 11½"; width 9½") of image of Buddha standing in gift-bestowing attitude (*varadamudrā*). Lower part below waist and right forearm missing. The modelling of the face shows a definite inferiority to Gupta work. Red colour. Back-slab plain. Chunār sandstone. Excavated in area to north-west of Main Shrine, 5' below surface.[5]

B (*c*) 134.—Fragment (ht. 1' 3"; width 9") similar to B (*c*) 133, but only feet missing. Small piece from top of back-slab also wanting. Chunār sandstone. Unearthed in 1904-05 east of Main Shrine.[6]

---

1 *A. S. R.*, 1904-05, p. 98, No. 292.
2 *Ibid.*, p. 98, No. 296.
3 *Ibid.*, p. 94, No. 116.
4 *Ibid.*, 1904-05, p. 94, No. 97.
5 *Ibid.*, 1907-08, p. 72, No. γ 34.
6 *Ibid.*, 1904-05, p. 94, No. 112.

B (*c*) 135.—Figure of Buddha (ht. 1′ 3½″; width 8″) standing inclined to left in gift-bestowing posture against rectangular back-slab. Treatment of hair and dress as in Gupta images, but workmanship distinctly inferior. Perhaps 8th or 9th century A.D.

Excavated in 1907-08 on site of Gupta monastery II, 2′ below surface.

B (*c*) 136.—Image (ht. 1′ 10″; width 9″) of Buddha standing; badly defaced. What remains of arms is, however, enough to show that it was in gift-bestowing (*varada*) attitude. There is no means of ascertaining the date. Probably preserved formerly in the Queen's College.

B (*c*) 137.—Legs (ht. 1′ 2″; width 1′) of standing Buddha image. Folds of upper robe (*saṅghāṭī*) along left leg. Toes worn away. Early mediaeval. Chunār sandstone. Excavated in 1904-05 south-east of Main Shrine.[1]

B (*c*) 138.—Image (ht. 1′ 5″; width 8½″), in high relief, of Buddha standing in gift-bestowing posture (*varadamudrā*). Broken into three pieces across the neck and the waist. The right hand which was held out at the level of the right thigh is broken off. Pieces also wanting in back-slab at level of shoulders. Devotees on either side of feet. The style appears to be of the early mediaeval period.

Back of the stone grooved after the fashion of a grindstone. All three pieces discovered in 1904-05, middle piece to north-east of Jagat Singh Stūpa.[2] Find-spot of other pieces not known.

B (*c*) 139.—Torso (ht. 1′ ½″; width across shoulders 8½″) of Buddha. Head, right forearm and legs below knees missing. Left hand, which is somewhat defaced, raises hem of robe to the level of the shoulders. This position of the left hand is invariably associated with the gift-bestowing attitude in Sārnāth sculptures. Chunār sandstone. Excavated in 1907-08 in area north of Main Shrine, 3′ below surface.

B (*c*) 140.—Torso (ht. 1′ 2″; width 7″) of Buddha standing in gift-bestowing posture (*varadamudrā*). Head, hands and feet lost. Legs and sides weathered. Girdle indicated. Excavated in 1904-05.[3]

B (*c*) 141.—Figure (ht. 1′ ¾″; width 5½″) of Buddha standing in gift-bestowing attitude (*varadamudrā*). Much defaced. Traces of kneeling figure below right hand. Unearthed in 1906-07 west of Jagat Singh Stūpa.[4]

B (*c*) 142.—Figure (ht. 11½″; width 6″) similar to B (*c*) 141. The right hip juts out. Hands and feet worn away. Traces of worshipper beneath right hand. Red paint. Margin of back-slab

---

[1] *A. S. R.*, 1904-05, No. 92.
[2] *Ibid.*, p. 93, No. 89.
[3] *Ibid.*, No. 64.
[4] *Ibid.*, 1906-07, p. 91, No. 24.

ornamented with bead and reel and curves, a remnant of the Gupta scallops. Early mediaeval. Chunār sandstone. Excavated in 1907-08 in area north of Main Shrine, 2′ below surface.[1]

B(c) 143.—Torso (ht. 10½″ ; width 5½″) of same type as B (*c*) 142. Too much defaced to allow of dating. Chunār stone. Unearthed in 1904-05[2].

B (*c*) 144.—Image (ht. 1′ 2″ ; width 6″) of Buddha with hands and feet broken off. Legs damaged. Head detached, but re-fixed with copper rod. Hair arranged in schematic curls. To judge from style, early mediaeval. Excavated in 1904-05 north of stūpa No. 5 near north-west corner of Main Shrine.[3]

B (*c*) 145.—Torso (ht. 1′ ; width 8½″) of Buddha standing. Head, both arms and feet wanting. The left hand evidently held the robe at the level of the left shoulder; the attitude was therefore that of bestowing a gift. No girdle. Traces of red colour. Border decoration of back-slab consists of bead and reel combined with scallops. Chunār sandstone. Unearthed in one of the recent excavations.

B (*c*) 146.—Lower portion (ht. 10¼″ ; width 9¾″) of an image of Buddha which from the disposition of the dress seems to have been in the gift-bestowing attitude (*varadamudrā*). Back-slab has bead and reel combined with curves. Chunār sandstone. Excavated in 1906-07 in the courtyard of mediaeval monastery I, 2′ 10″ below surface.

B (*c*) 147.—Three pieces making up the larger portion (ht. 11½″ ; width 8″) of an image of Buddha standing in the gift-bestowing posture. Legs below thighs wanting. Hands lost.

Chunār sandstone. Unearthed in 1904-05.

B (*c*) 148.—Fragment (ht. 9¾″ ; width 6″) with figure of Buddha in gift-bestowing attitude (*varadamudrā*). Right hand and feet missing. Left hand raises hem of robe to level of shoulder. Hair arranged in formal curls. Excavated in 1906-07 in mediaeval monastery I.[4]

B (*c*) 149.—Torso (ht. 8″ ; width 5½″) of Buddha standing. Head, arms and feet wanting. Chunār sandstone. Excavated in 1904-05.

B (*c*) 150.—Torso (ht. 7¾″ ; width 3½″) of Buddha standing. Head, right arm and feet missing. Left hand holds hem of robe at level of shoulder. The right hand must have been laid in the gift-bestowing attitude. Right hip protrudes a good deal. Right shoulder bare. Chunār sandstone. Unearthed in 1906-07 in area east of Main Shrine.

---

[1] *A. S. R.*, 1907-08, p. 71. β-16.

[2] *Ibid.*, 1904-05, p. 92, No. 47.

[3] *Ibid.*, p. 93, No. 81.

[4] *Ibid.*, 1906-07, p. 91, No. 23.

B (*c*) 151.—Torso (ht. 7½″; width 3½″) of same type as B(*c*) 150. Head, left hand and feet wanting. Chunār sandstone. Discovered in 1904-05 north of Jagat Singh Stūpa.[1]

B (*c*) 152.—Middle portion (ht. 8″; width 6″) of Buddha image in gift-bestowing attitude. Upper portion above waist, right arm, and legs below knees broken off. Chunār stone. Unearthed in 1907-08 between Dhamēkh Stūpa and 2nd gate of mediaeval monastery I.

B (*c*) 153.—Fragment (ht. 7¼″; width 11″) of standing image of Buddha in gift-bestowing attitude (*varadamudrā*). Head, legs, right forearm and left hand broken off. Chest defaced. Chunār sandstone. Found in 1906-07 or 1907-08.

B (*c*) 154.—Image (ht. 1′ 1½″; width 8½″) of Buddha in gift-bestowing attitude. Feet and hand missing. Much defaced. Hair arranged in curls. Chunār sandstone. Traces of red paint. Excavated in 1906-07 in area east of Main Shrine.

B (*c*) 155.—Figure (ht. 6½″; width 4½″) of Buddha standing in gift-bestowing attitude. Badly defaced. Discovered in 1906-07 north of structure No. 22 in area west of Main Shrine, 5′ below surface.

B (*c*) 156.—Bust (ht. 10″; width 6½″) of Buddha image. Both arms and lower part missing. Right shoulder bare. Elongated ear-lobes, and hair in short curls of usual form. Traces of halo behind shoulders. Late mediaeval. Chunār sandstone of reddish tint. Excavated in 1904-05.[2]

B (*c*) 157.—Base with lower part of legs (ht. 9″ with tenon; width 8″) of standing Buddha image. Chunār sandstone. Exact find-spot not known, but discovered in one of the recent diggings.

B (*c*) 158.—Fragment (ht. 8″ without tenon; width 7½″) similar to B (*c*) 157. Excavated in 1904-05.[3]

B (*c*) 159.—Base with feet and lower portion of legs (ht. 11½″; width 10″) of standing Buddha. Edges of lower garment (*antaravāsaka*) and upper robe (*saṅghāṭī*) above ankles. Traces of red colour. Chunār sandstone. Found in one of the recent excavations.

B (*c*) 160.—Bust (ht. 6″; width 5″) of figure of Buddha without head and forearms. Part of circular halo. Excavated in 1904-05.[4]

B (*c*) 161.—Waist and thighs (ht. 5″; width 5½″) of standing Buddha. Girdle indicated by plain band. Chunār sandstone. Unearthed in 1906-07 in area west of Main Shrine.

B (*c*) 162.—Fragment (ht. 2¾″; width 4¾″) from chest of Buddha figure. Defaced. Chunār sandstone. Excavated in 1907-08 in area around Jagat Singh Stūpa.

---

[1] *A. S. R.*, 1904-05, p. 98, No. 297.
[2] *Ibid.*, p. 97, No. 200.
[3] *Ibid.*, p. 93, No. 53.
[4] *Ibid.*, p. 96, No. 172.

B (*c*) 163.—Legs (ht. 6¼″; width 4″) of standing Buddha. Excavated in 1906-07 or 1907-08.

B (*c*) 164.—Chest and shoulders (ht. 4½″; width 7¾″) of Buddha image. Traces of red paint. Both shoulders covered. Chunār sandstone. Excavated in 1907-08 in area north of Main Shrine, 4′ below surface.[1]

B (*c*) 165.—Fragment (ht. 4½″; width 6″) similar to B (*c*) 164. Badly defaced. Chunār sandstone. Excavated in the same year and same area, 5′ below surface.

B (*c*) 166.—Fragment (ht. 5″; width 4¼″) representing the thighs of a standing Buddha. Chunār sandstone. Excavated in 1907-08 in area north of Main Shrine, 7′ below surface.

B (*c*) 167.—Bust (ht. 9½″; width 6¾″) with head and arms of Buddha. Back split away. Chunār sandstone. Discovered in 1906-07 in area east of Main Shrine.

B (*c*) 168.—Middle portion (ht. 10¼″; width 6″) of standing Buddha image. Back split away. Chunār sandstone. Excavated in 1906-07 to south of Gupta monastery III, 3′ below surface.

B (*c*) 169.—Fragment (ht. 4¾″; width 4¾″) similar to B (*c*) 174. Chunār sandstone. Discovered in 1907-08 in 2nd gateway of mediaeval monastery I.

B (*c*) 170.—Torso (ht. 1′ 1″; width 4″) of Buddha standing. Head badly defaced. Chunār sandstone. Excavated in 1907-08 near 2nd gateway of mediæval monastery I.

B (*c*) 171.—Base with legs (ht. 1′; width 9½″) of Buddha image standing on inverted lotus. Chunār sandstone. Excavated in 1906-07 in relic-chamber of *stūpa* 45 to south of first court on east of mediaeval monastery I.

B (*c*) 172.—Base with feet (ht. 10½″; width 10½″) presumably of Buddha standing on a lotus flower. Traces of red paint. Find-spot not known.

B (*c*) 173.—Right hand (ht. 4¾″; width 4″) which belonged to an image of Buddha in the attitude of granting security (*abhayamudrā*). That the hand is of a Buddha image is evidenced by the web which connects all the fingers. Chunār sandstone. Excavated in 1906-07 to south of Gupta monastery II, 11′ below surface.

B (*c*) 174.—Fragment of right hand (ht. 4½″; width 4″) which belonged to the same type of images as B (*c*) 179. The joints of the fingers are abnormally broad. Chunār sandstone. Excavated in 1904-05 in area around Jagat Singh Stūpa and Main Shrine.

B (*c*) 175.—Left hand and forearm (length 4″; width 1½″) of standing image of Buddha in reassuring attitude (*abhayamudrā*).

---

[1] *A. S. R.*, 1907-08, p. 68, *f. n.* 3.

The hand holds the hem of the upper robe (*saṅghāṭī*). Chunār sandstone. Unearthed in 1906-07 in area west of Main Shrine.

B (*c*) 176.—Fragment (ht. 8″; width 6″) bearing a figure of a celestial (*dēva*) in a cloud carrying a garland; broken from proper left upper corner of a Buddha or Bōdhisattva image. Left leg bent upwards, right in front to indicate flight.

Chunār sandstone. Discovered in 1904-05 in area around Jagat Singh Stūpa and Main Shrine.

B (*c*) 177.—Fragment (ht. 8″; width 4½″) with a figure of Maitrēya standing, with a fly-whisk in right hand and an ointment vessel, his characteristic attribute in the other hand.[1] He wears a head-dress characterized by large loops and evidently developed from that of the Bōdhisattva Avalōkitēśvara (B(d) 2). Behind his head, part of plain oval halo. The lower garment resembles the *antaravāsaka* of Buddha images. The upper part of the body is bare save for a thin band thrown across the chest. This is evidently meant for the deer-skin though this fact is not marked as in B (*b*) 172. The feet are lacking and the right cheek slightly injured.

The fragment is from the right side of a Buddha image presumably standing in the attitude of protection. On grounds of style the figure may be assigned to the early mediaeval period or perhaps a little earlier. Traces of red paint. Chunār sandstone. Unearthed in 1907-08 among *stūpas* to north of Dhamēkh Stūpa.[2]

B (*c*) 178.—Fragment (ht. 6½″; width 5⅛″), from proper right side of a Buddha image, with a figure of Maitrēya analogous to B (*c*) 177. The treatment of the hair is slightly different. The Bōdhisattva holds a fly-whisk in the right hand and what must have been a vessel in the left. The dress is similar to that of B (*c*) 177. Lower part of figure defaced. Nearly coeval with B (*c*) 177.

Chunār sandstone. Discovered in 1907-08 in area to north of Main Shrine, 4′ below surface.

B (*c*) 179.—Triangular piece (ht. 10″; width 6″) from left side of Buddha image. Contains figure of Avalōkitēśvara standing on a full-blown lotus which springs from the lotus throne of Buddha himself. Face damaged. Hair combed back. Right hand held fly-whisk above head. Left holds stalk of a lotus (*padma*).

Chunār sandstone. Excavated in 1906-07 in area to east of Main Shrine.[3]

B (*c*) 180.—Figure (ht. 6½″; width 4″) of Avalōkitēśvara from proper left side of an image of Buddha. Hair tied in a broad knot on

---

[1] In B (*c*) 110 Maitrēya holds a rosary in his left hand.
[2] *A. S. R.*, 1907-08, p. 61, No. η 164.
[3] *Ibid.* 1906-07, p. 92, No. 39.

top of head. Necklace around neck. Fly-whisk in right hand and stalk of lotus (*sanāla-kamala*) in left. Upper part of body nude to waist. Lower garment is bound to loins by a girdle (*kāyabandhana*).

Chunār sandstone. Discovered to south-west of 2nd gateway of mediaeval monastery I in 1907-08.

B (*c*) 181.—Figure (ht. 8½″; width 6″) of Avalōkitēśvara from proper left side of image of Buddha. Wears conical head-dress, ear-rings and necklace of beads, sacred thread (*yajñōpavīta*), bracelets and wristlets. Mark (*śrīvatsa*) on chest. Right hand which is missing was presumably in the gift-bestowing attitude (*varada-mudrā*); left holds stalk of lotus (*kamala*), his characteristic attribute. Lower part of body below waist missing. To judge from style, late mediaeval.

Chunār sandstone. Excavated in 1904-05 north-east of Jagat Singh Stūpa.[1]

B (*c*) 182.—Figure (ht. 7″; width 5″) of a Bōdhisattva attendant lacking feet; broken from proper left side of a Buddha image. No headdress. Hair combed back and hanging on neck. Upper body from waist nude. Lower garment (*antaravāsaka*) as in Buddha images. Scarf thrown round loins and tied in a large loop on left thigh. Right hand has fly-whisk. Object in left hand defaced, perhaps rosary, in which case the figure must be one of Maitrēya. Excavated in 1904-05 north of Jagat Singh Stūpa.[2]

B (*c*) 183.—Fragment (ht. 6¼″; width 3″) with a figure of a Bōdhisattva attendant from proper right side of a Buddha image. Legs and right hand defaced. Right hand held fly-whisk over right shoulder; left holds scarf on left hip. Hair hangs back on shoulders. Chunār stone. Discovered in 1904-05 in the same area as B (*c*) 182.[3]

B (*c*) 184.—Fragment (ht. 6″; width 3″) with upper half of a Bōdhisattva attendant, presumably Maitrēya, from proper right side of a Buddha image. The figure is ornamented with circular ear-rings, a necklace and wristlets. Right hand has fly-whisk; left arm broken off. Oval halo.

Chunār sandstone. Unearthed in 1906-07 south of first court on east of mediæval monastery I, 3′ below surface.

B (*c*) 185.—Fragment (ht. 7½″; width 7″) from proper left upper corner of a Buddha image, and containing a figure of Buddha standing in the gift-bestowing attitude (*varadamudrā*). Feet missing; head damaged. Repetitions of the main image generally are depicted in corners of sculptures showing the Śrāvastī miracle and this

---

[1] *Ibid.*, 1904-05, p. 98, No. 298.
[2] *Ibid.*, p. 98, No. 290.
[3] *Ibid.*, No. 291.

fragment may have belonged to a representation of that event. Excavated in 1904-05 north of Jagat Singh Stūpa[1].

B (c) 186.—Figure (ht. 9"; width 5½") of Maitrēya from proper right side of a Buddha image. Head and feet lost. Dress as in B (c) 177. Right hand held fly-whisk over shoulder but much damaged. Left holds rosary (*akshamālā*) on left hip. Reddish sandstone. Excavated in 1907-08 in area north of Dhamēkh Stūpa.

B (c) 187.—Figure (ht. 3"; width 2") of a Bōdhisattva attendant presumably from the proper right side of a Buddha image. His head is lost. The figure is standing on a double lotus and is dressed like a prince. The right hand is in the attitude of granting protection and the left on left hip. Blue stone. Late mediaeval. Probably carved in Magadha. Excavated in 1906-07 in area east of Main Shrine.

B (c) 188.—Figure (ht. 3¾"; width 1⅛") of Buddha in gift-bestowing attitude, without face. Dressed in usual monk's dress. *Cir.* 8th or 9th century A.D. Made of blue stone of Magadha and presumably brought from there. Exact find-spot not ascertainable.

B (c) 189.—Fragment (ht. 1'; width 2' 1") with the upper portion of a halo analogous to that in B (c) 2 and B (c) 35. On the proper right of it we notice a celestial (*dēva*) in a cloud carrying a garland. The fragment belonged to a Buddha or Bōdhisattva image. *Cir.* 8th or 9th century A.D. Chunār sandstone. Unearthed in 1907-08 in the long trench east of monastery I.

B (c) 190.—Rectangular fragment (ht. 10¾"; width 1' ⅜") bearing, in relief, a circular halo ornamented with a lotus pattern and surrounded by bead and reel and a scalloped border. To the proper right of the halo is a celestial, wanting head and left arm, in cloud. Below it is Maitrēya standing with a fly-whisk in his right hand and a rosary in the left. His upper robe is marked in imitation of a deer-skin. The fragment manifestly belonged to a Buddha image of which the head and shoulders can be traced on the lower part of the halo. Chunār sandstone. Find-spot not ascertainable.

B (c) 191.—Fragment (ht. 6"; width 10½") with a remnant of a Buddha head surrounded by a halo cut in lotus pattern. Late mediaeval style. Chunār sandstone. Excavated in 1906-07 in the area to the east of the Main Shrine.

B (c) 192.—Fragment (ht. 10"; width 9½") with a part of a halo, decorated with a lotus pattern and surrounded by a line of beads. To the proper right in a cloud flying in the opposite direction is a celestial (*dēva*) carrying a garland. Above the halo are carved the leaves of a *pīpal* tree. The fragment must therefore have belonged to a re-

---

[1] *A. S. R.*, 1904-05, p. 98, No. 301.

lief representing Buddha's temptation at the moment of his enlightenment. Mediaeval style. Chunār sandstone. Excavated in 1907-08 to the east of the 2nd gateway of mediaeval monastery I.[1]

B (*c*) 193.—Fragment (ht. 7½"; width 7½") with a figure of Buddha standing in the attitude of granting protection and another seated in meditation (*dhyānamudrā*). Probably from the proper right upper corner of a Buddha image. Late mediaeval. Chunār sandstone. Discovered in 1904-05 to the south of the Main Shrine.[2]

B (*c*) 194.—Head of Buddha (ht. 7½"; width 4½"). Ear-lobes slightly injured. Protuberance of the skull (*ushṇīsha*) prominent but free from curls. Modelling of features, particularly the nose, very inartistic.

Chunār sandstone. Unearthed in 1907-08 in the area to the north of the Main Shrine, 6′ below the surface.[3]

B (*c*) 195.—Face of image (ht. 9½"; width 5¾") of Buddha in two pieces, which must have split away and been re-fixed with iron nails. One of these nails still remains between the lips. The chin and the nose are damaged. There is a circular hole in the forehead above the nose which must have contained a precious stone to represent the *ūrṇā*. The hair is arranged in usual curls, but the style is definitely late.

Chunār sandstone. Excavated in 1906-07 in the area to the east of the Main Shrine.

B (*c*) 196.—Fragment (ht. 6½"; width 5¼") of Buddha's head with the front half broken off. The hair is arranged in conventional curls but the style is late. Chunār sandstone. Unearthed in the same year and in the same area as B (*c*) 195.

B (*c*) 197.—Head (ht. 4½"; width 2½") of Buddha. Protuberance on skull prominent. Treatment of hair of usual style. Remains of three folds (*rēkhā-traya*) on the neck. Early mediaeval. Chunār sandstone. Unearthed in 1906-07 in mediaeval monastery I, 4′ below the surface.

B (*c*) 198.—Face (ht. 3½"; width 2¼") of an image of Buddha. Hair arranged in schematic curls. The lateness of its date evidenced by the unskilled rendering of the features. Chunār sandstone of reddish tint. Excavated in supposed hospital (monastery to the west of the Dhamēkh *stūpa*), 4′ 3" below the surface.

B (*c*) 199.—Fragment (length 4¼"; width 4") of the skull of a Buddha head with formal curls. Mediaeval style. Chunār sandstone. Find-spot not known.

B (*c*) 200.—Head (ht. 5"; width 4½") of Buddha. Face damaged. Folds on neck. Mediaeval style. Chunār sandstone. Discovered in 1906-07 in the area to the east of the Mian Shrine.

---

[1] *A. S. R.*, 1907-08, p. 54, No. η 74.

[2] *Ibid.*, 1904-05, p. 78, No. 309.

[3] *Ibid.*, 1907-08, p. 68, f. n. 1· β 76.

B (c) 201.—Head (ht. 4½"; width 3¼") of Buddha. The chin is broken and the protuberance on the skull (*ūshṇīsha*) is pointed. Chunār sandstone. Found in the same area and same year as B (c) 207.

B (c) 202.—Head (ht. 4"; width 3") of Buddha in same style as B (c) 201. Nose and chin damaged. Both ears missing. Chunār sandstone. Excavated in 1907-08 in the second court on the east of the mediaeval monastery I.

B (c) 203.—Head (ht. 4½"; width 3¼") of a Buddha image; nose slightly injured. The protuberance (*ushṇīsha*) is indicated right at the back of the skull. Chunār sandstone. Unearthed in 1906-07 in the area to the east of the Main Shrine.

B (c) 204.—Fragment (ht. 4½"; width 3") of a Buddha head. Appears to be mediaeval. Chunār sandstone of reddish tint. Excavated in the same year to the east of the entrance of the mediaeval monastery I, 5′ below the surface.

B (c) 205.—Fragment (ht. 2"; width 2") of the head of a Buddha image. Chunār sandstone. Find-spot not ascertainable.

B (c) 206.—Head (ht. 2½"; width 1¾") of Buddha. Face injured. Skull too narrow. Chunār sandstone. Excavated in 1907-08 in the second gateway of the mediaeval monastery I.

B (c) 207.—Head (ht. 2½"; width 1¾") of Buddha. Well preserved. Reddish Chunār sandstone with traces of red paint. Found in 1906-07 on structure No. 23 on surface to the north-west of the Main Shrine.

B (*d*).—Bōdhisattva Images of the Gupta and Mediaeval periods.

*B (*d*) 1.—Statue (ht. 4′ 5¼″; width at base 1′ 3″) of the Bōdhisattva Avalōkitēśvara, carved in the round, standing on a finely executed full-blown lotus-flower issuing from an intricate mass of foliage. The statue is broken into three pieces, namely, across the knees and the throat. The nose is damaged and the left knee broken off. The right arm is wanting. The left arm was detached and has been re-fixed. It holds the stalk of a lotus-flower in accordance with the canon (*vāmē padmadharaṁ*). The flower itself has not been recovered nor the greater part of the stem. A broken fragment which fits on to the right thigh shows the right hand with the palm open to the front in the gift-bestowing attitude which we learn from the *sādhanas* is another characteristic of the images of this Bōdhisattva (*varadakaraṁ dakshiṇēna*).[1]

The statue is nude down to the girdle, the lower part being clad in a garment the edge of which hangs down between the feet. It is bound to the loins by means of a richly jewelled girdle tied into a loop beneath the navel. Over the lower garment we notice a scarf passed round the thighs and tied up in a knot behind the right forearm, the ends falling down in a graceful manner along the right leg. The ears and the neck are ornamented with circular ear-rings and a necklace of beads respectively, and a metallic chain is worn after the fashion of the Brahmanical thread (*yajñōpavīta*). On the left arm we notice an armlet with ends shaped like *makara* heads and a jewelled bracelet. The hair is fastened by means of a jewelled fillet over the forehead and then tied up with a chord in the fashion of an ascetic's top-knot (*jaṭāmukuṭa*), three curly locks falling down on each shoulder. In front of the head-dress is a figurine of the Dhyāni-Buddha Amitābha, the spiritual father of Avalōkitēśvara, seated in his characteristic posture of meditation (*dhyānamudrā*). On the top of the base at the Bōdhisattva's feet below his right hand are two tantalized spirits (*prēta*) with emaciated bodies[2] whom the Compassionate Lord is feeding (Skt. *tarpayantaṁ*) with the stream of nectar flowing from his right hand. There was a circular halo around the head, but it has entirely disappeared with the exception of a small piece behind the shoulders.

The front of the base has a Sanskrit inscription of two lines in characters of the 5th century A.D. It was first deciphered by Dr. Vogel and published by Mr. Oertel.[3] It runs as follows :—

1. 1.—*Ōṁ Dēyadharmmō=yaṁ paramōpāsaka-Vishayapati-Suyāttrasya.*

---

[1] Foucher, *Étude sur l'Iconographie Bouddhique de l'Inde*, Paris, 1905, p. 25.

[2] *Prētas* are spirits undergoing torment and are described in *sādhanas* (Foucher, *op. cit.* p. 26) as *mahākukshim=atikṛiśam atiśitivarṇam sūchimukham.*

[3] *A. S. R.*, 1904-5, p. 81 and Pl. XXXII, No. XVIII.

l. 2. *yad=attra puṇyaṁ tad=bhavatu sarvvasatvānām=anuttara-jñānāvāptayē.*

"*Ōṁ.* This [is] the pious gift of the very devoted layman, Suyāttra, the head of a district. Whatsoever merit [there is] in this [gift], let it be to the attainment of supreme knowledge by all sentient beings."

The sculpture is of particular interest as being the only Gupta statue carved fully in the round which has yet been found at Sārnāth. The sculptor has shown considerable skill in the portrayal of the upper naked portion of the body. The statue was discovered in 1904-05 west of structure No. 7 on south-west of Main Shrine.[1] The material is a fine quality of Chunār sandstone. Pl. XIII, b.

B (*d*) 2.—Image (ht. 4′ 6″; width 2′ 2″) of a Bōdhisattva, presumably Maitrēya, standing. Upper part of back-slab, both hands and feet missing. Nose, chin and ear-lobes slightly injured and legs much weathered. The lower part of the body is clad in a garment which is fastened to the waist by means of a band of which the tassels are visible beneath the navel. The upper half of the body is partly bare, only a narrow strip of cloth being shown across the breast. There are no ornaments. The hair is remarkably long and, though gathered in a high top-knot, it falls back in thick locks on the shoulders. In front of the top-knot is an effigy of the Dhyāni-Buddha Amōghasiddhi seated cross-legged on a lotus in his typical posture of imparting security (*abhayamudrā*). The Bōdhisattva must therefore be Maitrēya, the "Messiah" of the Buddhists. If this identification is correct, his left hand must have held a *nāgakēśara* flower, the stalk of which is still traceable. The smaller flower issuing from the same stem seems indeed to belong to the plant just mentioned.

The right hand was apparently held down in the gift-bestowing attitude (*varada-mudrā*) which is also characteristic of Maitrēya.

On account of its simplicity of treatment Mr. Oertel, who discovered the statue to south-west of shrine on the south-west of the Main Shrine, assigns it to the early Gupta period.[2] It is certainly earlier than B (*d*) 1 and possibly even belongs to the Kushāṇa epoch. It is made of red sandstone which must have been obtained from the Chunār quarries.

B (*b*) 3.—Statue (ht. 3′ 10½″; width 1′ 8¼″) of a Bōdhisattva seated cross-legged on the flat top of the base which projects 7″ from the back-slab. The lower garment is a simple cloth, the hem of which is visible below the knees. The Bōdhisattva wears ear-rings, a necklace of beads, armlets studded with jewels and bracelets. His hair is

---

[1] *A. S. R.* 1904-05, p. 81 and p. 94, No. 110. Pl. XXVII, *b* shows a photo of the statue without the left arm and the remnant of the right hand.

[2] *A. S. R.*, 1904-05, p. 82; Pl. XXVIII, *d* and p. 94, No. 118.

arranged in long curly ringlets and in his hands he holds a large bowl against his breast. On his right and left shoulder there are a male and a female figure standing facing to the front and holding bowls similar to that in the Bōdhisattva's hands. On the latter's head we notice a headless figure of Dhyāni-Buddha Amitābha seated on a lotus in his proper attitude of meditation (*dhyānamudrā*). This is the only clue we have for the identification of the central image which, we may assume, represents Avalōkitēśvara.

On account of the style the sculpture may be attributed to the Gupta period. It was discovered by Mr. Oertel in 1904-05 south-east of the Aśōka Column and published by him in his account of his excavations with a photo.[1] Made of Chunār sandstone of pale buff colour. Pl. XIV, *a*.

B (*d*) 4.—Replica (ht. 4′; width 1′ 4½″) of B (*d*) 3. It is broken into six pieces which have been re-fixed with copper dowels. Unlike B (*d*) 3, the present figure wears a garment which covers the left shoulder and breast. The armlets also are different; they resemble those of B (*d*) 1. The figure on the right shoulder is damaged and the head and right knee of the Dhyāni-Buddha on the head of the main image are lost.

Made of the same material as B (*d*) 3 and found in the same year and in the same locality.[2]

B (*d*) 5.—Replica (ht. 2′ 10″; width 1′ 7″) of B (*d*) 3, but broken across chest, also at the top and along the sides of the back-slab. Of the Dhyāni-Buddha Amitābha, seated on the head of the Bōdhisattva, as in the preceding two sculptures, only the crossed legs remain in a damaged condition. The figures standing on the Bōdhisattva's shoulders are also much injured.

Found by the side of B (*d*) 4 in the same year.[3]

*B (*d*) 6.—Image (ht. 3′ 10½″; width 1′ 7½″) of Bōdhisattva Mañjuśrī, the personification of wisdom, standing on a double conventional lotus. The head was found detached from the body, and the right leg is injured about the knee. The right hand, which is missing, was apparently stretched out in the gift-bestowing attitude (*varadamudrā*); whilst near the break a stalk issuing from the lotus throne of the Bōdhisattva still remains. The left hand held a lotus (probably a blue lotus or *utpala*), the entire stalk being still extant. The upper half of the body of the Bōdhisattva is apparently bare, the lower being clad in a garment the folds of which are indicated on the left thigh. The treatment of the hair is nearly analogous to that in B (*d*) 2. In the hair-dress we find a miniature effigy of the Dhyāni-Buddha Akshōbhya,

---

[1] *A. S. R.*, 1904-05, pp. 82-83; Pl. XXIX, *b* and p. 95. No. 141.
[2] *Ibid.* 1904-5, p. 82, and p. 95, No. 143.
[3] *Ibid*, p, 95, No. 142.

the spiritual father of Mañjuśrī readily recognized by his attitude of touching the earth (*bhūmisparśamudrā*). The ornaments are elaborate and numerous, for in addition to those noticed in B (*d*) 1 and B (*d*) 3-5 there is a heavy metallic chain around the waist and rings on the fingers. To the right of the Bōdhisattva standing on a lotus, is a figure of Bhṛikuṭī Tārā with a rosary (*akshamālā*) in her right and a water-pot (*kamaṇḍalu*) in her left hand.[1] Her hair is done up in a large top-knot and she wears a lower garment, a scarf and ornaments. To the left of the Bōdhisattva stands Mṛityuvañchana-Tārā, with her right hand in the gift-bestowing attitude and a blue lotus flower in her left.[2] On the back of the sculpture, a few inches above the base, is an inscription of two lines containing the Buddhist creed in Sanskrit followed by the syllables *Arōlik*. It has been suggested that these symbols possibly constitute the date. It is equally possible that it is the name of the donor. The characters belong to the end of the 7th century A.D.

The sculpture was excavated [3] by Mr. Oertel in 1904-05 to the south-east of Main Shrine. Made of Chunār sandstone of pale buff colour. Pl. XIII, c.

B (*d*) 7.—Image (ht. 2′ ¾″; width 1′ 6″) seated cross-legged in the attitude of contemplation (*dhyānamudrā*). The hair is bound by a fillet over the forehead. The image wears what appears to be a Brahmanical thread (*yajñōpavīta*), a broad torque, armlets and bracelets from which it may be concluded that it was probably meant for a Bōdhisattva. It is unfinished and the attributes of the Bōdhisattva are not shown. The style seems to be that of the late Gupta period. Chunār sandstone of the same kind as in B (*d*) 3-5.

The sculpture was formerly preserved in the Queen's College. That it originates from Sārnāth is shown by a sketch of it in Major Kittoe's Drawings where it is described as an 'unfinished figure of a deified prince Cir. 1000 to 1100 S. S. Sārnath.' [4]

*B (*d*) 8.—Slab (ht. 3′ 11½″; width 2′ 4″) with image in alto-relievo of the Bōdhisattva Avalōkitēśvara seated in the 'sportive' attitude (*lalitāsana* or *ardhaparyaṅka*) on a double conventional lotus. Right foot missing. The right hand with open palm which is marked with a little disk is laid against the right knee in the gift-bestowing attitude (*varadamudrā*) whilst the left, which rests on the other knee, holds the stalk of an expanded lotus which appears over the left shoulder. In the way of ornaments we observe a necklace, a double metallic chain worn in the fashion of the Brahmanical thread, elaborate armlets

---

[1] Foucher, *l'Iconographie Bouddhique* 1905, p. 69.
[2] *Ibid.*, p. 66.
[3] Vide *A. S. R.*, 1904-05, pp. 81-82; Pl. XXVIII, c and p. 94, No. 120.
[4] Vol. I, No. 29, Pl. 15.

and bracelets. The existence of the lower garment is merely indicated by its upper edge on which the richly decorated girdle is bound. The hair is fastened with a fillet over the forehead. In front of the high top-knot (*jaṭāmakuṭa*) is the figurine of the Dhyāni-Buddha Amitābha seated in his characteristic attitude of meditation. Around the head of the Bōdhisattva, is an oval halo of Magadha type resting on the back of a throne, carved in relief with bells suspended from its projecting ends. On the proper right of the halo is a miniature Buddha figure seated cross-legged on a full-blown lotus in the gift-bestowing attitude (*varadamudrā*). The left hand of this figure is broken. On the base is carved the Buddhist creed in characters of about the 9th century A.D. The image was presumably made by the same artist as B (*c*) 2 and B (*c*) 35. Chunār sandstone. Discovered in 1907-08 between *stūpas* Nos. 71 and 72 north of Dhamēkh Stūpa.[1] Pl. XII, b.

B (*d*) 9.—Figure (ht. 2′ 1″; width 11″) of the Bōdhisattva Avalōkitēśvara in relief in an oblong sunken panel with an arched head. The Bōdhisattva is standing facing to front, his right hand held down in the gift-bestowing attitude (*varadaṁ dakshinē hastē*), and the left holding a full-blown lotus with long stalk (*vāmē padmadharam*). The upper half of his body is bare down to the girdle. The garment covering the loins is a fine piece of cloth fastened to the waist by a plain band tied into a large loop in the centre. A double chord is worn after the fashion of the Brahmanical thread (*yajñōpavīta*). There is a double necklace of beads around the neck, but no armlets or bracelets, as we observed in the preceding Bōdhisattva images. The hair is fastened into a round top-knot in front of which is a figurine of the Dhyāni-Buddha Amitābha seated in the attitude of meditation (*dhyānamudrā*). Beneath the right hand of Avalōkitēśvara is a female figure kneeling with hands clasped before the breast, presumably the donor of the sculpture.

On grounds of style the sculpture may be assigned to about the early mediaeval period. The material is Chunār sandstone of light buff colour. Discovered in 1904-5 at the Chaukhaṇḍi Stūpa.[2]

B (*d*) 10.—Sculpture similar to B (*d*) 9 in style and posture and of identical dimensions. The treatment of the hair is somewhat different and in addition to the dress and ornaments observed in connection with the preceding figure, there are ear-rings, armlets, bracelets and a scarf tied round the thighs over the lower garment. There is no Dhyāni-Buddha in the head-dress; but as the left hand holds the stem of a flower which is probably *nāgakēsara* we may conclude that the

---

[1] *A. S. R.*, 1907-08, p. 60, and Pl. XVII, *a*.
[2] *Ibid.*, 1904-05, p. 82, Pl. XXIX, *a*; and p. 101, No. 471.

figure represents Maitrēya. Further proof in favour of this identification is the fact that this and the preceding sculpture have undoubtedly formed a pair and as one of them is Avalōkitēśvara, the other is probably Maitrēya.[1]

Made of the same kind of stone as B (*d*) 9 and discovered in the same year and locality.

B (*d*) 11.—Torso (ht. 2′ 1⅛″; width 1′ 4″) of a standing Bōdhisattva image ornamented with a necklace, armlets and an elaborate metallic girdle. Head, hands and feet broken off. The right hand was apparently in the attitude of bestowing a gift (*varadamudrā*). The left hand held a flower which is broken off. To the right of the Bōdhisattva we notice the left hand of a figure with what looks like a lotus-bud. To his left we notice another attendant, holding a fly-whisk (*chāmara*) in the left hand. His right hand is broken off. I am unable to identify the Bōdhisattva. On account of the workmanship the sculpture seems to belong to the early mediaeval period.

Made of Chunār sandstone. Excavated south of first court on east of mediaeval monastery I, 4′ 4″ below the surface.[2]

B (*d*) 12.—Lower part (ht. 2′ 2″; width 10″) showing the legs of a standing image, which seems to have been of the same type as B (*d*) 11.

The kneeling figure near its right foot seems to be the donor of the image.

Chunār sandstone. Excavated in 1904-05 south-east of Main Shrine.[3]

*B (*d*) 13.—Pedestal[4] (ht. 1′ 3¼″; width 1′ 11″) bearing the lower part of a well-draped figure, profusely adorned with ornaments, seated in the 'sportive' attitude (*lalitāsana*) on a lotus throne. The right leg is broken off with the exception of the foot which rests on a smaller lotus on the top of the base. On either side of the main image we notice a figure of a goddess in a fragmentary condition seated with the legs in the same position as the central image with the right hand raised in front of the chest and the left holding a lotus-stalk. Dr. Vogel identifies these figures as Tārā and surmises that the central figure must have been either Lōkēśvara or Tārā herself. The kneeling figurines, male and female, beneath the two Tārā figures at both ends of the sculpture are presumably the donor and his wife.

The front of the base is cut in recesses, two at each end, and the central facet contains an indistinct inscription of three lines measuring 10″, 10″ and 1″. It consists of the Buddhist creed in Sanskrit followed by *Dēyadha*[*r*]*mmō=yaṁ pravara=mahāyānānuyāyī*-[*pa*] *ramōpāsaka-Māgadhīya-śrī-Śāmaṅkasya* (?). "This [is] the pious gift

[1] *A. S. R.*, 1904-05, p. 82, Pl. XXIX, *a*; and p. 101, No. 472.
[2] *Ibid.*, 1906-07, p. 92, No. 36 and Pl. XXIX, *c*.
[3] *A. S. R.*, 1904-05, p. 96, No. 149.
[4] Described by Dr. Vogel in *A. S. R.*, 1903-04, pp. 223-4, Pl. LXIII, 4, and Pl. LXIV, 5.

of the follower of the excellent Mahāyāna, the lay-devotee, the illustrious Śāmaṅka (?) from Magadha."

The characters of the inscription belong to about the 11th century A.D. which must also be the date of the sculpture.

The sculpture is sketched in Major Kittoe's 'Drawings'[1] in the same fragmentary condition and must have been found at Sārnāth either by Major Kittoe himself or before him. It was presented to the Provincial Museum, Lucknow, by the Principal, Queen's College, Benaras, in December 1903, and has been returned to the Sārnāth Museum in 1911.

*B (*d*) 14.—Bust without head (ht. 10½"; width 11") of a Bōdhisattva wearing a necklace, armlets, bracelets and a girdle. The hands are held before the chest in the attitude of expounding the law (*vyākhyānamudrādharam*) for which reason the image may perhaps be identified as Mañjuśrī. The blue lotus flowers, the stalks of which are wound round his two arms, support this view, though it must be admitted that according to the Sādhana this flower should appear only in the left hand (*vāmēn=ōtpaladharam*).[2]

On the back of the sculpture is carved the Buddhist creed in characters of the 10th century A.D. Chunār sandstone of pink colour. Excavated in 1904-05.[3]

B (*d*) 15.—Bust (ht. 1' 6"; width 1' 5") of a Bōdhisattva with the head-dress decked with jewels (*ratnamukuṭinam*), and wearing circular ear-rings, a necklace, armlets, etc. The left fore-arm is broken off but traces of the right hand remain on the breast to show that the attitude was probably that of expounding the law (*vyākhyānamudrā*). The Bōdhisattva was presumably Mañjuśrī. At his right side is a female attendant perhaps Tārā with a fly-whisk (Sanskrit *chāmara*) in her right hand. Part of similar figure on left.

The style seems to be mediaeval. Chunār sandstone of buff colour. The image belonged to the Queen's College collection.

B (*d*) 16.—Relief (ht. 1' 4"; width 9½") with the figure of a Bōdhisattva, probably Avalōkitēśvara, seated in 'sportive' attitude (*lalitāsana*) on a conventional double lotus. The hair is tied up in a top-knot. He wears a *dhōtī* and the lower part of the figure is covered with several ornaments. The right hand, which is broken, probably rested on the right knee and held the stem of the lotus flower rising on this side. The left hand holds another lotus at the level of the shoulder. Mark on forehead, presumably meant for *ūrṇā*. There are the remains of two kneeling human figures at both ends of the base. The

---

[1] Vol. I, Pl. 30, No. 144.

[2] Foucher, *l'Iconographie Bouddhique*, 1905, p. 41 and edition of 1900, *fig.* 17, which illustrates an image of Mañjuśrī from Magadha now in the Calcutta Museum.

[3] *A. S. R.*, 1904-05, p. 96, No. 152.

one beneath the right hand appears to be a tantalized spirit (*prēta*) receiving the drops of nectar falling from the right hand of the deity. The other figure may be the donor.

Made of Chunār sandstone. The image is one of the thirteen Sārnāth sculptures which have recently been returned from the Lucknow Museum.[1]

B (*d*) 17.—Relief (ht. 1′ 1½″; width 7½″) which Dr. Marshall describes in the following terms.[2] "Avalōkitēśvara seated in *lalitāsana* on lotus. Right hand in *varadamudrā*, left hand holds rose. Above, five Dhyānibuddhas; in the centre, Amitābha in *dhyānamudrā*. To his right, Tārā, left hand holding blue lotus, right hand in explaining attitude; below her, Sudhanakumāra, his hands folded in supplicating attitude (*kṛitāñjalipuṭa*), holding a book in his left armpit; to Avalōkitēśvara's left, above, Bhṛikuṭī (?), sitting with left knee drawn up, right hand raised against the Bōdhisattva, left hand holding object (*kamaṇḍalu*). Below her, Hayagrīva (?), right hand raised towards the Bōdhisattva, left hand holding stick. On the base, under Avalōkitēśvara's right hand, Sūchimukha, his pointed face turned upwards. On the opposite corner two worshippers, male and female."

The style seems to be that of late mediaeval period. Made of stone of grey colour. Excavated in 1906-07.

B (*d*) 18.—Image of the Bōdhisattva Avalôkitēśvara (ht. 1′; width 10½″) seated in 'sportive' attitude (*lalitāsana*) on a conventional lotus flower, and wearing scarf across breast and *dhōtī* round loins, and several ornaments. The head and both arms below the shoulders are broken off, but the right hand remains on the knee in the gift-bestowing attitude (*varadamudrā*). Pair of feet to right and left of *Avalōkitēśvara*, perhaps Tārā and Bhṛikuṭī. Under the Bōdhisattva's right hand the spirit Sūchimukha with hands raised and pointed face turned upwards. Behind him, male figure with folded hands, presumably the donor. Beneath the left leg of the Bōdhisattva, seated male figure, presumably Hayagrīva, with protruding belly (*lambōdara*), his right hand raised towards Avalōkitēśvara and with a snake worn in the manner of the Brahmanical thread (*bhujaṅga-yajñōpavītin*). The staff (*daṇḍa*) is absent. At his side, male figure in devotional attitude.

For reasons of style, the image may be assigned to the 10th or 11th century A.D. Chunār sandstone of pale buff colour. Lower part discovered in 1907-08 in area north of Main Shrine, 2′ below the surface.[3] Upper part found in 1904-05 between the Jagat Singh Stūpa and the Main Shrine.

---

[1] For Dr. Vogel's description of this sculpture, *vide A. S. R.*, 1903-04, p. 225, and fig. 5.

[2] *A. S. R.*, 1906-07, p. 91, No. 32. *Cf.* also Pl. XIX, 8.

[3] *Ibid.*, 1907-08, p. 72, No. β 10.

B (*d*) 19.—Figure (ht. 1′ 3½″; width 10¼″) of the Bōdhisattva Mañjuśrī seated in 'sportive' attitude (*lalitāsana*) on a lion (*siṁhāsanastha*) and wearing jewelled ear-rings, necklace, armlets, bracelets and girdle, and a high pointed hair-dress. The fore-arms are broken, but parts of hands in the attitude of expounding the law (*vyākhyānamudrā*) are still extant on the breast. Of the blue lotus at the left side (*vāmēn=ōtpalam*) only the stalk remains in part. Similar lotus to right in perfect condition. In head-dress Dhyāni-buddha Akshōbhya, in the earth-touching attitude (*bhūmisparśamudrā*). Kneeling worshipper on either side. The one to the right of the Bōdhisattva is broken, the other which is intact is a female.

The style belongs to the late mediaeval period. Made of Chunār stone of greenish hue. Discovered in 1906-07 in area east of Main Shrine.[1]

*B (*d*) 20.—Figure (Ht. 1′ 7¼″; width 1′ ½″) of a Bōdhisattva, seated cross-legged, wearing a high conical hair-dress and ornaments. Broken into three pieces. Two large pieces of back-slab missing from right and left side. The deity's right hand holds a thunder-bolt (*vajra*) which remains in part, in front of his breast. His left hand holds a bell with thunderbolt top (*vajraghaṇṭā*) upside down. Around his head is an oval halo of Magadha style. In front of head-dress, Dhyānibuddha Akshōbhya in earth-touching attitude and in front of the lotus throne a figure of a bearded worshipper. In Tibetan paintings the thunderbolt symbol appears in the right hand of the Bōdhisattva Vajrasattva.[2] The figure under review is, therefore, probably to be identified with that deity, whose spiritual father is indeed Akshōbhya.

On the base is carved a fragmentary inscription of two lines consisting of the Buddhist creed followed by the words *Dēyadharmmō=yaṁ paramōpāsa* [*ka-*] "The pious gift of the very devoted ...." The characters are of the 11th century A.D. Made of stone of greenish colour. Discovered in 1906-07 on the approach to the Main Shrine from the east.[3]

B (*d*) 21.—Lower part of image (ht. 7½″; width 10″) similar to B (*d*) 20 with which it must be coeval. Upper half above the waist, right arm and left upper arm missing. The carving on the under side of the stone shows that it had originally been used for decorative face-work on the outside of a shrine or other monument.

Chunār sandstone. Excavated in 1907-08 in the same locality as B (*d*) 20, 6′ below the surface.

---

[1] *A. S. R.*, 1906-07, p. 92, No. 33 and Pl. XXIII, 10.

[2] *Cf.* Foucher *l'Iconographie Bouddhique*, edition of 1900, Pl. VI, 6; also image from Magadha now in Calcutta Museum in Fig. 19 on p. 122.

[3] For the lowest piece *cf.* *A. S. R.* 1906-07, p. 92, No. 37.

B (*d*) 22.—Relief (ht. 1′ 1″; width 9¼″) representing a Bōdhisattva, adorned with ornaments, seated in 'sportive' attitude (*lalitāsana*). Hair tied up in top-knot decked with pearls, etc. In his right hand is a bud of a flower; in the left a round object. He is surrounded by seven smaller figures seated in various styles. On base, in relief, horse standing shown in profile. Excavated in 1904-05.[1]

B (*d*) 23.—Lower part (ht. 5″; width 6″) of a figure of a Bōdhisattva, presumably Mañjuśrī seated on a cushion placed on the back of a lion, couchant, placed on an inverted lotus. The left leg of the Bōdhisattva lies flat, while the right leg must have been drawn up, and the right hand rested on it in easy pose (*līlāvasthita*). His left hand grasps the stalk of a blue lotus.

17 From the style, I assign the fragment to the late mediaeval period. Made of the same kind of stone as B (*d*) 19 and B (*d*) 20. Discovered in 1904-05 north-east of Jagat Singh Stūpa.[2]

B (*d*) 24.—Upper part (ht. 7″; width 7″) of a Bōdhisattva, from waist upwards, who, to judge from the Dhyānibuddha Akshōbhya in the earth-touching attitude in his head-dress, must be Mañjuśrī. The flower in the left hand, however, is apparently not a blue lotus and to this extent the identification remains uncertain. The Bōdhisattva has a lofty head-dress and is lavishly adorned with ornaments.

The style is that of the 11th or 12th century A.D. Chunār sandstone of buff colour. Found in 1907-08 on the approach to Main Shrine from the east 8′ below the surface.[3]

B (*d*) 25.—Torso (ht. 9½″; width 6½″) of a Bōdhisattva standing. Head, right arm and lower part of legs missing. His left hand holds a flower stalk. Wears *dhōtī*, scarf, armlets and bracelets. Presumably Gupta period.

Chunār sandstone. Discovered in 1907-08 outside north-east corner of mediaeval monastery I, some 3′ below the surface.

B (*d*) 26.—Figure (ht. 10″; width 8″) of a Bōdhisattva seated in 'sportive' attitude (*lalitāsana*) on a conventional lotus. The sides of the slab are damaged and the figure broken across the waist. Right hand on knee in gift-bestowing attitude. Left holds stalk of flower. Perhaps Avalōkitēśvara. Buff-coloured sandstone of Chunār. Lower part excavated in 1904-05.

B (*d*) 27.—Figure (ht. 8″; width 6½″) similar to B (*d*) 26. Much defaced.

Chunār sandstone. Unearthed in 1906-07 between the first court on the east of the mediaeval monastery I and *stūpa* No. 43.

B (*d*) 28.—Figure (ht. 6½″; width 4½″) of a Bōdhisattva, probably Avalōkitēśvara standing with his right hip jutting out. Much defaced.

---

[1] *A. S. R.*, 1904-05, p. 95, No. 125.
[2] *Ibid.*, p. 98, No. 305.
[3] *Ibid*, 1907-08, p. 67. No. γ7.

Legs below knees missing. High head-dress. Right hand in gift-bestowing attitude. Left hand holds lotus (*kamala*). Chunār sandstone of reddish colour. *Cir.* 11th century A.D. Excavated in 1907-08 in the first court on the east of the mediaeval monastery I.[1]

B (*d*) 29.—Breast and left upper arm (ht. 4″; width 7½″) of a Bōdhisattva adorned with a necklace and a garland of beads. Stalk of flower twined round his shoulder. Identification uncertain.

Chunār stone of buff colour. Unearthed in 1907-08 on the approach to the Main Shrine from the east 7′ below the surface.

*B (*d*) 30.—Figure (ht. 6″; width 3½″) of Bōdhisattva Maitrēya standing facing to front and wearing a high head-dress, a fillet over the forehead, a necklace, a scarf and a *dhōtī* which reaches down to the ankles. To the proper right of the head, in relief, is a miniature *stūpa* the characteristic attribute of the future Buddha. His right hand is in the gift-bestowing attitude which is also in keeping with tradition. The flower in the left hand, however, seems to be a lotus (*kamala*), whereas Maitrēya's prescribed flower is the *nāgakēśara*. On the base in the characters of about the 11th century A.D., are cut the words *Ōṁ yē dharmmā hē* . . . . The rest of the creed was not carved.

Made of very rough sandstone of a dark colour. Discovered in the area around the Jagat Singh *stūpa*.[2]

B (*d*) 31.—Fragment (ht. 11½″; width 7″) of a Bōdhisattva statuette, body, arms and feet missing. The lower part is clad in a well-draped under-garment, on which remain traces of a scarf as in B (*d*) 1. Folds of hem marked on the left thigh. Chunār sandstone. Unearthed in 1904-05 in the area around the Jagat Singh *stūpa* and the Main Shrine.

B (*d*) 32.—Head (ht. 6″; width 4½″) of Bōdhisattva Maitrēya. The face is cut away and the ears and chin damaged. The deity has a high head-dress, perhaps, made of the Bōdhisattva's own matted hair (*jaṭā-makuṭa*), on the front of which, in relief, is a miniature *stūpa*, the attribute of the future Buddha.

Chunār stone of pale buff colour. Unearthed in the courtyard of the mediaeval monastery I near the stair; 7′ 3″ below the surface.

B (*d*) 33.—Head (ht. 2¾″) presumably of an attendant Bōdhisattva which formed part of a larger statue. Chunār sandstone, with traces of red paint. Unearthed in 1906-07 in the area to the west of the Main Shrine.

B (*d*) 34.—Head of a Bōdhisattva which Mr. Hall describes as "3½″ high, broken off from a statuette, sandstone, of very marked character,

---

[1] *A. S. R.*, 1907-08, p. 49, No. 142.
[2] *Ibid.*, p. 65, No. J. S. 8.

hair parted in short bandeaux in the centre, ending in a series of short curls, with a short club of hair thrown back from the top of the head, high pencilled eyebrows; half-closed eyelids, forehead and nose in one straight line; facial angle about 80; smiling expression of mouth; coloured part of the under-lip marked in an exaggerated degree, almost like a protruded tongue, profile very Egyptian, throat marked with two folds; long ear-rings."[1] Mr. Hall mistook the head for that of a female. Dr. Vogel[2] in pointing this out suggests that this Bōdhisattva head has been copied from a Gandharan prototype. The style of the head belongs to the late Gupta period. The head is one of the 13 Sārnāth sculptures which were returned from the Lucknow Museum, to which institution they had been presented along with eight other sculptures by the Principal, Queen's College, in December 1903.

B (*d*) 35.—Upper part (ht. 7½"; width 7") of a relief with the five Dhyānibuddhas seated in their proper attitudes, and the Magadhan halo of the main figure. The central Dhyānibuddha in the attitude of granting protection is Amōghasiddhi, the godfather of the future Buddha Maitrēya. The main figure must, therefore, have been of Maitrēya. Further evidence is found in the miniature *stūpa*, the emblem of Maitrēya, carved in relief to the proper right of his halo.

The sculpture is made of blue stone of Magadha and the style belongs approximately to the 8th or 9th century A.D. Discovered in 1907-08 on the eastern approach of the Main Shrine, 7′ below the surface.

B (*d*) 36.—Head (ht. 7½"; width 4½") of a Bōdhisattva with a jewelled fillet and a high head-dress, presumably only his matted hair. The nose and mouth are broken, and the style of carving seems to be of the mediæval period. Chunār sandstone. Discovered in 1907-08 in the first court on the east of the mediæval monastery I.[3]

B (*d*) 37.—Top of head (ht. 4"; width 5") with curly hair arranged as in B (*d*) 3, which presumably belonged to a Bōdhisattva image. Chunār sandstone. Found in 1904-05 in the spoil earth which had been thrown up by Mr. Hall where the old sculpture shed now stands.[4]

B (*d*) 38.—Head (ht. 4"; width 2½") presumably of a Bōdhisattva image. Late mediæval style. Face boken off. Chunār sandstone. Find-spot not known.

B (*d*) 39.—Head (ht. 3½"; width 2") presumably of a Bōdhisattva image. The back is split away. Chunār sandstone. Mediæval style. Find-spot not known.

---

[1] *J. A. S. B.*, Vol. XXV (1856), p. 399, No. 5.
[2] *A. S. R.*, 1903-04, p. 225.
[3] *Ibid.*, 1907-08, p. 49, No. 168.
[4] *Ibid.*, 1904-05, p. 97. No. 371.

B (*d*) 40.—Top of a head (ht. 2½"; width 3¼") which presumably belonged to a Bōdhisattva image. Chunār sandstone. Find-spot not known.

B (*d*) 41.—Head (ht. 6"; width 3") with a figurine of the Dhyāni-buddha Amitābha on the front of the high head-dress. Probably Avalōkitēśvara. Mediæval style. Chunār sandstone of buff colour. Unearthed in the 2nd outer court of the mediæval monastery I, 2′ below the surface.[1]

*B (*d*) 42.—Lower part (ht. 7"; width 8½") of a figure of a Bōdhisattva, presumably Avalōkitēśvara, seated in easy attitude (*lalitāsana*) on a lotus throne, with the right foot which hangs down resting on a separate smaller lotus. Lower parts of both the arms survive. The right hand rests on the knee in the gift-bestowing attitude, the left holds the stalk of a flower. Below the right-hand of the Bōdhisattva is a worshipper kneeling to proper left, his hands joined in adoration. At the proper left side of the Bōdhisattva is Tārā seated on a lotus, her right hand held in front of her chest with the palm turned outwards, and left holding the stalk of a blue lotus. Below Tārā is a basin containing fire.

On the base is incised a line (length 5¾") of writing in characters of the 10th or 11th century A.D. which reads:—

Dānapati-Iṛiśōsya pōkasaḥ.

The material is blue stone of Gayā. Unearthed in 1906-07 in the area to the east of the Main Shrine.[2]

B (*d*) 43.—Fragment (ht. 7"; width 11") with the legs of a male figure. Its feet are broken off and the left hand is slightly injured. The latter seems to have held a vessel. If this is correct the image should be identified as Bōdhisattva Maitrēya. To his proper left is the bust of an attendant with his right hand stretched up towards the deity.

Mediæval style. Chunār sandstone. Unearthed in 1907-08 probably in the area north of the Main Shrine.

B (*d*) 44.—Bust (ht. 3½"; width 2¾") of a male figure without head and arms, adorned with a torque and a necklace, presumably a Bōdhisattva. Mediæval style. Greenish stone. Found in the second outer court of the mediæval monastery I, 1½′ below the surface.[3]

B (*d*) 45.—Base with the feet of a standing image (ht. 1′ ¾" with tenon; width 1′ 2") which to judge from the root of a flower-stalk rising near the left foot must have belonged to an image of a Bōdhisattva, (apparently Avalōkitēśvara or Mañjuśrī). Gupta work. Traces of red

---

[1] *A. S. R.*, 1907-08, p. 52, ¿ 44.

[2] *Ibid.*, 1906-07, p. 92, No. 43.

[3] *Ibid.*, 1907-08, p. 52, No. ¿ 1.

paint. Chunār sandstone of buff colour. Was probably formerly preserved in the Queen's College.

B (*d*) 46.—Base (ht. 1′ 6″; width 1′ 3″) with a tenon on underside and a pair of feet above. Between the feet we notice traces of the hem of the lower garment (*dhōtī*) as in B (*d*) 1, from which it may be inferred that the fragment belonged to an image of a Bōdhisattva. The style is evidently of the Gupta period. Traces of red colour.

Buff-coloured sandstone of Chunār. Excavated in 1907-08 in the area between the cloistered passage to the north-east of the Main Shrine and the mediæval monastery I, 1′ below the surface.

B (*d*) 47.—Base (ht. 1′; width 1′ 9″) of a sculpture with the feet of a Bōdhisattva standing on a lotus throne. To his proper left, root of a lotus plant. Further left, the feet of a goddess of smaller size, adorned with anklets. To judge from style late Gupta period. Chunār sandstone. Found in 1906-07 in the stair of mediæval monastery I, 6′ below the surface.

B (*d*) 48.—Fragment (ht. 7″; width 11″) bearing the lower part of a figure of a Bōdhisattva seated in easy attitude on a lotus. The left leg which hung down is broken off but the foot remains on the top of the base. Under the right leg of the deity is a lion couchant. The Bōdhisattva is therefore, perhaps, to be identified as Mañjuśrī. On the right and left of the deity is a kneeling worshipper with the head damaged, presumably the donor and his wife. Mediæval style. Buff-coloured sandstone of Chunār. Excavated in 1904-05 to the south of the Main Shrine.[1]

B (*d*) 49.—Fragment (ht. 10″; width 6¼″) from the proper left side of a bigger sculpture, bearing a standing figure of Yamāri or Yamāntaka without head and feet. His left hand holds a skull filled with blood (*raktapūrṇa-kapālam*) and right, a staff with human head (*muṇḍ-āṅkitasitadaṇḍa-dharam*).[2] Since Yamāri is the left hand attendant of Mañjuśrī,[3] the fragment must have belonged to an image of that Bōdhisattva.

To judge from style, late mediæval period. Chunār sandstone. Discovered in 1904-05.

B (*d*) 50.—Fragment (ht. 9″; width 6½″) with a figure of a male attendant, lacking feet, fly-whisk in right hand and what appears to be a thunderbolt in left. Perhaps Vajrasattva. Mediæval style.

The fragment is from the proper left side of a bigger sculpture. The main image was presumably a Bōdhisattva. Chunār sandstone with

---

[1] *A. S. R.*, 1904-05, p. 95, No. 122.
[2] Foucher, *l'Iconographie Bouddhique* 1905, p. 56.
[3] *Ibid.*, p. 40.

traces of red paint. Unearthed in 1906-07 in the area to the east of the Main Shrine.[1]

B (*d*) 51.—Left hand (length 1¼"; width 1½") holding the stalk of a flower, without any ornament, presumably of a Bōdhisattva image. Blue stone of Magadha. Find-spot not known.

B (*d*) 52.—Figure (ht. 6¾" ; width 4") of Dhyānibuddha Amōghasiddhi seated cross-legged on an expanded lotus in the attitude of granting protection (*abhayamudrā*). His right hand is broken off and left rests on lap. He has a circular halo around his head, and a dress as in ordinary Buddha images. The style belongs to the late Gupta period.[2]

Such figures occur on the top and in the corners of images of Bōdhisattvas and goddesses in later times. The figure under review is probably from an image of Maitrēya. Made of Chunār sandstone of buff colour. Unearthed in 1906-07 in the area on the east of the Main Shrine.

B (*d*) 53.—Figure (ht. 7¼" ; width 4") which conforms in all respects to B (*d*) 52. It was undoubtedly carved by the same artist and formed part apparently of the same sculpture. Found in the same locality and year.

B (*d*) 54.—Fragment (ht. 5¼"; width 7½"), from the top of a sculpture, bearing a figure of Dhyānibuddha Amōghasiddhi seated cross-legged on a blue lotus in the attitude of granting protection. Its late date is clearly indicated by the ornaments which the Dhyānibuddha wears and the absence of schematic curls and the skull protuberance (*ushṇīsha*).

The fragment seems to have belonged to an image of Maitrēya. Buff-coloured stone from Chunār. Unearthed in 1907-08 in the area to the north of the Main Shrine, 6' below the surface.

B(*d*) 55.—Upper part (ht. 4"; width 6") of an image of Bōdhisattva Maitrēya, with a part of the halo and Dhyānibuddha Amōghasiddhi seated in usual attitude. Buff-coloured stone of Chunār. Excavated in 1906-07 in the area on the east of the Main Shrine.

B (*d*) 56.—Fragment (ht. 5¼"; width 4½") with the same figure as B (*d*) 55. Presumably upper part of a Maitrēya image. Latest style. Greenish stone. Discovered in the same year and area.

B (*d*) 57.—Fragment (ht. 5½"; width 7¾") from proper right upper corner of a larger image. To the left we notice Dhyānibuddha Amōghasiddhi, in relief, seated cross-legged on a throne. The artist has failed to delineate the posture correctly for we find the left hand raised to the breast instead of the right and the latter on the knee with its

---

[1] *A. S. R.*, 1906-07, p. 95, No. 74.
[2] *Cf.* Stele C (*a*) 2 with four scenes from the Buddha's life.

palm turned outwards. The fragment presumably belonged to a Bōdhisattva, probably Maitrēya. Late mediæval style.

Made of Chunār stone of light colour. Excavated in 1907-08 in the area to the north-east of the Dhamēkh *stūpa*.

B (*d*) 58.—Figure (ht. 4¾"; width 3½") in alto-relievo of Dhyānibuddha Amōghasiddhi seated cross-legged in the attitude of granting security. Right hand damaged. Late Gupta. Chunār sandstone. Discovered in 1906-07 in the area to the west of the Main Shrine.

B (*d*) 59.—Statuette (ht. 2′ 5"; width 1′ 1⅛") of a Bōdhisattva presumably Avalōkitēśvara standing facing. Lower part of the sculpture with the deity's forearms and feet missing. Oval halo around the head which itself is broken off, but locks visible on shoulders. The lower part of the figure is clad in a well-draped *dhōtī* which is bound round the waist by means of a jewelled girdle. The upper body is naked. The right hand was apparently laid in the gift-bestowing attitude, while the left hand held the stalk of a lotus which remains in part.

The style seems to belong to the early mediæval period. Chunār sandstone of reddish colour. Find-spot not known.

B (*d*) 60.—Torso (ht. 5¼ ") of a miniature Bōdhisattva figure standing. The right hand was raised in the attitude of granting protection, the left holds the scarf on the hip. Presumably from side of a Buddha image. Gupta period. Chunār sandstone. Unearthed in one of the recent excavations.

B (*d*) 61.—Torso (ht. 5¼″) similar to B (*d*) 60 in all respects. Discovered in the area around the Jagat Singh *stūpa*.

B (*d*) 62.—Bust (ht. 6") of a figure which to judge from the remnant of a bowl which it held in front of the chest must have been a Bōdhisattva. The hair falls on the sides in long twisted curls and the figure wears a necklace. Gupta style. Chunār sandstone. Unearthed in one of the recent diggings.

B (*d*) 63.—Fragment bearing a head surrounded by a circular halo. The head-dress is richly decorated from which it may be assumed that the head belonged to a Bōdhisattva image. It is, of course, impossible to be sure in this matter for there are several mediæval figures of Buddha in the Museum, which have a similar headdress. Buff-coloured sandstone of Chunār. Unearthed in 1907-08 in the 2nd court on the east of monastery I, 6′ below the surface.

B (*d*) 64.—Head (ht. 3¼") of a Bōdhisattva figure carved in the round. The hair is tied in a knot at the top and then arranged in concentric rings on the back. Traces of a scarf on the breast and back. Gupta style. Vestiges of red paint. Unearthed in 1907-08 in the trench crossing the south boundary wall of monastery I, 4′ below the surface.

B (*d*) 65.—Head (ht. 3¼″) of a Bōdhisattva (?) figure with a three-peaked head-dress. Mediæval style. Discovered in one of the recent excavations.

B (*d*) 66.—Fragment (ht. 2¼″) of a head which presumably belonged to a Bōdhisattva figurine. The hair is parted in the middle. Gupta style. Chunār sandstone.

B (*d*) 67.—Face (ht. 2¾″) of a Bōdhisattva (?) figurine with ornamental head-dress. Gupta period. Excavated in one of the recent diggings.

B (*d*) 68.—Base (ht. 6¼″) with the left leg of a Bōdhisattva in sportive attitude. Gupta work. Chunār sandstone. Discovered in 1906-07 in the monastery to the west of the Dhamēkh *stūpa*, 3′ below the surface.

B (*e*).—Images of Minor Deities.

*B (*e*) 1.—Sculpture (ht. 2′ 2½″; width 1′ 8½″) representing a group of Kubēra or Jambhala, the Buddhist god of wealth and his female counterpart (Sanskrit Śakti) Vasundharā, the goddess of plenty, standing side by side facing to the front. The images are carved in alto-relievo but the stone has been cut away from behind them to give them the appearance of statues in the round. The sides of the sculpture are carved in the shape of ornamental pilasters their caps being surmounted by flying figures of celestial beings (*dēvas*) carrying garlands. Both caps are detached. One of them has been re-fixed, the other is too much worn on the underside. The upper part of the slab between the celestials as well as the head of the goddess is missing. Hāritī is standing on a conventional lotus, Kubēra on his vehicle, a man (*nara*) lying full length on his back on a lotus. This figure wears a high diadem and ornaments. Its feet are broken off. Kubēra is represented as completely nude, and the usual armlets, bracelets and anklets are replaced by cobras. He wears also a snake in the manner of a Brahmanical thread. His teeth are visible between his lips and from the corners of his mouth protrude crooked tushes, a characteristic of the Yaksha. He bears a rectangular mark on his forehead and has a prominent abdomen and legs disproportionately short. On his head he wears a figurine of the Dhyāni-buddha Amitābha surrounded by a flaming halo of oval shape[1]. As in Mathurā sculptures, the right hand of Kubēra holds a bowl which is partly broken. The left hand is missing, but it may be assumed to have held a mongoose the tail of which is still traceable. The goddess wears a long garland reaching down to a little beneath the knees and is profusely adorned with ornaments of all sorts. In her right hand was an object which has disappeared. Her left hand is wanting. We may perhaps assume that she held the same objects as the miniature figures of the goddess Vasundharā in No B(*f*) 19, namely an ear of corn and a fruit (?) On the top of the pedestal at the feet of the deities are two kneeling figures, a male and a female, presumably the donor and his wife, while in front of it beneath the goddess is carved a pair of vases (Sanskrit *ratnaghaṭa*) a symbol of abundance over which she presides. The remaining portion of the pedestal is taken up with a fragmentary Sanskrit inscription of five lines in characters of the 11th or 12th century A.D. consisting of the Buddhist creed followed by :—

l. 3. *Dē*[*yadharmmō=yaṁ*] *mahāyā*[*nā*]*nuyāyinaḥ paramōpāsaka-Mā*......

---

[1] According to the *sādhanas* the Dhyāni-buddha on the head of Kubēra should be either Ratnasambhava or Akshōbhya.

l. 4. ...... [*yad=atra pu**]*ṇyaṁ tad=bhavatv=āchāryōpādhyāya-mātā—*

l. 5. [*pitrōḥ*]......*sarvasattvānāñch=ānuttarajñānāvāptayē*

"This is the pious gift of the follower of the Great Path, the supremely devoted......Whatever merit there is in it, may it be to the attainment of unsurpassed knowledge by his preceptors, teachers, parents, ... and all sentient beings."

Groups of the god of wealth and the goddess of fertility are common in Mathurā and Gandhāra sculpture[1] where they are invariably represented as seated. For the difference in the position and the addition of the corpse the later sculptors must have been responsible. It is also worth noting that, whereas in the schools referred to, it is Kubēra who occupies the right position, in the sculpture under review the order is changed.

Made of Chunār stone of pale grey colour and discovered in 1907-08 on eastern approach of Main Shrine 7′ below the surface[2]. Pl. XV, *a*.

B (*e*) 2.—Sculpture (ht. 1′; width 1′ 2½″) representing a pair of corpulent figures, presumably goblins (*yakshas*) crouching side by side. The heads of both and one arm of each are missing. They wear lower garments, necklaces, armlets and bracelets. The left hand of the right, and right hand of the other, rest on the knees. The style seems to belong to the mediæval period. It is made of Chunār sandstone of buff colour and was probably found at Sārnāth.

B (*e*) 3.—Corpulent male figure (ht. 8″ including tenon on underside; width 8¼″) apparently a goblin or *yaksha*, seated with the left knee drawn up. Both arms are wanting, but the right hand exists on the knee. The tenon on the underside shows that the statuette was fixed in a pedestal. The image does not seem to be of Kubēra. Small figures of this deity occur on several facing stones preserved in the Sārnāth Museum and there is quite a collection of them in the Mathurā Museum, but all of them have one or other emblem of the deity. Late Gupta work.

Made of Chunār sandstone. Discovered in 1906-07 in so-called Hospital (monastery) west of Dhamēkh Stūpa 2′ 6″ below the surface.

B (*e*) 4.—Torso (ht. 10½″; width 6″) of statuette seated after the fashion of Kubēra (*Cf.* the long Gupta lintel D (*d*) 1). The left leg is laid flat on the ground, the right, which is broken off, was probably drawn up. Head and arms missing. Presumably a goblin (*yaksha*).

Chunār sandstone of reddish colour. Excavated in 1906-07 in so-called Hospital (monastery) west of Dhamēkh Stūpa 6′ below the surface.

---

[1] *Cf.* Vogel, *Mathurā Catalogue*, B 65 and C 2, 4, 5, 10, 11, etc.; and for a Sahribahlol group *A. S. R.*, 1906-07, p. 117, Pl. XXXII, *c*.

[2] *Ibid.*, 1907-08, p. 67, and Plate XIX, *d*.

B (*e*) 5.—Torso (ht. 9½″; width 6½″) of corpulent male figure. The head, arms and legs are broken off. There is a broad band on breast and a part of an elaborate necklace also remains. Chunār sandstone of pale buff colour. The style is similar to that of B (*e*) 4. Excavated in 1904-05 south-west of the Main Shrine.[1]

B (*e*) 6.—Slab (ht. 1′ 6″; width 2′ 2″) with group of three deities seated cross-legged side by side on conventional lotuses, all of which rise from the same root. The central figure is larger than the side ones, and the one at the proper left end is a female while the other two are males. In other respects they are identical, each having a plain circular halo and four arms. The lower hands are clasped before the breast, the other two hold a rosary (*akshamālā*) and a full-blown lotus flower respectively[2]. Their hair is done up in high top-knots. They wear *dhōtīs*, the upper half of the body being nude.

Under the lotus thrones are four miniature figures, two of which in the middle seem to uphold the central throne, the other two have hands joined in adoration. The back-slab is cut away from behind the lower part and at both sides of the central figure. The significance of this group of deities cannot be made out. Mr. Oertel proposed to identify them as the three-jewels (*triratna*) of the Buddhist church, [3] but this identification is untenable. On account of the conventional style and multiplicity of ornaments I assign the sculpture to the mediæval period.

Chunār sandstone. Unearthed in 1904-05 north-west of Jagat Singh Stūpa.[4] Pl. XIV, *b*.

B (*e*) 7.—Fragment (ht. 5¼″; width 8″) with similar group of three deities. The head of the central figure and the upper halves of the other two are broken off. Contemporaneous with B (*e*) 6 and made of the same kind of stone. Excavated in the same year north-east of Jagat Singh Stūpa.[5]

*B (*e*) 8.—Three fragments which fit together (ht. 1′ 2″; width 8″) of a relief with a group of three deities seated side by side similar to B (*e*) 6. The figure at the proper right end is fairly preserved, though the hands are damaged. The lower two hands were clasped in adoration in front of the breast. The upper ones must have held a rosary (*akshamālā*) and a lotus flower (*padma*). Around the head is a circular halo decorated with a lotus pattern. Of the remaining two figures only the lower halves survive, but there is no doubt that they were of the

---

[1] *A. S. R.*, 1904-05, p. 96, No. 148.
[2] It will be observed, that the attributes in the upper hands are those of Avalōkitēśvara.
[3] *A. S. R.*, 1904—5, p. 87.
[4] *Ibid.*, p. 95, No. 130.
[5] *Ibid.*, p. 98, No. 299.

same type as B (e) 6. The date of the sculpture is supplied by an inscription of two lines carved on the base and containing the Buddhist creed in characters of the 11th century A.D.

The material is a pale grey variety of Chunār stone. The fragment at the proper right end was discovered in 1907-08 in the area around the Jagat Singh Stūpa[1]; the middle fragment came to light in 1906-07 in the area west of the Main Shrine. The provenance of the third piece is not known.

*B (e) 9.—Fragment (ht. 5¼"; width 3") containing the figure of a four-armed deity seated cross-legged on a conventional lotus, with a pointed halo around the head. Lower hands joined in front of the breast. The upper hands are broken but must have held a rosary (*akshamālā*) and a lotus (*padma*) respectively. The fragment is evidently from the proper right end of a relief similar to B (e) 6-8. On the base is a fragmentary inscription *Ōṁ dēyadha*...... in characters of about the 11th century A.D. Made of the same kind of stone as B (e) 8. Discovered in 1906-07 in area to the east of the Main Shrine[2].

*B (e) 10.—Fragment (ht. 4¼"; width 5½") of sculpture similar to B (e) 6 containing the crossed legs of two of the three deities which composed the whole group. The figure at the proper right end is wanting. It was evidently a male figure and smaller than the one in the centre. On the top of the base beneath the central deity, is a kneeling figure in bold relief, probably meant for the donor and in front of it, a fragmentary inscription in characters of 11th century A.D. which runs :—

[*Dēyadharmmō=yaṁ para**]*mōpāsaka Ākshapaṭalika-śrī* ...... *suta* .... *sya*

" This is the pious gift of the supremely devoted, the son of the illustrious ...... the record-keeper ...."

The material of the relief is the blue stone of Gayā. It must, therefore, have been carved there. Find-spot not known.

B (e) 11.—Fragment (ht. 3¼"; width 3¾") with the lower half of a deity seated corss-legged on a lotus throne. It seems to be from the proper left end of a group of three deities similar to B (e) 6. Blue stone of Gayā. Nearly contemporaneous with B (e) 10.

Discovered in 1907-08 in the area on the north-east of the Dhamēkh Stūpa.[3]

B (e) 12.—Fragment (ht. 4"; width 2¾") with a part of a figure seated cross-legged on a lotus throne. The appearance of the fragment seems to show that it is from the middle of a group of three deities similar to B (e) 6.

---

[1] *A. S. R.*, 1907-08, p. 66, No. J. S. 1.
[2] *Ibid.*, 1906-07, p. 92, No. 38 and photo on Plate XXIII, 2.
[3] *Ibid.*, 1907-08, p. 62, No. K 4.

Blue stone of Gayā. Excavated in 1906-07 in area to the east of the Main Shrine.

B (e) 13.—Imperfect statuette (ht. 4½″) seated, apparently a goblin (*yaksha*) carved in the round with a prominent abdomen. Head and left arm broken off. The right hand was raised to the level of the breast. The upper body is bare and the legs clad in a lower garment. Gupta style. Chunār sandstone with traces of red paint. Excavated in one of the recent excavations.

B (e) 14.—Fragment (ht. 5¾″; width 7¼″) of a sculpture showing the heads of two Nāgas facing towards each other, perhaps a Nāga and a Nāgī. Each of them has a hood of three snake-heads over its head. At the proper left end of the piece is a headless male worshipper kneeling with folded hands in the attitude of adoration. Late Gupta style. Chunār sandstone. Found in 1907-08 in spoil earth near the Old Sculpture Shed.

B (e) 15.—Head (ht. 5″) of a demon (*rākshasa*) with a flat face and grinning mouth, his teeth being visible between the lips. The hair is straight and shoots out in a thick mass on the right side. Late Gupta period. Chunār sandstone of reddish colour. Discovered in 1906-07 in the monastery west of the Dhamēkh Stūpa, 3′ below the surface.

B (e) 16.—Fragment (ht. 9″; width 11″) with the head of a demon or *yaksha*. The mouth is open and the hair, which hangs down on either side, seemingly decked with jewels. The right hand is raised and so presumably was the left, which is broken off. Perhaps Gupta. Buff-coloured sandstone of Chunār. Found in 1904-05 north of the Main Shrine.[1]

B (e) 17.—Head (ht. 4″) of similar figure. Discovered in 1906-07 in the area to the east of the Main Shrine.

---

[1] *A. S. R.*, 1904-05, p. 97, No. 214.

B (*f*).—Images of goddesses and other female images.

B(*f*) 1.—Image (ht. 3′ 4″; width 1′ 3½″) of a goddess, probably Tārā—Bhṛikuṭī, standing to the front, in alto-relievo against a back-slab. The back-slab is rounded at the top and adorned along the margin with a scalloped and beaded border as in the Buddha images of the Gupta period.[1] The feet and right hand are wanting and the proper left side of the back-slab is much mutilated from the elbow of the figure upwards. The nose and lips are injured. The dress of the goddess seems to consist of a simple cloth of the type of *sāṛhī* which is indicated on the legs by raised lines and covers the whole of the upper body with the exception of the right arm. The ends of the garment falling over the left arm are carefully marked. The hair is, curiously enough, partly treated in short spiral curls similar to those of Buddha images with a fringe of ringlets along the forehead and the rest of the hair is done up in a roundish knot, while some locks are indicated on the left shoulder. An ornamental fillet with a crest in the middle adorns the forehead. The other ornaments are large circular ear-rings, a double necklace, a long string of beads, fastened between the breasts, richly studded armlets and bracelets and an elaborate girdle (*kāñchī*) consisting of five strings of beads which are secured in a large circular diamond in the centre.

The left hand of the goddess holds a water-pot (*tridaṇḍi-kamaṇḍalu*) on the hip and the right which is broken off was apparently stretched out in the gift-bestowing attitude (*varadamudrā*). It is for these two reasons that the image is identified as Tārā Bhṛikuṭī.[2]

The workmanship of the image is quite as good as that of B (*d*) 1. The material is Chunār sandstone of the same kind. It will be noticed that the breasts are made very large and the waist thin, from which it follows that the exaggerated female forms of mediæval sculpture were not altogether unknown in the Gupta period. This is the earliest representation of a goddess found at Sārnāth. Discovered in 1904-05 to the south of the Main Shrine.[3]

B (*f*) 2.—Image (ht. 4′ 8″; width of back-slab 2′ 2½″) of the goddess Tārā standing, facing, on a lotus in high relief and with the stone cut away at the back of the figure. The image is broken across the waist and a large piece is wanting in the proper left side of the back-slab. The nose and ears are damaged. The forearms are missing, but deep circular holes in the joints indicate that they were separate pieces joined to the image by metal rods. The right hand was apparently in the gift-bestowing attitude (*varadamudrā*). The left hand held a blue

---

[1] *Cf.* B (*b*) 6 above.

[2] *Cf.* Foucher, *l'Iconographie Bouddhique* 1905, p. 69.

[3] *A. S. R.*, 1904-05, p. 95, No. 139.

lotus of which the stem still remains in part. A similar plant rises at the proper right side.

In the way of dress the goddess wears presumably only a lower garment whereas the upper half of the body is bare. But she is lavishly adorned with ornaments which would throw useful light on the Indian jewellery of the mediæval period. The most elaborate ornament is the girdle (*kāñchī*). The head-dress consists of a five-peaked crown (*makuṭa*) set with jewels and pearls and held with a band resembling a garland of *mālatī* flowers. On the middle crest of the crown is a miniature headless figure of the Dhyānī-buddha Amōghasiddhi seated cross-legged with his right hand raised in the attitude of imparting security (*abhayamudrā*). The hair of the goddess is tied into a long thick knot behind the head, which may be seen above the right shoulder. The female attendant to the proper right of Tārā is Mārīchī, the goddess of Dawn without head and right arm. She is readily recognised by her usual attributes of a thunderbolt (*vajra*) held in front of her breast and an *aśōka* flower in the left hand. The figure on the other side of Tārā is the angry Ēkajaṭā the forehead marked with deep furrows, with a protruding abdomen (*lambōdarā*) and a loin cloth (perhaps a tiger's skin) on the thighs. The hands are broken but we may assume that they held a sword (*khaḍga*) and a skull.[1]

It is interesting to note that the sculpture is in perfect accord with the *sādhana*[2] and must have been carved under the supervision of an intelligent monk or a sculptor acquainted with the canon. The image affords also a typical specimen of feminine beauty, as conceived in the mediæval period of Indian art, which forms such a marked contrast to the simple and chaste style of the earlier periods. This is manifest in every part of the sculpture. The breasts are very large and prominent, the waist is inordinately thin (*tanumadhyamā*) and the posture exaggerated to a degree.

Made of Chunār sandstone. Discovered by Mr. Oertel in 1904-05 some distance to the north of the Dhamēkh Stūpa.[3] Pl. XIII, *a*.

B (*f*) 3.—Image (ht. 2′ 6″; width of back-slab 1′ 10″) standing with the right hip thrust out and upper body inclined to the left. Head, forearms and feet missing, also upper part of the back-slab. The right hand was apparently in the gift-bestowing attitude (*varadamudrā*), and the left held a flower of which the stem still remains. The image may perhaps be identified as Tārā. The attendant female figures, one

---

[1] With this sculpture may be compared another Sārnāth one sketched in Major Kittoe's Drawings, Vol. I, No. 113, Pl. 13. In this case, however, the figure on the right of Tārā is a repetition of herself.

[2] *Cf.* Foucher *l'Iconographie Bouddhique* 1905, p. 65, for Tārā; and pp. 75-76 for a *sādhana* of Ēkajaṭā. There is no separate image of the latter in the Museum.

[3] *A. S. R.*, 1904-05, p. 86, and photo on Pl. XXXI, *a*; also p. 95, No. 132.

on either side of her, are too much defaced to allow of identification.

The style of the sculpture is undoubtedly of the mediæval period. Its material is Chunār sandstone. It was formerly preserved in the Queen's College, and most probably originates from Sārnāth, although it is not sketched in Major Kittoe's Drawings.

B (*f*) 4.—Figure (ht. 2′ 7½″; width of back-slab 1′ 11″) of a goddess seated to proper right in Indian fashion with the right foot swung over the left thigh. The head, left arm and right forearm are broken off and the right leg is damaged below the knee. The latter was fastened to the waist by a broad band. The hair hangs down the back almost to the ground. She wears ornaments similar to those in B (*f*) 2. To the proper left of the goddess is a flower-stalk, but as the flower itself is broken off it does not help us to identify the image.

The style is of the late mediæval period. The sculpture was found in 1906-07 in the first outer court of the mediæval monastery I, close to the stair, 6′ below the surface.[1] I am inclined to think that it was placed at the entrance of the building just as river goddesses are in Brahmanical temples. This is borne out by the fact that another figure [B (*f*) 5] of the same style and size was found in the same year on the south of the same court.[2] Pl. XVI.

B (*f*) 5.—Figure (ht. 2′ 2½″; width at base 1′ 6″) similar in all respects to B (*f*) 4 which must have formed a pair with it. Head and left arm wanting. Back-slab broken off. Find-spot indicated under B (*f*) 4.

B (*f*) 6.—Figure (ht. 1′ 10″; width 1′ 4½″) of a goddess in alto-relievo projecting from a rectangular back-slab of the same type as B (*f*) 4 and 5 . Head, both arms and right leg broken off. Near her right shoulder is a miniature elephant in fragmentary condition apparently standing on a lotus. Traces of a similar figure exist on the other side. Is the goddess perhaps Śrī or Lakshmī ? The sculpture is made of Chunār sandstone but is much weather-stained. Discovered[3] in 1907-08 in the first outer court of mediæval monastery I.

B (*f*) 7.—Slab (ht. 1′ 10″; width 1′ 3½″) with a figure of Tārā seated in an easy attitude (*lalitāsana*) on a lotus throne with the right foot hanging down and placed on a smaller lotus. With the exception of the right forearm, which is damaged, the sculpture is in an excellent state of preservation. The goddess wears a lower garment and a number of ornaments, her hair being tied in a round knot behind the head. Her right hand is, as usual, in the gift-bestowing attitude (*varadamudrā*) and the flower in the left hand is undoubtedly a blue lotus (*nīlōtpala*).

---

[1] *A. S. R.*, 1906-07, p. 92, No. 46 and photo on Pl. XXVI, 4.
[2] *Ibid.*, No. 47.
[3] *Ibid.*, 1907-08, p. 49, " 18.

To her left, is a standing female figure with similar dress and ornaments and probably a repetition of herself. On the front of the base is another figure with an indistinct object, perhaps a flower or a thunderbolt (*vajra*) in the right raised hand and what seems to be an incense-burner in the left. This is probably a human worshipper. The back of the throne consists of a horizontal bar supported by a pair of pilasters with bracket-capitals and a pair of rampant leogryphs. Above its ends are *makara* heads emerging from foliage. Around the head of the goddess is a circular halo in the shape of a full-blown lotus flower, on either side of which projecting from a cloud is a flying celestial being shown in the act of showering flowers.

The sculpture seems to date from the late mediæval period. It is made of buff-coloured Chunār sandstone and was discovered in 1904-05 to the south-east of the Main Shrine[1]. Pl. XVII, *a*.

B (*f*) 8.—Bust (ht. 1′ 7″ ; width 1′ 3″) of Tārā in the form of Vajra-Tārā,[2] carved in the round with four heads (*chaturvaktrā*) and eight arms (*ashṭabāhu*). All the left arms are missing, but portions of those to the right side are extent. The goddess wears an elaborate torque with a large jewel in the middle and a necklace consisting of three strings of beads. On the fore-head of the front lead is a square diamond-shaped mark probably meant for the third eye of the goddess (*trinētrā*). The hair is arranged in a conical knot visible between the four heads. The head-dresses are profusely adorned with strings of pearls and in the head-dress of the principal head are introduced four miniature figures of Dhyāni-buddhas, namely, two of Akshōbhya in the earth-touching attitude, one of Amitābha in meditation and the fourth in the attitude of teaching, presumably Vairōchana. The head on the back has only one figure of Amōghasiddhi in the attitude of protection (*abhayamudrā*). There are no Dhyāni-buddhas on the other two heads.

The image belongs to the mediæval period, as is sufficiently evident from the abnormally large breasts and the elaborate ornaments. The material is a grey kind of fine-grained stone. The sculpture was excavated in 1904-05 south-west of the Main Shrine[3].

B (*f*) 9.—Slab (ht. 1′ 1″ ; width 10″) with a four-armed figure of a goddess seated cross-legged on a lotus throne. The figure is broken into two across the waist, and a triangular piece is missing at the proper right upper corner. The goddess wears an under-garment and a scarf (*uttarīya*) over her shoulders, the ornaments on her person being a jewelled fillet over her fore-head, ear-rings, a torque, a necklace, armlets, bracelets, a girdle and anklets. The lower right hand

---

[1] *A. S. R.*, 1904-05, p. 85, and photo on Pl. XXX, *d* ; also p. 95, No. 131.
[2] For the *sādhana* of this goddess *cf.* Foucher, *l'Iconographie Bouddhique* 1905, p. 70.
[3] *A. S. R.*, 1904-05, p. 88 and photo in Fig. 11 on p. 87 ; also p. 95, No. 133.

is in the gift-bestowing attitude (*varadamudrā*); the upper right hand is missing. The lower left hand holds a stalk with two full-blown lotus flowers and the upper left some flaming object. The goddess seems to be Tārā, though none of the *sādhanas* mentions the flaming object which the present figure holds in one of the hands.

The style is of the mediæval period. Chunār sandstone of pink colour. Excavated in 1906-07 in the area to the east of the Main Shrine.[1]

*B (*f*) 10.—Fragmentary relief (ht. 11″; width 1′) with the lower half of the figure of a goddess, presumably Tārā, standing on a lotus. Her right hand was apparently stretched downwards in the gift-bestowing attitude (*varadamudrā*) and the left must have held a blue lotus of which only the stalk remains in part. To her right is a miniature figure seated holding a thunderbolt in front of its breast and a bell under its left armpit. This is evidently Vajrasattva. To the left of the goddess is a standing figure holding a sword in its right hand. Its left hand is missing but the figure was probably Ekajaṭā. The attendant on the right side of the goddess should have been Mārichī and the identification of the principal image cannot, therefore, be considered as certain. Along the proper right side of the sculpture is the beginning of the Buddhist creed in Nāgarī characters of about the 9th century A.D.

Chunār sandstone. Unearthed in 1904-05 in the area east of the Main Shrine.[2]

B (*f*) 11.—Slab (ht. 1′ 5½″; width 10½″) with pointed top bearing a standing figure of a goddess, probably Tārā. Her right leg is injured and both forearms missing. Her right hand was apparently held down in gift-bestowing attitude (*varadamudrā*); while the left hand holds a blue lotus (*utpala*) which is intact. The goddess wears a high three-peaked tiara on her head, a garment around her loins and a scarf (*uttarīya*) thrown on her arms. The left hip juts out. Ornaments as usual. The style is of the mediæval period. Buff-coloured sandstone of Chunār. Discovered in 1904-05 north-west of Jagat Singh Stūpa.[3]

*B (*f*) 12.—Slab (ht. 1′ 3″; width 7″) with figure of Tārā standing facing. Feet broken off. Rest in excellent preservation. The hair is fastened in a flat knot on the top of the head. Around the loins is a well-draped garment, but there is no scarf. The image is adorned with a necklace, a garland (*hāra*), armlets and bracelets. The right hand is in the gift-bestowing attitude (*varadamudrā*) and the left holds the stem of a blue lotus (*nīlōtpala*). The head is surrounded by a horse-shoe-shaped halo with a lotus pattern roughly carved on it.

---

[1] For upper half see *A. S. R.*, 1906-07, p. 92, No. 45.
[2] *A. S. R.*, 1904-05, p. 96, No. 151.
[3] *Ibid.*, p. 95, No. 127.

On the left flank of the slab is the Buddhist creed in nine lines in Nāgarī characters of about the 8th century A.D. and on the back of the sculpture another inscription of five lines which is obliterated.

Chunār sandstone of buff colour. Excavated in 1904-05, south-west of Jagat Singh Stūpa.[1]

B (*f*) 13.—Fragmentary sculpture (ht. 1′ 8″; width 10½″) with the figure of a female deity standing with the left hip thrust out. Legs below knees wanting. From the similarity of the dress and the ornaments to those in B (*f*) 11, it may be inferred that the sculpture is Buddhist, though what goddess is represented here cannot be ascertained. The left hand which was raised to the level of the shoulder is broken off and the object in the right hand is not recognizable. To the right of the goddess is the bust of a female worshipper with hands joined before her breast.

Weather-stained. Chunār sandstone. Major Kittoe has left a sketch of the sculpture in his volume of Drawings where he calls it a Brahmanical Śakti.[2] Unfortunately he has not indicated the provenance.

B (*f*) 14.—Fragmentary slab (ht. 1′ 1″; width 11½″) with the bust of a four-armed goddess, perhaps Tārā. Her right upper hand, left upper arm and lower forearm are broken off. The lower right hand was apparently in the gift-bestowing attitude (*varadamudrā*). There are traces of a scarf (*uttarīya*) on the lower arms and ornaments as usual. Circular halo with a lotus pattern around the head. In the proper right upper corner is a miniature *stūpa*.

To judge from style early mediæval period. Made of Chunār sandstone. Found lying outside the Śvētāmbara Jaina temple near Sārnāth Railway Station.

*B (*f*) 15.—Figure (ht. 1′ 1½″; width 8½″) of a goddess presumably Tārā seated in easy posture (*lalitāsana*) on an inverted lotus flower with her right leg placed on the ground. The right arm is broken off with the exception of the hand which is held in front of the knee in the gift-bestowing attitude (*varadamudrā*). The left fore-arm is broken off and the left leg damaged. The remaining portion is broken into three pieces. The hair of the goddess is gathered in a knot above her right shoulder. She wears a tiara and ornaments. Traces of a scarf on the left arm. On the right and left side of the goddess are a male and a female figure kneeling, which probably represent the donor and his wife.

On the projecting portion of the base is an inscription of four lines in characters of the 11th century A.D. It was first deciphered by

---

[1] *A. S. R.*, 1904-05, p. 95, No. 136; and p. 104, inscription No. XXXVIII.
[2] Vol. I, No. 90 on Pl. 81.

Dr. Konow and consists of the Buddhist creed followed by *Dēya-dharmmō=yam=upāsaka-Mābhūkasya* (?) "This (is) the pious gift of the layman Mâbhūka[1] (?)"

All the three pieces of the sculpture came to light in 1906-07, the lower portion and detached knee in the area to the east of the Main Shrine and the bust to the south of the first outer court of mediæval monastery I, 4′ below the surface.[2]

B (*f*) 16.—Slab (ht. 10½″; width 7″) with a figure of the goddess Tārā seated in easy attitude (*lalitāsana*) on a lotus throne. Her right knee and abdomen are chipped off and the sculpture broken into two above the waist. The image wears a lower garment, a scarf and the usual ornaments. The right hand which is broken off rested on the knee in the gift-bestowing attitude (*varadamudrā*); the left hand holds a blue lotus (*nīlōtpala*). In front of the head-dress is the Dhyāni-buddha Amitābha in the attitude of meditation (*dhyānamudrā*). To the proper right of the goddess is carved a miniature *stūpa* in relief and to her proper left, a female figurine kneeling, presumably the donor. The style is of the late mediæval period. Chunār stone of pale buff colour. Discovered in 1907-08 on the approach to the Main Shrine from east, 6′ below the surface.[3]

B (*f*) 17.—Lower half (ht. 7½″; width 9″) of a figure of a goddess seated in easy attitude (*lalitāsana*) on a lotus throne. She is adorned with an elaborate girdle (*kāñchī*) and anklets. Unlike other images in this attitude, it is noticed that in the present sculpture it is the left leg which hangs down and not the right. The hands which would supply the means of identification are missing. Beneath the throne in the stalks of a lotus is a goose or duck on a leaf, a device which also occurs among the carvings on the Dhamēkh Stūpa. On the top of the base near the left foot is a figurine of a worshipper with hands joined before the breast.

Made of pale buff stone from Chunār and excavated in 1904-05 to the south of the Main Shrine.[4]

B (*f*) 18.—Fragmentary slab (ht. 11½″; width 9″) with the bust of a goddess, in which to judge from the figurine of the Dhyāni-buddha Amitābha (*Amitābha—mukuṭāṁ*) carved above her head, we must recognise the Red Tārā. The right hand, which is broken off, must have been in the attitude of granting security. The flower in the left hand is, in accordance with the canon, a red lotus (*raktōtpala*) and not a

---

1 *A. S. R.*, 1906-07, p. 100, No. XII.

2 For lower half *cf. ibid.*, p. 92, No. 41.

3 *Ibid.*, 1907-08, p. 67, U 25.

4 *A. S. R.*, 1904-05, p. 85; and p. 95, No. 129. *Cf.* also Pl. XXX, *d*, middle figure; but it must be noticed that the upper part (B (*f*) 18 in this catalogue) evidently does not blong to this sculpture as will be apparent from the photo itself.

blue lotus (*nīlōtpala*). The goddess has an elaborate diadem and ornaments. Near her left hand is a miniature *stūpa* in relief. The style is of the late mediæval period. Pale buff stone of Chunār. Found in the same locality as B (*f*) 17.[1]

B (*f*) 19.—Fragmentary sculpture (ht. 2′ 1″; width 1′ 3″) with a headless figure of Vasundhārā, the goddess of abundance, standing facing on a semi-circular lotus throne. The upper part of the slab and the forearms of the goddess are missing. The sculpture was also fractured across at the ankles and has been re-fixed. The ornaments are numerous but the dress consists, as usual, of a lower garment which completely covers the entire lower part of the body, and a scarf over the arms, the upper half of the body remaining bare. The right hand was apparently in the gift-bestowing attitude and from the stalk beneath the left hand it seems probable that this hand held an ear of corn (*dhānyamañjarī*), the ordinary emblem (*chihna*) of this goddess. The other attribute, the vase of treasure (*ratnaghaṭa*) is represented by a pair of vases one under each foot. According to the *sādhana* both these objects should be in the left hand (*dhānyamañjarī-nānā-ratnavarshaghaṭa-vāmahastā*[2]). On either side of the goddess is a repetition of herself. These smaller figures exhibit the same dress and ornaments as the central one, but the one on the proper right holds the ear of corn in the right hand and the treasure-vase in the left. (*Cf.* the group B (*e*) 1.)

On grounds of style the sculpture may be assigned to the late mediæval period. The material is pale buff stone of Chunār. Discovered in 1904-05.[3] Pl, XV, *b*.

*B (*f*) 20.—Fragmentary sculpture (ht. 1′ 3½″; width 1′ 3½″) with the lower half of an image of Vasundhārā seated in easy attitude (*lalitāsana*) on a lotus throne. The right foot is placed on an inverted vase which rests on a lotus flower. This vase is apparently a treasure vase, the attribute of Vasundhārā. The line of seven similar vases lying upside down on the top of the base was added manifestly by the sculptor to emphasise the idea of Vasundhārā's control over the wealth of the world. The breakage in the right knee indicates that the right hand was laid on it in the gift-bestowing attitude (*varadamudrā*). To the right and left of the goddess we notice two kneeling worshippers, a male and a female, respectively. These must be the donor and his wife.

On the front of the base was an epigraph of which only three characters of about the 11th century A.D. remain. The image is made of the same kind of stone as B (*f*) 19 but is badly weather-stained. It

[1] *Cf.* remarks under B (*f*) 17.

[2] Foucher, *l'Iconographie Bouddhique*, 1905, p. 85.

[3] *A. S. R.*, 1904-05, p. 95, No. 121; also p. 86 and photo in Pl. XXX, *a*.

belonged to the Queen's College collection but it is evident that it originated from Sārnāth.

B (*f*) 21.—Fragment (ht. 6"; width 8") similar to B (*f*) 20. There are, however, two inverted vases under the right foot and the row on the top of the base consists of five vases only. The male worshipper is also absent. Made of the same kind of stone as B (*f*) 19 with which it is co-eval. Excavated in 1906-07 in the area to the east of the Main Shrine.

B (*f*) 22.—Relief (ht. 11½"; width 8½") with the upper right corner broken off, bearing a figure of a four-armed goddess seated in Indian style with her feet crossed on a jar guarded by a snake on either side. Her lower hands are placed on the knees but are damaged. The upper right arm is missing and the upper left hand holds a vase, presumably the vase of treasure (*bhadraghaṭa*). We may therefore assume that the goddess here represented is Vasundharā. In the upper proper left corner there is probably an ear of corn (*dhānyamañjarī*) the second attribute of this goddess. Along the proper left side of the relief, is a row of four snake heads with a miniature figure of Gaṇēśa above. There were similar snake heads on the other side. The presence of Gaṇēśa on a Buddhist sculpture is noteworthy.

The style belongs to the mediæval period. Made of Chunār sandstone and discovered in 1907-08 in area on north side of Dhamēkh Stūpa.[1]

*B (*f*) 23.—Slab (ht. 1' 10"; width 1' ½") with a figure of the goddess Mārīchī standing in the attitude of an archer (*pratyālīḍha-padā*). The lower half of her body is clad in a garment which is fastened to the waist with a plain girdle (*kāñchī*). The upper half of the body is naked with the exception of a scarf (*uttarīya*) thrown over two of her arms. She has three faces and six arms. The central face is larger than the other two and the proper left face is that of a boar. The uppermost right hand is damaged, but it is evident that it held a thunderbolt (*vajra*). The second hand holds an arrow which is somewhat damaged and the third or lowest has an elephant goad (*aṅkuśa*). Of the left hands, the uppermost is broken, but a reference to other known images of this goddess leaves no doubt that it must have held an *aśōka* flower. In the next lower hand on this side we notice a bow (*chāpa*), whereas the third is held in front of the breast with the forefinger raised in a menacing attitude (*tarjanīdhara*). The central head wears a conical mitre on front of which in accordance with the canon is represented a figure of the Dhyāni-buddha Vairōchana in the attitude of expounding the law (*vyākhyānamudrā*).

On the front of the base, carved in relief, is a row of seven boars, the central one facing to the front, the rest running in opposite

[1] *A. S. R.*, 1907-08, p. 61, ¶ 123 and photo on Pl. XIX, c.

directions, which draw the car of Mārīchī (*saptaśūkara-rathārūḍhā*ḥ). The corpulent female (?) figure riding astride on the central boar is evidently the charioteer, though we do not find her referred to in the *sādhana.*[1] There is no further indication of the car itself. Its wheels are clearly carved in the next sculpture (B (*l*) 24). The kneeling figurines, a male and a female, at the proper right end of the base below the boars must be the donor and his wife. The remaining space of the base is taken up by an inscription which is now altogether obliterated. The style is clearly mediæval and the material reddish sandstone of Chunār.

It is interesting to compare this sculpture with three complete images of Mārīchī, all orginating from Magadha and now preserved. one in the Lucknow Museum, the other two in the Indian Museum., Calcutta.[2] The former has been discussed in detail by Dr. Vogel.[3] The goddess is a personification of the morning dawn. Her three faces have probably some connection with certain three-faced images of Vishṇu found in Kashmir and Kuḷū. The idea of the car drawn by seven pigs is analogous to that of the Sun's (Sūrya's) chariot drawn by seven horses, just as the anonymous charioteer is manifestly to be traced to Aruṇa, who drives the car of Sūrya.

The Sārnāth image under review differs from the three Magadha representations quoted above in several points. Whereas all those have eight arms, the former has only six. Nor does it show the head of a demon (Rāhu) which figures on all those either above or beneath the central boar, nor the repetitions of the goddess one in each of the four corners of the sculpture (*dēvīchatushṭaya-parivṛitā*).

The sculpture was discovered in 1904-05.[4] Pl. XVII, *b.*

B (*l*) 24.—Fragment (ht. 1′ 4½″; width 1′ 5½″) representing the base of a similar Mārīchī statue. The goddess herself is missing, but her chariot is quite intact. The female charioteer who sits astride on the demon is placed on the flat top of the base in the centre. She holds a thunderbolt (*vajra*) in her right hand. Her head and breast are broken. The wheels of the car are shown one on each side of the base. The execution of the seven pigs on front of the base, though in bold relief, is very inartistic and gives the impression of so many mice. To the proper left of the charioteer is a figure with a single boar's face, a bow (*chāpa*) in left hand and in her right an arrow which she draws out of her quiver. The lower part of a similar figure remains on the other side of the charioteer. That these are

---

[1] Foucher, *l'Iconographie Bouddhique* 1905, p. 92.

[2] *Ibid.*, p. 92 and fig. 7; and edition of 1900, p. 149, fig. 27. Dr. Vogel draws attention to a fragmentary image of Mārīchi in the Kangra Valley (*A. S. R.*, 1903-04, p. 218) and *A. S. R., V.*, p. 178, Pl. XLII.

[3] *A. S. R.*, 1903-04, pp. 217-218 and Pl. LXII, 4.

[4] *Ibid.*, 1904-05, p. 87, and photo on Pl. XXX, *d*, 3; also p. 95, No. 126.

merely repetitions of the goddess herself is plain from the Magadha images referred to under B (*f*) 23, in which we find such figures in the corners of the sculptures.

The style of the sculpture is of the late mediæval period. The material is grey-coloured stone of Chunār. Excavated in 1904-05 south-east of the Main Shrine.[1]

B (*f*) 25.—Bust (ht. 1′ 6¼″; width 1′ 2½″) of a goddess. Her hair is gathered in a round knot behind her head and she wears a jewelled fillet over her forehead, large ear-rings and a necklace. Made of Chunār sandstone in mediæval style. It was formerly preserved in the Queen's College.[2]

B (*f*) 26.—Bust (ht. 8½″; width 1′ 6″) of a goddess with eight arms lavishly adorned with ornaments. The forearms and hands are broken off, for which reason the image cannot be identified. The style seems to be that of the late mediæval period and the sculpture is made of grey-coloured stone from Chunār. Broken into three fragments which were all found in 1904-05.[3]

B (*f*) 27.—Slab (ht. 1′ 2″; width 9¾″) with a figure of Sarasvatī[4] the goddess of learning, seated in easy attitude, on a cushion (?) and playing on a lute (Sanskrit *vīṇā*). She has the same dress and ornaments as the other goddesses described above. Above her head is foliage of a tree. To her proper right is a jar standing upside down. The sculpture seems to date from the early mediæval period. It is made of reddish Chunār sandstone and was discovered in 1904-05.

B (*f*) 28.—Base (ht. 6″; width 10″) of a sculpture representing the lower part of a goddess, possibly Tārā seated on a lotus in 'easy attitude' (*lalitāsana*). Her right hand is stretched out in front of the knee in the gift-bestowing attitude (*varadamudrā*). Left arm missing. Mediæval style. Chunār sandstone of reddish colour. Discovered in 1907-08 on the approach to the Main Shrine from east, 8′ below the surface.[5]

B (*f*) 29.—Fragment (ht. 5″; width 8½″) of similar figure. To the proper left of the goddess is a miniature figure seated in Indian style. Found in 1906-07 in entrance chamber of the mediæval monastery I, 2′ 3″ below surface.

B (*f*) 30.—Figure (ht. 5½″; width 7″) of a goddess, presumably Tārā if we may judge from the position of the right hand on the knee.

---

[1] *A. S. R.*, 1904-05, p. 88, Pl. XXXI, *c*, 1 and p. 95, No. 144.

[2] Four such busts from Sārnāth are sketched in Major Kittoe's Drawings, Vol. I, No. 83, Pl. 31.

[3] *A. S. R.*, 1904-05, Nos. 145, 247, and 315 on pp. 95, 97 and 99, respectively.

[4] *Ibid.*, p. 86 and fig. 9; also p. 95, No. 134. Dr. Vogel points out that the only other representation of this goddess found on a Buddhist site is the one from Gandhāra first identified by Grünwedel (*Buddhistische Kunst*, 1900, p. 101).

[5] *A. S. R.*, 1907-08, p. 67, U 66.

Body and head missing. She is ornamented with a girdle and anklets and has part of the stalk of a flower to her proper left. Mediæval style. Same kind of stone as in B (*f*) 28. Excavated in 1907-08 on the approach to the Main Shrine from east 7′ below the surface.

B (*f*) 31.—Fragment (ht. 5¾″; width 8″) with the legs of a goddess seated cross-legged on a lotus throne. Right knee broken. Girdle and anklets. To the proper right of the goddess, traces of a worshipper, and to her left, stalk of lotus. Late mediæval. Grey-coloured stone. Excavated in 1904-05 north of Jagat Singh Stūpa.[1]

B (*f*) 32—Figure (ht. 6″; width 7″) of Tārā (?) seated in 'easy attitude' (*lalitāsana*) on a lotus; her bust, head and arms are broken off. Right hand laid against the knee in gift-bestowing attitude (*varadamudrā*). She is ornamented with the usual ornaments. On either side of the goddess is the stalk of a lotus. Mediæval style. Chunār sandstone of reddish colour. Found in the western precinct of monastery I, near the surface.[2]

B (*f*) 33.—Fragment (ht. 7″; width 5½″) representing the left leg of a goddess seated on a lotus. Mediæval style. Pale buff stone of Chunār. Excavated in 1907-08 in the second outer court of mediæval monastery I, 1′ below the surface.

B (*f*) 34.—Fragment (ht. 6½″; width 5″) similar to B (*f*) 33. Find-spot not known.

B (*f*) 35.—Fragment (ht. 9″; width 6½″) with the bust of a goddess. Right arm broken off. Left hand held a blue lotus (*nīlōtpala*). In the goddess we may therefore recognise Tārā. The style belongs to the late mediæval period. Chunār stone of pale buff colour. Excavated in 1709-08 among the group of *stūpas* on the north side of Dhamēkh Stūpa.[3]

B (*f*) 36.—Fragment (ht. 3¼″; width 4½″) with a bust of Tārā much defaced. Her right hand which is missing was apparently held down in the gift-bestowing attitude. Left hand holds a blue lotus (*nīlōtpala*). Chunār stone, badly weather-stained. Dates from the mediæval period. Find-spot not known.

B (*f*) 37.—Fragment (ht. 4½″; width 3½″) representing a blue lotus flower (*nīlōtpala*) which may be from the left side of a Tārā image. Mediæval style. Grey stone presumably from Chunār. Unearthed in 1904-05 to the east of the Main Shrine.[4]

---

[1] *A. S. R.*, 1904-05, p. 97, No. 227, where it is described as a Buddha image.
[2] *Ibid.*, 1907-08, p. 47, a 1.
[3] *Ibid.*, p. 61, 107
[4] *Ibid.*, 194-05, p. 98, No. 307.

B (*f*) 38.—Fragment (ht. 10½"; width 5¼") bearing a female figure standing, which from its close affinity to the left hand attendant of Tārā in B (*f*) 2, I identify as Ekajaṭā. This is borne out by the fact that the fragment is evidently broken from the proper left side of a bigger sculpture. The hands are broken. The right hand presumably held a sword (*khaḍga*). The feet are missing. To the right of Ekajaṭā, we observe the stalk of a flower which must have been a blue lotus, the well-known emblem of Tārā. The miniature figure squatting at the left foot of the goddess must be a worshipper. Mediæval style. Chunār sandstone of reddish colour. Discovered in 1907-08 in the area to the north of the Dhamēkh Stūpa.[1]

B (*f*) 39.—Fragment (ht. 10½"; width 6") from the proper left upper corner of a bigger sculpture, representing a figure of Mārīchī seated cross-legged on a lotus which rests on the top of a pilaster. The goddess holds a thunderbolt (*vajra*) in the right hand. The left hand held an *aśōka* flower but it is broken off. To her proper right is the arched top of a niche which contained the main figure which presumably was Tārā. This is favoured by the blue lotus flower projecting from the pilaster on which the goddess sits. Mediæval style. Grey stone. Discovered in 1904-05 to the south-east of the Main Shrine.[2]

B (*f*) 40.—Fragment (ht. 10½"; width 7") from the proper right upper corner of a bigger sculpture similar to B (*f*) 39. The goddess seated on the capital of the pilaster has a flower in her left hand which cannot be identified. The right hand may have held a sword over the head. High head-dress and usual ornaments. Made of the same kind of stone and found in the same locality as B (*f*) 39.

B (*f*) 41.—Fragment (ht. 7"; width 4") from the proper right side of a bigger sculpture bearing a figure of a goddess, presumably Tārā, standing inclined to the right. Her feet are missing. Her right hand is disposed in front of her breast (*vikāśayantī*); while the left holds a flower. High head-dress and ornaments. To her proper left is the stalk of a flower which must have been held in the right hand of the main figure. Mediæval style. Chunār sandstone. Excavated in 1904-05 north-west of Jagat Singh *stūpa*.[3]

B (*f*) 42.—Fragment (ht. 9½"; width 7") representing the torso of a goddess wearing a well-draped *dhōtī* and attended by a female attendant who may have held an umbrella over her head. The head, right hand and feet of the goddess are wanting. She is standing in the position of an archer (*pratyālīḍha-padā*), with her left hand

---

[1] *A. S. R.*, 1907-08, p. 61, η 16.
[2] *Ibid.*, 1904-05, p. 96, No. 154.
[3] *Ibid.*, p. 98, No. 295.

disposed before her breast in menace, and may be identified as Mārīchī or Vajravārāhī.

Mediæval style. Pale buff stone of Chunār. Unearthed in 1904-05.[1]

B (*f*) 43.—Fragment (ht. 9″; width 8½″) showing the bust of a standing figure of a goddess holding an *aśōka* (?) flower in her left hand; presumably Mārīchī. Her right hand is broken off. The mark on her forehead is probably meant for the third eye. Dress and ornaments as usual. Grey-coloured stone. Mediæval style. Excavated in 1906-07 in the area to the east of the Main Shrine.

B (*f*) 44.—Fragment (ht. 8¾″; width 6½″) with the bust of a similar goddess. But the flower seems to be a blue lotus (*nīlōtpala*) in which case we might recognize, in the figure, the goddess Tārā. The third eye is indicated between her brows. Lavishly adorned with ornaments. Chunār stone of reddish colour. Mediaeval style. Unearthed in 1904-05 east of the chapel on the south-west of the Main Shrine.[2]

B (*f*) 45.—Fragment (ht. 5½″; width 5½″) showing the bust of a goddess with a figurine of the Dhyāni-buddha Amitābha in her head-dress, and therefore some form of Tārā. Both arms broken off. The flower in her left hand seems to be a red lotus instead of a blue lotus. Made of blue stone of Gayā, in mediæval style. Discovered in 1907-08 on the approach to the Main Shrine from the east 8′ below the surface.[3]

B (*f*) 46.—Breast and left arm (ht. 4½″; width 4½″) of a goddess holding in her left hand what seems to be an ear of corn. The identification is uncertain. Mediæval style. Pale buff stone of Chunār. Excavated in 1904-05 to the south of the Main Shrine.[4]

B (*f*) 47.—Fragment (ht. 3½″; width 3″) bearing the bust of a four-armed goddess, holding a sword in her upper right hand behind her head and an object, resembling a dagger, in the second hand. The left arms are broken off. She wears a high head-dress and usual ornaments. It is possibly Prajñāpāramitā though it must be admitted that the attitude of expounding the law (*vyākhyānamudrā*) is absent. Late mediæval. Chunār stone of buff colour. Unearthed in 1907-08 in the area to the north of the Main Shrine, 8′ below the surface.[5]

B (*f*) 48.—Bust (ht. 6½″; width 5″) of a three-faced goddess, profusely adorned with ornaments, presumably Ūshṇīshavijayā. The mark

---

[1] *A. S. R.*, 1904-05, p. 97, No. 226.
[2] *Ibid.*, p. 95, No. 122.
[3] *Ibid.*, 1907-08, p. 67, U 68.
[4] *Ibid.*, 1904-05, p. 99, No. 368.
[5] *Ibid.*, 1907-08, p. 72, 7 25.

on the forehead of her middle head is meant for her third eye. The Dhyāni-buddha Amitābha is seated on the front of her headdress.

There seem to have been only six arms, though the *sādhanas* attribute eight arms to this goddess. This reduction must have been due to the sculptor. But why he placed a figure of Amitābha in the headdress instead of on one of the right hands cannot be easily explained[1].

Mediæval style. Grey-coloured stone. Unearthed in 1906-07 in the so-called hospital (really a monastery) to the west of the Dhamēkh *stūpa*, 4′ below the surface.

B (*f*) 49.—Head and right arm (ht. 4″; width 3½″) of a goddess. Her right hand holds a pointed object overhead. Mediæval style. Chunār sandstone. Excavated in the western precinct of the mediæval monastery I, 5′ below the surface.

B (*f*) 50.—Fragment (ht. 7″; width 4″) showing the left arm of a female holding a child, perhaps from an image of Hāritī, the goddess of plenty. Mediæval. Chunār stone of reddish colour. Unearthed in 1904-05 to the north-west of the Jagat Singh *stūpa*.[2]

B (*f*) 51.—Bust (ht. 10″; width 9″) of a goddess, the head and right forearm being broken off. She wears the usual ornaments. Her left hand holds an ear of corn (*dhānyamañjarī*) while the right was apparently laid in the gift-bestowing attitude (*varadamudrā*). The image must therefore be one of Vasundhārā, the Buddhist goddess of wealth. Late mediæval. Chunār sandstone of reddish colour. Excavated in 1904-05.[3]

B (*f*) 52.—Bust (ht. 11″; width 10″) without head and arms, of a goddess carved in the round. She wears a necklace and a garland of beads, their tassels being indicated on the back. Date uncertain. Made of white stone of Makrānā in Jodhpur state. Excavated in 1906-07 or 1907-08 in the monastery to the west of the Dhamēkh *stūpa* 2½′ below the surface.

B (*f*) 53.—Torso (ht. 11½″; width 7″) of a goddess standing facing. Her head, right arm and feet are missing. Her lower part is clad in a well-draped *dhōtī*. There are traces of a scarf (*uttarīya*) on her left arm. She wears the usual ornaments. Pale buff stone of Chunār. Mediæval style. Find-spot not known.

B (*f*) 54.—Bust (ht. 7″; width 8″) of a goddess without head and arms. She wears a broad torque and a garland (*hāra*) hanging between her breasts. Mediæval. Chunār sandstone. Unearthed in 1906-07 in the area to the east of the Main Shrine.

---

[1] *Cf.* Foucher, *l'Iconographie Bouddhique*, 1905, p. 86 and fig. 6.

[2] *A. S. R.*, 1904-05, p. 98, No. 300.

[3] *Ibid.*, p. 95, No. 123.

B (*f*) 55.—Legs (ht. 9½"; width 5") broken into two pieces, of a goddess standing holding an uncertain object in front of her thighs. Her feet are missing. Mediæval. Chunār sandstone.

Unearthed in 1904-05 in the area around the Main Shrine and Jagat Singh Stūpa.[1]

B (*f*) 56.—Fragment (ht. 11½"; width 7") of an image of a goddess from the waist to the knees, profusely adorned in mediæval style. It is made of grey-coloured stone. Excavated in 1904-05 to the west of the Main Shrine.[2]

B (*f*) 57.—Waist and thighs (ht. 9"; width 7½") of an image of a goddess with an elaborate girdle and pendant chains. Mediæval style. Chunār stone of greyish colour. Excavated in 1904-05.[3]

B(*f*) 58.—Fragment (ht. 11½"; width 7') with the bust of a goddess, of which the left arm and the right forearm are missing. Halo around the head. Plain ornaments. The right hand seems to have been in the gift-bestowing attitude (*varadamudrā*). Mediæval style. Chunār sandstone of pink colour. Unearthed in 1907-08 in the area to the north of the Main Shrine 2' below the surface.[4]

B (*f*) 59.—Torso (ht. 8½"; width 6½") of a goddess much defaced. The left hand is raised to the shoulder. Mediæval. Chunār sandstone. Unearthed in 1907-08 in the 2nd outer court of the mediæval monastery I, 2' below the surface.[5]

B (*f*) 60.—Breast (ht. 7½"; width 6½") of a goddess lavishly adorned with ornaments. Mediæval. Chunār sandstone. Excavated in 1907-08 in the first outer court of mediæval monastery I.[6]

B (*f*) 61.—Waist and legs (ht. 7½"; width 3½") of a statuette of a goddess profusely adorned. Mediæval. Grey stone. Unearthed in 1907-08 in the 2nd outer court of monastery I.

B (*f*) 62.—Fragment (ht. 6¾"; width 5¼") showing the lower half of a goddess standing with a portion of a female attendant to her left holding a thunderbolt (*vajra* ?) in her right hand. The latter goddess is presumably Mārīchī, the central figure may therefore have been Tārā. Mediæval. Chunār stone of buff colour. Unearthed in 1907-08 in the area on the north of the Dhamēkh *stūpa*.[7]

B (*f*) 63.—Lower part (ht. 8"; width 6") without feet of a standing figure of a female deity, wearing a well-draped *dhōtī*. Mediæval.

---

[1] *A. S. R.*, 1904-05, p. 96, No. 184 and p. 99, No. 328.
[2] *Ibid.*, p. 95, No. 146.
[3] *Ibid.*, No. 135.
[4] *Ibid.*, 1907-08, p. 72, β 7.
[5] *Ibid.*, p. 52, ι 4.
[6] *Ibid.*, p. 49, η 24.
[7] *Ibid.*, p. 61, γ 97.

Chunār sandstone. Excavated in 1907-08 in the area on the north of the Main Shrine, 7′ below the surface.[1]

B (*f*) 64.—Legs without feet (ht. 6″; width 3½″) of a goddess. Her right hand rests on the right hip. Mediæval. Chunār sandstone. Unearthed in 1904-05 between the Jagat Singh *stūpa* and the Main Shrine.[2]

B (*f*) 65.—Waist and thighs (ht. 4½″; width 2½″) of a statuette of a goddess in mediæval style and Chunār sandstone. Found in the same locality as B (*f*) 64.[3]

B (*f*) 66.—Fragment (ht. 5″; width 4½″) representing the waist of a statuette of a goddess carved in the round. Grey stone. Mediæval. Find-spot not known.

B (*f*) 67.—Bust without head and arms (ht. 5″; width 5½″) of a statuette of a goddess. Much chipped. Find-spot not known.

B (*f*) 68.—Fragment (ht. 5″; width 5½″) similar to B (*f*) 67. Grey stone. Unearthed in 1906-07 in mediæval monastery I, 3′ below the surface.

B (*f*) 69.—Fragment (ht. 4¾″; width 3¾″) with the legs of a female figure. Mediæval. Chunār sandstone. Excavated in 1906-07 in the monastery to the west of the Dhamēkh *stūpa* 2′ 9″ below the surface.

B (*f*) 70.—Fragment (ht. 9½″; width 6½″) with portions of two female figures standing side by side wearing well-draped lower garments. Bodies chipped. Traces of red paint. Mediæval. Chunār sandstone of light colour. Excavated in 1904-05.[4]

B (*f*) 71.—Head (ht. 7½″; width 10″) of a goddess wearing an ornamental diadem adorned with strings of pearls. Her hair is gathered in a cylindrical mass to the proper left side. She wears large circular ear-rings which are broken. Folds of flesh on the neck. Mediæval style. Grey-coloured stone. Excavated in 1907-08 in the area on the north of the Dhamēkh *stūpa*.[5]

B (*f*) 72.—Head (ht. 6″; width 8″) with three faces, the left one being one of a boar, which must have belonged to a statuette of Mārīchī, the goddess of the rising sun. All three heads have lavishly adorned head-dresses and on the top of the central one we notice the lower half of a seated Dhyāni-buddha who must have been Vairōchana in the teaching attitude (*vyākhyānamudrā*). Mediæval style. Greenish stone. Excavated in 1907-08 in the second outer court of the mediæval monastery I.[6]

---

1 *A. S. R.*, 1907-08, p. 68, η 33 in f. n. 3.
2 *Ibid.*, 1904-05, p. 99, No. 320.
3 *Ibid.*, No. 322.
4 *Ibid.*, p. 96, No. 176.
5 *Ibid.*, 1907-08, p. 61, η 128.
6 *Ibid.*, p. 52, η 10.

B (*f*) 73.—Head (ht. 9¼″; width 8″) of a goddess wearing a high tiara and ear-rings. Nose damaged. Mediæval style. Chunār sandstone of buff colour. Discovered in 1904-05 to the south-east of the Jagat Singh Stūpa.[1]

B (*f*) 74.—Head (ht. 8½″; width 5″) of a goddess wearing a high diadem richly adorned with strings of pearls. Third eye marked on the forehead. Mediæval style. Chunār sandstone of reddish colour. Excavated in 1906-07 or 1907-08 outside the south-east corner of the mediæval monastery I, 3′ below the surface.

B (*f*) 75.—Head (ht. 8½″; width 5″) of a goddess with a similar diadem. Much defaced. Chunār sandstone of reddish hue. Found in the same locality.

B (*f*) 76.—Head (ht. 8½″; width 5″) of a goddess adorned with strings of pearls and a diadem which is elaborated with a figure of the Dhyāni-buddha Amitābha. The ears are damaged and the face much defaced. Mediæval style. Chunār sandstone of reddish hue. Excavated in 1906-07 in monastery I, 6′ below the surface.

B (*f*) 77.—Head (ht. 6½″; width 5″) of a goddess with the hair gathered in a round mass at the back and tied with a fillet over the forehead. Large ear-rings. Mediæval style. Chunār sandstone of buff colour. Excavated in 1904-05 to the south of the Main Shrine.[2]

B (*f*) 78.—Head (ht. 6″; width 4″) of a goddess with the hair treated in the same way as in B (*f*) 77. Much defaced. Chunār sandstone. Mediæval style. Found in 1906-07 in monastery I.

B (*f*) 79.—Head (ht. 6¼″; width 4″) with the hair gracefully waved back. The right ear is missing and the nose injured. The style seems to belong to the mediæval period. Chunār sandstone of buff colour. Excavated in 1904-05.[3]

B (*f*) 80.—Fragment (ht. 9″; width 7″) with the head of a goddess, presumably Tārā, ornamented with strings of pearls and a miniature figure of the Dhyāni-buddha Amitābha. The circular mark on the forehead probably indicates the third eye. The right ear is broken off, the left adorned with a circular ear-ring. Mediæval style. Pale buff stone of Chunār. Excavated in 1907-08 in the area on the north side of the Dhamēkh Stūpa.[4]

B (*f*) 81.—Fragment (ht. 8″; width 10½″) representing the head of a goddess with the hair gathered up in a disc-like mass and surrounded by a halo with a lotus pattern. A string of beads adorns her forehead.

---

1 *A. S. R.*, 1904-05, p. 97, No. 211.

2 *Ibid*, 1904-05, p. 99, No. 368.

3 *Ibid.*, 1904-05, p. 99, No. 366.

4 *Ibid.*, 1907-08, p. 50, *n* 98.

Mediæval style. Chunār sandstone of buff colour. Excavated in 1904-05 to the south of the Main Shrine.[1]

B (*f*) 82.—Head (ht. 6″; width 4½″) of a goddess with the hair tied up in a lofty knot. The chin is broken off and the ears and the nose are damaged. Mediæval style. Chunār sandstone of buff colour. Unearthed in 1907-08 in the area on the north of the Main Shrine 5′ below the surface.

B (*f*) 83.—Fragment (ht. 5″; width 4″) of the head of a goddess with a low head-dress and a circular mark on the forehead. Chunār sandstone of buff colour. Mediæval style. Excavated in 1906-07 in the mediæval monastery I, 9′ below the surface.

B (*f*) 84.—Fragment (ht. 4½″; width 3¾″) of the face of a goddess with the third eye indicated on the forehead. Mediæval style. Chunār stone of buff colour. Found in 1907-08 in the first outer court of the mediæval monastery I.

B (*f*) 85.—Head (ht. 4″; width 4″) of a goddess, with large ear-rings and a circular mark on the forehead. Pale buff stone of Chunār. Mediæval style. Discovered in 1907-08 on the approach to the Main Shrine from the east 3′ below the surface.

B (*f*) 86.—Head (ht. 4″; width 2¾″) of a goddess with the hair gathered in a circular mass at the back. Mediæval style and Chunār sandstone of buff colour. Unearthed in 1907-08 in the area on the north of the Dhamēkh Stūpa.[2]

B (*f*) 87.—Bust (ht. 6″; width 4″) of a goddess without arms. Circular ear-rings. Mediæval style. Pink-coloured stone of Chunār. Found in 1907-08 in the trench on the south of the 2nd outer court of the mediæval monastery I.

B (*f*) 88.—Bust (ht. 5½″; width 3½″) of a goddess wearing a tiara, a necklace and ear-rings. Mediæval style. Chunār sandstone. Excavated in 1906-07 in the area on the east of the Main Shrine.

B (*f*) 89.—Fragment (ht. 3½″; width 3″) of a female head. Chunār sandstone. Discovered in 1906-07 in the mediæval monastery I, 6′ below the surface.

B (*f*) 90.—Fragment (ht. 3¾″; width 3″) bearing the head of a goddess wearing a fillet overhead and ear-rings, and surrounded by a beaded halo of Magadha type. The face is broken off. At the top of the fragment is a grotesque head of a lion (*kīrtimukha*). The style seems to belong to the late mediæval period. Made of blue stone of Gayâ and unearthed in 1907-08 in the 1st outer court of the mediæval monastery I.[3]

---

[1] *A. S. R.*, 1904-05, p. 97, No. 202.

[2] *Ibid.*, 1907-08, p. 61, η 162.

[3] *Ibid.*, p. 49, η 192.

B (*f*) 91.—Fragment (ht. 8″; width 7½″) with the four right arms of an eight-armed goddess. The hands and attributes in them are missing and the identity of the goddess cannot be determined. Each arm is adorned with armlets and bracelets. The forearms are detached. The style is mediæval and the material grey stone of Chunār. Excavated in 1904-05 to south of the Main Shrine.[1]

B (*f*) 92.—Fragment (ht. 5″; width 2″) bearing five left arms of a goddess. Each hand is holding what seems to be a plate containing sweets. Mediæval style. Blue stone of Gayā. Find-spot not known.

B (*f*) 93.—Hand (length 11″) of a goddess finely executed and adorned with finger-rings. It holds an object resembling a thunderbolt (*vajra*), and belonged presumably to a statuette of Mārīchī. Grey stone of Chunār. Mediæval style. Found in the monastery to the west of the Dhamēkh Stūpa, 4′ below the surface.[2]

B (*f*) 94.—Left hand (length 4½″) of a goddess holding the stalk of a flower, and adorned with rings and a bracelet. The execution and stone are similar to those of B (*f*) 93. Found in the 2nd outer court of the mediæval monastery I, 11′ below the surface.

B (*f*) 95.—Hand (length 3″) of a goddess holding the stalk of a lotus. It is much defaced and bears traces of a bracelet. Grey-coloured stone. Mediæval style. Discovered in 1906-07 in the 1st outer court of monastery I, near the stair, 2′ below the surface.

B (*f*) 96.—Hand (length 4½″) of a goddess holding the stalk of a lotus and adorned with a bracelet and finger-rings. It is similar in the style of execution to B (*f*) 93 and is made of the same kind of stone. Unearthed in 1904-05 near the Jagat Singh *stūpa*.[3]

B (*f*) 97.—Forearm and part of hand (length 6″) of a goddess wearing a bracelet. Grey-coloured stone. Mediæval style. Found in the same locality[4] as B (*f*) 96.

B (*f*) 98.—Hand (length 3¼″) of a goddess resting against a flower, and made of the same kind of stone as B (*f*) 97 and in similar style. Excavated in 1906-07 in the area on the west of the Main Shrine.

B (*f*) 99.—Hand (length 3″; width 4″) of a goddess adorned with finger-rings and holding a lotus-stalk. Similar in style and stone to B (*f*) 93. Unearthed in 1904-05 in the area around the Jagat Singh *stūpa* and the Main Shrine.[5]

B (*f*) 100.—Fore-arm (length 4½″) of a goddess ornamented with a bracelet. It is made of a grey-coloured stone and is finely executed. Found in the same locality[6] as B (*f*) 99.

---

[1] *A. S. R.*, 1904-05, p. 97, No. 248.
[2] *Ibid.*, 1906-07, p. 94, No. 65.
[3] *Ibid.*, 1904-05, p. 99, No. 340.
[4] *Ibid.*, No. 348.
[5] *Ibid.*, No. 364.
[6] *Ibid.*, p. 99, No. 350.

B (*f*) 101.—Fragmentary left arm (ht. 4¼″; width 4½″) of a goddess bent at the elbow, adorned with an armlet and a remnant of a lotus-stalk which was twined round it. Fine mediæval style. Same kind of stone as in B (*f*) 100. Find-spot not known.

B (*f*) 102.—Forearm (length 3½″) of a goddess wearing a bracelet. Grey-coloured stone. Mediæval work. Discovered in 1906-07 in the area on the east of the Main Shrine.

B (*f*) 103.—Fragment (length 3½″; width 2¼″) of a palm of a goddess similar in style and material to B (*f*) 102. Find-spot not known.

B (*f*) 104.—Fragment (length 5¼″; width 1¾″) representing a hand and wrist of a goddess, ornamented with a bracelet. The fingers are broken off. Mediæval style. Chunār sandstone with traces of red paint. Unearthed in 1904-05 in the area around the Jagat Singh Stūpa and the Main Shrine.[1]

B (*f*) 105.—Fragment of the right arm (length 3¾″; width 3″) of a goddess, ornamented with an armlet. Grey-coloured stone. Mediæval style. Discovered in 1906-07 in the area on the east of the Main Shrine.

B (*f*) 106.—Hand (length 6″; width 2½″), probably left, of a goddess holding the stalk of a lotus and ornamented with a bracelet. Chunār sandstone of buff colour. Mediæval work. Find-spot not known.

B (*f*) 107.—Hand (length 4½″; width 4½″), probably left, of a goddess, adorned with a bracelet and holding a lotus-stalk.

Mediæval. Chunār sandstone of buff colour. Found in 1907-08 probably in the 1st outer court of the mediaeval monastery I.

B(*f*) 108.—Hand (length 4″; width 1¾″) holding a lotus-stalk and adorned with a bracelet. Mediæval. Chunār stone of buff colour. Find-spot not known.

B (*f*) 109.—Hand (length 6″; width 2¼″) of a goddess lavishly adorned with ornaments and holding an uncertain object. Mediæval work. Chunār sandstone of buff colour. Excavated in 1907-08 on the approach to the Main Shrine from the east, 8′ below the surface.

B(*f*) 110.—Fragment (length 4½″; width 3½″) of a hand of a goddess adorned with ornaments, which must have held a bowl or a similar object. Mediæval. Chunār sandstone of reddish colour. Unearthed in the area around the Jagat Singh Stūpa and the Main Shrine.[2]

B (*f*) 111.—Fragment (length 5½″; width 2½″) of the palm of a hand of a goddess with a large circular mark in the middle. Mediæval. Buff-coloured stone of Chunār. Found in the same locality.[3]

---

[1] *A. S. R.*, 1904-05, p. 99, No. 327.
[2] *Ibid.*, p. 99, No. 334.
[3] *Ibid.*, No. 330.

B (*f*) 112.—Fragmentary hand (length 3"; width 2½") of a goddess which must have held the stalk of a lotus. Mediæval style. Chunār sandstone. Unearthed in 1906-07 in monastery I.

B (*f*) 113.—Hand (length 5") of a goddess which was excavated at Sārnāth by Professor F. E. Hall. It was presented to the Lucknow Provincial Museum by the Principal of the Queen's College in December 1903 and returned to the Sārnāth Museum at the instance of Dr. Vogel in 1911. Professor Hall describes it as follows :—

" Alto-relievo fragment; sandstone, 5 inches long, a female right hand holding a custard apple, armlet bordered above with kawris and below with gems cut in facets, and kawris alternately; phalanges of the fingers not marked, but running into curves; ring on the little finger."[1] Mediæval style, very fine.

B (*f*) 114.—Left hand (length 4½") of a goddess holding a custard apple. Mediæval. Sandstone of Chunār. Unearthed in 1906-07 in the court of mediæval monastery I, near the well, 2½' below the surface of the mound.

B (*f*) 115.—Hand (length 6"), probably right, of a goddess wearing a bracelet. It held an uncertain object. Mediæval style. Buff-coloured sandstone of Chunār. Unearthed in 1904-05 in the area around the Jagat Singh *stūpa* and the Main Shrine.[2]

B (*f*) 116.—Forearm (length 5") of a goddess adorned with a bracelet. Mediæval epoch. Chunār sandstone. Excavated in 1906-07 to the south of the 1st outer court of mediæval monastery I, 3' below the surface.

B (*f*) 117.—Fragment (length 4½") similar to B (*f*) 116. Excavated in 1906-07 in the mediæval monastery I, 6' below the surface.

B (*f*) 118.—Forearm (length 4½") of a goddess. Mediaeval. Chunār sandstone. Unearthed in 1906-07 near stūpa No. 21 to the north-west of the Main Shrine.

B (*f*) 119.—Left hand and fore-arm (length 6½") of a goddess with a bracelet, which seems to have been held up in the attitude of granting protection. Mediæval epoch. Chunār sandstone. Find-spot not known.

B (*f*) 120.—Fragment (length 3¾") of an arm of a goddess. Chunār sandstone. Mediæval style. Excavated in 1907-08 in the 2nd outer court of mediæval monastery I, 4' below the surface.

B (*f*) 121.—Fragment (ht. 3½"; width 4") representing a part of the left leg of a goddess who must have been seated in easy attitude

---

[1] *J. A. S. B.*, Vol. XXV (1856), pp. 399-400, No. 7; and *A. S. R.*, 1903-04, p. 225, No. 15.

[2] *A. S. R.*, 1904-05, p. 99, No. 345.

(*lalitāsana*) or cross-legged. Draped closely. Tassel of beaded girdle on thigh. Grey stone. Mediæval epoch. Find-spot not known.

B (*f*) 122.—Breast (ht. 4¼") of a goddess, ornamented with a garland of beads (*hāra*). Chunār sandstone. Mediæval style. Unearthed in 1906-07 in the 1st outer court of mediæval monastery I, 6' below the surface.

B (*f*) 123.—Fragment (ht. 3¾") similar to B (*f*) 122. Find-spot not known.

B (*f*) 124.—Fragment (ht. 1¼") representing a highly ornamented ear-ring of a goddess. Grey stone. Mediaeval. Find-spot not known.

B (*f*) 125.—Fragment (ht. 3"; width 7½") representing the feet of a goddess on a lotus throne. The feet are adorned with anklets. Mediæval style. Chunār sandstone. Unearthed in 1904-05 between the Jagat Singh Stūpa and the Main Shrine.[1]

B (*f*) 126.—Fragment (ht. 4"; width 10½") with the feet of a goddess on a lotus. Chunār sandstone. Mediæval. Unearthed in 1906-07 in mediæval monastery I.

B (*f*) 127.—Base (ht. 11"; width 11") of a sculpture with the feet of a goddess standing on a lotus. To her proper right is a kneeling female worshipper, and behind her a standing male presenting an uncertain object. Mediæval. Chunār sandstone. Found in 1907-08 on the approach to the Main Shrine from the east, 6' below the surface.

B(*f*) 128.—Lower part (ht. 11"; width 9") of a sculpture with the legs of a goddess—presumably Tārā—standing. To her right we notice Mārīchī holding an *aśōka* flower in her left hand and what must have been a thunderbolt (*vajra*) in the other. To her left is represented a male figure with a moustache and a nimbate head. His breast is encircled by a snake. This figure is presumably Hayagrīva.

Mediæval style. Pale buff stone of Chunār. Excavated in 1906-07 in the area to the north-west of the Main Shrine.

B (*f*) 129.—Base (ht. 7"; width 1' 2") with the feet of a standing goddess remaining on it. To her right and left we notice a part of a lotus stalk. The front of the fragment is ornamented with scroll work. Mediæval style. Pale buff stone. Excavated in 1904-05.[2]

B (*f*) 130.—Head (ht. 5") of a goddess. Mediæval style. Chunār sandstone. Discovered in 1907-08 to the south of the 2nd gateway of monastery I.

B (*f*) 131.—Left leg (ht. 4½") of a figure of a goddess which must have been seated in easy attitude (*lalitāsana*). Mediæval. Bluish stone. Discovered in one of the recent excavations.

---

[1] *A. S. R.*, 1904-05, p. 99, No. 316.

[2] *Ibid.*, p. 95, No. 138.

B (*f*) 132.—Part (ht. 4¼") of a leg of a goddess in the same kind of stone and coeval with B (*f*) 131. Unearthed in 1907-08 to the east of monastery IV.

B (*f*) 133.—Fragment (ht. 6") with the three heads of a Mārīchī figure. The left head is, as usual, that of a boar. The other two are much damaged. The central head has a high head-dress resembling a *stūpa* in form. Mediaeval style. Chunār sandstone. Discovered in one of the recent excavations.

B (*g*).—Jaina Images.

B (*g*) 1.—Relief (ht. 9½"; width 8½") with a standing Jaina saint or Tīrthaṅkara. His right hand, which is broken off, was held in the gift-bestowing attitude while the left holds the hem of the garment to the level of the shoulder. Hair arranged in schematic curls. Umbrella over his head. Feet broken off. Found in 1904-05.

B (*g*) 2.—Relief (ht. 6½"; width 6½") with the bust of a Jaina saint or Tīrthaṅkara who must have been sitting in meditation. Umbrella over his head and a miniature *stūpa* on either side of it. Mediæval. Found in 1904-05.

B (*g*) 3.—Relief (ht. 6"; width 8¾") with the head of a Jaina saint or Tīrthaṅkara under a *pīpal* tree. Hair in formal curls. Mediæval. Buff stone of Chunār. Found in 1904-05.

B (*g*) 4.—Head (ht. 5") of a Jaina saint or Tīrthaṅkara canopied by a seven-hooded snake. Buff stone. Mediæval. Found in 1906-07 in monstery I, 3' below the surface.

B (*g*) 5.—Bust (ht. 4") of a Jaina saint or Tīrthaṅkara canopied by the hoods of a snake. Unfinished. Buff stone. Mediæval. Found in 1906-07 east of *stūpa* No. 22.

B (*g*) 6.—Head (ht. 3½") of a Jaina saint or Tīrthaṅkara with the hair treated in formal curls. Mediæval. Buff stone. Found in 1906-07 in monastery I, 4' below the surface.

B (*h*).—Brahmanical Sculptures.

B (*h*) 1.—Dr. Marshall describes this sculpture as a "colossal figure of Śiva[1] in relief, measuring 12′ 1¼″ high × 3′ 11″ broad and 1′ 10″ thick. The god is represented spearing his adversary, Tripura (?) on his trident, which he holds with one l. and one r. hand. A second r. hand holds a sword; a third holds two arrows and a fourth his *ḍamaru*, while the fifth grasps an uncertain object which is broken at the upper end. The second l. hand holds the mace, adorned with a skull (*khāṭvāṅga*); the third grasps a shield, the handle of which is visible; the fourth supports the bowl for catching the blood of Śiva's enemy; and fifth holds a bow of double flexure (*pināka*).

The demon Tripura grasps a sword in his right hand; his left forearm is broken. Beneath Śiva's left foot is another figure fighting upwards, with sword in right hand and shield in left and by the side of the last mentioned, a buffalo (?bull) head looking upwards.

The carving of this sculpture was never finished and the ornaments which the god wears on his body and upper part of legs are incomplete.

The image was found in the débris above monastery IV * * at a height of about 8′ above the floor level. Near it were two other large stones, one a rough block, 9′ 5″ long, the other seemingly intended to be used as a pedestal for the statue." Pl. XVIII.

B (*h*) 2.—Slab (ht. 1′ 10″; width 1′) with a figure of Śiva engaged in a wild dance (*tāṇḍava*). His head and feet are broken off, so also the right hand which was thrown up. He wears a long garland of human skulls (*muṇḍa-mālā*) and holds a trident (*triśūla*) in the left hand. The prongs of the trident are broken off. To the right of Śiva, in a shallow niche is a kneeling male figure presenting a jar (?) and to the left, in a similar niche, a female figure kneeling and presenting a flower.

Mediaeval style. Unearthed in 1907-08 in the 2nd outer court of monastery I.

B (*h*) 3.—Slab (ht. 2′; width 1′ 1″) with a representation of the Brahmanical trinity, the Trimūrtti (Brahmā, Vishṇu and Mahēśa) with three faces and four arms. The upper right hand held a trident (*triśūla*), the emblem of Śiva, from which we may gather that the artist by putting the attribute of Śiva in this hand evidently sought to emphasise the supremacy of this deity. The female figure whom the upper left arm of the god clasps must therefore be identified as Pārvatī. The emblem of Brahmā, the Generator, which is a water-pot or *kamaṇḍalu*, is naturally enough placed in the lower left hand. The lower right hand probably held a conch (*śaṅkha*), the attribute of Vishṇu, the Preserver.

---

[1] *A. S. R.*, 1907-08, p. 52. f 138.

The multiplicity of ornaments with which both figures are adorned as well as the exaggerated pose of the goddess assigns the sculpture to the late mediæval period.

Discovered in the 2nd outer court of monastery I, 9′ below the surface. [1]

B (*h*) 4.—Slab (ht. 1′ 3½″; width 9½″) with an unfinished figure of Śiva dancing on a demon lying full length on the base. Śiva wears, as usual, a garland of human skulls (*muṇḍa-mālā*) and holds a club capped with an unfinished human head (*khaṭvāṅga*) in his left hand. He has two long tushes and the dot on his forehead is evidently meant for his third eye (*Tryambaka*). Late mediæval. Excavated in 1906-07 in *stūpa* No. 40 to the north-east of the Main Shrine. [2]

B (*h*) 5.—Slab (ht. 1′ 7″; width 1′ 10″) with a seated figure of Gaṇēśa. It seems to have had four arms. The sculpture is too much defaced to allow of dating. Greenish stone of Chunār. Excavated in 1904-05. [3]

B (*h*) 6.—Top (ht. 5½″) of a club (*khaṭvāṅga*) [4] encircled with a serpent, which must have been held in the left hand of an image of Śiva. Mediæval. Excavated in 1906-07 in the area on the east of the Main Shrine.

B (*h*) 7.—Fragment (ht. 4½″; width 5″) with a couchant bull (Nandi), vehicle of Śiva. The figure of Mahādēva himself is missing with the exception of his left hand. Mediæval. Unearthed in 1906-07 in monastery I, 7′ below the surface.

B (*h*) 8.—Fragment (ht. 6″; width 11″) of a pedestal with a relief which possibly represents the fight of Vishṇu and Gaṇēśa when Śiva maliciously cut off his son's head. Pārvatī's austere penance compelled him to agree to restore it. The severed head of Gaṇēśa could not be found and it was determined to fix on his trunk the head of the first animal that should make its appearance, which happened to be an elephant with but one tusk.

In the relief we see Gaṇēśa standing by the side of Śiva's bull. Of the elephant only two legs remain. The feet of a female and a standing male are also extant.

Buff-coloured sandstone of Chunār. Excavated in 1904-05. [5]

B (*h*) 9.—Fragment (ht. 6″; width 6½″) with the feet of a goddess perhaps Durgā trampling on an uncertain object. Mediæval. Unearthed in 1907-08 in the area to the north of the Dhamēkh Stūpa.

---

[1] *A. S. R.*, 1907-08, p. 52, 104.

[2] *Ibid.*, 1906-07, p. 81, and Pl. XXIII, 11. Dr. Konow did not then agree to this identification of the sculpture but a comparison with B (*h*) 2 will show that it can be nothing else.

[3] *Ibid.*, 1904-05, p. 96, No. 153.

[4] *Cf.* B (*h*) 1.

[5] *A. S. R.*, 1904-05, p. 95, No. 140.

B (*h*) 10.—Fragmentary sculpture (ht. 10″; width 1′ 4½″) showing a female figure which seems to have been standing in the attitude of an archer (*pratyālīḍha-padā*). She holds a mace adorned with a pair of human skulls (*khaṭvāṅga*) on her left shoulder. Her hair falls down her back and the lower part of her body below the waist, and the hands are missing. Presumably Durgā. Chunār sandstone. Mediæval style. Excavated in 1907-08 in the trench on north-west of Dhamēkh Stūpa.[1]

B (*h*) 11.—Hand holding a club (ht. 8″) encircled with a snake similar to that in B (*h*) 10. The hand is ornamented with a bracelet and finger-rings. Mediæval. Unearthed in 1906-07 to the north of the Aśōka Column.

B (*h*) 12.—Fragmentary plaque (ht. 3½″; width 3″) showing Durgā piercing the buffalo demon (Mahishāsura) with her trident (*triśūla*) which she holds in her right hand. With her left hand she holds the tail of the demon. Late mediaeval style. Excavated in 1907-08 in the trench crossing the south boundary wall of monastery I, north of the Main Shrine, 6′ below the surface.[2]

B (*h*) 13.—Human skull (ht. 5¾″) which manifestly formed the top of Śiva's club (*khaṭvāṅga*). Mediæval. Discovered in 1907-08 in the western precinct of monastery I, 5′ below the surface.[3]

B (*h*) 14.—Figure of Bhairava (ht. 4½″; width 2½″) riding a dog to proper right. He wears a high-peaked head-dress and holds a mace in the right hand and a bowl in the left. Late mediæval. Excavated in 1907-08 in the first outer court of monastery I.[4]

B (*h*) 15.—Fragment (ht. 3″; width 4½″) of a pedestal with the feet only of the main figure remaining. The standing bull to the proper right would indicate that the relief represented Śiva In front of the bull is a kneeling figure, presumably the donor of the sculpture. Mediæval style. Unearthed in 1907-08 in the trench around the south-west angle of monastery I, 6′ below the surface.

B (*h*) 16.—Fragment (ht. 3″; width 3″) of a relief of doubtful character. Mediæval. Discovered in 1907-08 in the trench crossing the south boundary wall of monastery I, north of the Main Shrine, 6′ below the surface.

B (*h*) 17.—Figure (ht. 1′ 2½″; width 5½″) representing the dwarf incarnation (*vāmanāvatāra*) of Vishṇu, when he humbled the pride of the demon Bali. The deity wears a circular halo around his head and holds a staff in his left hand. The face is cut off and the sculpture was

---

[1] *A. S. R.*, 1907-08, p. 62, K. 6.
[2] *Ibid.*, 1907-08, p. 72, β-58.
[3] *Ibid.*, 1907-08, p. 48, α 13 and Fig. 3.
[4] *Ibid.*, p. 49, η 190 and Fig. 5.

not finished. Mediæval. Chunār sandstone. Excavated in 1906-07 in the monastery west of Dhamēkh Stūpa, 5′ 6″ below the surface.

B (*h*) 18.—Hand (ht. 9½″) holding a conch (*śaṅkha*) which must have belonged to a colossal statue of Vishṇu. Chunār sandstone. Excavated in 1904-05 to the north-west of the Jagat Singh Stūpa.[1]

B (*h*) 19.—Female figure (ht. 8″) without feet, standing holding a fly-whisk (*chāmara*) in the right hand. The figure is evidently from the proper left side of an image of Vishṇu whose left hand remains on her head. Mediæval. Chunār sandstone. Discovered in 1906-07 in the monastery to the west of the Dhamēkh *stūpa*, 2′ 3″ below the surface.

B (*h*) 20.—Votive plaque (ht. 4½″; width 2½″) showing a four-armed figure of Vishṇu standing facing. He wears a high head-dress, a sacred thread, a *dhōtī* and a garland (*banamālā*). The right hands hold a lotus and a conch respectively, and the left hands a mace and a wheel. Mughal period. Chunār sandstone. Unearthed in 1907-08 in the trench to the north-east of the Dhamēkh *stūpa*.[2]

B (*h*) 21.—Votive plaque (ht. 3½″; width 2″) similar to B (*h*) 20. The arrangement of the objects in the hands of the deity is different. Grey sandstone. Excavated in one of the recent diggings.

B (*h*) 22.—Votive plaque (ht. 5½″; width 3½″) showing a four-armed male figure wearing a turban. The upper hands hold the ends of what must be a garland (*banamālā*). The lower hands hang down and rest on uncertain objects. The figure presumably represents Vishṇu. Mughal period. Reddish sandstone of Chunār. Excavated in the trench to the south of monastery II, 7′ below the surface.

B (*h*) 23.—Votive plaque (ht. 6″; width 3″) similar to B (*h*) 22. Discovered in 1906-07 in the area to the west of the Main Shrine.

B (*h*) 24.—Votive plaque (ht. 5½″; width 3½″) similar to B (*h*) 21 and 22. Discovered in 1907-08 in the trench crossing the south boundary wall of monastery I, 9′ below the surface.

B (*h*) 25.—Votive plaque (ht. 3½″; width 2″) with a four-armed female figure standing facing. Her lower hands hang down and rest on uncertain objects. The objects in the upper hands cannot be identified. Style similar to that of B (*h*) 22—24. Find-spot not known.

---

[1] *A. S. R.*, 1904-05, p. 97, No. 237.
[2] *Ibid.*, 1907-08, p. 62, K. 2.

B (i)—Fragments of Miscellaneous and Doubtful Sculptures.

Mediæval.[1]

*B (i) 1.—Dr. Vogel describes this fragment in the following terms :—"A curious fragment (ht. 1′ ½″ ; width 1′ 5½″) of sandstone from Sārnāth must likewise belong to the expiring days of Indian Buddhism. This is evident from the character of the inscription (Pl. LXIII, No. 6) which consists of two lines of Nāgarī of 23 and 28·5 cm. It contains only the Buddhist creed. We are thus justified in attributing it to the Bauddha religion with which the sculpture itself does not show any connection. Over the inscription there is a nude male figure, of which the head is broken, stretched out on its back, between two kneeling figures much injured, of which that to the proper left is a woman. The other seems to be identical. They wear a girdle and a necklace. Both seem to hold a garment as an offering. Possibly the fragment belongs to a Tantric sculpture, the lying figure representing a corpse on which the deity stands. It cannot have any relation to Buddha's *parinirvāṇa*."[2] The sculpture is sketched in Major Kittoe's Mss. Drawings[3], where we learn that it originates from Sārnāth. The fragment is one of the thirteen sculptures which were returned from the Lucknow Provincial Museum.

B (i) 2.—Figure (ht. 1′ 8⅜″ ; width 9⅞″) of a male wearing an ornamental diadem, and other ornaments. The left leg, which is damaged, was bent upwards and as the hands hold a garland, the figure may be assumed to represent a celestial (*dēva*). But it did not form part of a bigger sculpture for it is clear from the stone projecting from the back of the figure that it was meant to be fixed in a wall independently. From the multiplicity of ornaments and the style of execution, the figure is assignable to the mediæval period. Grey-coloured sandstone of Chunār. It was formerly preserved in the Queen's College and probably originates from Sārnāth.

B (i) 3.—Fragment (ht. 1′ 4½″ ; width 1′ 8″) representing an oval-shaped halo cut in lotus pattern. On either side of it, in a cloud, carved in relief is a celestial figure carrying a garland, one end of which is held in a hand of his consort, who is perched on his legs and whom he embraces with one arm. Their legs are displayed in the usual position. The space between them just above the top of the halo is occupied by a miniature figure of Dhyānibuddha Vairōchana seated cross-legged in the attitude of expounding the law (*vyākhyānamudrā*). We may consequently assume that the fragment under review belonged to an

---

[1] The sculptures described under this head are all of the mediæval period and made of buff-coloured Chunār sandstone unless specified to the contrary.

[2] *A. S. R.*, 1903-04, p. 224 and Fig. 3 on the same page.

[3] Vol. I, No. 20, Pl. 9.

image of Mārichī or a Bōdhisattva. Belonged to the Queen's College Collection.

B (*i*) 4.—Fragment (ht. 1′ 4½″; width 10½″) showing a celestial figure flying in a cloud, carved in relief and carrying a garland. His hair is treated after the style of a female. Below him is carved a crocodile (*makara*) raising a conventional lotus. Unearthed in 1904-05 to the north-east of the Jagat Singh Stūpa.[1]

B (*i*) 5.—Fragment (ht. 11″; width 9″) from the proper right upper corner of a bigger sculpture, bearing a part of an ornamental halo and a celestial carrying a garland between both hands while his consort or a nymph (*apsaras*) sits in the same position on his right leg. These figures are placed on the capital of a pilaster in relief. The style belongs to the late mediæval period. Unearthed in 1904-05.[2]

B (*i*) 6.—Fragment (ht. 1′; width 7½″) from the proper left side of a bigger sculpture, showing a figurine kneeling on a lotus (?) in adoration (*namaskāra*). Its head is broken off. Mediæval style. Buff-coloured sandstone of Chunār. Unearthed in 1904-05.[3]

B (*i*) 7.—Fragment (ht. 5″; width 3¼″) similar to B (*i*) 6 but smaller. Unearthed in 1904-05.[4]

B (*i*) 8.—Fragment of a halo (ht. 9½″; width 5¼″) which seems to have been oval. Around the margin, it is adorned with a rope pattern and floral scroll. Unearthed in 1904-05.[5]

B (*i*) 9.—Fragment (ht. 6″; width 10¼″) of a circular halo cut in lotus pattern. Excavated in the area on the east of the Main Shrine in 1906-07.

B (*i*) 10.—Fragment (ht. 7½″) from the proper left upper corner of a sculpture bearing a part of a fretted halo with a celestial (*dēva*) wearing a high diadem and carrying a garland. His hair is gathered in a mass behind the head. The style is distinctly mediæval. Discovered in 1907-08 in the area to the north-east of the Dhamēkh Stūpa.[6]

B (*i*) 11.—Fragment (ht. 6″; width 5″) from the proper left upper corner of a sculpture. To the proper left we notice a miniature *stūpa* in relief and projecting from what seems to have been a flower or a similar object. To the proper right are the traces of a halo adorned with a lotus pattern.

Excavated in 1906-07, east of *stūpa* No. 22 in the area to the west of the Main Shrine.

---

[1] *A. S. R.*, 1904-05, p. 97, No. 238.
[2] *Ibid.*, p. 96, No. 155.
[3] *Ibid.*, No. 179.
[4] *Ibid.*, p. 98, No. 306.
[5] *Ibid.*, p. 97, No. 266.
[6] *Ibid.*, 1907-08, p. 62, K. 18.

B (*i*) 12.—Fragment (ht. 5¾″; width 6″) from the proper left upper side of a sculpture bearing traces of a fretted halo surrounded by a lotus pattern. Grey-coloured stone. Excavated in 1904-05.[1]

B (*i*) 13.—Fragment (ht. 7″; width 5½″) from the proper right upper corner of a sculpture, bearing traces of a halo with a lotus pattern with a miniature *stūpa* in relief. Unearthed in 1907-08 on the approach to the Main Shrine from the east, 8′ 3″ below the surface.

B (*i*) 14.—Fragment (ht. 6″; width 5½″) from the proper right upper side of a sculpture with a headless figure of a Bōdhisattva seated on a lotus in easy attitude. His right hand is broken off; his left hand holds a flower. The figure is perhaps one of Maitrēya. The stalk of another flower is carved at his right, while to his proper left is a foliated scroll. Late Gupta period. Unearthed in 1904-05 to the north of the Jagat Singh *stūpa*.[2]

B (*i*) 15.—Fragment (ht. 7″; width 8″) from the back-slab of an image showing a part of a throne in relief similar to B (*c*) 36. Excavated in the trench crossing the south boundary wall of monastery I, 1½′ below the surface.

B (*i*) 16.—Fragment (ht. 9¾″; width 9″) from the side of a statue, bearing a lotus carved in relief. Excavated in 1907-08 in the 2nd gateway of monastery I.

B (*i*) 17.—Fragment (ht. 8¼″; width 10½″) with a part of a pierced halo surrounded by a beaded border and other decoration. Above it traces of a flying celestial figure. Finely carved. Presumably Gupta work. Blue stone. Excavated in 1904-05 near shrine to the east of the Jagat Singh Stūpa[3].

B (*i*) 18.—Fragment (ht. 5¼″; width 4″) from the proper left side of a sculpture with traces of a halo and a blue lotus (*nīlōtpala*). Excavated in 1906-07 in the area to the east of the Main Shrine.

B (*i*) 19.—Fragment (ht. 7½″; width 5″) from the proper left side of a sculpture, bearing traces of an oval halo. Unearthed in 1907-08 on the approach to the Main Shrine from the east, 4′ below the surface.

B (*i*) 20.—Fragment (ht. 9″; width 13″) with a flying celestial (*dēva*) carrying a garland. Unearthed in the 1st outer court of monastery I.

B (*i*) 21.—Fragment (ht. 5″; width 4½″) with traces of a pierced halo. Find-spot not known.

B (*i*) 22.—Fragment (ht. 5½″; width 4¾″) with traces of a circular halo and a crocodile (*makara*) head, and below them the throne pattern. Late Gupta period. Excavated in 1906-07 in the mediæval monastery I.

---

[1] *A. S. R.*, 1904-05, p. 96, No. 163.
[2] *Ibid.* 1904-05, p. 98, No. 289.
[3] *Ibid.*, No. 304.

B (*i*) 23.—Fragment (ht. 6¾"; width 3½") from the proper right side of a sculpture, bearing traces of a halo and a flower. Excavated in 1906-07 in the area on the east of the Main Shrine.

B (*i*) 24.—Fragment (ht. 5½"; width 4") with traces of a halo and a figure of a Buddha seated in meditation in a square niche. To the proper right is a part of a leogryph. Excavated in 1906-07 in the area on the east of the Main Shrine.

B (*i*) 25.—Fragment (ht. 6½"; width 4¾") from the back-slab of a sculpture with the legs of a male figure and scroll. Found in 1907-08 in the trench to the south of mediæval monastery I, 2' below the surface.

B (*i*) 26.—Fragmentary head (ht. 1' 2"; width 8") wearing an elaborately bedecked high diadem with a circular mark between the eyebrows. Fine work. Excavated in 1906-07 in the area on the east of the Main Shrine.

B (*i*) 27.—Fragment (ht. 5¾"; width 5") of a head with a radiated halo probably belonging to an attendant. Of the main figure, traces of a hand remain.[1] It is one of the 13 sculptures which have come back from the Lucknow Provincial Museum.

B (*i*) 28.—Bust (ht. 4"; width 3") of a male figure with the hair combed back, in the act of blowing a conch (*śaṅkha*) which it holds between both hands. The upper arms are broken off. Unearthed in 1907-08.

B (*i*) 29.—Head (ht. 5¾"; width 4¾") of a statuette with the hair fastened on the top by means of a fillet. Late Gupta work. Traces of red paint. Unearthed in 1907-08 in the western part of the Gupta monastery II, 6' below the surface.[2]

B(*i*) 29*a*.—A head, 9¼" high and 7½" thick, from the tip of the nose to the back, sex uncertain. It is carved in the round and well preserved. The ears are decorated with ornaments of the shape of the plantain flower. The hair in front is arranged in a wavy line over the forehead, the middle curve being occupied by a circular pendant resembling the *ṭikulī*. Over the forehead the hair is fastened with a fillet consisting of five lines of beads and adorned with jewels. From that point the hair hangs down straight as far as the neck where it is interlaced and parted off into locks. Dr. Marshall assigns the sculpture to the late Gupta period.

B (*i*) 30.—Bust (ht. 5"; width 4½") of a sturdy looking male statuette carved in the round. The right arm is broken off; the left hand holds a long flat object under the chin. The hair falls down in curls of typical Gupta style. No ornaments or dress. Excavated in 1906-07 in the area on the east of the Main Shrine.

---

[1] *A. S. R.*, 1903-04, p. 226.
[2] *Op. cit.* 1907-08, p. 56, § 1.

B (*i*) 31.—Fragment (ht. 4″) of a head of which only the right cheek and ear remain. Unearthed in 1906-07 near the north-east corner of mediæval monastery I, 9′ below the surface.

B (*i*) 32.—Bust (ht. $3\frac{1}{4}$″; width $3\frac{1}{2}$″) of a figurine of a Brahmanical mendicant, with his hair combed back and a pointed beard. His left forearm is broken off, and the right hand rests on a flat object. Late mediæval style. Excavated in 1906-07 between the 1st outer court of mediæval monastery I and *stūpa* No. 44 on south of it, 5′ 4″ below the surface.

B (*i*) 33.—Face and throat (ht. $3\frac{3}{4}$″; width $3\frac{1}{2}$″) of a statuette with the upper part above the lips and the ears broken off. Find-spot not known.

B (*i*) 34.—Unfinished head (ht. $3\frac{1}{2}$″; width 3″) which to judge from the protuberance on the skull must have been meant for a Buddha head. Unearthed in 1906-07 in the 1st outer court of mediæval monastery I, $2\frac{1}{2}$′ below the surface.

B (*i*) 35.—Fragment (ht. 5″; width 4″) with a bust of a female figurine, both arms broken off. Much defaced. Found in the same locality but 4′ 4″ below the surface.

B (*i*) 36.—Fragment (ht. $4\frac{1}{2}$″; width $4\frac{1}{2}$″) with a badly defaced head. Chunār sandstone of reddish colour. Find-spot not known.

B (*i*) 37.—Head (ht. $3\frac{3}{4}$″; width 3″) with the back and top split away. The eye-brows are indicated by incised lines. Unearthed in 1904-05.[1]

B (*i*) 38.—Bust (ht. $4\frac{1}{2}$″; width 3″) of a female figure carved in the round. Much defaced. Both arms are broken in part. The hair is gathered in a long mass on the back. Gupta or earlier.

Traces of red paint. Excavated in 1906-07 in the area on the east of the Main Shrine.

B (*i*) 39.—Head (ht. $2\frac{1}{4}$″; width $1\frac{3}{4}$″) of the Gupta period, presumably of a Bōdhisattva attendant. Unearthed in 1907-08 in the trench which crosses the south boundary wall of mediæval monastery I, to the north of the Main Shrine, 6′ below the surface.

B (*i*) 40.—Fragment (ht. 3″; width $2\frac{1}{2}$″) of a head with shaven skull, which presumably belonged to an image of a Buddhist monk. The fragment may have formed part of a representation of the Buddha's first sermon at Sārnāth. Gupta work. Excavated in 1907-08 in the western precinct of mediæval monastery I, 4′ below the surface.

B (*i*) 41.—Head (ht. 2″) of a miniature figure which to judge from its treatment may have belonged to a Bōdhisattva attendant. Late

---

[1] *A. S. R.*, 1904-05, p. 99, No. 373.

Gupta work. Excavated in 1906-07 in the area on the east of the Main Shrine.

B (*i*) 42.—Head (ht. 2 3/16" ; width 1 3/4") with the back split away. The hair is brushed back. The circular dot on the forehead marks the third eye. The head presumably belonged to a figure of a goddess.

Excavated in the same year in front of the entrance of mediæval monastery I, 6′ below the surface.

B (*i*) 43.—Head (ht. 3/4" ; width 2") of a miniature male figure, presumably a Bōdhisattva. The hair falls on the sides in long curls. Gupta style. Unearthed in 1906-07 outside the south boundary wall of mediæval monastery I, 4′ 5" below the surface.

B (*i*) 44.—Torso (ht. 1′ 2 1/4" ; width 9") of a statuette with the head, arms and legs broken off. It wears a necklace and another ornament consisting of a circular ring on the breast on which terminate two bands, one going round the breast and the other round the neck. Much defaced. Unearthed in 1906-07 in the 1st outer court of mediæval monastery I, 2′ below the surface.

B (*i*) 45.—Fragment (ht. 9" ; width 5 1/2") with the torso of a standing figure. Much defaced. Excavated in 1906-07 in the 1st outer court of monastery I, 3′ 3" below the surface.

B (*i*) 46.—Fragment (ht. 5 1/4" ; width 5 3/4") with the legs of a standing figure in relief. Excavated in 1907-08 in the area north-west of the Main Shrine, 3′ 9" below the surface.

B (*i*) 47.—Fragmentary relief (ht. 7 1/4" ; width 5 1/2") with the legs of a figure running to proper right. There is a hand over the loins. Discovered in 1907-08 on the approach to the Main Shrine from the east, 6′ below the surface.

B (*i*) 48.—Fragment (ht. 8 1/2" ; width 4 1/2") with the legs of a celestial (*dēva*) flying to proper left, which belonged to a bigger image. Found in 1906-07 in the area on the east of the Main Shrine.

B (*i*) 49.—Torso (ht. 7 3/4" ; width 3") of a male figure wearing a *dhōtī*, with a protruding abdomen. Discovered in 1906-07 west of *stūpa* No. 17 in the area north-west of the Main Shrine, 6′ below the surface.

B (*i*) 50.—Fragment (ht. 6" ; width 3 1/2") representing the legs of a standing figure. Find-spot not known.

B (*i*) 51.—Fragment (ht. 4 3/4" ; width 3 3/4") with the feet and hem of a garment. Find-spot not known.

B (*i*) 52.—Relief (ht. 4 3/4" ; width 3") with the legs of a standing figure. There are traces of a worshipper to the proper left. Unearthed in 1907-08 in the 1st outer court of mediæval monastery I.

B (*i*) 53.—Fragment (ht. 4 1/2" ; width 3") showing the legs of a standing figure holding a staff, presumably an attendant Bōdhisattva or possibly Indra holding the staff of an umbrella. In the latter case the fragment must have belonged to a representation of Gautama Buddha's descent at Sāṅkāśya from the "heaven of the thirty-three gods." The identification is not to be looked upon as certain.

Gupta style. Unearthed in 1907-08 on the approach to the Main Shrine from the east, 7′ below the surface.

B (*i*) 54.—Fragment (ht. 4¼″; width 3″) with the closely draped legs of a female figure, which, to judge from the manner in which the legs are crossed, must have been a dancing girl. This is apparent from a comparison with the central dancing girl in the third compartment from the proper left of the long Gupta lintel D(*d*)[1]. Good Gupta style. Discovered in 1906-07 in the mediæval monastery I.

B (*i*) 55.—Fragment (ht. 5″; width 2¾″) with a miniature figure. Its head is destroyed, but it has long wavy hair behind the shoulders. The right hand is bent over the breast, the left is missing. Gupta work. Unearthed in 1907-08 in the western precinct of mediæval monastery I, 2′ below the surface. [1]

B (*i*) 56.—Fragment (ht. 3¾″; width 5″) of a relief with the top of a tree in Gupta style. Traces of red paint. Unearthed in Gupta monastery III in 1907-08.

B (*i*) 57.—Base (ht. 6″; width 1′ ½″) of a statue of a female deity of which only the right foot remains on the head and chest of a human figure lying fully stretched out. Find-spot not known.

B (*i*) 58.—Lower part (ht. 6¼″ including tenon; width 11½″) of a statuette carved in the round and seated cross-legged on a lotus. Provenance not ascertainable.

B (*i*) 59.—Fragment (ht. 3″; width 6½″) with the lower part of a figure seated cross-legged on a lotus. There is an uncertain object on the left thigh. Provenance not known.

B (*i*) 60.—Left leg (ht. 3¼″; width 4¼″) bent in a manner which suggests its connection with a statuette seated in easy attitude (*lalitāsana*) peculiar to Bodhisattvas and goddesses. Excavated in 1906-07 in the monastery to the west of the Dhamēkh *stūpa*, 5½′ below the surface.

B (*i*) 61.—Fragment (ht. 2½″; width 3¾″) representing a leg bent at the knee as in the cross-legged position. Found in 1906-07 in the area on the east of the Main Shrine.

*B (*i*) 62.—Base (ht. 4″ including tenon beneath it; width 4″) with the left foot of a standing figure which must have been a Buddha or a Bōdhisattva. On the front of the base is a fragmentary inscription in characters of about the 7th century A. D. which reads *Sagadasēnasya* "Of Sagadasēna."

Find-spot not known.

---

[1] *A. S. R.*, 1907-08, p. 48, *c* 11.

B (*i*) 63.—Fragment (ht. 1¼″; width 2¾″) representing a pair of feet adorned with anklets on a lotus throne. Unearthed in 1906-07 in the area to the north-west of the Main Shrine.

B (*i*) 64.—Base (ht. 3″ including tenon on underside; width 3½″) bearing the right foot of a standing image of a Buddha or a Bōdhisattva. Late Gupta work. Grey-coloured sandstone of Chunār. Excavated in 1906-07 near the Aśōka Column.

B (*i*) 65.—Base (ht. 2″; width 5″) of a sculpture with the feet of a figure, which, to judge from the position of the left, foot must have been standing to left. Provenance not known.

B (*i*) 66.—Fragment (ht. 2¼″; width 4½″) consisting of a moulded base of a statuette of which only the feet remain. Perhaps Gupta work. Excavated in 1906-07 in the area on the east of the Main Shrine.

B (*i*) 67.—Fragment (ht. 4½″; width 5¼″) of the base of a statue with parts of three toes of the right foot remaining. Traces of red paint. Find-spot not known but apparently unearthed in one of the recent excavations.

B (*i*) 68.—Fragment (ht. 4¼″; width 4″) of a pierced relief with a pair of feet on the base. Excavated in 1906-07 in the area on the east of the Main Shrine.

B (*i*) 69.—Fragment of the base (ht. 2¼″; width 4¼″) of a sculpture bearing the left foot of the main image with the right foot of an attendant to the proper left. The fragment most probably belonged to a Buddha statuette. The smaller foot must then be of an attendant Bōdhisattva. Gupta work. Found in the same locality, as B (*i*) 68.

B (*i*) 70.—Fragment (ht. 4¾″; width 5″) with the major part of the left foot of a statuette and toes of another foot which was presumably crossed behind it. It is, however, to be noted that these toes seem to be of a smaller statue. Traces of floral decoration on the front of the base and of red paint. Typical Gupta style. Found in 1906-07 in the area on the east of the Main Shrine.

B (*i*) 71.—Fragment (ht. 6″; width 11″) with the feet of a female adorned with anklets and rings on the toes. The underside of the fragment is moulded in the shape of a capital. Apparently found in one of the recent excavations.

B (*i*) 72.—Left (?) arm (ht. 5½″; width 6½″) of a statuette bent at the elbow. The head is missing but there are traces of a bracelet on the wrist and an uncertain object above the elbow. The fragment was painted red. Apparently found in one of the recent excavations.

B (*i*) 73.—Fragment (ht. 11″; width 7½″) representing an arm of a colossal statue, bent at the elbow. Find-spot not known but probably discovered in one of the recent diggings.

B (*i*) 74.—Fragment (ht. 9″; width 5″) of an arm of a large-sized statue. Excavated in one of the recent diggings.

B (*i*) 75.—Fragment (ht. 1¾″; width 4″) similar to B (*i*) 74. Excavated in 1906-07 in the area on the east of the Main Shrine.

*B (*i*) 76.—Fragment (ht. 6¾″; width 7½″) of a relief with a part of an arm adorned with an armlet, which must have belonged to an image of a Bōdhisattva or a goddess. To the proper right we notice a portion of the Buddhist creed in Nāgarī characters of the 10th or 11th century A.D. Excavated in 1906-07 on the approach to the Main Shrine from the east, 6′ below the surface.

B (*i*) 77.—Hand (length 6″) of a colossal statue holding a rosary, which may have belonged to a statue of Maitrēya or the Brahmanical god Brahmā. Late Gupta style. Probably found in one of the recent diggings.

B (*i*) 78.—Hand (length 4½″) wearing a bracelet and holding an object resembling a dagger. Gupta style. Unearthed in 1907-08 in the area between the 2nd gateway of mediæval monastery I and the Dhamēkh Stūpa.

B (*i*) 79.—Left hand (length 6½″) adorned with a bracelet and holding the stalk of a flower. Gupta style. Excavated in 1906-07 in the area on the east of the Main Shrine.

B (*i*) 80.—Hand (length 4¾″), probably left. Found in the same year as B (*i*) 79.

B (*i*) 81.—Hand (length 7½″) adorned with a bracelet. The fingers are joined by a web like those of the Buddha images. Gupta style. Excavated in 1907-08 in the long trench east of monastery I.

B (*i*) 82.—Hand (length 3½″) with the ring-finger (*anāmikā*) decked with a ring and a mark on the palm. The hand is probably the right hand of a standing goddess, which was held down in the gift-bestowing attitude. Behind it on the stone by which it was connected with the back-slab of the image we notice a flower, presumably a blue-lotus (*nīlōtpala*). The material is grey-coloured stone from Chunār. Late Gupta style. Excavated in 1904-05 in the area around the Jagat Singh *stūpa* and the Main Shrine. [1]

B (*i*) 83.—Upper arm (length 5½″) adorned with an armlet. Excavated in 1906-07 in the area on the east of the Main Shrine.

B (*i*) 84.—Fragment of a hand (length 5″) with a circular mark on the palm. The thumb is broken off. Unearthed in 1907-08 in the area between the Dhamēkh Stūpa and the 2nd gateway of mediæval monastery I.

B (*i*) 85.—Hand (length 7½″), presumably the right hand, disposed in the gift-bestowing attitude, of a Bōdhisattva or a goddess, adorned

---

[1] *A. S. R.*, 1904-05, p. 99, No. 338.

with a bracelet on the wrist. Gupta style. Excavated in 1907-08 on the approach to the Main Shrine from the east, 4′ below the surface.

B (*i*) 86.—Fragment (length 4½″) with a hand holding something, in Gupta style. Excavated in 1906-07 in the area on the east of the Main Shrine.

B (*i*) 87.—Hand (length 4½″) adorned with a bracelet. Unearthed in 1907-08, south of mediæval monastery I, 3′ below the surface.

B (*i*) 88.—Hand (4″×3″) carved in the round, ornamented with a lotus flower (*padma*) in relief on the plam. The fingers are damaged. Unearthed in the trench crossing the south boundary wall of mediæval monastery I on the north of the Main Shrine, 6′ below the surface.

B (*i*) 89.—Hand (length 4½″), presumably left, of an attendant figure holding the handle of a fly-whisk (Sanskrit *chāmara*). Red colour. Gupta style. Excavated in 1906-07 in the area on the east of the Main Shrine.

B (*i*) 90.—Upper part of an arm (length 5½″) adorned with an elaborate armlet. To the proper right we notice the traces of a necklace. The fragment is made of the blue stone of Gayā and must have belonged to a Bōdhisattva or a goddess. Find-spot not known but presumably discovered in one of the recent excavations.

B (*i*) 91.—Fragment (ht. 2¾″) representing a hand holding an oval-shaped object, perhaps a water-pot (*kamaṇḍalu*). Probably Gupta work. Found in 1906-07 in the area on the east of the Main Shrine.

B (*i*) 92.—Left hand (length 3″) adorned with a bracelet and holding the hem of a garment. Traces of red colour. Unearthed in 1906-07 in the monastery west of the Dhamēkh *stūpa*, 5′ 6″ below the surface.

B (*i*) 93.—Fragment (length 2½″) of an arm bearing traces of red paint. Excavated in 1906-07 in the area on the east of the Main Shrine.

B (*i*) 94.—Hand (length 2¼″) of which the fingers are broken off. Found in 1906-07 in the area on the east of the Main Shrine.

B (*i*) 95.—Fragment (ht. 3¼″; width 1¾″) with the right hand, holding a garland, of a celestial (*dēva*) flying in a cloud to proper left, which must have formed part of a statue of a Buddha, a Bōdhisattva or a goddess in the late Gupta style. Excavated in 1906-07 in the area on the east of the Main Shrine.

B (*i*) 96.—Fragment (ht. 1½″; width 3″) representing a left leg, clad in a *dhōtī* which must have belonged to a figure of a Bōdhisattva seated in easy attitude (*lalitāsana*). Grey-coloured stone of Chunār. Found in the same year and locality as B (*i*) 95.

B (*i*) 97.—Left arm (ht. 2″; width 1½″) bent at the elbow, adorned with a bracelet on the wrist. Found in the same year as B (*i*) 96.

B (*i*) 98.—Hand (length 5¼″) with a flower carved in relief on the palm and a bracelet on the wrist, which was connected with the back-slab by a plain mass of stone. The fragment may have belonged to a statuette of a goddess.

B (*i*) 99.—Fragment of an arm (length 3¼"). Excavated in 1906-07 in the area on the east of the Main Shrine.

B (*i*) 100.—Left arm (length 8") from the shoulder down to the elbow adorned with an armlet, with the remains of two long locks of hair on the shoulder. Find-spot not known.

B (*i*) 101.—Fragment (ht. 6½"), presumably of a pilaster, decorated with a geometric pattern. Excavated in 1907-08 in the trench crossing the south boundary wall of monastery I, north of the Main Shrine.

B (*i*) 102.—Hand (length 6") holding the snout of a crocodile, (*makara*) apparently broken from a *tōraṇa* lintel. Unearthed in 1906-07 on the east wall of the entrance chamber of monastery I, 5′ 4″ below the surface.

B (*i*) 103.—Pair of hands (length 6") one of which, adorned with finger-rings, is caught in the other. Excavated in 1906-07 in the area on the east of the Main Shrine.

B (*i*) 104.—Left knee (ht. 2¼"; width 3") of a figure, which was fastened to the body by a broad band, and may have belonged to a figure of a goblin (*yaksha*).[1] Find-spot not known.

B (*i*) 105.—Leg below the knee without feet (length 4") clad in an under-garment, which may have belonged to a Bōdhisattva image. Excavated in 1906-07 in the area on the east of the Main Shrine.

B (*i*) 106.—Fragment (length 3½") which to judge from the edge of the garment on its underside must have belonged to an arm of a Buddha image standing in the attitude of granting protection (*abhaya-mudrā*). Gupta work. Find-spot not known, but apparently found in one of the recent diggings.

B (*i*) 107.—Fragment (ht. 4¾"; width 3½") from the left profile of a head, with a part of the ear and folds on the throat. Excavated in 1906-07 in the area on the east of the Main Shrine.

B (*i*) 108.—Fragment (ht. 4¾"; width 5½") of the base of a statue of which only three right toes remain on it. To the proper right of the toes, we notice a long groove for an iron clamp. Late Gupta style. Discovered in 1906-07 in the area on the east of the Main Shrine.

B (*i*) 109.—Part of a right foot (length 4½"), with a lotus flower in the middle of the sole which must have faced upwards and an anklet. The fragment apparently belonged to a figure of a goddess or perhaps a Bōdhisattva—for Bōdhisattvas have ornaments too—seated in easy attitude (*lalitāsana*). Grey-coloured stone of Chunār. Excavated in 1907-08 in the 1st outer court of mediæval monastery I.

---

[1] Vogel, *Mathura Catalogue*, C 3, and Pl. XIV.

B (*i*) 110.—Fragment (ht. 8½"; width 3½") representing the right leg of a corpulent standing figure, perhaps a goblin (*yaksha*). Found in 1907-08 in the 2nd outer court of the mediæval monastery I, ½′ below the surface.

B (*i*) 111.—Fragment (ht. 7"; width 7½") with a knee or elbow of a figure and folds of a garment. To what kind of sculpture it belonged cannot be made out. The style appears to be Gupta. Unearthed in 1904-05 [1].

B (*i*) 112.—Fragment (ht. 3½"; width 2½") bearing traces of a pierced halo with a lotus border. To the proper left is a headless figure of a celestial (*dēva*) flying to proper right with a garland between his hands. Discovered in 1906-07 near the stair to the mediæval monastery I, 3′ below the surface.

B (*i*) 113.—Top of a parasol (diam. 3⅝") the staff of which must have been held in the hands of a figure of Indra who accompanied the Buddha on his descent from the heaven of the thirty-three gods at Sāṅkāśya. Excavated in 1906-07 in the area on the east of the Main Shrine.

B (*i*) 114.—Fragment (ht. 5"; width 3½") from the proper right side of a sculpture bearing a miniature *stūpa* in relief. Discovered in 1907-08 on the approach to the Main Shrine from the east, 7′ below the surface.

B (*i*) 115.—Fragment (ht. 4¼"; width 3½") with a full-blown lotus (*padma*) and stalk, from the proper right side of a statue, in Gupta style. Excavated in 1906-07 in the area on the east of the Main Shrine.

B (*i*) 116.—Fragment (ht. 2"; width 1⅞") with a *stūpa* in relief. Find-spot not known.

B (*i*) 117.—Full-blown lotus and stalk (ht. 3"; width 1") in *alto-relievo*, made of blue stone of Gayā. Found in the same year and the same locality as B (*i*) 116.

*B (*i*) 118.—Fragment (ht. 2⅝"; width 1⅞") from the proper right side of a sculpture, with a *stūpa* carved in relief, and on the back a part of the Buddhist creed in Nāgarī characters of about the 10th century A.D. Unearthed in 1906-07 between the Main Shrine and *stūpa* No. 22 on the west of it.

B (*i*) 119.—Fragment of a lotus flower (diam. 1") found in the area on the east of the Main Shrine.

B (*i*) 120.—Part of a halo (ht. 2½"; width 3¼") with a defaced head. Found in the same area, as B (*i*) 119.

B (*i*) 121.—Fragment (ht. 2½"; width 2½") with a fully expanded flower and stalk detached from the proper right side of a statue, made of blue stone of Gayā. Unearthed in 1906-07 in the area on the east of the Main Shrine.

---

[1] *A. S. R.*, 1904-05, p. 97, No. 258.

B (*i*) 122.—Fragment (ht. 3″; width 3″) from the back slab of a statue. Found in the same year and locality as B (*i*) 121.

B (*i*) 123.—Fragment (length 4″) without any carving. Unearthed in 1906-07 near *stūpa* No. 21 on the north-west of the Main Shrine.

B (*i*) 124.—Figure (ht. 3″; width 4¼″) of the Dhyānibuddha Amōghasiddhi seated on a lotus throne. His upper body is broken off. The left hand holds the hem of the robe on the left thigh; the right, which is missing, must have been raised in the attitude of granting protection. The figure formed part of a statue of a Bōdhisattva or a goddess. Unearthed in 1907-08 in the trench crossing the south boundary wall of monastery I, north of the Main Shrine, 6′ below the surface.[1]

B (*i*) 125.—Figure (ht. 3¼″; width 4¾″) of the same Dhyānibuddha in the same attitude as in the previous sculpture. His head is broken off. Discovered in 1906-07, south of *stūpa* No. 22 on the west of the Main Shrine, 4′ below the surface.

B (*i*) 126.—Fragment (ht. 2½″; width 4¾″) of the base of a sculpture with parts of the toes of the right foot. Found in 1907-08 in the area north-west of the Main Shrine, 3′ below the surface.

B (*i*) 127.—Head (length 5½″) of a crocodile (*makara*) with a coiled snout almost as big as an elephant's trunk. Carved with skill in Gupta style. Excavated in 1907-08 in the area north of the Dhamēkh *stūpa*.[2]

B (*i*) 128.—Fragment (length 4¾″) representing the head of a leogryph (?) in Gupta style. Found in the same year and locality[3] as B (*i*) 127.

B (*i*) 129.—Head (length 3½″) of a crocodile (*makara*) in Gupta style. Found in 1906-07 in the area on the west of the Main Shrine.

B (*i*) 130.—Hind part (length 2½″) of a figure of a bull in Gupta style. Unearthed in 1906-07 in the area on the east of the Main Shrine.

B (*i*) 131.—Fragment (length 4″) representing a branch of a tree, in fine Gupta style. Find-spot not known.

B (*i*) 132.—Hind foot (ht. 3½″) of an elephant. Unearthed in 1906-07 in the first outer court of monastery I, 3′ below the surface.

B (*i*) 133.—Hand (ht. 2¾″) disposed in front of the knee, in Gupta style. Found in the trench on the south of the 2nd outer court of monastery I, 8′ below the surface.

B (*i*) 134-135.—Two small fragments (length 3½″ and 3½″) which cannot be identified, of no interest. One of them was found in 1906-07 in the area east of the Main Shrine, the other, north-west of it.

---

[1] *A. S. R.*, 1907-08, p. 72, No. β 59.
[2] *Op. cit.* p. 61, η 160.
[3] *Ibid.*, No. η 139.

B (i) 136.—Fragment (ht. 8½″) from the proper right upper corner of a bigger sculpture. To the proper left we notice the traces of an ornamental halo of the main figure, and to the right, those of a celestial with his spouse on his thigh. Mediæval style. Excavated in 1907-08 in the 2nd outer court of monastery I, 1′ below the surface.

C. BAS-RELIEFS.

C (*a*).—Scenes from Buddha's life.

* C (*a*) 1.—Stele (ht. excluding tenon 4′ 5″ ; width 1′ 2¼″) or high slab (*ūrdhvapaṭa*) rectangular in shape and terminating at the top in a small *stūpa* carved in the round, which, however, has lost its finial (*hti*). The bas-relief carved on the face of the sculpture is divided into four compartments placed one above the other and containing the four principal scenes of the Buddha's life, which are arranged chronologically, starting from below[1] :—

(*a*) The lowest panel illustrates the birth of Gautama Buddha or rather Bōdhisattva in the Lumbinī garden (modern Rummindēi) near Kapilavastu. His mother Māyādēvī stands in the centre, in the same posture as in the representations of this scene in Gandhāra and Mathurā sculptures,[2] her right hand catching hold of a branch of a *sāla* tree (*Shorea Robusta plaksha*), which forms, as it were, an arched canopy over her head. She has a plain circular halo around her head and a scarf (Hindi *dupaṭṭa*) is visible on her arms. The carving to her proper right is defaced, but a comparison of the stele under review with another complete Sārnāth specimen (ht. 90 cm.) bearing the same four scenes now in the Indian Museum[3], makes it absolutely certain that this part of the sculpture was occupied by a figure of Śakra receiving the new-born infant. To the proper left of Māyādēvī is the defaced figure of her sister Prajāpati standing with her right hand resting on her hip. In Gandhāra sculpture she is always represented as supporting Māyādēvī. To the left of Prajāpati again was the child Buddha receiving his first bath. The child itself is effaced, but we still distinguish the 'half-bodied' Nāga-kings, Nanda and Upnanda standing in the air[4] with their heads canopied by snake-hoods and pouring water over the infant's head from pitchers which they hold between their hands. Above the Nāgas we notice two celestial beings (*dēva*) apparently

---

[1] One of the Buddha's last exhortations to his chief disciple Ānanda was that his followers should visit the four places associated with his birth, his enlightenment, his first sermon and his demise. Kern, *Manual of Buddhism*, p. 43.

[2] *Cf.* Vogel, *Mathurā Catalogue*, No. H 1 and Pl. VI, *a*.

[3] Foucher, *l'Iconographice Bouddhique*, 1900, p. 163, fig. 29 *b*.

[4] In the Mathurā sculpture alluded to above, the Nāgas are issuing from masonry wells. *Cf.* also Dr. Vogel's remarks in *A. S. R.*, 1906-07, pp. 152-153, where it is pointed out that the Sārnāth representation is in perfect agreement with the *Lalitavistara* (1902), p. 83.

showering down flowers. The corresponding space on the other side may similarly have been occupied by divine beings, but they are now altogether defaced. At both ends of the panel in narrow separate compartments are two Buddha figures standing in the attitude of protection.

(*b*) The next division contains the scene of Buddha's enlightenment (*bôdhi*) at Gayā. In the centre is the Buddha seated, as usual, in the earth-touching attitude (*bhūmisparśamudrā*) under the *pīpal* tree. To his right we recognize the Evil One (Māra) holding a bow (*chāpa*) in his left hand and an arrow in the right. Behind him is a figure which Dr. Vogel rightly identifies as an attendant of Māra holding his crocodile standard (*makara-dhvaja*). The seated figure in front of this attendant with the head supported on its left hand is presumably Māra again, his attitude expressing despair after his defeat. The two female figures to the left of the Buddha are two of Māra's three daughters. In stele No. C (*a*) 2 all the three are represented.[1] In the upper corners of the panel two demons (*rākshasa*) are shown, the one to the proper right holding up a finger in menace, the other wielding a sword in his right and clasping a snake in his left hand. On the front of the throne beneath the Buddha's right hand there must have been a figure of the earth goddess as in B (*b*) 172. It is now obliterated. In the middle of the base is a female figure, perhaps a daughter of Māra flying away and to her proper left two kneeling figures of uncertain meaning.

(*c*) Buddha's first sermon in the Deer-park (modern Sārnāth). The Buddha is seated in the centre of the panel on a couch in the attitude of expounding the law (*dharmachakramudrā*). To his right is the Bōdhisattva Maitrēya standing on a full-blown lotus (*padma*) with a fly-whisk (Sanskrit *chāmara*) in his right hand and a rosary (*akshamālā*) in the left. To the left of the Buddha we see the Bōdhisattva Avalōkitēśvara standing on a lotus and holding a full-blown lotus flower in his left hand, while his right hand is stretched down in the gift-bestowing attitude (*varadamudrā*). The two standing Buddha figures on either side of the Buddha's halo are probably also meant to represent Gautama Buddha. In the upper corners of the panel are two celestial beings (*dēva*) carrying garlands. It deserves notice that they are provided with wings, an unusual device in Indian art except

---

[1] In the Mathurā sculpture referred to, only one daughter of Māra is shown.

in that of Gandhāra. The relief on the front of the throne on which the Buddha sits, consists of the wheel-and-deer symbol between six kneeling figures, Buddha's first five disciples (*pañchabhadra-vargīya*) to whom the sixth figure seems to have been added for the sake of symmetry.

(*d*) The uppermost compartment illustrates the Buddha's decease (*mahāparinirvāṇa*), which has been represented in the usual fashion in strict agreement with the version.[1] The Buddha is lying on his right side facing to the front, with pillows under his head and his feet, on a couch with stout tapering legs which is placed between the twin *sāla* trees of Kuśinagara. In front of the couch is a group of five mourning figures evidently comprising both monks and lay-members. The figure seated cross-legged with the back turned to the front must be identified as the recluse (*parivrājaka*), Subhadra of Kuśinagara, the last convert of Buddha, as would appear from the three staves tied together (*tridaṇḍa*) with the water-pot (*kamaṇḍalu*) resting on them. The figure at the feet of the Buddha is his great disciple, Mahākāśyapa of Rājagriha who according to the Buddhist scriptures adored the Master's feet immediately before the cremation. The figure near the Buddha's head fanning him must be the monk Upavāna. Behind the Buddha, in the background are four more mourning figures each with the right hand raised in grief. The female figures issuing from the foliage of the two *sāla* trees are the tree-spirits engaged in showering flowers on the Buddha.[2]

The *stūpa* at the top of the stele contains, in a niche with arched head, a figure of Buddha seated cross-legged in meditation. The flanks of the slab are rounded off and on its back at the top is the Buddhist creed in six lines in characters of about the 5th century A.D. It is obvious that the stele was meant to stand by itself and not to be engaged in a wall.

The slab is broken into two across the middle of the second panel from below. The lower part was unearthed by Mr. Oertel in 1904-05 in the cloistered passage to the north-east of the Main Shrine, and the upper part, by Dr. Marshall and Dr. Konow in the area west of mediæval monastery I, 4′ below the surface.[3] Pl. XIX, *a*.

---

[1] *Cf.* Kern, *Manual of Buddhism* p. 43.

[2] This identification is due to Dr. Vogel. *Cf.* his *Mathurā Catalogue*, p. 129, H 8. These fairies are first figured in Gandhāra sculptures and it appears very likely that they were borrowed from that school.

[3] *Cf. A. S. R.* for 1904-05, p. 83, Pl. XXX, *a*, and p. 97, No. 231, and for 1907-08, p. 47, *a* 42.

C (*a*) 2.—Stele (ht. excluding tenon 3′ 2″; width 1′ 7½″) with three panels illustrating a series of events of Gautama Buddha's life arranged as in C (*a*) 1 from bottom upwards. It will however be noticed that here the lowermost panel includes also Buddha's conception, that the second panel from the bottom comprises several scenes relating to the great Renunciation (*mahābhinishkramaṇa*) and that the enlightenment (*bōdhi*) and First Sermon are placed side by side in the third panel the top of which is broken. There was apparently a fourth panel at the top which contained the last scene, namely, the Buddha's extinction (*parinirvāṇa*). The extant portion is broken across the second panel from the bottom. The following scenes are depicted[1] :—

(*a*) Lowest panel. Dream of Māyādēvī in the proper right lower corner. Māyādēvī is reclining on her right side[2] on a couch with short legs. One female attendant rubs her feet, three others stand behind her head one with a fan, the other two with fly-whisks. Above, in the air, we notice the Bōdhisattva descending from the Tushita heaven in the form of a white elephant. Two celestials (*dēvaputra*) pay him obeisance.

Birth of Buddha in the proper left part of the same panel. Māyādēvī stands, as usual, holding a branch of a *sāla* tree with her left hand. Her right hand is broken.[3] To her proper right, stands Indra receiving the child which is coming out of her right side. To her left is her sister Prajâpati, her right hand resting on her breast and the left holding a water-pot (?).

Between these two scenes is shown the first bath of the new-born Bōdhisattva. He stands on a full-blown lotus, his right hand raised in the attitude of protection[4] and the left held against the hip. On either side of him we notice the Nāga kings Nanda and Upananda as in C (*a*) 1. The two male figures standing with clasped hands to the proper right of the Bōdhisattva may be Indra and Brahmā, but they have nothing to distinguish them.

(*b*) The flight of Buddha from Kapilavastu (*mahābhinishkramaṇa*) in the proper right lower corner of the second panel. The event is shown in the profile. The Buddha is astride on his horse Kaṇṭhaka, which has the usual trappings but no stirrups. The figure under the horse's head is his groom

---

[1] Described by Dr. Marshall and Dr. Konow in *A. S. R.*, 1906-07, pp. 93—94, Pl. XXVIII, and *ibid*, 1907-08, p. 49, *η* 170, and Pl. XIII, *b*.

[2] In Gandhāra sculpture Māyā is more correctly shown lying on her left side.

[3] According to the texts she seizes the tree with her right hand.

[4] Dr. Vogel has noticed this in connection with a Mathurā sculpture (*A. S. R.*, 1906-07, pp. 152—153, and Pl. LIII, *a*). In the sculpture under review the Bōdhisattva's hair also appears to be treated in the formal curls of a Buddha.

Chhandaka receiving from the Buddha's hands his royal robes and ornaments. The smaller figure under the body of the horse is of uncertain meaning.[1] Behind the horse is the Bōdhisattva cutting off his hair with his sword. The female figure holding a bowl is perhaps the girl Sujātā offering the Buddha a pot of rice-milk, after his long fast. We see the Buddha a fourth time evidently in conversation with a Nāga king, perhaps Kālika.

Finally the Bōdhisattva is shown seated on a lotus in meditation under an umbrella. His head is broken off. To the Bōdhisattva's left is a headless corpulent figure standing, with right hand raised and probably holding a fly-whisk. Its left hand holds an object resembling a purse.

It will be noticed that in the panel here described the Bōdhisattva is shown not less than six times.

(c) The third panel contains two scenes. The one to the proper right shows Buddha's enlightenment. He is seated, as usual, in the earth-touching attitude. To his right, the Evil One (Māra) stands with a bow in his left hand; and to his left, Māra's three daughters (Desire, Pleasure and Lust). On front of the throne beneath the Bōdhisattva's right hand the earth-goddess is seen emerging from the earth with a treasure vase in both hands. In the centre, we notice the daughter of Māra fleeing away. The three kneeling figures at both ends of the relief must be worshippers. The second scene which occupies the proper left half of the panel, is Buddha's first sermon. The Buddha is seated in the attitude of expounding the law (*dharmachakramudrā*). In front of the throne, is a wheel between a pair of deer. The five disciples were seated on both sides of the Buddha, namely, three on the right and two on the left. Of the latter, traces of the lower figure only remain. Both the Buddha figures are headless.

From the close conformity of its style to C (a) 1, this sculpture may be assigned to the Gupta period. The lower part of the stele was excavated in 1906-07 in the first outer court of mediæval monastery I[2] and the upper part in 1907-08 in the same locality.[3] Pl. XX.

C (a) 3.—Slab (ht. 3′ 2½″; width 2′ 2″) sculptured with the eight principal scenes from the Buddha's life. It has been restored from

---

[1] In Gandhāra sculptures the horse's hoofs are shown supported by the earth-goddess or by goblins (*yaksha*). *Cf.* Grünwedel-Burgess, *Buddhist Art in India*, figs. 50—53.

[2] *A. S. R.*, 1906-07, p. 87, sculpture No. 52.

[3] *Op. cit.* 1907-08, p. 40, 170, and Pl. XIII, *b*.

three fragments, two of which were found by Dr. Marshall and Dr. Konow on the approach to the Main Shrine from the east, while the third piece forming the proper left lower corner must have been unearthed by Major Kittoe as it is sketched in his "Drawings."[1] The whole sculpture was published with a photograph by Dr. Marshall and Dr. Konow and subsequently fully discussed by M. Foucher[2]. M. Foucher points out that the sculptor evidently on purpose made the scenes with a seated Buddha in the centre alternate with the others containing standing figures. The scenes are as follows :—

(*a*) Nativity in proper right lower corner. Māyādēvī stands, in her usual pose, holding a branch of the *sāla* tree with her right hand. To her proper right are traces of two standing figures evidently Indra and Brahmā, of whom the former must have been receiving the infant. To the left of Māyā, is represented the Bōdhisattva's first bath. The infant stands facing with his hands hanging down on both sides, while the two Nāga kings pour water on his head from pitchers[3]. Two maid servants are shown kneeling on both sides at the Bōdhissattva's feet.

(*b*) In proper left lower corner, Buddha's enlightenment (*bōdhi*) at Gayā. He is seated in the earth-touching attitude with Māra, the Evil One, standing to the right with a flower-arrow in his left hand and one of his daughters to the left. Above each of them is a demon (*rākshasa*).

(*g*) In the proper right upper corner, Buddha's first sermon in the Deer-park (*Mṛigadāva*). The Buddha is seated in the centre in the attitude of expounding the law (*dharmachakramudrā*) on a lion-throne (*siṁhāsana*). To his right is a Buddha figure standing in the gift-bestowing attitude. A similar figure is on the other side. In C (*a*) 1 and other images the Buddha has figures of Maitrēya and Avalōkitēśvara on his right and left. On front of the throne, between the lion figures we notice the wheel and deer, the ordinary symbol of the sermon in the Deer-park.

(*h*) In the proper left upper corner, Buddha's demise at Kuśinagara. The Buddha is lying in the usual manner on a couch. Behind him we notice four mourners and in front of the couch three. The central figure seated facing to the Buddha is probably the ascetic Subhadra, his last convert.

---

[1] Vol. I, No. 130, Pl. VI.

[2] *A. S. R.* for 1906-07, pp. 92, 93, No. 50, Pl. XXVIII, 4 ; and Foucher, *J. A.*, 10th Series, Vol. XIII (1909), pp. 5 *et. seq.*

[3] They are the *dvē udakadhārē* of the Pali text, which regularly occur in Græco-Buddhist representations of this scene. The Nāga kings, on the contrary, are never shown in Gandhāra. Cf. *A. S. R.* 1906-07, p. 152.

(e) In the panel beneath *g* we find the Buddha's descent from the Trāyastriṁśa heaven at Sāṅkāśya (modern Sankisā). The Buddha stands in the gift-bestowing attitude between Indra, who holds an umbrella over his head and Brahmā with his water-gourd (*kamaṇḍalu*) in his left hand. The flight of steps and the nun, Utpalavarṇā, who received the Buddha first of all on his descent, have been omitted, evidently for want of space.

(*f*) Beneath the Nirvāṇa we have the miracle of Śrāvastī which consisted in the Buddha being seen preaching at the same time in different places in order to confound the heretical teachers. The preaching Buddha figure in the centre is indeed repeated on either side on a somewhat smaller scale, each of the three figures being seated on a full-blown lotus-flower. The two remaining figures in the lower corners of the panel seem to represent, one a true believer kneeling with folded hands in the attitude of adoration, the other one of the heretical teachers collapsing under the weight of Buddha's miraculous display. Possibly the former figure is meant for Prasēnajit, the king of Śrāvastī, in whose presence the event is said to have taken place.

(*c*) Presentation of honey to Buddha by a monkey in the Pārilēyyaka forest near Kauśāmbī, to which the Buddha had retired for some time in his ninth retreat owing to the quarrels of his disciples. The monkey with a bowl on his hands approaches from the right the Buddha, who is seated in the middle on a lion-throne with a similar bowl in both hands. To the proper left of the Buddha we notice the feet and tail of the monkey, who is disappearing in a well. For it is said that after his meritorious act he committed suicide in this manner, immediately to be reborn as a celestial being (*dēva*). The figure holding a sword in its left hand, in the proper left upper corner of the panel seems indeed to represent the monkey thus reborn to a more blessed state.

(*d*) The last scene, in the panel to the proper left of *c*, immediately above the enlightenment scene is the miracle of Rājagṛiha. Buddha is standing in the middle. To his left is the ferocious elephant, Nālāgiri or Ratnapāla, which at the instigation of Dēvadatta had been let loose in order that it might kill the Buddha on his way to the house of a Brāhmaṇa who had invited him and his 500 disciples to a meal. The elephant was, as we know, readily subdued and is seen in the relief kneeling at Buddha's feet in submission. The figure to the left of Buddha may be identified as Ānanda his favourite disciple, who alone, remained with Buddha when all the other monks had fled.[1] The long staff in his right hand may be the *khakkhara* carried by Buddhist friars.[2]

It may be noted that the four secondary scenes as found in a sculpture from Mathurā are different.[3] The omissions of details and personages in the scenes in the sculpture under review may have been due, as pointed out above, to scarcity of space. The style of execution is of the Gupta period. The material is Chunār sandstone of buff colour. Pl. XIX, *b*.

C (*a*) 4.—High slab (*ūrdhvapaṭa*. Ht. 3′ 3½″; width 1′ 6″) divided into three horizontal compartments one above the other. The sculpture apparently illustrated the four chief events of Buddha's life such as we find delineated on C (*a*) 1.

(*a*) The first scene, *i.e.*, the brith of Budhda, in the lowest panel, to the proper left, is all but effaced. The feet of Māyā and a twig of the *sāla* tree, however, still remain. To the right of Māyā we can trace a kneeling figure, *i.e.*, Indra, and another standing to her left which must have been her sister Prajāpati. The proper right portion of this section is altogether destroyed, but we may assume, that it represented the Enlightenment of Buddha.

(*b*) The middle panel contained two scenes. The proper left portion represents the miracle of Śrāvastī. The Buddha is seated in the attitude of expounding the law. To his right and left we notice traces of two standing Buddhas and above each of these three, a seated Buddha figure with a pair of miniature *stūpas* between them. At the foot of the lotus on which the Buddha is seated we notice a corpulent figure seated on a low stool and supported by an attendant. This must be one of the heretical teachers with a pupil. On the sculpture under review this scene is mostly destroyed, but the same subject is figured on a larger scale on two other slabs (Ca 6 and 7) where it is much better preserved.

(*c*) The other scene in the middle panel is almost effaced. Traces, however, do remain to show that it was probably the first sermon of Benares. A pair of celestials carrying garlands are intact in the upper corners.

(*d*) The event shown in the uppermost compartment is the demise of Buddha. He is reclining as usual on his right side on a couch. One figure is standing at his head; another, evi-

---

[1] Rockhill, *Life of Buddha*, p. 93.
[2] Kern, *Manual of Buddhism*, p. 80.
[3] Vogel. *Mathurā Museum Catalogue*, p. 166, N 2.

dently Mahākāśyapa, worships his feet. In front of the couch are nine seated figures, the central one being Subhadra, his last convert. Behind Buddha is a line of mourners. Of the twin *sāla* trees under which the Buddha attained extinction only the one at the proper left end remains. To judge from the style the sculpture must be assigned to a period intervening between Ca 1 and Ca 3.

The back of the slab is incised with a *stūpa* with elaborate *hti* (*harmikā*). The material is buff-coloured Chunār sandstone. Unearthed in 1906-07 standing *in situ* in south side of *stūpa* No. 19.[1]

C (*a*) 5.—Three fragments (ht. 2′ 6″) all of which belonged to a stele illustrating events from Buddha's life. Two of these fragments fit together and have been re-fixed with a copper dowel. These fragments represent portions of two panels placed one over the other. The upper one illustrated the first sermon of Gautama Buddha at Sārnāth. The Buddha himself is missing. His throne was supported on a pair of lions standing to front. Between them we notice traces of three monks and a pair of deer, the wheel being absent. To the right of the Buddha is the Bōdhisattva Maitrēya standing on a lotus and wearing a deer skin. He holds a rosary (*japa-mālā*) in his right hand; his left hand is broken off. The Bōdhisattva on the other side is Avalōkitēśvara, holding a lotus (*padma*) in his left hand.

The scene in the lower compartment is the enlightenment of the Buddha at Gayā. The Buddha is missing. To his right, no doubt, stood the Evil One (Māra). The latter is missing but his attendant holding a flag with a crocodile head (*makaradhvaja*) is extant. In the upper corners are carved eight demons (*rākshasa*) with terrific faces, hurling weapons. One of them in the proper left corner is lifting a rock.

A fourth fragment (ht. 10″; width 6″) is evidently the proper left lower corner of the same stele. On it we notice the legs below knees of a female figure standing to front and to her proper left another female figure turned towards the former. These must be Māyā and Prajāpati, her sister, from the scene of Buddha's birth.

The style of carving is Gupta.

Three of the fragments were found in the 2nd outer court of monastery I at depths of 1½′ to 3′ below the surface.[2] The fourth fragment was found in the courtyard of the same monastery near its well, 4′ 3″ below the surface.

C (*a*) 6.—Slab (ht. 3′ 2½″; width 1′ 7″), round at the top, illustrating the great miracle performed by Gautama Buddha at Śrāvastī in order

---

[1] *A. S. R.*, 1906-07, p. 75 and p. 93, No. 51.

[2] For two of these, *cf. A. S. R.*, 1907-08, p. 51, 72, Pl. XIII, *c*, and p. 52, *c* 49.

to confound the six heretical teachers, the opponents of his doctrine.[1] The Buddha himself is seated cross-legged in the attitude of expounding the law, on a fully expanded lotus which is supported by a pair of Nāgas with their upper half bodies visible. Above and on either side of Buddha, are eight other Buddha figures, two of which above his head are seated in meditation, two others one on each side of his halo in the earth-touching attitude and the remaining four standing in the gift-bestowing or protecting attitude. In the upper corners of the slab we notice two celestials flying in opposite directions.

The corpulent figure seated on a stool in the proper right lower corner of the sculpture is presumably one of the six heretics (*tīrthika*) falling back under the fear of the Buddha's wonderful power. The figure supporting him from behind and the other figure right in the corner must be the adherents or disciples of the heretic. The corpulent figure seated in a devotional attitude on the other side is Prasēnajit, king of Śrāvastī, in whose presence the miracle was performed.

To judge from the style the sculpture is nearly coeval with C (*a*) 5. Reddish sandstone of Chunār. Discovered in 1906-07 on the top of *stūpa* No. 17 to the north-west of the Main Shrine, 2½′ below the surface.[2] Pl. XXI.

C (*a*) 7.—Slab (ht. 2′ 8″; width 1′ 7½″) similar to C (*a*) 6 and illustrating the same subject. It is interesting to note in this sculpture a figure of an elephant standing to front behind the king Prasēnajit in the proper left lower corner. This was evidently introduced to show the royal rank of the personage.

Unearthed in 1906-07 between *stūpas* Nos. 16 and 17 to the north-west of the Main Shrine, 3′ below the surface.[3]

C (*a*) 8.—Relief (ht. 2′ 1″; width 1′ 8½″) showing the presentation of honey to Gautama Buddha by a monkey in the Pārilēyyaka forest near Kauśāmbī, which is one of the eight main events of Buddha's life represented on the stele C (*a*) 3. The lower part of the sculpture is missing, while the upper part of the back slab is broken into two pieces and a large piece is missing from the proper left side. The Buddha is seated cross-legged with a bowl in his hands on a lotus throne which was supported by lions. The monkey who presented the honey stands to his right. The Buddha is clad in a well-draped upper robe. Around his head is an oval halo with a celestial figure (*dēva*) carrying a garland on either side. On grounds of style the sculpture may be assigned to the early mediæval period. It is made of blue stone and must have been carved in Magadha. Unearthed in 1907-08.

---

[1] The same scene is represented in stele No. C (*a*) 3, *f*, and C (*a*) 7.
[2] *A. S. R.*, 1906-07, p. 94, No. 54 and Pl. XX, 4.
[3] *A. S. R.*, 1906-07, p. 75 and p. 94, No. 55.

C (*a*) 9.—Fragment (ht. 8″; width 5½″) containing small portions of two panels of a stele sculptured with scenes from Buddha's life. In the upper panel a monk and a deer facing to left show that the proper left portion represented the first sermon at Sārnāth. To the proper right we observe a lion and the lower part of a human figure seated in the fashion of a mourner. This is apparently a part of the scene of Buddha's demise.

The lower panel contained a representation of the Buddha's enlightenment, of which only two demons in the act of hurling a rock and a missile are extant. Another fragment (ht. 5″; width 5⅓″) belongs to this sculpture. It shows part of crossed legs of Buddha on a throne supported on a lion. To his right we notice a pair of feet and below him a worshipper with joined hands. The scene concerned must have been one of the four minor events of the Buddha's career.

The style seems to be of the late Gupta period. Buff-coloured sandstone of Chunār. Unearthed in 1904-05 north-east of the Jagat Singh *stūpa.*[1]

C (*a*) 10.—Fragment (ht. 6″; width 4½″) representing the upper part of a figure of Māyā standing under a *sāla* tree. Her right hand, which is missing, must have held a branch of the tree. The fragment belonged, no doubt, to a representation of the Buddha's Nativity. Gupta style. Traces of red paint. Buff-coloured sandstone of Chunār. Excavated in 1906-07 in the courtyard of monastery I, 3′ below the surface.

C (*a*) 11.—Fragment (ht. 6½″; width 4½″) similar to C (*a*) 10. Unearthed in the same year in the area to the east of the Main Shrine.

C (*a*) 12.—Fragmentary relief (ht. 1′ 5¼″; width 1′ 4½″) bearing a figure of a child seated in Indian fashion with what looks like a writing board (*lipiphalaka*) on its knees. The writing board is partly broken and the sculpture badly weathered all over. It is tempting to connect the relief with Gautama Buddha's first visit as a child to the writing school (*lipiśālā*) when he amazed the teacher, Viśvāmitra by his knowledge of sixty-four scripts of which the teacher did not even know the names. This subject is portrayed on an imperfect Gandhāra relief now preserved in the Lahore Museum.[2] Another illustration of the same scene is afforded by the miniature *stūpa* drum from Sikri now also in the Lahore Museum, where we find this subject among other events from Buddha's life and immediately after Asitadēvala's visit to the infant Gautama Buddha.[3] In these Gandhāra sculptures the Buddha is represented as a grown-up man. It is interesting, there-

[1] *A. S. R.*, 1904-05, p. 101, No. 469.
[2] *A. S. R.*, 1903-04, p. 245f. and Pl. LXVI, 1, and M. Boyer, *B. E. F. E. O.*, Vol. IV (1904), p. 685.
[3] *A. S. R.*, 1903-04, p. 247, and fig. 1 on p. 246.

fore, to note that the Sārnāth relief under review if referring to the same scene represents him distinctly as a child with long locks falling on the shoulders.

The style of the sculpture, as far as it can be judged from its damaged condition, points to the late Gupta period. It is also evident from the flanks of the sculpture that it was never finished. The material is Chunār sandstone. The sculpture was formerly preserved in the Queen's College, but was most probably found at Sārnāth.

C (*a*) 13.—Sculpture (ht. 1′ 3″; width 1′ 4½″) representing the death or Nirvāṇa of Gautama Buddha. He is lying on his right side as in the preceding sculptures with Mahākāśyapa standing at his feet. Five figures are seated in front of the couch. The second figure from proper right, which is damaged, was Subhadra seated turned to the Buddha. Behind the Buddha, two mourners are standing; a third issues from the *sāla* tree at the proper left end. The other tree is broken off. The sculpture is coeval with C (*a*) 4 and made of the same kind of stone. Major Kittoe has left us a sketch of this sculpture in his "Drawings" and he may have excavated it.[1]

C (*a*) 14.—Fragment (ht. 1′ 3″; width 1′ 3″) from the top of a stele (*ūrdhvapaṭa*) on which only the uppermost panel with the scene of Buddha's death (*parinirvāṇa*) remains. The Buddha is shown lying in the usual fashion with one figure standing at his head and Mahākāśyapa worshipping his feet. In front, there are four mourning figures of which the second one from the proper right is Subhadra, the last convert of the Buddha. It is noteworthy that, unlike the arrangement on other steles, he is seated in the present sculpture facing to front. In the background we observe the traces of four mourners and the twin *sāla* trees. The style is similar to that of C (*a*) 13. Excavated in 1904-05.[2]

C (*a*) 15.—Fragment (ht. 1′ 11½″; width 1′ 10″) of a sculpture representing the same subject as on C (*a*) 6 and C (*a*) 7. The upper part of the slab is broken off. The Buddha is seated in the attitude of expounding the law on a lotus which was supported by Nāgas. The lower corners were no doubt occupied by one of the heretics and Prasēnajit, King of Śrāvastī. Much defaced and weather-stained. The sculpture was formerly preserved in the Queen's College, but the material and the style leave no doubt that it originates from Sārnāth.

C (*a*) 16.—Slab (ht. 1′ 4″; width 10″) with a figure of Buddha seated cross-legged in the earth-touching attitude on a lotus. Behind him is carved a pattern of throne and halo in low relief. Above Buddha's

---

[1] Vol. I, No. 161, Pl. 8.

[2] *A. S. R.*, 1904-05, p. 96, No. 180.

head we notice a twig of the *pīpal* tree and at the top of the slab a figure of the Dying Buddha. Traces of six Buddhas on the sides. The front of throne is entirely defaced. The style seems to belong to the mediæval period. Pale buff stone of Chunār. Unearthed in 1907-08 in the 2nd outer court of monastery I, 2′ below the surface.

C (*a*) 17.—Fragment (ht. 1′ 5″; width 1′ 5″) with the head of a Buddha image under a *pīpal* tree. To the proper left projecting from a cloud is a celestial figure carrying a garland and flying to the proper right. Below it, we notice a miniature Buddha seated in meditation. The fragment evidently belonged to a representation of Buddha's enlightenment. The style seems to be mediæval. Buff-coloured sandstone of Chunār.

It would seem that this stone was brought by Mr. Oertel from Sassaram and added to the Sārnāth Collection.

C (*a*) 18.—Relief (ht. 1′ 2½″; width 11″) representing Gautama Buddha's descent from the 'heaven of the thirty-three gods' at Sāṅkāśya (modern Sankisā in the district of Farrukhābād). In the middle of the composition is the Buddha standing in the attitude of protection[1] on the top of a ladder of five steps. To his right, is a figure of Brahmā standing with a fly-whisk (Sanskrit *chāmara*) in his right hand and his attribute the rosary (*akshamālā*) in the left. To the left of the Buddha is Indra standing, holding an umbrella over his head. On the base to the proper right of the ladder we observe traces of two worshippers, one of whom must be identified as the nun Utpalavaraṇā who was the first to receive the Buddha on his descent. To the left of the ladder are represented two more kneeling figures.

The sculpture undoubtedly dates from the Gupta period. The earliest representation of this scene occurs on the Bharhut *stūpa*,[2] where the Buddha himself is, however, absent. The next two examples are afforded by the Mathurā school.[3] In these two sculptures the Buddha is shown actually descending by a triple ladder. He is accompanied by Brahmā and Indra with clasped hands on the side ladders. The idea of the umbrella presumably originated with the masons of Sārnāth.

Unearthed in the 2nd outer court of monastery I.[4]

C (*a*) 19.—Relief (ht. 8½″; width 6¼″) representing the same subject as C (*a*) 18 with which it is apparently contemporaneous. The

---

[1] In mediæval representations of this scene the Buddha stands in the gift-bestowing attitude. *Cf.* C (*a*) 21 and 23.

[2] Kern, Manual of Buddhism, p. 33, foot-note 4; and Cunningham, *Bharhut Stūpa*, Pl. XVII, central compartment.

[3] Vogel, *Mathurā Catalogue*, p. 125, H 1, *c* and Pl. VI; and p. 167, N-2.

[4] *A. S. R.*, 1907-08, p. 51, No. *η* 1, and Pl. XIII, *g*.

upper part of the sculpture is broken off carrying away the head of the Buddha. The base of the sculpture is effaced.

Discovered in 1906-07 south of south-east angle of monastery I, 3′ below the surface.

C (*a*) 20.—Fragment (ht. 6½″; width 5″) similar to C (*a*) 18 and 19. The upper part of the sculpture is missing and the rest somewhat defaced. The Buddha stands in the middle of the composition in the attitude of granting protection, attended by Brahmā on the right and Śakra on the left. The top of the umbrella, which Indra holds, is broken off.

Gupta style. Buff-coloured stone of Chunār. Discovered in 1906-07 to the west of the Jagat Singh *stūpa*.[1]

* C (*a*) 21.—Relief (ht. 1′ 2½″; width 9½″) representing Gautama Buddha's descent from the heaven of 'the thirty-three gods' where he had preached his doctrine to his mother for three months. The upper part of the slab is broken off; and the rest defaced. The central figure without head standing in the gift-bestowing attitude (*varadamudrā*) is the Buddha himself. The figures standing on his right and left are Brahmā and Indra respectively. Of the umbrella which Śakra held over Buddha's head only the staff remains in his hands. The ladder is not indicated. At the right end of the base is a kneeling figure, no doubt Utpalavarṇā the nun. An inscription of four lines in Nāgarī characters of the 8th or 9th century A.D. occupies the rest of the base. The first two lines contain the Buddhist creed. The third begins with the words *dēyadharmmōyaṁ*. The remaining portion is obliterated. Buff-coloured sandstone of Chunār. Excavated in 1904-05 to the north-west of the Jagat Singh *stūpa*.[2]

C (*a*) 22.—Relief (ht. 1′ 5½″ without the tenon under the base; width 1′ 2″) illustrating the same subject as C (*a*) 21 and of about the same date. The right side of the slab is broken off. The rest is broken into three pieces which have been re-fixed. The head and the left knee of the Buddha are damaged and both his fore-arms are wanting. To the Buddha's right is carved a pair of feet which must have belonged to a figure of Brahmā. Indra who stands on the left of the Buddha, holds an umbrella over his head.

Chunār sandstone. Traces of red paint. Unearthed in 1907-08 on the approach to the Main Shrine from the east at depths of 7 to 8 feet below the surface.[3]

*C (*a*) 23.—Relief (ht. 2′ 4½″; width 1′ 6″) representing Gautama Buddha's descent from the 'heaven of the thirty-three gods' at Sankisā.

---

[1] *A. S. R.*, 1906-07, p. 91, No. 18.
[2] *Ibid*, 1904-05, p. 96, No. 166.
[3] *A. S. R.*, 1907-08, p. 67, U 65 which is the lowest of the three fragments.

The upper portion and the sides of the back-slab are missing, and the rest broken into six pieces which have been re-fixed. The Buddha is standing between Brahmā and Indra. Both of them wear the Brahmanical thread (*yajñōpavīta*) and whereas the god of creation holds his characteristic water-gourd in his left hand, Śakra holds an umbrella over the Buddha's head. The top of the umbrella is missing. On the base below the lotus on which the Buddha stands is incised an inscription of two lines containing the Buddhist creed in characters of the 9th or 10th century A.D.

Chunār sandstone of buff colour. Excavated in 1904-05 to the north-west of the Jagat Singh *stūpa*.[1]

C (*a*) 24.—Lower portion (ht. 1′ 5″; width 1′ 4″) of a relief showing the descent of Gautama Buddha from the heaven of the thirty-three gods. The upper part above the thighs and the feet of the Buddha are missing; so also the figure of Brahmā from his right side. To his left stands Indra holding the staff of an umbrella followed by an attendant.

The style of execution is exceedingly inartistic and must be assigned to the late mediæval period.

Chunār standstone. Unearthed in 1904-05.[2]

C (*a*) 25.—Fragmentary relief (ht. 5½″; width 6½″) showing the presentation of honey (Sanskrit *madhu*) to the Buddha by a monkey in the Pārilēyyaka forest. The upper portion of the Buddha above the waist is wanting. He is seated in European style with a bowl in his hands on the lap. To his right stands the monkey in the act of offering honey in a bowl. Below it is another monkey seated cross-legged.

Chunār stone of grey colour. Discovered in 1904-05 between the Jagat Singh *stūpa* and the Main Shrine.[3]

C (*a*) 26.—Fragment (ht. 8½″; width 10″) of a relief showing the same subject as on C (*a*) 25. The Buddha is seated cross-legged with a bowl in his hands which rest on his lap. His upper part above the waist is damaged. To his right we notice only the feet of the monkey who presented the honey.

Mediæval style. Buff-coloured sandstone. Unearthed in 1904-05 to the south of the Main Shrine.[4]

C (*a*) 27.—Fragment (ht. 4½″; width 7½″) similar to C (*a*) 26. Discovered in 1907-08 in the 2nd outer court of mediæval monastery I.

C (*a*) 28.—Fragment (ht. 1′ 2″; width 1′ 10½″) of a sculpture showing an emaciated figure prostrating itself to the proper left. On its back we notice the left foot of a larger figure, while its right foot rests

---

[1] *A. S. R.*, 1904-05, p. 94, No. 101.
[2] *Ibid*, p. 94, No. 106.
[3] *Ibid*, p. 99, No. 312.
[4] *Ibid* p. 93, No. 65.

on the base of the sculpture. The identification is uncertain. It can not be a representation of the Sumēdha-Jātaka; for in the numerous representations of this scene in the Gandhāra sculptures the Buddha is never shown as stepping over Sumēdha.

Made of pale buff stone of Chunār. The sculpture was formerly preserved in the Queen's College.

C (*b*).—Decorative bas-reliefs.

C (*b*) 1.—Sculptured slab (ht. 2′ 11″; width 1′ 10½″) showing a leogryph rising in the air and ridden by a warrior armed with a sword. He holds one of its curved horns with his left hand. The dragon has protruding eyes, leaf-shaped ears, a well-executed mane and paws; its head shows no likeness to that of a lion. The hair of the warrior is parted in the middle and falls on the sides in wig-like curls. He wears ear-rings, a necklace and a *dhōtī* fastened by a plain band. The tail of the leogryph is twined round the waist of a second warrior beneath, who seems to be piercing its right fore-paw with a sword and, as Mr. Oertel has pointed out, seems to be transported himself in the air.

The panel was unearthed at the Chaukhaṇḍī *stūpa* in 1904-05 by Mr. Oertel who is of opinion that it decorated one side of the stair to the upper terrace of that *stūpa*, being matched on the other side by the similar sculpture C (*b*) 2[1]. The sculpture which is wonderfully well preserved dates from the Gupta period. Pale buff stone of Chunār. Pl. XXII.

C (*b*) 2.—Sculpture of the same dimensions as C (*b*) 1 which was found close to it and must have been carved by the same artist to correspond to it on the opposite side of a stair. This view is supported by the fact that the leogryph and the lower warrior are turned in the opposite direction. The other warrior however faces away from the dragon and displays his sword as if in the act of exchanging a blow with a foe. The warrior beneath the animal holds its tail with his left hand, the weapon in his right hand being a short dagger. Pl. XXII.

C (*b*) 3.—Sculpture (ht. 2′ 6″; width 1′ 7½″) analogous to C (*b*) 2, showing a leogryph flying to the left. It has a thick foliated tail and is ridden astride by a headless warrior who holds the reins passed through its lower jaw, with his left hand. The proper left side of the panel is broken off with the head of the rider. The remainder is broken into five pieces. Fine Gupta style. Traces of red paint. Pale buff stone of Chunār. Discovered in 1906-07 on the south side of the large court or open hall east of the Main Shrine, below the concrete terrace.[2]

C (*b*) 4.—Fragment (ht. 1′ 7″; width 1′ 2″) of a panel which served as a counterpart to C (*b*) 3. The fragment retains only the bust of the leogryph who flies to the proper left and the left hand of the rider holding the reins of the dragon on the front. The other hand of the warrior must have held a sword. Found near C (*b*) 3.

C (*b*) 5.—Fragment (ht. 1′ 6″; width 6½″) with the bust of a warrior holding a sword in his right hand, which might have belonged to C (*b*) 4, though as it is, it does not fit on to that sculpture.

---

[1] *A. S. R.*, 1904-5. Pl. XXXI, *b*; p. 88 and p. 101, No. 474.
[2] *Ibid*, 1906-07, p. 94, No. 60.

Unearthed near C (*b*) 4 in 1906-07.

C (*b*) 6.—Panel (ht. 2′; width 1′ 6½″) showing a rampant leogryph with a bushy tail, ridden astride by a warrior holding its reins in his left hand and a whip in the right. The hair of the warrior is fastened at the top and falls in plaits on the back of the head. The workmanship is decidedly inferior to that of the preceding panels. Probably late Gupta period. The fragment was formerly preserved in the Queen's College. It is made of a reddish sandstone of Chunâr and must have been discovered at Sārnāth.

C (*b*) 7.—Sculpture (ht. 2′ 7″; width 1′ ½″) showing a figure of a leogryph with three paws raised in the air and head turned backward. Its tail is caught in the trunk of a miniature elephant standing beneath. Such rows of figures occur on door-jambs and I have no doubt that this fragment served the same purpose.

The style seems to be late Gupta or mediæval. It is made of the same kind of stone as C (*b*) 6 and belonged to the Queen's College Collection.

C (*b*) 8.—Fragment (ht. 1′ 4″; width 10″) with a figure of a leogryph without the hind legs. On its back is a human figure clasping an uncertain object. The mane of the animal is indicated by very shallow wavy lines. Possibly late Gupta, but more probably mediæval. Buff-coloured sandstone of Chunār. Formerly preserved in the Queen's College.

C (*b*) 9.—Fragmentary sculpture[1] (ht. 1′ 6″; width 3′ 4¾″) which must have formed part of the top piece of a door-architrave. To the proper left is the corner of the architrave, surrounded by bands of ornament, two of which simulate the garland pattern and two others contain flowing vine and lotus designs, the intervening curves in them being filled up with bunches of grapes and leaves, and lotus buds, flowers and fruits respectively. The birds pecking at the bunches of fruit are particularly interesting.

The portion at the proper right end is taken up by a square panel representing a *stūpa* which presumably illustrates the legend of the Rāmagrāma *stūpa* narrated by Hiuen Thsang.[2] In the sculpture under review the *stūpa* is surrounded by a railing of the usual type and has a smaller railing at the top, which supports the *hti*. The latter is decorated with a fly-whisk (Sanskrit *chāmara*) at each end and an umbrella hung with streamers standing in the middle. The interlaced triple-hooded snakes which encircle the drum of the *stūpa* represent the dragon or Nāga who, according to tradition, guarded the Rāmagrāma *stūpa* and dissuaded Aśōka from destroying it for the sake of

---

[1] Described and illustrated in *A. S. R.*, 1904-05, p. 89, and fig. No. 12 on p. 88.

[2] *Ibid*, and Beal, *Buddhist Records of the Western World*, Vol. I, introduction, pp. i-ii.

the Buddha relics enshrined in it. The elephant presenting the nosegay of lotus flowers must be the elephant which, in the absence of human beings, worshipped the *stūpa* with flowers and perfumes. Above the elephant is a winged harpy (*suparṇa*) with a long tail carrying a long garland as an offering.

Dr. Vogel has drawn attention to the similarity of this last figure to similar figures on Mathurā sculptures. The style of execution is elegant and the sculpture may presumably be assigned to the late Kushāṇa period.

The two semi-circular grooves on the top of the slab must have received the tenons of the face-stone immediately above it in the wall. The square hole in the middle may have held a gargoyle. Made of pale buff stone of Chunār and unearthed in 1904-05 east of the Main Shrine.[1] Pl. XXIII, b.

C (*b*) 10.—Fragment (ht. 10″; width 7″) of an architrave with bands of decoration, similar to C (*b*) 9 and probably by the same mason. Unearthed in 1904-05 north of shrine on the north-east of the Jagat Singh *stūpa*.[2]

C (*b*) 11.—Fragment (ht. 1′ 2″; width 7″) similar to C (*b*) 10 and evidently made for the same structure by the same artist. It is adorned with five bands of ornament analogous to those on C (*b*) 9. Probably found in the same year and locality.

C (*b*) 12.—Votive slab (*āyāgapaṭa*) (length 1′ 8″; width 9½″) broken on all sides. To the proper left we notice a rosette surrounded by four 'three-jewel' (*triratna*) symbols with blue lotus flowers between them. Perhaps the rosette is meant for the 'wheel of the law' (*dharma-chakra*). To the proper right is a symbol resembling the honey-suckle, which occurs on the Hāthī Gumphā cave at Khaṇḍagiri, on Gupta terra-cotta seals from Basāṛh and Bhīṭā, on coins of the Āndhra dynasty, on the umbrella of the Bōdhisattva statue [B (*a*) 1] in the Sārnāth Museum and many other Mathurā sculptures. The proper right end of the slab is adorned with a column with a diminishing base.

The style seems to be of the 1st century B. C. Chunār sandstone of reddish colour with vestiges of red paint. The slab formed part of the stone floor on which the concrete terrace on the east of the Main Shrine was laid.[3]

C (*b*) 13.—Rectangular votive slab (*āyāgapaṭa*) (length 1′ 4½″; width 10″) bearing an ornamental thunderbolt (*vajra*) and the Indian cross (*svastika*). This diagram was presumably continued towards the proper left in simulation of the Greek fret. Āndhra period. Found at the same place as C (*b*) 12.

---

[1] *A. S. R.*, 1904-05, p. 100, No. 427.
[2] *Ibid*, p. 97, No. 261.
[3] *Ibid*, 1906-07, p. 77.

C (*b*) 14.—Slab (ht. 1′ 1″; width 1′ 1″) with the legs of a standing male deity in a sunken panel, with the stalk of a flower to his right. To his left we observe a short male figure holding a club (?) in its left hand, the right being raised in front of the breast. Mediæval style. Reddish sandstone of Chunār. Unearthed in 1904-05 to the north-east of the Jagat Singh *stūpa.* [1]

C (*b*) 15.—Slab (ht. 10½″; width 9″) with a defaced figure standing facing. To its right are the traces of a female figure wearing a *sāṛhī* and anklets turned towards it. If this had been a male figure, it could have been identified as Indra receiving the new-born Buddha. The date cannot be ascertained. Traces of red paint. Chunār sandstone. Unearthed in the area on the east of the Main Shrine.

C (*b*) 16.—Two fragments which fit together (ht. 1′ 4″; width 2′ 1½″) of a door-lintel with two bands of figures. The upper one shows an object resembling the acanthus flower with a large jewel disposed in its centre being transported in a dish by a pair of flying celestials (*dēva*). Each of them has his consort perched on his back. The lower band retains portions of three celestials, the middle one carrying a garland. Below, there is some foliated decoration.

Gupta style. Chunār sandstone. The bigger fragment was unearthed in 1907-08 in the trench to the south of the 2nd outer court of the mediæval monastery I, 1′ below the surface [2], the other in 1904-05 to the east of the Jagat Singh *stūpa.* [3]

C (*b*) 17.—Fragment (ht. 1′ 9″; width 1′ 8″) of a door-lintel with a double border at the top and a fine floral pattern in the corner. The upper band shows a pair of male celestials (*dēva*) carrying their spouses on their thighs and what appear to be leaf-cups (*drōṇa*) containing flowers in their hands. The hair of the male figures is arranged in wig-like curls, that of the females in masses on the sides of their heads. The lower band contains only male celestials. In vertical continuation of this ring on the proper right side there are two panels containing a goblin (*yaksha*) dancing and another playing a tabor (*mṛidaṅga*) which he holds under his left arm-pit.

The style is Gupta and the material Chunār sandstone. The fragment is sketched in Major Kittoe's Mss. Drawings, but evidently he did not know its provenance.[4]

C (*b*) 18.—Slab (ht. 7″; width 2′ 2¾″) with two long panels. The upper panel contains twenty-six Buddha (or Tīrthaṅkara?) figures seated in the attitude of meditation (*dhyānamudrā*) on the front and five on each of the sides. In the lower panel we observe two worship-

---

[1] *A. S. R.*, 1904-05, p. 96, No. 168.

[2] *A. S. R.*, 1907-08, p. 54 ; 45 and Pl. XIII, *h*.

[3] *Ibid*, 1904-05, p. 100, No. 417.

[4] Vol. I, No. 151, on Pl. 149.

pers at the proper right end and one at the other. The remaining space is taken up with a series of articles of worship which beginning from the proper left end are a conch (*śaṅkha*) on a tripod, a lamp-stand (*dīpadāna*), an incense-burner (*dhūpadāna*), a basin with sweets (?), a pair of fire basins (?), a pitcher with a conch (*śaṅkha*), an umbrella (*chhattra*) with a streamer, a bed with a pair of fly-whisks (*chāmara*) on it and three uncertain objects under it, a female with a fly-whisk in her right hand, and last of all a vessel containing fruit (?).

The stone must have been used in the facing of a shrine or *stūpa*. This is clearly shown by grooves for clamps on its top and its rough surface on the back. The style of execution is attributable to the mediæval period. Buff-coloured sandstone of Chunār. Discovered in 1904-05 near the north-west corner of the Main Shrine.[1]

C (*b*) 19.—Slab (ht. 5¾"; width 1′ 4″) with two rows of Buddhas in the attitude of meditation, which are continued on the sides. The total number of the Buddhas amounts to thirty-four. Mediæval style. The sculpture must have served as a face-stone on a shrine or a *stūpa*. This is proved by the fact that the drum of a mediæval votive *stūpa* D (*b*) 8 in the Sārnāth Museum is decorated with similar rows of Buddha figures. The slab is one of the thirteen Sārnāth sculptures returned from the Lucknow Provincial Museum.

C (*b*) 20.—Slab (ht. 1′ 9″; width 7″) with a single row of Buddhas seated in the attitude of meditation (*dhyānamudrā*) which must have decorated a *stūpa* or a shrine. Excavated in 1904-05 to the south of the Aśōka Column.[2]

C (*b*) 21-25.—Five slabs (ht. 9″ each) with four rows of Buddhas seated in the attitude of meditation, which must have been used in the facing of a *stūpa* or a shrine. Mediæval style. Found near the same shrine as C (*b*) 18.

C (*b*) 26.—Frieze (ht. 9″; width 1′ 10″) with a cornice above and below. The projecting portion contains five sunken panels containing figures of Gautama Buddha, two in the attitude of meditation, two others in the earth-touching attitude, while the fifth one in the centre holds a bowl on the lap. The last mentioned scene recalls the presentation of cups by the four guardians of the quarters (*lōkapāla*) or of honey by the monkey of the Pārilēyyaka forest. Another niche to the proper left contains a figure of Buddha in the gift-bestowing attitude.

The style is referrable to the mediæval period. The sculpture is made of grey granite stone and was presented by Mr. Oertel who brought it from elsewhere.

---

[1] *A. S. R.*, 1904-5, p. 56, No. 158.
[2] *Ibid*, p. 97, No. 194.

* C (*b*) 27.—Slab (ht. 5″ ; width 2′ 2″) with a row of seven miniature *stūpas* in relief on which is incised the Buddhist creed in Sanskrit in characters of the 9th century A. D. Buff-coloured sandstone of Chunār. Excavated in 1904-05.[1]

C (*b*) 28.—Fragment (ht. 6″ ; width 8½″), evidently a spandrel of an arch, carved with a figure of a woman seated in Indian style, absorbed in grief, her face buried in her arms which rest on her knees. Her hair hangs down back as far as the waist and her upper body seems to be naked while the lower part is clad in a *dhōtī* which is tied to her loins by a girdle (*kāñchī*) resembling a metal chain. She wears anklets and her feet are missing. Behind her we see a blue lotus and in front, an uncertain object which tapers upwards. The carving is singularly fine. Dr. Marshall who unearthed it in 1906-07 in the area on the east of the Main Shrine assigns it to the Maurya period.[2]

C (*b*) 29.—Slab (ht. 1′ 11″ ; width 1′ 8″) with a bust of a dancing female figure. Her hair is gathered in a round mass above her left shoulder and she wears an elaborate necklace and a scraf. Mediæval style. The sculpture was formerly preserved in the Queen's College.

C (*b*) 30.—Fragmentary relief (ht. 8½″ ; width 5″) containing a bust of a female figure in a shrine. Mediæval. Chunār sandstone. Excavated in 1906-07 in the area on the east of the Main Shrine.

C (*b*) 31.—Fragment (ht. 5″ ; width 10½″) with traces of two monkeys (?) crouching face to face. Buff-coloured sandstone of Chunār. Mediæval. Excavated in the monastery to the west of the Dhamēkh *stūpa*, 2′ below the surface.

C (*b*) 32.—Fragment (ht. 8″ ; width 6½″) of a column (?) or stele with two panels placed one above the other. The upper compartment contains a pair of celestials flying in opposite directions and carrying a bowl of sweets and a garland respectively. The lower panel shows a pair of geese (*haṁsa*) standing facing each other and holding the ends of a garland with their bills. Below, we observe traces of the head-dress of a female figure and at the top the feet of figures. There are traces of two square sockets on the proper left flank. The style seems to belong to the mediæval period. Buff-coloured sandstone of Chunār. Find-spot not known.

C (*b*) 33.—Fragment (ht. 9″ ; width 5½″) with a figure of a Buddha without feet standing in the gift-bestowing attitude. To his right is carved a lotus. Late Gupta style. Buff-coloured sandstone of Chunār. Unearthed in 1904-05 in the chapel near the south-east corner of the Main Shrine.[3]

---

[1] *A. S. R.*, 1904-05, p. 96, No. 167; and p. 104, inscription No. XXXVII.
[2] *Ibid*, 1906-07, p. 94., No. 71.
[3] *Ibid*, 1904-05, p. 98, No. 273.

C (*b*) 34.—**Fragment** (ht. 11¾"; width 7") carved with two panels, which seems to have belonged to a door-jamb. The upper panel contains a male standing with his left arm passed round a female who stands to his left. The heads of both are broken off. The male wears a short *dhōtī* covering his things and a scarf above it, with its ends falling on his right side. The *dhōtī* worn by the female reaches down to her ankles, but her scarf is laid on her arms. In the lower panel we notice only the heads of two figures, which from their head-dresses must be a male and a female. Late Gupta style.

The fragment is delineated in Major Kittoe's Mss. Drawings,[1] but the provenance is not stated. The Chunār sandstone of which it is made and the style of carving, however, are enough to show that the sculpture must have been discovered at Sārnāth.

C (*b*) 35.—**Fragment** (ht. 4¼"; width 3½") probably of a jamb of a window, with portions of two panels remaining on it. The upper panel contains the legs of two goblins (*yaksha*) dancing, and the lower, a male head facing to the left. Gupta style. Buff-coloured sandstone of Chunār.

Discovered in one of the recent excavations. The precise find-spot cannot be ascertained.

C (*b*) 36.—Part of a stele (*ūrdhvapaṭa*) (ht. 7¼"; width 6") with portions of three panels. In the uppermost compartment, only the feet of a male and a female figure remain. The position of the feet of the female shows that she must have been engaged in a dance. The middle panel contains two atlantes or supporting figures, supporting the top of the panel with their heads. One of the figures has the legs bent upwards and rests its weight on the arms. Both of them have corpulent bellies which are bound with wide bands. The lowest panel retains only the heads of a male and a female figure which were standing side by side.

Gupta style. Chunār sandstone with vestiges of a red paint. Discovered in 1904-05.[2]

C (*b*) 37.—Bust (ht. 9¾") of a male figure, without arms, wearing a band round the belly, similar to the atlantes in C (*b*) 36. Gupta style. Chunār sandstone with traces of a red paint. Excavated in 1906-07 near the north-east corner of the open hall on the east of the Main Shrine.

C (*b*) 38.—Head (ht. 6½") of a male which must have belonged to an atlante or supporting figure. His hair falls in twisted curls, and he has a crescent mark on his forehead. Gupta style. Chunār sandstone with traces of a red paint. Unearthed in 1904-05.[3]

---

[1] Vol. I, No. 166 on Pl. 114.
[2] *A. S. R.*, 1904-05, p. 96, No. 182.
[3] *Ibid*, p. 99, No. 365.

C (*b*) 39.—Slab (ht. 9¼″; width 6″) with a corpulent supporting figure or atlante in relief, with its belly and knees damaged. The sculpture must have served as a face-stone in a building. Gupta style. Chunār sandstone. Provenance not known.

C (*b*) 40.—Fragment (ht. 6″; width 4¾″) with an atlante or supporting figure in relief. Its right hand was raised upwards, and portions of its left arm and leg are broken off. The face is damaged. Gupta style. Unearthed in 1907-08 in the western precinct of monastery I, 3′ below the surface.

C (*b*) 41.—Fragment (ht. 7″) with the right half of a figure sitting in oriental fashion in a niche with a circular pilaster on the proper right. The hands of the figure were presumably joined in front of the chest. The lower side of the stone is ornamented with lotus-petals. Late Gupta or mediæval period.

Discovered in 1907-08 in the 1st outer court of monastery I.[1]

C (*b*) 42.—Fragment (ht. 4½″; width 6″) with the bust of a Buddha in the attitude of expounding the law. Late Gupta or mediæval period. Excavated in 1904-05 to the north of the Jagat Singh *stūpa*.[2]

C (*b*) 43.—Fragment (ht. 4″; width 4½″) probably of a jamb of a window with a defaced figure seated in 'easy attitude' like a Bōdhisattva. Mediæval style.

Reddish sandstone of Chunār. Found in the western precinct of monastery I, 2′ below the surface.[3]

C (*b*) 44.—Fragment (ht. 6″; width 5½″) of a door jamb bearing the upper portion of a female above the waist, who holds with her left hand a cord which goes round the neck of a male figure standing facing her. Traces of foliage are visible above the female figure. Late Gupta (?) style. Excavated in 1906-07 in monastery I.

C (*b*) 45.—Fragment (ht. 6″; width 6″) bearing a celestial figure carrying a dish of flowers and a leg of a similar figure to the proper left. The fragment undoubtedly belonged to a door lintel similar to C (*b*) 16. Late Gupta style. Buff-coloured sandstone of Chunār. Excavated in 1907-08 in the area to the south of monastery II, 6′ below the surface.[4]

C (*b*) 46.—Fragment (ht. 5½″; width 7″) carved with the foliage and fruit of a mango tree. Traces of a red paint. Gupta style. Unearthed in 1906-07 in the area on the east or west of the Main Shrine.

C (*b*) 47.—Fragment (ht. 9½″) probably of a pillar, showing the bust of a figure with hands joined before the breast. There is a branch of

---

[1] *A. S. R.*, 1907-08, p. 49, η 207.

[2] *Ibid*, 1904-05, p. 98, No. 303.

[3] *Ibid*, 1907-08, p. 48, [illegible] 14

[4] *Ibid*, p. 72, γ 29.

a tree on the proper left. Mediæval style. Buff-coloured sandstone of Chunār. Unearthed in 1904-05.[1]

C (*b*) 48.—Fragment (ht. 9"; width 11") of a lintel with a celestial figure carrying a garland as an offering. Below and on the proper left side of it is carved a conventional garland pattern. Late Gupta style. Buff-coloured sandstone of Chunār. Excavated in 1904-05 to the north-east of the Main Shrine.[2]

C (*b*) 49.—Sculptured fragment (length 5¼"; width 3¾") showing a part of a lotus flower. Mediæval style. Find-spot not known.

C (*b*) 50.—Fragment (ht. 2½"; width 4") with the feet of a female figure, wearing anklets. Mediæval style. Chunār stone. Unearthed in 1907-08 in the western precinct of monastery I, 5′ below the surface.

C (*b*) 51.—Fragment (ht. 3¾") with foliage and the head of a bird. Chunār sandstone. Find-spot not known.

C (*b*) 52.—Fragment (ht. 4") with a side pilaster of a niche in mediæval style, excavated in 1906-07 in the monastery to the west of the Dhamēkh *stūpa*.

C (*b*) 53.—Fragment (ht. 3") carved with a miniature *stūpa* at the top. Mediæval. Excavated in 1907-08 on the approach to the Main Shrine from the east, 7′ below the surface.

C (*b*) 54.—Fragment (ht. 9¾") with a lotus in relief. Mediæval period. Unearthed in one of the recent excavations.

C (*b*) 55.—Similar fragment (ht. 9¼") discovered in 1904-05.[3]

C (*b*) 56.—Two fragments (ht. 3¾"; width 3¾") of a frieze with three Buddha figures seated in the attitude of meditation, similar to C (*b*) 18, etc. Mediæval. Chunār sandstone. Excavated in 1907-08 on the approach to the Main Shrine from the east, 8′ below the surface.

---

[1] *A. S. R.*, 1904-05, p. 97, No. 228.
[2] *Ibid*, 1904-05, p. 97, No. 234.
[3] *Ibid*, p. 97, No. 232.

D. ARCHITECTURAL PIECES AND INSCRIBED SLABS.

D(*a*).—Railing posts, coping stones and cross-bars.

D(*a*) 1-12.—Twelve posts of a railing of about the 1st century B. C., which Dr. Marshall and Dr. Konow found fixed into a floor made of brick and mud in the open space east of the paved passage situated to the north-east of the Main Shrine. The learned discoverers are of opinion that [1] "when complete in the place where it was found, the rail must have comprised 14 uprights, *i.e.*, five on the north and south sides, and four on the east and west, forming a rectangle of approximately 7′ 6″ × 8′ 6″. One upright, however, on the north and one on the west are missing as well as all the coping stones and cross-bars." The posts vary in length from 4′ 2″ to 4′ 4″ of which the base up to a height of 6″ to 9″ was left rough, the rest of the surface being smoothed, dressed and carved. Three of the corner posts are sculptured on the two outer faces; the fourth corner post at the north-east corner and the rest of the intermediate posts are carved, as usual, on one face only. Dr. Marshall and Dr. Konow have also shown that these pillars were not standing in their original position, for which reason they have been taken out and deposited in the Museum. Pl. VI.

Beginning at the north-west corner of the rectangle referred to and going round in the *pradakshiṇa* direction as the columns stood we have:

D(*a*) 1.—Corner post sculptured on two faces (ht. 4′ 4″; section 8″ × 6″). One of these faces shows a long panel with a bead and reel border along each vertical edge. The devices beginning from below are (*a*) Vase with honeysuckle placed on a triple pedestal; (*b*) Vase with lotus plant bearing flowers and buds; (*c*) Symbol resembling a double trident placed on a triple pedestal with the Buddhist railing in front. The presence of the throne and the railing would show that the symbol is not a merely decorative motif. It is meant for the three jewels (*triratna*) of the Buddhist church. (*d*) *Stūpa* decorated with garlands and surmounted with *hti* supported on railing and on top of it an umbrella (Sanskrit *chhattra*) with pendant streamers. On the other face, (*a*) identical with (*c*) on above-mentioned face; (*b*) Persepolitan pillar on triple pedestal with a vase-shaped base and a cap surmounted with a lotus, a three-jewel symbol (*triratna*), a sixteen-spoked wheel and an umbrella resting one above the other.

On each of the remaining two faces, we notice three lozenge-shaped sockets for the reception of cross-bars.

---

[1] *A. S. R.*, 1907-08, pp. 68, 69, and Pl. XX.

D(*a*). 2.—(Ht. 4′ 3½″; section 8″×6½″). Carved on one face only with three complete and one half medallions containing respectively an *acanthus* (?), a honey-suckle, a lotus rosette and an *acanthus* (?). On the sides there are three sockets of the same form to hold the ends of the cross-bars and traces of a square tenon at the top.

D(*a*) 3.—(Ht. 4′ 4″; section 8½″ × 6″.) Carved on front with three complete and one half lotus rosettes. There are mortices on two opposite sides.

D(*a*) 4.—(Ht. 4′ 3½″; section 8¼″ ×6″.) Ornamented from below with a lotus rosette; a lion in a circular medallion; a medallion containing a *stūpa* with railing, *hti* and streamers; and a half medallion with an *acanthus* (?). There are sockets for cross-bars on two sides and at the top a rectangular tenon, 2″ high.

D(*a*) 5.—(Ht. 4′ 4″; section 8″×4″.) Carved with a medallion containing a honey-suckle (?) in the middle and two full and one half rosettes in the upper part. On two sides, we notice lozenge-shaped sockets for cross-bars and at the top a tenon 1¾″ in height.

D(*a*) 6.—(Ht. 4′ 2″; section 8½″ × 6″.) Adorned with a medallion showing a fabulous deity with a human bust, elephant's ears and a double fish-tail; two full lotus rosettes and a half medallion representing a winged dragon with a lion's head and paws and a fish tail. Sockets on the sides as usual and a tenon at the top 2″ in height.

D(*a*) 7.—Corner post (ht. 4′ 4″; section 8″×7″) engraved on two faces. On one of them, from below, we notice a pot with an acanthus (?); a pair of leogryphs standing back to back; a temple (*gandhakuṭī*) with a railing in front, and two arched doors with a smaller railing between them and a row of four finials on the top; and a *stūpa* with a double railing, *hti*, parasol, garlands and streamers. On the other face, from the bottom, we see an acanthus; a pot with a lotus plant and a pillar as on D (*a*) 1 referred to.

D(*a*) 8.—(Ht. 4′ 3½″; section 8″×6″.) Engraved with two medallions containing a honey-suckle and a pot with a lotus plant, and one full lotus-rosette at the bottom and a half such rosette at the top. Sockets on sides for cross-bars and a tenon at the top, 2″ high.

D(*a*) 9.—Post broken at the base (ht. 3′ 2½″; section 7″×5½″) engraved with a medallion containing a winged lion with the tail of a fish; and one full and parts of two other lotus rosettes.

D(*a*) 10.—(Ht. 4′ 2″; section 8″×6″.) Medallion with a honey-suckle (?) and two full and one half lotus rosettes. Mortices on sides for cross-bars and a tenon at the top.

D(*a*) 11.—Corner post (ht. 4′ 5″; section 8½″×6½″). Carved on one face, from below, with honeysuckle and acanthus decoration; a tree surrounded by a railing; a *pīpal* tree with a railing and pendant garlands; and a *stūpa* with a railing and a parasol.

On the other face, we have a *stūpa* with a railing and a parasol top, the rest of the space being taken up by floral decoration. The remaining two sides have sockets as usual.

D(*a*) 12.—(Ht. 4′ 4″ ; section 7½″ ×5½″). Carved with acanthus and two full and one half lotus rosettes. Sockets on two sides for cross-bars.

* D(*a*) 13.—Railing pillar (ht. 2′ 10″ ; section 10¼″ ×9″) broken at the base. On the front, 6″ below the top, is a Prakrit inscription of two lines (10″ and 5½″ in length) in Brāhmī characters of the 2nd century B. C. which I read:

1. 1. . . . *niyā Sōnadēvi*[*yē**]
1. 2. . . . *thabhō dāna*[*ṁ**]

" The pillar, the gift of Suvarṇadēvī. . . ." On two sides, there are two lozenge-shaped mortices (11¾″ ×4¾″) for the reception of the ends of the cross-bars (*sūchī*). There were originally three sockets on each side. To judge from its size this post would seem to have belonged to the railing which surrounded the open court or hall on the east of the Main Shrine, of which a small portion still remains *in situ*.[1] To the same railing evidently also belonged D(*a*) 14 to D(*a*) 20 and the coping stone D(*a*) 39. In the top is cut a circular mortice hole (diam. 3″, depth 2″).

Buff-coloured sandstone of Chunār. Traces of red paint. Discovered in 1904-05 near the Aśōka Column.[2] The grooves for cramps on the front show that the stone must have been used at a later period as a paving slab, perhaps in the stone paving around the Aśōka Column.

* D(*a*) 14.—Railing pillar (ht. 3′ 8½″ ; section 10¼″ ×8¾″) broken at the lower end. On the front, 5″ below the top, is a Prakrit inscription of one line, 10″ long, and in characters of the 2nd century B. C. It reads as follows [3] :—

Sīhayē sāhi Jaṁtēyikāyē thabhō.

" The pillar [is the gift] of Jaṁtēyikā with Sihā "

On two sides there are three lozenge-shaped sockets (ht. 1′ ¾″; width 5″) of which the lower one is partly broken off. The post apparently belonged to the same railing as D(*a*) 13. In the top is cut a mortice hole (3″ × 2″ × 2½″). Unearthed in 1904-05 near the Aśōka Column.[4]

*D(*a*) 15.—Fragmentary pillar (ht. 2′ 7½″ ; section 10¼″ ×10″) which may be surmised to have belonged to the same railing as D(*a*) 13.

On the front, below the top, is a Prakrit epigraph of one line (10″ long) in characters of the 2nd century B. C. I read it :

---

[1] *A. S. R.*, 1906-07, pp. 78-79, and Pl. XXI, *c*.
[2] *A. S. R.*, 1904-05, p. 66 ; also p. 91, No. 2.
[3] *Cf. A. S. R.*, 1906-07, p. 95, II.
[4] *Ibid.* 1904-05, p. 91. No. 2.

...*kayē bhikhuni-Vasutaragutāyē dānaṁ tha*[*bhō*]. "The pillar [is] the gift of the nun-Vasudharaguptā(?)". There are two lozenge-shaped sockets for the reception of cross-bars on each of two sides.

That the pillar was, in the Gupta period, used as a lamp-stand is evidenced by two small niches scooped out near the lower end and each accompanied by a dedicatory inscription in characters of that age. The inscription belonging to the upper niche consists of four lines (9", 9¾", 10" and 5") and runs as follows:—

1. 1. *Dēyadharmmō=yaṁ paramōpā-*
1. 2. *sika-Sulakshmaṇāya mūla-*
1. 3. [*gandhakuṭyāṁ bha*[1]]*gavatō Buddhasya*
1. 4. *pradīpaḥ.*

"This lamp [is] the pious gift of the supremely devoted Sulakshmaṇā at the principal temple of the Lord Buddha."

The inscription attached to the lower lamp niche consisted of three lines carved on either side of it. This epigraph is mostly destroyed. The word *pradīvaḥ* (*paḥ*) meaning a lamp is, however, distinct in the last line.

In the top is cut a circular mortice (diam. 2¾"; depth 2½") for a cramp which shows that finally the pillar has done duty for a paving slab.

Excavated in 1904-05 near the Asōka Column.[2]

*D(*a*) 16. Pillar (ht. 4' 4½"; section 10½"×8") of a railing with three lozenge-shaped mortices (ht. 1'; width 4¾") on each of two sides On the front, 6½" below the top, is a Prakrit inscription of one line (length 9") in characters of the 2nd century B. C. which reads:

[*Bha*]*riniyē sahaṁ Jatēyikā*[*yē thabhō dānaṁ.**] "[This pillar is the gift] of Jatēyikā together with Bharinī."[3]

Some 8" lower down on the same side is incised another inscription of three lines in characters of the 4th or 5th century A. D. which has been read by Dr. Konow[4] as follows:—

1. 1. *Dēyadharmmō=yaṁ paramōpā-*
1. 2. [*sa*]*ka-Kīrttēḥ* [*mūla-ga*]*ndhaku-*
1. 3. [*ṭyāṁ pra*]*dī*[*p..........ddhaḥ*]

"This is the pious gift of the devoted worshipper Kīrtti, a lamp put up in the Principal Shrine."

It is thus apparent that this post was also converted into a lamp-stand in the Gupta period. The pointed niche in which the earthen

---

[1] The loss of these syllables was caused by a groove for a metal cramp, but portions of them which remain favour the proposed restoration. *Cf.* also terracotta sealing No. F. (*d*) 4 found to the west of the Main Shrine in 1906-07 (*A.S.R.*, 1906-07, p.75 and p.97, V).

[2] *A. S. R.*, 1904-05, p. 66; p. 91, No. 3 and p. 103, Inscription XI.

[3] *Ibid*, 1906-07, p. 95, II.

[4] *Ibid*, p. 97, No. V.

lamp was placed is still intact and a line of soot still adheres to the surface above the niche.

Buff-coloured sandstone of Chunār. The pillar probably originally belonged to the railing around the open court on east of Main Shrine. Unearthed in 1906-07 near the south wall of the court to the east of the Main Shrine immediately below the concrete terrace.[1]

D(*a*) 17.—Fragment (ht. 2′ 5″; section 11″ ×8″) of a railing pillar with one lozenge-shaped mortice (1′ ×4¾″) on each of two sides which may have belonged to the same railing as D(*a*) 13 and the intervening pillars. Lastly, it must have been used as a building stone.

Unearthed in 1904-05 [2], near the Aśōka Column or the Main Shrine.

*D(*a*) 18.—Fragment (ht. 1′ 11″; section 10¾″ ×11″) of a railing post with a lozenge-shaped mortice for a cross-bar on two sides. Near the top of the stone is a line (8″ long) of writing in characters of the 6th century A.D. which Dr. Konow reads as follows :—

[*Śākyabhi*] *kshu* (*ō*) *r=Vōdhishēṇasya*

" [Gift] of the Buddhist friar Vōdhishēṇa." Below this inscription is a lamp niche pointed at the top and beneath it again an inscription of a single line (length 8″) which reads :—

[*Paramōpāsa*]*ka-Bhavarudrasya pradīpa*[*ḥ*].

" [This] lamp is [the gift] of the devoted worshipper Bhavarudra ".[3]

Found in 1906-07 near the south-east corner of the Main Shrine.[4] The fragment probably belonged to the same railing as D(*a*) 13.

D(*a*) 19.—Fragmentary pillar (ht. 2′ 5″; section 10″ ×8¾″) from the same railing as the preceding ones with a lozenge-shaped mortice (1′ ×4¾″) on two sides.

Unearthed in 1904-05 near the Main Shrine.[5]

*D(*a*) 20.—Fragment of a pillar (ht. 2′ 8½″; section 10½″ ×9½″) presumably from the same railing as D(*a*) 13. Two lozenge-shaped sockets (1′ ×4¾″) for cross-bars on two sides. On the front, there are the traces of a Prakrit inscription in the Brāhmī script of the 2nd century B.C. consisting of two lines. It is badly defaced but *dāna*[*ṁ*] in the second line is distinct.

In the top is a rectangular mortice (3″ ×2″ ×2¼″) for the metal dowel which received the coping stone.

Sandstone of Chunār. Traces of red paint. Unearthed in 1904-05 near the Main Shrine.[6]

D(*a*) 21.—Fragmentary pillar (ht. 2′ 2½″; section 10½″ ×8¾″) of a railing with one full and one imperfect mortice on two sides. Traces of red colour. Probably found in 1904-05 in the same locality as D(*a*) 20.

---

[1] *A. S. R.*, 1906-07, p. 77.
[2] *Ibid.*, 1904-05, p. 91, No. 2 or 3.
[3, 4] *Ibid*, 1906-07, p. 77 & p. 100, Nos. IX and X.
[5, 6] *Ibid*, 1904-05, p. 91, No. 3.

D(*a*) 22.—Corner post (ht. 2′ 4½″; section 6½″×6½″) of a railing with the lower part broken off. It is carved on two faces on one of which starting from the bottom we have a vase with a lotus plant; a temple in front elevation showing two doors side by side; and a *stūpa* with a railing, a *hti*, streamers and a parasol. The other side presents floral scroll with the intervening curves filled with artistically executed lotus rosettes. On the remaining two faces are noticed two complete and one imperfect socket (ht. 7¾″; width 2¼″) of the usual shape of a lozenge for the reception of cross-bars. The style is of about the 1st century B.C. Pale buff stone of Chunār with traces of red paint. Discovered in 1906-07 in the south-west corner of the open hall or court on the east of the Main Shrine.[1]

D(*a*) 23.—Lower part (ht. 1′ 10½″; section 7″×5″) of a pillar of a railing with an imperfect lotus rosette on the front and a part of a lozenge-shaped socket on two sides. Style similar to that of D(*a*) 22 and made of the same kind of stone.

D(*a*) 24-30.—Seven posts (section 6″×5″) of the same railing varying in height from 1′ 11″ to 2′ 5″. The upper part of every one of these, from the middle of the central socket is broken off. They are carved on one side only with lotus rosettes and honeysuckle patterns, with the exception of one pillar which is engraved on two sides and must have occupied a corner. The bases of these posts which were meant to be concealed in the ground are rough for 9″ to 11″. On grounds of style these posts must be assigned to about the 1st century B.C.

The material is a very rough kind of Chunār sandstone. Unearthed most probably in 1904-05 around the Aśōka Column and the Main Shrine.[2]

D(*a*) 31.—Upper part (ht. 1′ 6″; section 5¼″×4¾″) of a railing pillar carved on the front with a pattern resembling the honeysuckle. On two sides we have lozenge-shaped sockets (ht. 8″; width 2¼″) for the reception of cross-bars. *Cir.* 1st century B. C. Found in 1906-07 in the stone paving around the Aśōka Column.[3]

D(*a*) 32.—Railing pillar (ht. 3½″; width 5½″) with the back half cut away. On the front side we notice flowing floral scroll with four lotus rosettes in the curves, and traces of three lozenge-shaped sockets on two sides for the reception of cross-bars. *Cir.* 1st century B. C. Excavated in 1906-07 in the stair to monastery I, 3′ below the surface.

D(*a*) 33.—Railing post (ht. 3′ 2½″; width 8½″) with the back half split away. Traces of three lozenge-shaped sockets for cross-bars on two sides. On front side, four rosettes much defaced. The style is

---

[1] *A. S. R.*, 1906-07, p. 79 and Pl. XXVIII, 3.
[2] *Ibid*, 1904-05, p. 91, No. 3.
[3] *Ibid*, 1906-07, p. 68 and photo. in Pl. XIX, 3.

analogous to that of D(*a*) 32. Traces of red paint. Excavated in 1906-07 between the Main Shrine and *stūpa* No. 22 on west of it.

D(*a*) 34.—Fragment (ht. 2′ 3″; width 6″) of a railing pillar which exhibits two sockets of the usual form on one side. It may have been excavated in 1904-05.

D(*a*) 35.—Fragment (ht. 1′ 10½″; width 6″) of a railing pillar with the back cut off. On two sides, traces of two lozenge-shaped sockets for cross-bars. No carving. Discovered in 1906-07, but the exact find-spot cannot be ascertained.

D(*a*) 36.—Fragment (ht. 9″; width 6″) of a railing pillar with one lotus rosette, which must have belonged to the same railing as D(*a*) 32. Probably found in 1906-07.

D(*a*) 37.—Fragment (ht. 1′ 4½″; section 8¼″×5″) of a railing post. The front side has bevelled edges and parts of two medallions with an expanded lotus and a part of a leogryph of which the head, one wing and tail are extant. Portions of two lozenge-shaped sockets for cross-bars remain on two sides. *Cir.* 1st century B. C. Buff-coloured sandstone of Chunār. Discovered in 1906-07 in the area on the east of the Main Shrine.

D(*a*) 38.—Top portion (ht. 1′ 3½″; section 8½″×6¼″) of a corner post of a railing. On one side we notice a *stūpa* with *hti*, a parasol, streamers and garlands. On another side, may be seen the cap of a pillar supporting an elliptical object with a dot in the centre, perhaps meant for a wheel (*dharmachakra*) adorned with a pair of streamers and above it again, an umbrella with a tall staff, ornamented with garlands. The remaining two sides exhibit lozenge-shaped sockets for cross-bars. The style is referable to about the 1st century B.C.

Excavated in 1904-05 north of Jagat Singh *stūpa*.[1]

*D(*a*) 39.—Coping stone (length 6′ 5½″; width 11″; ht. 1′ 1½″) of a railing, with rounded edges at the top. On the front is carved an inscription of one line (1′ 8″ in length) in the Brāhmī characters of the 2nd century B.C. which was first deciphered by Dr. Konow. It reads as follows :[2]—

Bhikhunikāyē Saṁvahikāyē dānaṁ āla[ṁ]banaṁ*

"[This] base stone [is] the gift of the nun Saṁvahikā."

It is curious that in the epigraph the coping stone is referred to as a base stone.

To judge from dimensions, the stone may have belonged to the railing which surrounded the open hall on the east of the Main Shrine and to which some of the pillars described above undoubtedly belonged.[3]

---

[1] *A. S. R.*, 1904-05, p. 100, No. 407.
[2] *Ibid*, 1906-07, p. 95, I; and facsimile on Pl. XXX, 1.
[3] *Cf.* D(*a*) 13—20 above.

On the under side, there are two mortices (3″×2¼″×3″) at a distance of 2′ 7″ from each other, for the reception of the tenons of pillars.

Buff-coloured sandstone of Chunār.

Unearthed in 1906-07 near the south wall of the open hall referred to above immediately below the concrete floor around the Main Shrine.[1]

D(*a*) 40.—Coping stone (length 4′ 9½″; width 6″; ht. 10½″) of a railing carved on one side only. Above, a band of lotus petals; below, to proper left a row of animals, namely an elephant, a buffalo, a rhinoceros and a bull; to right, a female figure offering a garland to a *stūpa* of which only the parasol streamers survive.

On the under side we notice four mortice holes (3¼″×2½″×2½″) to receive the tenons of the columns on which it rested. The style is of about the 1st century B. C.

Pale buff stone of Chunār. The stone seems to have been discovered in one of the recent excavations.

D(*a*) 41.—Coping stone (length 3′ 10½″; width 6″; ht. 8¾″) of a railing rounded at the top, smoothed and dressed but with no carving. On the under side, two mortices measuring 7½″×3″×2″ and 5″×3″×1½″ at a distance of about 1′ from each other.

Buff-coloured sandstone of Chunār. Unearthed in one of the recent excavations.

D(*a*) 42.—Fragment (length 2′ 4½″; width 10½″; ht. 11¼″) carved on two sides. On one of the sides in the middle is a wheel (*dharmachakra*) surrounded by four ornamental tridents and an equal number of blue lotuses. To the right and left, and separated by garlands hanging vertically, is a circular ring placed on a triple pedestal and supporting the three-jewel symbol (*triratna*). On the other side in the centre, we notice a tree resembling the cypress adorned with pendant garlands and surrounded by a throne. To the proper right is a circular pillar with a Persepolitan cap and an uncertain object above. The remaining surface is taken up by elaborate palmettes (?).

The stone has square mortice holes both in the top and in the bottom and is presumably a portion of a lintel of a *tōraṇa* gateway.

On grounds of style Dr. Marshall who discovered the stone near structure No. 7 on the south-west of the Main Shrine 3′ below the concrete terrace around it, assigns it to about the 1st century B. C.[2]

D(*a*) 43.—Fragment (length 1′ 8¾″; width 4¾″; ht. 9″) of a coping stone of a railing carved on one side only. Above, we notice a band of lotus petals and below, a *stūpa* with streamers which is being approached by a fabulous being, half man half beast, carrying a stalk of a lotus plant. *Cir.* 1st century B.C.

---

[1] *A. S. R.*, 1906-07, p. 77.
[2] *Ibid*, p. 73 and Pl. XX, 1 and 2.

Pale buff stone of Chunār.

It was found lying among the architectural stones excavated in 1904-05 on the structure to the north-east of the Jagat Singh *stūpa* and must have been unearthed in that area.

D(*a*) 44.—Cross-bar (length 2′; ht. 1′; width 4½″) of a railing. The ends are lozenge-shaped like the mortices of the pillars described above. It is carved on one side with a badly executed lotus rosette. *Cir.* 1st century B. C. Unearthed in 1906-07 in the area to the west of the Main Shrine.

D(*a*) 45-46.—Two lozenge-shaped railing cross-bars (length 2′ 1″; ht. 11½″; width 4¾″). They have lost their numbers but they were most probably found in the same area as D(*a*) 44 in 1906-07.

D(*a*) 47-48.—Two lozenge-shaped cross-bars (length 2′ 5½″; ht. 11½″; width 4½″) which must have belonged to the same railing. Probably unearthed in 1904-05.[1]

D(*a*) 49.—Railing cross-bar (length 1′ 10″; ht. 10″; width 3″) of the same style as D(*a*) 47-48. Found in one of the recent diggings.

D(*a*) 50.—Railing cross-bar (length 2′ 2½″; ht. 10¼″; width 4½″). Find-spot not known but evidently discovered in one of the recent excavations.

D(*a*) 51.—Fragment (length 11¾″; ht. 7½″; width 2¼″) of a railing cross-bar with a medallion containing a lotus rosette on one side. *Cir.* 1st century B. C. Must have been found in one of the recent excavations.

D(*a*) 52-53.—Fragments (width 10″ and 1′) of cross-bars each adorned with a lotus rosette. Chunār sandstone. One of them [D(*a*) 52] was found in 1906-07 in the area to the east of the Main Shrine.

---

[1] *A. S. R.*, 1904-05, p. 91, Nos. 2 and 3.

D(*b*).—Votive stūpas.

D(*b*) 1.—Votive *stūpa* (ht. 1′ 9″; width 1′ 1″) carved out of a single block of stone. The basement which is square has a plain cornice above and below. The middle portion or drum is octagonal with a rectangular niche, capped with a pediment, at each cardinal point. These niches contain the four important events of Buddha's life in chronological order.

(*a*) In the first niche we notice the birth of Gautama Buddha. Māyā is standing holding a branch of a *sāla* tree with her right hand. To her proper right is Indra kneeling to receive the Bōdhisattva and to her left, Prajāpati supporting her. In the proper right upper corner is represented the Bōdhisattva's first bath by the Nāgas Nanda and Upananda who pour water over his head. The Bōdhisattva has a halo and stands facing with his right hand raised in the attitude of imparting protection.

(*b*) In next niche, Buddha's enlightenment (*bōdhi*). He is sitting as usual, in the earth-touching attitude (*bhūmisparśa-mudrā*). To his right, is a figure with a fly-whisk; and to his left, another figure holding a garland. Above, two demons (*rākshasa*).

(*c*) The third niche shows the first sermon at Sārnāth, with the Buddha sitting in the attitude of expounding the law and the five converts on the front of the base, with the wheel-and-deer symbol below it.

(*d*) In the last niche is represented the great demise. The Buddha is lying in the usual style, with four mourners below and two flying celestials, perhaps the spirits of the twin *sāla* trees, above. The pediments surmounting the niches have each a figure of a Buddha in meditation. The drum is hemispherical. The *hti* and the pinnacle are missing.

The style seems to be Gupta. Buff-coloured sandstone. The *stūpa* belonged to the Queen's College Collection. It is not pictured in Major Kittoe's Manuscript Drawings.

D(*b*) 2.—Votive *stūpa* (ht. 1′ 9″; diam. 1′ 2″) with one half cut away from the top to the bottom. The basement was presumably a separate piece. The drum, which is circular, was adorned with trefoil niches enclosed in plain pilasters and containing figures of Buddha. One of these figures is seated on a lotus throne expounding the first sermon. Two others, which are preserved in part, are in the attitude of meditation. The spaces between the niches have rosettes. Above the niches we notice ornamental pediments with lion-heads (*kīrttimukha*) in circular panels. The dome is hemispherical and the *hti* broken off. The *stūpa* shows a close resemblance to a Mathurā votive *stūpa*[1] and though, on account of its material, it cannot have been carved at Mathurā, we may assume that it has been copied from a Mathurā model.

Gupta style. It is made of a reddish sandstone of Chunār, and was probably discovered in 1904-05 to the east of the Main Shrine.[2]

D(*b*) 3.—Votive *stūpa* (ht. 1′ 9½″; width 9¾″), square in the basement, circular above. On the front is a projecting niche with arched head, containing a figure of Buddha seated cross-legged preaching the first sermon, and above it, a relic-casket of the type of the Piprāhvā casket between a pair of lions. On the proper right side is a smaller niche with a trefoil arch containing a Buddha standing in the attitude of granting protection. On the other side, similar niche with Buddha in the earth-touching attitude. The niche on the back contains Buddha seated with a bowl on his hands. This may have reference to the presentation of the bowl by the guardians of the quarters or by the monkey in the Pārilēyyaka forest.

The style seems to be mediæval. Chunār sandstone of dark buff colour. Formerly preserved in the Queen's College.

D(*b*) 4.—Votive *stūpa* (ht. 2′ 3″; width 1′3″) cut out of a single block. Basement low and square with recessed corners. The upper portion is circular and the drum adorned on four sides with rectangular projecting niches. The figures in these niches are Buddha in the earth-touching attitude, Tārā, Avalōkitēśvara and Mañjuśrī arranged in the direction of *pradakshiṇa*. The last three figures are seated in 'easy attitude' and have their ordinary attributes. Mañjuśrī has the Prajñāpāramitā on a lotus flower at his left side. From the top of the drum projects the *hti* with a square mortice for the pinnacle which is missing. Mediæval period. Buff-coloured sandstone of Chunār. Excavated in 1904-05 to the north of the Jagat Singh *stūpa*.[3]

D(*b*) 5.—Votive *stūpa* (ht. 2′ 5″; width 1′ 3½″) without the pinnacle. Drum circular with three cornices and a bold torus moulding below them. On all four sides, niches with trefoil arches supported on plain pilasters and surmounted with spires (*śikhara*). These niches contain figures of Buddha, two of which are seated in the attitude of expounding the law, one other in the earth-touching attitude, while the fourth one holds a bowl in the lap. It is noteworthy that all these Buddha figures are dressed like Bōdhisattvas and have high diadems. The *hti* which projects from the top of the drum has a square mortice sunk into it for the reception of the pinnacle.

[1] Vogel, *Mathurā Catalogue*, No. 1 on Pl. IV.
[2] *A. S. R.*, 1904-05, p. 99, No. 386.
[3] *A. S. R.*, 1904-05, p. 99, No. 385.

It is interesting to find the spire of the mediæval Brahmanical temple on this and other *stūpas* to be described below. Buddhist architecture did not differ from the Brahmanical.

Reddish sandstone of Chunār. Discovered in 1904-05.[1]

D(*b*) 6.—Votive *stūpa* (ht. 1′ 10½″). The basement is rectangular 1′-1″×1′ and has a bevelled top. The drum is adorned with four cornices. In the top of the dome, is a circular mortice surrounded by a raised border to receive the pinnacle.

Mediæval style. Buff-coloured sandstone of Chunār. Excavated in 1904-05 north-west of the Jagat Singh *stūpa*.[2]

D(*b*) 7.—Votive *stūpa* (ht. 1′ 10½″) square at base, circular above. On the front is a niche with a trefoil arch, a spire (*śikhara*) and an *āmalaka*, containing a figure of Buddha at the moment of enlightenment. The artist has given him a high diadem and ornaments because he has not yet attained Buddhahood. On the remaining three sides the drum is carved with figures of Buddha of ordinary type seated in niches of smaller size, two of which show the Master as preaching the first sermon, the third with a bowl on his lap. The last figure has reference to the presentation of four bowls by the guardians of quarters or of honey by the monkey in the forest near Kauśāmbī. The *hti* which springs from the top of the dome retains traces of the pinnacle.

Mediæval style. Buff-coloured sandstone of Chunār. Unearthed in 1904-05 north-east of Jagat Singh *stūpa*.[3]

D(*b*) 8.—Votive *stūpa* with separate base and pinnacle (total ht. 1′ 8″). The base is square with double recessed corners and adorned with a row of miniature Buddha figures in the attitude of meditation all round. The drum, which is circular, is carved at the cardinal points with niches with trefoil arches supported on pilasters which have vase-shaped bases, round tapering shafts and bracket-capitals.[4] These niches contain four scenes from the Buddha's life :—

(*a*) His enlightenment expressed by the Buddha seated, as usual, in the earth-touching attitude, with a figure of the earth-goddess holding a vase beneath his right hand and a figure of one of Māra's three daughters at the other end of the throne.

(*b*) His first sermon at Sārnāth. The Buddha is seated in the attitude of teaching with a wheel and pair of deer on front of the throne. The five monks who were converted on this occasion have been omitted.

---

[1] *A. S. R.*, 1904-05, p. 99, No. 394.

[2] *Ibid*, p. 99, No. 392.

[3] The number has been wiped off, but I have no doubt that the sculpture is identical with *A. S. R.*, 1904-05, p. 99, No. 383.

[4] This is the design of Magadha pillars.

(*c*) Presentation of honey by the monkey at the Pārilēyyaka forest near Kauśāmbī (modern Kōsam). Buddha is seated on a lotus throne with a bowl on his hands in the lap. On the front, at the proper left end of the throne, is a figure raising a round object, evidently the monkey with the bowl of honey. The figure behind it on this side holds a long object in the left hand. I cannot identify it. On the other side of the throne we notice a masonry well with a figure jumping into it and by the well another figure with arms thrown up in the air. Is it the monkey itself before jumping into the well. This scene is pictured on C(*a*) 3,*c*.

(*d*) The miracle of Śrāvastī. The Buddha is seated on a lotus throne in the attitude of teaching. At either end of the throne is a corpulent squatting figure as on C(*a*) 6 and 7, evidently a heretical teacher and King Prasēnajit. The spaces between the niches are filled up with rows of miniature Buddha figures seated in meditation.

The place of the *hti* at the top of the dome is taken up by a square mortice for the tenon of the pinnacle which is a square shaft tapering upwards and ornamented with cornices. Mediæval style. Sandstone of Chunār.

Finial unearthed in monastery I, in 1906-07, 4′ below the surface. The *stūpa* was unearthed in 1904-05 in the chapel near the south-east corner of the Main Shrine.[1]

D(*b*) 9.—Votive *stūpa* (ht. 2′) carved on four sides with figures of the Buddha in the attitude of meditation, enlightenment, expounding the law and final extinction (*parinirvāṇa*) in arched niches or chapels surmounted with spires (*śikhara*) and *āmalaka* finials. Of the smaller rectangular niches which alternate with the bigger ones three contain figures of Buddha standing in the gift-bestowing attitude and the fourth to the proper right of the Buddha in meditation, a female figure, perhaps Māyā at the moment of Gautama Buddha's birth. It has to be noted that the child is represented as coming out of the left side of his mother. The representation of the demise is also uncanonical inasmuch as the Teacher is shown as reclining on his left side.

On the top of the dome is a *hti* with a square mortice for the pinnacle. Mediæval. Buff-coloured sandstone of Chunār. Unearthed in 1904-05 south-east of Main Shrine.[2]

*D(*b*) 10.—Votive *stūpa* (ht. 1′ 5″; width 11″) with the pinnacle broken off. The basement is square and has recessed corners. It is

---

[1] *A. S. R.*, 1904-05, p. 99, No. 380.
[2] *Ibid*, p. 99, No. 377.

carved on each face with a niche with a trefoil arch. Of the figures in these niches two represent Tārā in 'easy attitude', her right hand held in the gift-bestowing attitude. The third is a Bōdhisattva supporting his head on his right hand. The fourth figure is of a female seated cross-legged with a bowl in the lap.

The drum is adorned with eight scenes following the direction opposite to the *pradakshiṇa* :—

(*a*) Nativity. Māyā stands alone holding a branch of a tree with the child coming out of her right side. *Cf.* steles C(*a*) 1-3.

(*b*) The miracle of Śrāvastī. The Buddha is seated in the attitude of teaching with a corpulent figure falling back with a flower-like object before it on the front of the base. This is evidently one of the heretical teachers whom the Buddha confounded by a display of his miraculous powers.

(*c*) Buddha standing in the gift-bestowing attitude, presumably descending from the Trāyastriṁśa heaven for on the base of it is sketched a figure holding a water-pot in the left hand, which may be identified as Brahmā. The absence of Indra on the other side is to be noted. This scene is depicted on stele C(*a*) 3,*e*.

(*d*) Buddha's enlightenment without any details.

(*e*) Rājagṛiha miracle expressed by the Buddha standing with the elephant Nālāgiri prostrating itself at his feet. *Cf.* C(*a*) 3,*d*.

(*f*) First sermon at Sārnāth. Buddha seated in the teaching attitude. On front, wheel between a pair of deer.

(*g*) Buddha's extinction (Nirvāṇa). The Buddha is lying on the right side on a couch which is placed diagonally on account of inadequate space. Above him a *stūpa*.

(*h*) Buddha receiving honey from the monkey. The latter is roughly incised at the proper left end of the base, offering a bowl, which is repeated in the Buddha's hands. *Cf.* C(*a*) 3 and 8.

On the base of the *stūpa* was carved the Buddhist creed in characters of the 8th or 9th century A.D. of which a portion *ēvaṁ vā* remains on the basement beneath the Bōdhisattva figure referred to and *mahāśrama a* beneath the goddess with the bowl.

Reddish sandstone of Chunār. Unearthed in 1904-05 south of the Main Shrine.[1]

D(*b*) 11.—Votive *stūpa* (ht. 2′; width 11″) carved with four large niches and four smaller ones in the corners. The former have trefoil

[1] *A. S. R.*, 1904-05, p. 99, No. 384.

arches and spires (*śikhara*) with *āmalaka* finials. The smaller niches are rectangular and have pediments. The larger niches contain figures of Buddha, two of which on opposite faces are in the teaching attitude and represent the sermon at Sārnāth and the miracle at Śrāvastī. The third is seated in the earth-touching attitude and the fourth has a bowl in the lap and probably represents the presentation of honey by the monkey of the Pārilēyyaka forest. Of the Buddha figures in the smaller niches two are standing in the attitudes of granting protection and bestowing a gift. The next smaller niche shows the Buddha subduing the elephant at Rājagriha and the last one, his demise with the Buddha lying as in D(*b*) 10, *g* with a mourner below and a *stūpa* above him.

Hti with mortice at the top. Mediæval style. Buff-coloured stone of Chunār. The *stūpa* belonged to Queen's College collection.

D(*b*) 12.—Votive *stūpa* (ht. 2′ ; width 11½″) carved round the drum with figures of Buddha seated in the attitudes of enlightenment and teaching, then a figure holding a bowl on the lap and another in the attitude of teaching. The second figure in the attitude of expounding the law presumably represents the great miracle enacted by the Buddha at Śrāvastī. The niches in which these figures are seated are analogous to those in D(*b*) 11. On the four sides of the basement, we have (*a*) Kubēra the god of wealth seated in easy attitude, with *vījapūraka* (Hindi *bijaura*) in his right hand and the pearl-vomiting mongoose (*nakula*) in the left, (*b*) Hāritī or Vasundhārā, her right hand in the gift-bestowing attitude, and the left holding a flower and her right foot resting on a vase lying upside down, (*c*) Tārā in easy attitude, her right hand on the knee in the same attitude as Vasundhārā, the left holding a blue lotus (*nīlōtpala*), (*d*) Avalōkitēśvara seated in the usual style of Bōdhisattvas in the gift-bestowing attitude, while his left hand grasps the stalk of a red lotus (*padma*).

The style of the sculpture seems to be of the late Gupta period. Buff-coloured sandstone of Chunār. Formerly preserved in the Queen's College.

D(*b*) 13.—Votive *stūpa* (ht. 1′ 7½″ ; diam. 11″) consisting of a drum, dome and *hti*, but with no carving barring three plain cornices and a torus moulding around the drum. The square mortice in the *hti* was meant for the tenon of the pinnacle. Excavated in 1904-05, north-west of the Jagat Singh *stūpa*.[1]

D(*b*) 14.—Votive *stūpa* (ht. 1′ 3″; diam. 10″) similar to D(*b*) 13. Found in the same locality.[2]

D(*b*) 15.—Votive *stūpa* (ht. 2′). The basement is 9½″ square ; the drum octagonal with three cornices one above the other, and the dome

[1] *A. S. R.*, 1904-05, p. 99, No. 392.
[2] *Ibid*, 390.

hemispheric. The top is flanged for the finial to fit on. Buff-coloured sandstone of Chunār. Discovered in 1904-05 south-east of the Main Shrine.[1]

D(*b*) 16.—Votive *stūpa* (ht. 1′ 7″; width at base 8½″) with a square base adorned with empty trefoil arches. Rest quite plain. On the top is a projecting *hti* with a square mortice for the pinnacle. Buff-coloured sandstone of Chunār. Find-spot not known.

*D(*b*) 17.—Votive *stūpa* (ht. 1′ 5″; width 7¼″) with square drum carved on four sides with figures of Buddha. One of them is seated in the earth-touching attitude, one other standing in the gift-bestowing attitude and the remaining two seated in the attitude of expounding the law (*dharmachakramudrā*). One of the last mentioned figures wearing a high diadem and other ornaments apparently represents the great miracle of Śrāvastī. On the proper left pillar of the niche in which this event is illustrated is a short record in characters of 9th or 10th century which may be read as

l. 1. *Déva (ya) dharmō=yaṁ*

l. 2.—*Varṇṇikasya*

"The pious gift of Varṇṇika."

On the base of the same niche is the Buddhist creed which is continued below the Buddha in the earth-touching attitude.

The finial is wanting. Buff-coloured sandstone of Chunār. Discovered in 1904-05 in the chapel near the south-east corner of Main Shrine.[2]

*D(*b*) 18.—*Stūpa* (ht. 1′ 8″) with a square drum on each side of which is a figure of Gautama Buddha seated cross-legged in the attitude of expounding the law. Pinnacle missing. The basement has peeled off on two of the four faces. On the other two we have the symbol of wheel and deer with traces of a dedicatory epigraph. Unearthed in 1904-05 south-west of the shrine near the south-west corner of Main Shrine.[3] Pale buff sandstone of Chunār.

D(*b*) 19.—Votive *stūpa* (ht. 1′) with star-shaped recessed basement. Pinnacle broken off; around the drum on four sides, figures of Buddha seated cross-legged in arched niches. Two of these figures are in the attitude of meditation, the other two in that of expounding the law. Alternating with these figures are miniature lions' heads (*kīrttimukha*) in similar niches. Mediæval style. Red sandstone of Chunār. Discovered in 1904-05 north-west of Jagat Singh *stūpa*.[4]

*D(*b*) 20.—Votive *stūpa* (ht. 1′ ½″) lacking the pinnacle. On front in a deep sunken niche is Buddha seated in the earth-touching attitude, with a roughly carved tree over his head. The base was inscribed

---

[1] *A. S. R.*, 1904-05, p. 99, No. 388.
[2] *Ibid*, p. 99, No. 380.
[3] *Ibid*. p. 99, No. 376 and p. 104, inscription No. XXXVI.
[4] *Ibid*, p. 99, No. 379.

with a record of which a small piece 4½" in length remains to the proper left of the niche containing the Buddha figure. The character is of about the 11th century A.D. It reads *Yadē* (*dēya*) *dharmmō-yaṁ* ....‘ This the pious gift..’

This *stūpa* is one of the thirteen sculptures which were returned from the Lucknow Provincial Museum. It is made of reddish sandstone of Chunār.

*D(*b*) 21.—Votive *stūpa* (ht. 1′ 1″; width 6¼″) carved round the circular drum on four sides, following the *pradakshiṇa* direction, with a figure of Buddha in earth-touching attitude, another Buddha in the attitude of expounding the law, the Bōdhisattva Avalōkitēśvara in the gift-bestowing attitude and Tārā. The basement is square. On it beneath the Buddha in the earth-touching attitude is an inscription of four lines in Nāgarī characters of 8th or 9th century A.D. consisting of the Buddhist creed followed by what appears to be *yadattra puṇyaṁ tad =bhavatu* ‘ what merit there is in it, may it be...............’

Buff-coloured sandstone of Chunār. Discovered in 1904-05.[1]

D(*b*) 22.—Votive *stūpa* (ht. 1′ 5″; width 8½″) with a square basement adorned with a torus moulding at the top. Around the drum, in *pradakshiṇa* order, we notice the Buddha in the earth-touching attitude; Avalōkitēśvara in easy attitude, his right hand on the knee, the left holding stem of a lotus (*padma*); Tārā in the same attitude, with a blue lotus (*nīlōtpala*) at her left side; and Buddha in the attitude of expounding the law. All these figures are contained in niches with circular heads. Pinnacle as well as *hti* wanting.

Presumably late Gupta period. Buff-coloured sandstone of Chunār. Formerly preserved in the Queen's College.

D(*b*) 23.—Votive *stūpa* (ht. 1′ 3″) consisting of a drum, a dome and *hti*. The drum is carved on all four sides with scenes from Buddha's life. The first shows him in the earth-touching attitude; the next his sermon at Sārnāth. The third event must be the presentation of honey in the Pārilēyyaka forest or the gift of bowls by the four guardians of the quarters. The last scene is probably meant for the Śrāvastī miracle.

The niches containing these figures are surmounted with trefoil arches supported on pillars which taper upwards as in D(*b*) 8.

Mediæval style. Buff-cloured sandstone of Chunār. The *stūpa* belonged to the Queen's College collection.

D(*b*) 24.—Votive *stūpa* (ht. 1′ 2″). On the front is a big niche with a trefoil arch, containing a three-faced and six-armed Mārīchī, the goddess of dawn, standing in the position of an archer. Her left face is that of a boar. Her lowest right hand is on the thigh, the upper ones hold a thunderbolt (*vajra*) and an arrow (*śara*). The lowest left hand

[1] *A. S. R.*, 1904-05, p. 99, No. 375 and p. 104, inscription No. XXXV.

is held in menacing attitude on the breast. The upper two hands have a leaf (*aśōka-pallava* ?) and a bow (*chāpa*). The seven pigs who draw her car are not indicated, but we notice a figure of the driver between the goddess's legs.

On the remaining three sides, are smaller niches with Maitrēya (?); Mañjuśrī, with thunderbolt bell (*vajraghaṇṭā*) under his left armpit; and Avalōkitēśvara respectively. *Hti* and pinnacle as well as part of basement broken off.

Mediæval style. Chunār sandstone. Formerly preserved in the Queen's College.

D(*b*) 25.—Votive *stūpa* (ht. 10¾") with the *hti* broken off. On the four sides in niches with trefoil heads supported on round tapering pillars, are figures of Buddha touching the earth at the moment of his enlightenment; preaching his first sermon; holding a bowl on the lap; and showing his miracle at Śrāvastī. Date not ascertainable. Buff-coloured sandstone of Chunār. Unearthed in 1906-07 in the area on the north-west of the Main Shrine.

*D(*b*) 26.—Votive *stūpa* (ht. 11¼"; width 6¼") carved around the drum on four sides with figures of Buddha seated in the earth-touching attitude, Avalōkitēśvara seated in easy attitude, Buddha in the attitude of expounding the law and Tārā in easy posture. On the basement beneath the last-mentioned figure is an inscription of five lines. The writing is too roughly incised to admit of decipherment. The expression *dēyadharmō* occurs in the fourth line.

Chunār sandstone of buff colour. Unearthed in 1906-07 south of the approach to the Main Shrine from the east.[1]

D(*b*) 27.—*Stūpa* (ht. 1' ½") on a fully expanded lotus flower with a figure of Buddha seated on a throne in European fashion in the atttiude of expounding the law (*dharmachakramudrā*). Double cornice around the drum. Pinnacle broken off. The *stūpa* must have been attached to something. Style distinctly Gupta. Buff-coloured sandstone of Chunār. Discovered in 1904-05 west of the Main Shrine.[2]

D(*b*) 28.—Votive *stūpa* (ht. 11") of which only a half remains. Basement and *hti* missing. It was carved on four sides with figures of Buddha in niches of which one seated in meditation and parts of two others remain. Mediæval style. Red sandstone. Excavated in 1906-07 in the area on the north-west of the Main Shrine.[3]

D(*b*) 29.—Base (ht. 10") of a votive *stūpa* 1' 3" square, ornamented with cornices, and carved on all four sides with figures of Buddha in trefoil niches. Two of these figures are in the attitude of expounding the law, one other in the earth-touching attitude, while the fourth has a

---

1 *A. S. R.*, 1906-07, p. 94, No. 59.
2 *Ibid.*, 1904-05, p. 99, No. 378.
3 *Ibid.*, 1906-07, Pl. XIX, 9, p. 72 and p. 94, No. 58.

bowl on the lap. Mediæval style. Buff-coloured sandstone of Chunār. Discovered in 1904-05 north-east of Jagat Singh *stūpa.*[1]

D(*b*) 30.—Base (1′ 2½″ square ; ht. 6¾″) of a votive *stūpa* with Buddha figurines in arched niches on all sides. Two of these figurines are in the attitude of teaching, one in meditation and the fourth in the earth-touching attitude. Mediæval style. Buff-coloured sandstone of Chunār. Excavated in 1904-05.[2]

D(*b*) 31.—Part of drum (ht. 11″) of a votive *stūpa* with two figures of Buddha in the attitude of touching the earth and of protection respectively seated in rectangular niches. Late mediæval style. Chunār sandstone. The sculpture seems to have been one of the Queen's College collection.

D(*b*) 32.—Base (1′ 3″ square; ht. 3″) with recessed corners, adorned with a row of miniature Buddha figures seated in the earth-touching attitude. Mediæval style. Chunār sandstone. Discovered in 1904-05.

D(*b*) 33.—Base (1′ 3½″ square ; ht. 4½″) similar to D(*b*) 32, but with two rows of Buddha figurines in the same attitude.

D(*b*) 34.—Base (1′ 1½″ square ; ht. 9″) of a votive *stūpa* with double recessed corners. On two opposite faces, we notice Buddha standing in the gift-bestowing attitude with an indistinguishable object to his right, perhaps the elephant Nālāgiri. On the third side, is a female figure standing holding a branch of a tree (?) with the right hand, probably Māyā. On the fourth face, is shown the Dying Buddha lying on his left side which is at variance with the accepted tradition. Above him is a miniature *stūpa.*

Late mediæval style. Chunār sandstone. Unearthed in 1904-05 in the chapel near the south-east corner of the Main Shrine.[3]

D(*b*) 35.—Dome (diam. 2′ 6″ ; ht. 1′) of a large-sized votive *stūpa* in two pieces which were held together by metal cramps. No decoration. At the top is a broad mortice for the tenon of the *hti.* Buff-coloured sandstone of Chunār. Unearthed in 1906-07 near the open courtyard east of the Main Shrine.

D(*b*) 36.—Dome (diam. 1′ 3″ ; ht. 8″) similar to D(*b*) 35. Discovered in 1904-05 west of shrine near the south-west corner of the Main Shrine.

D(*b*) 37.—Half dome (diam. 1′ 11½″ ; ht. 11¼″) of a votive *stūpa.* Top flanged for *hti* to fit on. Mediæval. Buff-coloured sandstone of Chunār. Discovered in 1904-05 south of Main Shrine.[4]

*D(*b*) 38.—Part of the drum (diam. 2′ 4″ ; ht. 1′) of a votive *stūpa* with three Buddha figures seated cross-legged in trefoil-arched niches,

---

[1] *A. S. R.*, 1904-05, p. 99, No. 393.
[2] *Ibid.*, No. 395.
[3] *Ibid.*, No. 382.
[4] *Ibid.*, No. 387.

two in the earth-touching attitude, the third in that of imparting security. On the base of the central figure, is an inscription of three lines in characters of the 11th or 12th century A.D. consisting of the Buddhist creed followed by *Dēyadharmō=yaṁ Śāksha(kya)bhikshōḥ sthavira-[śrīKāśyapasya]* "This is the pious gift of the senior monk, the illustrious Kāśyapa". The fragment possibly belonged to the same *stūpa* as D(*b*) 37 but the dome slightly overlaps the drum.

Buff-coloured sandstone of Chunār. Discovered in 1904-05 south of the Main Shrine.

D(*b*) 39.—Part (ht. 1′ 1½″) of the drum of a votive *stūpa*, quite plain. Probably excavated in 1904-05.

D(*b*) 40.—Votive *stūpa* (diam. 1′ 6″; ht. 8″), quite plain. The dome and *hti* form a distinct piece. The drum is made up of two pieces which were joined by iron-cramps. Found in 1907-08 on approach to the Main Shrine from the east.

D(*b*) 41.—Part (ht. 1′; width 1′ 9″) of star-shaped base of a votive *stūpa* with figures of Buddha seated in rectangular niches on three faces. Two of the figures are in the earth-touching and teaching attitude respectively. The third figure has a bowl in the lap.

Mediæval. Buff-coloured sandstone of Chunār. Discovered in 1904-05 south-west of the Main Shrine.[1]

*D(*b*) 42.—Fragment (ht. 1′ 1½″) of the pinnacle[2] of a votive *stūpa* with a square tenon at base and three cornices above, on the uppermost of which occurs a dedicatory record which reads—

[*Dēya*]*dharmmō=yaṁ*........*sūtradhā*[*ra*]........ "This is the pious gift ......the architect..."

Mediæval. Excavated in 1907-08 on the approach to the Main Shrine from the east, 8′ below the surface.

D(*b*) 43.—Pinnacle (ht. 1′ 1½″) with a tenon at the base which must have belonged to a votive *stūpa*. Discovered in 1907-08 in the 1st outer court of monastery I.

D(*b*) 44.—Fragment (ht. 7″) of the pinnacle of a votive *stūpa* with two cornices. Excavated in 1907-08 on the approach to the Main Shrine from the east.

D(*b*) 45.—Pinnacle (ht. 1′ 6″) tapering upwards and adorned with a series of cornices. Top broken. Discovered in 1907-08 in second outer court of monastery I, 8′ below the surface.

D(*b*) 46.—Part (ht. 9″) of the pinnacle of a votive *stūpa* with three cornices. Excavated in 1906-07 in *stūpa* 44 on south of first outer of monastery I, 3′ below the surface.

---

[1] *A. S. R.*, 1904-05, p. 101, No. 463.
[2] All pinnacles registered here seem to be mediæval.

D(*b*) 47.—Pinnacle (ht. 1′ 1″) broken at the top and adorned with raised bands or cornices which diminish upwards. Excavated in 1906-07 in the area on the east of the Main Shrine.

D(*b*) 48.—Pinnacle (ht. 8¾″) broken at both ends. Found in 1906-07 in the entrance chamber of monastery I, 3½′ below the surface.

D(*b*) 49.—Pinnacle (ht. 1′) broken at the top; of usual shape. Mediæval. Unearthed in one of the recent diggings.

D(*b*) 50.—Pinnacle (ht. 1′ ½″) of a votive *stūpa*, complete. Usual form, with cornices. Find-spot not known.

D(*b*) 51.—Pinnacle (ht. 1′ 1″) of a votive *stūpa*. The finial has the shape of a lotus bud. Part split away on one side. Excavated in 1906-07 in the area on the east of the Main Shrine.

D(*b*) 52.—Pinnacle (ht. 1′ 5″) broken at both ends; of usual type. Mediæval. Find-spot not known.

D(*b*) 53.—Pinnacle (ht. 11″) broken at both ends; of usual form. Find-spot not known.

D(*b*) 54.—Pinnacle with part of *hti* (ht. 7″). Mediæval. Discovered in 1906-07 in the area west of the Main Shrine.

D(*b*) 55.—Fragmentary pinnacle (ht. 1′) of a votive *stūpa* of usual style. Mediæval. Excavated in 1906-07 in area east of the Main Shrine.

D(*b*) 56.—Fragment (ht. 10″) of a pinnacle of usual type. Mediæval. Found in the same year and area as D(*b*) 55.

D(*b*) 57.—Fragment of a pinnacle (ht. 9″) found in 1906-07 in the same area as D(*b*) 56.

D(*b*) 58.—Fragment (ht. 2½″) of a small pinnacle corrugated like the *āmalaka* fruit at the base. Mediæval. Found in 1906-07 between *stūpa* No. 45 and the first outer court of monastery I, 7′ below the surface.

D(*b*) 59-60.—Two fragmentary pinnacles (ht. 6½″ and 3¾″) of mediæval date. Provenance not known. Sandstone of Chunār.

D(*b*) 61.—*Hti* and part of pinnacle (ht. of both 4½″) of a votive *stūpa*. The *hti* is star-shaped. Blue stone of Gayā. Probably mediæval. Unearthed in 1904-05 north-east of Jagat Singh *stūpa*.

D(c)—UMBRELLAS.

D(c) 1.—Top of a stone umbrella (diam. 4′ 1″) of the form of a mushroom, convex on the upper side. The circular mortice (diam. 4½″) in the centre has a raised rim carved in the manner of a lotus flower. There was some petal decoration around it, but it is now almost obliterated. The outer rim is pierced on the outside with fine holes for the reception of flower garlands with which it must have been decorated. It may have been placed over a statue or a *stūpa*. The date cannot be later than the early Gupta period. Traces of red paint. Discovered in 1907-08.

D(c) 2.—Top of a stone umbrella (diam. 4′ 5½″). A large segment 2′ 8″ in chord is broken off. The extant portion shows three mortices inside the outer rim at equal distances which must have received the upper ends of additional props. The mortice (diam. 9½″) for the main post is cut through the stone. The surface has not been smoothed and the umbrella may not have been finished. The date cannot be ascertained. Unearthed in 1904-05 among the *stūpas* west of the Jagat Singh *stūpa*.[1]

D(c) 3.—Top of an umbrella (diam. 4′) similar to D(c) 1 and 2. The rim around the mortice which held the staff is broken off. Around it is carved a ring of lotus petals. Two large pieces broken off the rim. Early Gupta period. Unearthed in 1906-07 in the trench on the west of the old sculpture shed close to the surface.

D(c) 4.—Top of an umbrella (diam. 3′ 2½″). The outer rim and the one around the mortice in the centre are damaged. Discovered in 1904-05, probably west of Jagat Singh *stūpa*.

D(c) 5.—Top of an umbrella (diam. 2′ ½″) of usual form. Rim around the edge 1¼″ high. The mortice in the centre which held the top of the staff has a double flange like the umbrella of B (a) 1 and is surrounded by a raised rim resembling a lotus flower. Early Gupta or Kushāṇa period. Excavated in 1906-07 in the first outer court on the east of monastery I, 20′ below the surface.

D(c) 6.—Top of an umbrella (diam. 2′ 3¾″) of the usual form. Outer rim damaged in parts. The raised rim around the mortice is carved like a lotus flower. Gupta period. Excavated in one of the recent diggings.

D(c) 7.—Top of an umbrella (diam. 1′ 7½″) similar to D(c) 6. Excavated in 1907-08 in second outer court on east of monastery I.

D(c) 8.—Fragment (chord 2′ 6″) of the top of an umbrella of Gupta date. Probably discovered in 1906-07 in the trench west of the old sculpture shed.

---

[1] *A. S. R.*, 1904-05, p. 101, No. 468.

D(*c*) 9.—Fragment (chord 2′) of the top of an umbrella. Find-spot not known.

D(*c*) 10.—Fragment (length 2′ 9″; width 1′ 3″) of the top of an umbrella. In the centre is a mortice with a lotus-shaped raised rim. Gupta period. Probably excavated in one of the recent diggings.

*D(*c*) 11.—Fragment (chord 1′ 5½″) of the top of an umbrella with a raised rim, 1½″ high. On it is carved a Pālī inscription of four lines containing the four great truths of the Buddhist doctrine which formed the subject of Gautama Buddha's first sermon at Sārnāth. The characters are of the late Kushāṇa period, *Cir.* 2nd or 3rd century A.D. Dr. Konow remarks that this is the only Pālī inscription found in Northern India and proves that the Pālī canon existed and was known in Benares in the late Kushāṇa period. The inscription runs as follows :—

l. 1. *Chattār=imāni bhikkhavē ar*[*i*]*ya-sachchāni*

l. 2. *katamāni* [*cha*]*ttāri dukkha*[*ṁ*] *di*(*bhi*)*kkhavē arā*(*i*)*ya-sachchaṁ*

l. 3. *dukkha-samuday*[*ō*] *ariyasachchaṁ dukkhanirōdhō ariyasach-chaṁ*

l. 4. *dukkha-nirōdha-gāminī* [*cha*] *paṭipadā ari*[*ya**]*sachchaṁ.*

Dr. Konow translates as follows[1] :—

" Four are, ye monks, the Noble Axioms. And which are these four ? The Noble Axiom about suffering, ye monks, the Noble Axiom about the origin of suffering, the Noble Axiom about the cessation of suffering, and the Noble Axiom about the way leading to the cessation of suffering."

Buff-coloured sandstone of Chunār. Discovered in 1906-07 between *stūpas* Nos. 13 and 14 to north-west of Main Shrine, 4½″ below the surface.[2]

D(*c*) 12.—Fragment (chord 10½″) of the top of an umbrella of Gupta date unearthed in 1906-07 in the area on east of Main Shrine.

D(*c*) 13.—Fragment (chord 10″) of the top of an umbrella of Gupta date. Unearthed in one of the recent diggings.

D(*c*) 14.—Fragment (chord 1′ 1″) of the top of an umbrella ornamented with a lotus pattern on the underside. Mediæval style. Buff-coloured stone of Chunār. Unearthed in one of the recent excavations.

---

[1] *A. S. R.*, 1906-07, pp. 95, 96.
[2] *Ibid.*, p. 74.

*D(c) 15.—Fragment (chord 8½″) of the top of an umbrella. On the upper curved surface is an inscription of four lines in mediæval characters. The epigraph reads as follows [1]:—

l. 1. *Rājaputra-śrī-Mā-*
l. 2. *junadēvasa śubha*
l. 3 *rājaputra-Hathari-*
l. 4. *dēvasa.*

"For the welfare of the king's son, the illustrious Mājunadēva; of the king's son Hatharidēva."

Find-spot not known, but presumably unearthed in one of the recent excavations.

D(c) 16.—Upper part (ht. 3′ 8½″) of an umbrella post (Sanskrit *chhattra—yashṭi*). It is octagonal at the base, sixteen-sided in the middle and circular above. The lowest portion must have been square. This is the design of the umbrella posts of the Kushāṇa statues B (*a*) 1-3. It may be concluded that the present fragment is also Kushāṇa.[2] Chunār sandstone of reddish colour. Presumably excavated in 1904-05.

D(c) 17.—Upper part (ht. 1′ 8½″) of a similar umbrella post. Chunār sandstone. Probably discovered in 1904-05.

D(c) 18.—Upper part (ht. 3′) of an umbrella post, sixteen-sided below, circular above. The tenon is 2¼″ high. Kushāṇa (?) period. Chunār sandstone. Probably excavated in 1904-05.

D(c) 19.—Lower part (ht. 3′ 4″) of an umbrella post. The fragment has not been smoothed or dressed. It is octagonal in section except the base which was intended to be buried in the ground. The date cannot be ascertained. Chunār sandstone. Find-place not known.

D(c) 20.—Fragment (ht. 2′ 1″) of an umbrella octagonal below, round above. Chunār sandstone. Excavated in one of the recent diggings.

D(c) 21.—Upper part (ht. 3′ 5″; diam. at base 7″) of an umbrella post. It is round in section and, like all the other umbrella posts described above, tapers upwards. The surface is well-dressed. Probably Gupta. Chunār sandstone. It was found among the stones stacked by Mr. Oertel in the north-east corner of the Main Shrine.

D(c) 22.—Upper-part (ht. 2′ 1½″) of an umbrella post octagonal in section which tapers upwards. Chunār sandstone. Probably excavated in one of the recent diggings.

D(c) 23.—Fragment (ht. 1′ 8″) of an octagonal umbrella post. Chunār sandstone. Probably unearthed in one of the recent excavations.

---

[1] *A. S. R.*, 1907-08, p. 76, XXI.
[2] The section of the Bēsnagar *garuḍadhvaja* is of the same style.

D(*c*) 24.—Fragment (ht. 1′ 9″) of an umbrella post octagonal below, sixteen-sided above. To judge from section, Kushāṇa (?). Chunār sandstone. Probably found in one of the recent excavations.

D(*c*) 25.—Fragment (ht. 1′ ½″) of an umbrella post octagonal in section. Chunār sandstone. Probably excavated in one of the recent diggings.

D(*c*) 26.—Upper part (ht. 1′ 11″) of a circular post. The top is round and the tenon which is pierced with a mortice very narrow. It may have been an umbrella post. Chunār sandstone. Probably unearthed in one of the recent excavations.

D(*c*) 27.—Fragment (ht. 9″) from the top of an umbrella post. Back half broken off. Tenon at the top. Chunār sandstone. Excavated in one of the recent excavations.

D (*c*) 28.—Top (ht. 4½″) of an umbrella post adorned with petal decoration in Gupta style. Excavated in one of the recent diggings.

D(*d*).—Lintels of doorways.

D(*d*) 1.—Lintel (length 16′; ht. 1′ 10″; thickness 1′ 3½″) of a large doorway. The face is divided into six fields separated by two representations of shrines and three pediments or tops of temples. The shrines have diminishing roofs surmounted with *āmalaka* finials flanked by leogryphs facing in opposite directions. In front of the shrines are trefoil niches in one of which is a female standing facing and giving something to a child squatting on either side. The niche of the other shrine contains a similar female standing between a pair of jars filled with gold or sweets. She holds a lotus in her left hand and a bunch of buds in the right. These figures presumably represent *Hārītī*, the female energy of Kubēra, the god of wealth, whom we find pictured in the fields at the ends of the lintel. The vases and children associated with her support this identification. The three pediments which alternate with the shrines contain each two niches, one above the other. The upper niches which present lions' heads (*kīrttimukha*) are flanked by lions *sejant* in two cases and Kubēra figures in the third. In each of the lower niches we notice a group of three musicians. The lower portion of the lintel is adorned with lines of dentils and floral scroll.

Of the six panels referred to above, the one at the proper left extremity (Pl. XXIV) exhibits Kubēra or Jambhala, the Buddhist god of wealth[1] sitting in easy posture with a *bījapūraka* (Hindi or Gujarati *bijaura*) fruit in his right hand and a money purse, originally made of mongoose's skin, in the left hand.[2] He has, as usual, a fat belly and wears a diadem, a necklace of beads, bracelets and a lower garment round his loins. To his right is an amorous couple.

Another figure of Kubēra occurs in the panel at the other end of the lintel (Pl. XXIX). He has the same attributes in his hands and is attended by a female with a bowl of sweets in one hand and a fly-whisk (Skt. *chāmara*) in the other on the right and a similar figure holding a fly-whisk on the left.

The intervening four compartments illustrate the *khantivādi-jātaka* according to which Gautama Buddha, in one of his previous existences, was tortured to death by a cruel king named Kalābu of Benares, for preaching the truth of patience to his nautch girls after they had lulled him to sleep by their musical entertainments. In the first of these four panels, *i.e.*, the second from the proper left end (Pl. XXV), we notice the Bōdhisattva seated in the attitude of meditation surrounded by five girls, two on one side and three on the other seated with

---

[1] He is also the mammon of the followers of the Brahmanical faith.

[2] Dr. Vogel, whose researches have thrown valuable light on the iconographic history of this god, has shown that in early specimens Kubēra actually holds a live mongoose (*nakulī*) which vomits pearls, which later artists have ingeniously converted into a purse (Skt *bhastra*) of treasure.

folded hands and apparently listening to the ascetic. These girls are, no doubt, the dancing girls referred to above. The next two sections (Pls. XXVI—XXVII) represent the same five girls engaged in a musical performance. The central girl, who is dancing, is clad in a loin cloth, a scarf falls over her arms while a third garment covers her breast.[1] The remaining four girls are playing a flute (Sanskrit *vaṁśī*), cymbals, a drum and a pair of tabors (*mṛidaṅga*). It is to be noted that the king himself is absent from both of these scenes. These two panels should strictly speaking have preceded the sermon alluded to and seem to have been put in their present position for considerations of symmetry. The last panel, *i.e.*, the second from the proper right, shows the torture of the Bōdhisattva (Pl. XXVIII). He is seated with a rosary in his left hand while his right hand is being cut off with a sword by a male figure who is being restrained from the act by two girls, one holding his legs and the other pulling him from behind by his shoulders. The aggressor must be the executioner who, according to the story, cut off the hand, feet, nose and ears of the Bōdhisattva.

At either end of the lintel we notice a bold garland moulding which must have been continued on the uprights of the doorway. The lintel must have belonged to a large portal. It was discovered in 1907-08 by Dr. Marshall under a brick platform to the east of the paved passage on the north-east of the Main Shrine. On grounds of style the learned discoverer has attributed the lintel to the Gupta period[2]. It is made of Chunār sandstone and must have been painted red. Pl. XXIII, *a* ; and Pls. XXIV—XXIX.

D(*d*) 2.—Two fragments (length 5′ 9″ ; ht. 1′ 5″ ; thickness 1′ 2″) of a lintel or architrave. Above, a bold foliated pattern which must have been continued on the uprights. Below it there are two compartments alternating with representations of tops of shrines surmounted with *āmalaka* finials. In the proper left panel we notice a celestial carrying a garland in his hands and his spouse who is looking at a mirror on his thighs. In the other compartment is Buddha seated in the attitude of expounding the law between two male attendants, perhaps meant for Bōdhisattvas though they do not hold their emblems.

Late Gupta or early mediæval. Pale buff stone of Chunār. The lintel belonged to the Queen's College Collection, but it must have been found at Sārnāth.

D(*d*) 3.—Two fragments which fit together (length 6′ 6½″ ; ht. 1′ 7½″ ; thickness 10″) of a door architrave or lintel divided into three

---

[1] This cloth is a sort of waistcoat, with hooks on the back which is still worn by the women of Rajputana and other parts of India.

[2] *A. S. R.*, 1907-08, pp. 70-71 and Pl. XX.

compartments by pediments containing niches surrounded by ornamental borders. Two of the pediments are surmounted with *āmalaka* finials. Of the niches, the central one, which marks the middle of the lintel, contains Buddha seated on a couch in European style, in the attitude of expounding the law; the other two contain lions' heads (*kīrttimukha*). Among the panels the first from the proper left shows Buddha seated with his fingers making the sign of expounding the law. He has a male fly-whisk bearer on either side. In each of the other two panels is a celestial (*dēva*) in flight, holding a lute (*vīṇā*) in one instance and a flower (?) in the other, and carrying his spouse on his thighs. The spaces between the projections in the upper part are taken up with bold foliated designs. The style points to the late Gupta epoch as the date of the sculpture.

The larger fragment is sketched with slight restorations in Major Kittoe's Drawings, where it is described as a Sārnāth sculpture.[1] Perhaps he excavated it himself. The other fragment was unearthed in 1906-07.

D(*d*) 4.—Fragment (length 3′ 5½″; ht. 1′ 5″; thickness 11½″) similar to D(*d*) 2 and 3. To proper left in a panel, Buddha seated in the posture of expounding the law between attendants. The sculpture may have belonged to the same building as the preceding two sculptures.

Chunār sandstone. The sculpture was formerly preserved in the Queen's College.

D(*d*) 5.—Lintel (length 5′; ht. 1′) of a doorway adorned with bands of foliated design. Early mediæval. Traces of red paint. Chunār sandstone. Excavated in 1904-05 south of the Aśōka Column.[2]

D(*d*) 6.—Proper left part (length 3′ 8″; ht. 10″) of an architrave or lintel of a doorway, adorned with a bold garland pattern and *āmalaka* finial which belonged to a representation of the top of a shrine such as we notice in D(*d*) 1-5. Early mediæval. Pictured in Major Kittoe's manuscript drawings and may have been excavated by him.[3]

D(*d*) 7.—Fragment (length 3′ 1″; ht. 1′ 1½″) of an architrave similar to D(*d*) 6 sketched in Major Kittoe's manuscript Drawings.[4]

D(*d*) 8.—Fragment (length 3′ 11″; ht. 8½″) of the top piece of a door architrave, with a corpulent figure seated in easy attitude in a niche between *āmalaka* projections. Mediæval. Excavated in one of the recent excavations.

D(*d*) 9.—Proper left end (length 1′ 1″; ht. 1′ 1″) of a lintel with a figure of Kubēra the god of wealth, seated in easy attitude and hold-

---

[1] Vol. I, Pl. 24.
[2] *A. S. R.*, 1904-05, p. 100, No. 436.
[3] Vol. I, No. 101, Pl. 25.
[4] Vol. I, No. 125, Pl. 26.

ing a purse in his right hand and a citron (*bījapūraka*) in the left. He has a halo around his head. Co-eval with D(*d*) 1. Seems to be one of the Queen's College sculptures. But it must have been discovered at Sārnāth.

D(*d*) 10.—Top piece of an architrave or lintel (length 4′ 3½″; ht. 1′ 2½″) of a doorway. At the top we notice a broad band representing a pair of crocodiles (*makara*) facing each other, with long foliated tails. At each end, *i.e.*, where the lintel was supported by uprights is a lion's head (*kīrttimukha*). Early mediæval. Delineated in Major Kittoe's manuscript Drawings.[1] The provenance is not stated there, but it may be assumed that this is one of the numerous sculptures which before the museum was erected were carried to Benares and deposited in the Queen's College.

D(*d*) 11.—Lintel (length 2′ 4½″; ht. 1′ 1″) of a doorway decorated with three floral and ornamental bands. In the centre in a trefoil sunken niche is Tārā seated in easy attitude, her right hand in gift-bestowing attitude, her left holding her attribute, the blue lotus. Early mediæval. Unearthed in 1907-08 in the second outer court on the east of monastery I, 1′ below the surface.[2]

D(*d*) 12.—Lintel (length 4′ 11″; ht. 9″) of a doorway, with floral bands. In the centre, in a trefoil niche, Buddha seated in the earth-touching attitude. Much defaced. Late Gupta style. Excavated in 1907-08 near the Dhamēkh *stūpa*.

D(*d*) 13.—Proper left portion (length 2′ 1″; ht. 9½″) of a lintel with two bands of garland pattern and rosettes. Below, geometric decoration. Early mediæval. Delineated in Major Kittoe's Manuscript Drawings where it is labelled as a Sārnāth sculpture.[3]

D(*d*) 14.—Fragment of a lintel (length 4′ ½″; ht. 8½″) with geometric decoration. Found in 1904-05. Its find-spot has not been recorded.

D(*d*) 15.—Fragment (length 2′ 3½″; ht. 1′ 1″) of a lintel which was formerly preserved in the Queen's College.

D(*d*) 16.—Fragment (ht. 2′ 3″) of a lintel or pediment adorned with a celestial carrying a lotus flower to proper right, a lion and part of a worshipper. Gupta style. Chunār sandstone. Excavated in 1906-07 in area north-east of the Main Shrine.

D(*d*) 17. Fragment (ht. 11¼″; width 1′ 7″) from the middle of a lintel. In centre, Buddha seated in the earth-touching attitude in a chapel supported on circular columns. On either side scroll work and other decoration. Mediæval. Unearthed in one of the recent excavations.

---

[1] Vol. I, No. 118, Pl. 148.
[2] *A. S. R.*, 1907-08, p. 53, ι 3 and fig. 7.
[3] Vol. I, No. 125, Pl. 26, *a*.

D(*e*).—Window Screens.

D(*e*) 1.—Frame (ht. 1′ 11½″; width 2′ 2½″) of a perforated window screen. The *jāli* work has disappeared with the exception of a single row of square holes along the proper right jamb. They are filled with square flowers placed diagonally and their total number must have been sixteen. On the base or sill, is carved some floral decoration in the centre and couching lions at the ends. The style shows close affinity to the innumerable carvings unearthed in 1906-07 in monastery I, and there seems to be no doubt that this window must have belonged to that building.

D(*e*) 2.—Window screen (ht. 1′ 8″; width 1′ 10″; thickness 2¾″) pierced with triangular holes formed by one square placed in a bigger one and their diagonals, all points of intersection being ornamented with lotus rosettes. It is one of the few Gupta antiquities which Dr. Marshall discovered[1] right on the floor of the Gupta monastery III and has supplied one of the two patterns which have been employed in the windows of the verandah of the Sārnāth museum. The other pattern was furnished by D (*e*) 12.

The material is, as usual, the sandstone of Chunār.

D(*e*) 3.—Window screen (ht. 1′ 6¼″; width 1′ 4″; thickness 3″) pierced with an arched niche (ht. 1′ 1″; width 6″). Dr. Marshall who unearthed it in the Gupta monastery IV has drawn attention to the identity of the form of the outer line of the arch with that of the arches decorating the wall around the tomb of Zainu-l-'Ābidīn and in the parapet around the Jyēshṭhēśvara temple on the Takht-i-Sulaimān in Śrīnagar, and concludes that these two buildings cannot be as late as the Muhammadan period to which Mr. Fergusson assigned them.[2]

D(*e*) 4.—Window screen (ht. 1′ 6″; width 1′ 1″; thickness 3″) pierced with two niches side by side, which are of the same form as the one in D(*e*) 3. At each end of the slab and between the arches are pillars in relief. The screen seems to have been used in an enclosure wall decorated with a series of such screens, as in the two Kashmir monuments alluded to under D (*e*) 3.

Chunār sandstone of buff colour. Discovered in 1907-08 in Gupta monastery III probably on the floor.[3]

D(*e*) 5.—Slab (ht. 1′ 2½″; width 1′ 4″; thickness 2¾″) adorned with two arched niches side by side. The niches are, however, not cut through the stone as in D(*e*) 4. The shape of the arches is identical.

---

[1] *A. S. R.*, 1907-08, p. 58, ŋ 144, and Pl. XIV, *b*. *Cf.* Smith, *Jaina Stūpa*, Pl. XLI, fig. 1.

[2] *A. S. R.*, 1907-08, p. 58, and Pl. XIV, *c*. Also, Marshall, *Note on Archæological work in Kashmir*, p. 32.

[3] *Ibid.*, p. 58, ŋ 130.

It was found near the stair to the monastery I, 4′ 4″ below the surface and would seem to have been built in that building.[1]

D(*e*) 6.—Window screen (ht. 1′ 7½″; width 1′ 7″; thickness 4″) similar to D (*e*) 3. Unearthed in 1906-07 near the north flanking wall of the stair to monastery I, 3′ 4″ below the surface.

D(*e*) 7.—Window screen (ht. 1′ 7¼″; width 1′ 7½″; thickness 5″) of the same type as D(*e*) 6. The niche is 1′ 2¼″ high and 8″ wide. Discovered in 1904-05 north-west of Jagat Singh *stūpa*.[2]

D(*e*) 8.—Proper left upper corner (ht. 10″; width 10″; thickness 5½″) of a window screen similar to D(*e*)1, showing a figure of a celestial (*dēva*) with a garland. Mediæval. May have belonged to monastery I.

D(*e*) 9.—Proper left lower corner (ht. 1′ 1″; width 7″; thickness 5½″) of a window screen of the same type as D(*e*) 8. Female dancer above, part of lion couchant, below. Mediæval. Found in the trench south of the monastery I, 1′ below the surface.

D(*e*) 10.—Fragment (ht. 10″; width 5″; thickness 6½″) of the proper left jamb of a pierced window screen, with a figure of Buddha in the earth-touching attitude. Found in 1907-08 in the western precinct of monastery I, 4′ below the surface and was most probably used in that monastery.

D(*e*) 11.—Upper piece (length 1′ 10¾″; ht. 4½″; thickness 3¾″) of a pierced window screen of mediæval date. In the centre, Buddha seated in the earth-touching attitude. To proper left, a celestial (*dēva*) carrying a garland. The fragment must have been found in monastery I.

D(*e*) 12.—Fragment (length 10¼″; width 7¾″; thickness 4½″) of a pierced window screen adorned with lotus rosettes on the front. Mediæval style. This type has also been employed in the verandah of the Sārnāth Museum.

---

[1] *A. S. R.*, 1906-07, p. 85, and Pl. XXVI, 3.
[2] *Ibid.*, 1904-05, p. 100, No. 435.

D(*f*).—Pillars and Door-Jambs.

D(*f*) 1.—Fragment (ht. 3′ 11″) of a column, octagonal below, sixteen-sided above and circular at the top. From the similarity of its section to the umbrella posts of B (*a*) 1-3, it seems to be Kushāṇa in date. Unearthed in one of the recent excavations.

*D(*f*) 2.—Column (ht. 4′ 6″) broken into two pieces. Base shaped like a vase with foliage (*ghaṭa-pallava*). Capital square and carved on three faces with lions' heads. The shaft is circular with a slight taper upwards and decorated with two bands of floral pattern. Necking ornamented with torus moulding and lotus petals.[1] Above the base is cut a Sanskrit inscription of five lines (length 8¼″) in Gupta characters which I read :

l. 1. *Dēyadharmmō=yaṁ śākyabhikshōḥ Si...vika Siṁhamatēḥ* (?)
l. 2. *Yad=atra puṇyaṁ tad=bhavatu mātāpitrōr=āchāryōpādhyā=*
l. 3. *yānāṁ sarvvasatvānāṁ ch=ānuttara-jñānāvāptayē*
l. 4. .... *Lōka=*
l. 5. *nāthasya*........

Translation.

This [is the pious gift of Siṁhamati ...... Whatever merit [there is] in it, [may it be] for the attainment of supreme knowledge of [his] parents, preceptors and teachers and of all sentient beings........... of Lōkanātha.........

The column was formerly preserved in the Queen's College but as it is made of buff-coloured sandstone of Chunār it was probably discovered at Sārnāth.

D(*f*) 3.—Lower part (ht. 4′ 2″) of a column circular in section. Base moulded in the form of a vase with foliage with atlantes disposed in the four corners. Shaft plain except for a band of lions' heads with festoons of beads. The style resembles that of D(*f*) 2, hence Gupta. Buff-coloured sandstone of Chunār with vestiges of red paint. Presumably excavated in one of the recent diggings.

D(*f*) 4.—Top-portion (ht. 2′ 8″) of a column with the cap moulded into a vase with foliage. Shaft circular and plain. Late Gupta style. Discovered in 1904-05. Chunār sandstone.

D(*f*) 5.—Lower part (ht. 3′ 10″) of a column with the base moulded into a vase with foliage. Shaft octagonal and ornamented with a frieze of lions' heads with festoons of pearls. Late Gupta period. Chunār

---

[1] *Cf.* similar pillars in Gupta monastery III, *A. S. R.*, 1907-08, Pl. XV. It is interesting to note the similarity of design between the Gupta columns of Sārnāth and those of Mathurā. The vase and foliage which occurs both at the base and under the cap, friezes of lions' heads with pendant chains, and crescents are motives which we find on columns of both places.

sandstone. Traces of red paint. Excavated in 1906-07 in the monastery I.

D(*f*) 6.—Lower part (ht. 4′ 1″) of a column similar to D(*f*) 5 which must have been employed in the same building with it.

D(*f*) 7.—Half column (ht. 4′ 6″ ; width 7′ 7½″) which must have been engaged in a wall. The cap was moulded after the style of a vase with foliage. Below it, lions' heads with half lotus medallions above. Late Gupta work. The back of the column is cut into a bold half lotus such as we find on ceiling stones of the mediæval period. The stone presumably belonged to the Queen's College collection.

*D(*f*) 8.—Column (ht. 4′ 2″ ; width 7″) rectangular in section. On the front is a niche containing a figure of Buddha in the attitude of expounding the law with the usual deer, wheel and five disciples below his lotus throne. Below the niche are traces of an inscription of four lines in 4th or 5th century characters. The extant portion reads as follows :—

l. 1. *Dēya [dharmmō=yaṁ śā] kyabhikshōḥ*
l. 2.
l. 3. . . . . . . *ścha*
l. 4. *sēnamuddiśya.*

Excavated in 1907-08.

D(*f*) 9.—Upper part (ht. 4′ 1½″) of a column with a square cap in the form of a vase. The shaft is octagonal and ornamented with a broad band consisting of festoons of beads containing geese alternating with floral patterns. Above this band is a row of lunettes or crescents and other decoration. Excavated in 1904-05 south-west of Main Shrine.[1]

D(*f*) 10.—Column (ht. 4′ 4″) with square, octagonal and sixteen-sided section. The decoration consists of two friezes of lions' heads with festoons of beads below and half lotus rosettes above them.[2] Late Gupta. Find-spot not ascertainable.

D(*f*) 11.—Upper part (ht. 2′ 5½″) of a column decorated after the style of D(*f*) 10, and of the same period. The cap is square (8½″ along each side), and plain. Excavated in 1904-05 south-west of Main Shrine.[3]

D(*f*) 12.—Lower part (ht. 2′ 1½″) of a column, square in section, adorned with pattern of vase with foliage near the base and a band of lions' heads with chains and half lotus rosettes above. Late Gupta style. Pale buff stone of Chunār. Unearthed in one of the recent excavations.

D(*f*) 13.—Upper part (ht. 2′ 4″) of a column in late Gupta style. The cap has the shape of a vase with foliage. Lower down, we notice

---

[1] *A. S. R.*, 1904-05, p. 101, No. 455.
[2] *Cf.* similar decoration on a Mathurā column, Smith, *The Jain Stūpa*, Pl. XLVI, fig. 3.
[3] *A. S. R.*, 1904-05, p. 100, No. 443.

a broad band of foliated pattern with geese introduced into it. The column is sketched in Major Kittoe's Manuscript Drawings where it is called a Sārnāth pillar.[1]

D(*f*) 14.—Upper part (ht. 2′ 4″) of a column with a circular shaft. The cap is moulded like a vase filled with foliage. Lower down, there is a band of floral design with jewels introduced in it. Back half split away. Late Gupta style. Chunār sandstone. Excavated in 1904-05 north-east of Jagat Singh *stūpa*.[2]

D(*f*) 15.—Upper part (ht. 2′ 2″) of a column, similar to D(*f*) 14 and most probably from the same building. Unearthed in 1904-05 south-west of Main Shrine.[3]

D(*f*) 16.—Fragment (ht. 1′ 8½″) of the circular shaft of a pillar with a band of floral pattern. Late Gupta. Reddish sandstone of Chunār.

D(*f*) 17.—Fragment (ht. 1′ 11½″) of the circular shaft of a pillar of the Gupta period. In the middle, a band of foliated pattern as on D(*f*) 2. Unearthed in 1907-08 in area around Jagat Singh *stūpa*.[4]

D(*f*) 18.—Upper part (ht. 2′ 8″) of a pillar, with a square cap adorned on each face with a lion's head. Rest covered with ornament. Early mediæval. Chunār sandstone. The fragment was formerly preserved in the Queen's College, but to judge from style it may have been discovered at Sārnāth.

D(*f*) 19.—Upper part (ht. 2′ 8½″) of a pillar carved after the fashion of D(*f*) 18. It belonged to the Queen's College collection.

D(*f*) 20.—Fragment (ht. 2′ 2″) of a pillar with the top moulded after the fashion of a vase with foliage. Late Gupta work. Chunār sandstone. Probably from the Queen's College collection.

D(*f*) 21.—Lower part (ht. 2′ ½″) of a pilaster which must have been engaged in a wall. Base ornamented with a vase filled with foliage. At the top, a band of decoration as on D(*f*) 10. Gupta style. Reddish Chunār sandstone. Excavated in 1904-05.[5]

D(*f*) 22.—Short pilaster (ht. 2′ 6″) with vase and foliage pattern at the base and the top. In the middle there is a band of ornament as on D(*f*) 21. Gupta style. Excavated in 1907-08 in monastery III.[6]

D(*f*) 23.—Pilaster (ht. 2′ 5½″) of a slightly variant style but evidently from the same building. Found in monastery I.

D(*f*) 24.—Pilaster (ht. 2′ 6″) similar to D(*f*) 22 and 23. The ornament in the middle presents geese. Excavated in one of the recent diggings.

---

[1] Vol. I, No. 145, Pl. 27.
[2] *A. S. R.*, 1904-05, p. 100, No. 430.
[3] *Ibid.*, p. 101, No. 461.
[4] *Ibid.*, 1907-08, p. 66, J. S. 6.
[5] *Ibid.*, 1904-05, p. 100, No. 428.
[6] *Ibid.*, 1907-08, Pl. XIII, a.

D(*f*) 25.—Pilaster (ht. 2′ 6″) with the same kind of decoration as on D(*f*) 22. Discovered in 1907-08 near the second gateway of monastery I.

D(*f*) 26.—Pilaster (ht. 2′ 5″) similar in style to D(*f*) 25, which has been rescued from a temporary viaduct over a *nālā* west of the site of Sārnāth.

D(*f*) 27.—Fragment (ht. 1′ 9½″) of a pilaster. In the middle, a band of lions' heads with pendant chains and half lotus rosettes. Gupta style. Found in one of the recent excavations.

D(*f*) 28.—Fragment (ht. 2′ 4″) of a pilaster, adorned with various ornaments. Late Gupta style. Find-spot not known.

D(*f*) 29.—Pilaster (ht. 3′ 2″) of late Gupta period. The motifs employed in its decoration are a vase with palmettes at the corners, at the base and at the top; jewel-work, a crocodile with elaborate tail, geese in festoons, a vertical line of rosettes, a female standing in trefoil niche, etc. Sandstone of Chunār, with traces of red paint. Unearthed in 1906-07 in monastery I.[1]

D(*f*) 30.—Pilaster (ht. 3′ 2″) which to judge from its size and the carving on it must have formed a pair with D(*f*) 29.

Exact provenance cannot be determined, but it must have been found in one of the recent excavations.

D(*f*) 31.—Fragment (ht. 1′ 9″) of a pillar, with a plain square cap, vase-shaped necking and octagonal and sixteen-sided shaft with a frieze of lions' heads. Late Gupta. Chunār sandstone. Unearthed in 1904-05 south-east of the *stūpa* on south of *stūpa* No. 7.[2]

D(*f*) 32.—Upper part (ht. 1′ 8½″) of a pillar with vase-shaped cap and rope necking with pendant chains. Gupta style. Chunār sandstone. Discovered in the monastery to west of Dhamēkh *stūpa*, 5′ 6″ below the surface.

D(*f*) 33.—Upper part (ht. 1′ 6″) of a column, with recessed cap adorned with palmettes. The necking has the shape of a vase with palmettes in corners. Late Gupta work. Excavated in one of the recent diggings.

D(*f*) 34.—Pilaster (ht. 4′ 2″). On the front Śiva is standing facing wearing high head-dress, a scarf, a *dhōtī* and a long garland of skulls (*muṇḍa-mālā*) which reaches down to his ankles. His face is cut off. The ornaments on his person are cylindrical ear-trinkets, a necklace, armlets, a girdle and anklets. He has four arms, all four hands broken off or damaged. Above his head, is a canopy with a kneeling figure on a lotus to the proper left. There must have been a similar figure on the other side. These figures are perhaps meant for celestials (*dēva*). Śiva's vehicle, Nandi, is crouching at his left side.

---

[1] *A. S. R.*, 1906-07, Pl. XXVI, 7 and p. 85, 1.
[2] *Ibid.*, 1904-05, p. 100, No. 406.

Early mediæval. Discovered in 1907-08 in the first outer court of monastery I.[1]

D(*f*) 35.—Fragment (ht. 3′ 4″) of a pilaster. The lower part, which is broader than the upper, has a figure of Pārvatī standing under an arch with smaller figures under her arms. To her proper right, we notice a female fly-whisk bearer and to her left, a defaced figure which held a trident (*triśūla*) in the right hand. The upper part presents two rectangular panels with a border of flowers and a row of musicians along each edge. The lower panel contains a four-armed standing figure of Gaṇēśa with broad elephantine ears and trunk. His lower right hand holds a mace; lower left, a bowl of sweets. His upper hands are raised up. In the upper panel we notice an emaciated figure of Chāmuṇḍā with four arms, holding a bowl of blood in her lower right hand. Late mediæval, or later. This pilaster, like D(*f*) 34, must have belonged to a Śaiva temple.

It was probably found at Sārnāth.

D(*f*) 36-40.—Five fragments (ht. 1′ 10½″ to 4′ ½″) of columns with recessed corners. Their faces are adorned with carvings which, to quote Dr. Marshall's words,[2] are bold and flowing in outline, but quite flat on the surface, and with none of the vitality and realism which characterize the work on the Dhamēkh *stūpa* and other sculptures of the Gupta age.

These columns were found in the mediæval monastery I, and were no doubt employed in it.

D(*f*) 41.—Fragment (ht. 2′ 8″) of a door-jamb, with a border of boldly executed warriors alternating with lions. The pilaster of the jamb is semi-octagonal in section and ornamented with chains with bells which issue from conventional lions' heads. Mediæval. Found in the first outer court of monastery I, 5′ below the surface. It must have been employed in the same building.[3]

D(*f*) 42.—Fragment (ht. 1′ 10½″) of a door-jamb with three borders of musicians, etc., on each side. The central facet shows a four-armed figure of Pārvatī standing with a miniature bull (Nandi) at her proper left side. Discovered in 1906-07 in the entrance chamber of monastery I, 3′ below the surface.

D(*f*) 43.—Fragment (ht. 1′ 4″) similar to D(*f*) 42. The figure on the central face seems to be Chāmuṇḍā. Found in 1906-07 presumably in area north-west of Main Shrine.

D(*f*) 44.—Window-jamb (ht. 3′ 1½″) adorned with a female figure at the base and lions' heads (*kīrttimukha*) with pendant chains above.

---

[1] *A. S. R.*, 1907-08, p. 50, *η* 36, Pl. XIII, *f*.

[2] *Ibid.*, 1906-07, p. 83. A specimen of such carving is illustrated in fig. 7 on the same page.

[3] *Ibid.*, 1906-07, p. 85, Pl. XXVI.

The rough portion at the back which was let into the wall is 1' 4" in depth. Mediæval. Discovered in monastery I, for which it was evidently intended, 5' below the surface.

D(*f*) 45.—Jamb stone (ht. 3' 1") with a double pilaster of which the front one is broken off. It is evident from the style of its carving that it belonged to the mediæval monastery I.

D(*f*) 46.—Fragment (ht. 3' ½") of a jamb stone with one border of rosettes and another of flowing arabesque. The pilaster has a pair of lions' heads at the top and a vase with palmettes at the base. Late Gupta style. Discovered at Sārnāth.[1]

D(*f*) 47.—Jamb stone (ht. 3' 1") similar to D(*f*) 44. It was undoubtedly employed in monastery I.

D(*f*) 48.—Fragment (ht. 1' 6½") of a jamb stone with borders of musicians and lions attacked by warriors as in D(*f*) 42 and 43. On the central face, above, Śachi with the elephant Airāvata crouching at her proper left side. Below, a goddess, much defaced. Mediæval. Discovered in 1906-07 in the first outer court of monastery I, 4' below the surface. The fragment must have belonged to a Brahmanical temple at Sārnāth.

D(*f*) 49.—Fragment (ht. 10") similar to D(*f*) 48. Mediæval or later. Excavated in 1906-07 in the first outer court of monastery I, 3' below the surface.

D(*f*) 50.—Fragment (ht. 1' 8") of a pillar adorned after the style of D (*f*) 10. Gupta style. Found in one of the recent excavations.

D(*f*) 51.—Top portion (ht. 1' 11") of a pilaster with vase-shaped cap. Gupta style. Probably found at Sārnāth.

D(*f*) 52.—Base (ht. 1' 7") of a pillar adorned with the design of a vase with palmettes. Gupta work. Traces of red paint. Excavated in 1907-08 in the western precinct of monastery I, 6' below the surface.

D(*f*) 53.—Fragment (ht. 1' 11") of a pillar with the back broken off from mediæval monastery I.

D(*f*) 54.—Fragment (ht. 1' 6") similar to D(*f*) 53 and from the same building.

D(*f*) 55.—Jamb stone (ht. 1' 6") of a window of late mediæval date. Excavated in 1906-07 on the approach to the Main Shrine from east.

D(*f*) 56.—Jamb stone (ht. 1' 6") which belonged to the same window as D(*f*) 55.

D(*f*) 57.—Jamb stone (ht. 1' 6") in the same style as D (*f*) 55-56. Found in the same area.

D(*f*) 58.—Jamb stone (ht. 1' 11") of mediæval date. Unearthed in one of the recent excavations.

---

[1] Kittoe, Manuscript Drawings, Vol. I, No. 101, Pl. 25.

*D(*f*) 59.—Door jamb (ht. 3′ 7″) with inscription[1] of one line in characters of the 9th Century A. D. Dr. Konow reads: *Viśvapālaḥ*] *daśa chaityāṁs=tu yat=puṇyaṁ kārayitv=ārjjitaṁ mayā* [1*] *sarvvalōkō bhavē[t=tēna] sarvvajñaḥ karuṇāmayaḥ* || *Śrī-Jayapāla* .... *ētān=uddiśya kāritam=Amṛitapālē[na].*

Translation.

Viśvapāla. By the merit which has been acquired by me after having caused ten *chaityas* to be made, let the whole world become omniscient, filled with compassion. Jayapāla . . . . has been made with reference to those (*Chaityas*?) *by* Amṛitapāla.

Found in 1907-08.

D(*f*) 60.—Fragment (ht. 1′ 2½″) of a door jamb. In the middle, a corpulent figure without head seated in Indian style. His right hand rests on his knee; his left arm is broken off. Perhaps Kuvēra. Gupta style. Chunār sandstone. Unearthed in 1906-07.

---

[1] *A. S. R.*, 1907-08, p. 75, VI.

D (*g*).—Capitals.

D (*g*) 1.—Bell-shaped capital (ht. 1′ 2½″; diam. 1′ 1½″) of Persepolitan type. The necking is ornamented with rope pattern; the abacus is plain. On the top, in centre, we notice a mortice hole (depth 4″, diam. 3″) for the tenon of the upper cap which must have been a figure of some sort. 2nd or 1st century B. C. There is no trace of polish. Chunār sandstone. Excavated in 1904-05 north-east of Main Shrine.[1]

D (*g*) 2.—Four fragments (ht. 1′; diam. 1′ 2″) of a bell-shaped capital of Persepolitan character. Tenons at the top and the base. 2nd or 1st century B. C. Traces of red paint, but no polish. Chunār sandstone. Discovered probably in 1904-05.

D (*g*) 3.—Fragment (ht. 10½″) of a bell-shaped capital of Persepolitan type, with rope pattern around necking and a low abacus. Much weathered. Same kind of stone as in D (*g*) 2. Find-spot not ascertainable.

D (*g*) 4.—Capital (ht. 1′ 1½″; width 2′) which Dr. Marshall describes[2] as "a fine capital of a pillar, found 4′ 9″ below the level of the concrete floor, 10′ from the north-west corner of the *Main Shrine*. The capital belongs to about the 1st century B. C., and is finely carved. On one face is represented a horse and rider, and on the other an elephant with two mahauts, while on the sides are Perso-Ionic volutes and palmettes." The capital has two brackets, one of which is partly broken and must have been employed in some sort of an arcade, presumably in the verandah of a monastery. In the top and the base, are mortice holes (3½″ in diam. and same in depth). Pl. V.

D (*g*) 5.—Capital (ht. 11½″; length 2′ 10″; width 2′ 1″) rectangular in horizontal shape with recessed corners. All four projecting faces have scenes from Gautama Buddha's life. They are the following:—

(*a*) The enlightenment (*bōdhi*) represented by a figure of Buddha seated, as usual, in the earth-touching attitude on a throne whose back is adorned with a pair of crocodiles (*makara*). On either side of Buddha is a *stūpa*.

(*b*) Broken off.

(*c*) The death (*mahāparinirvāṇa*). The Buddha is lying in the usual manner with three mourners in front. The water-pot and the three-pronged staff (*tridaṇḍa*) between them show that one of them is Subhadra, the last convert of the Buddha.[3]

---

[1] *A. S. R.*, 1904-05, p. 97, No. 233.
[2] *Ibid.*, 1906-07, p. 72 and Pl. XIX, 4, 5 and 6.
[3] *Cf.* steles Nos. C (*a*) 1, 3 and 4.

(*d*) Gautama Buddha seated in meditation under the hood of the snake-king (Nāgarāja) Muchilinda who guarded him during a thunder-storm after his enlightenment at Gayā.[1] On either side of the Buddha is a standing figure, which cannot be identified. Each recessed corner contains a standing worshipper. The capital was found in 1904-05 at the eastern entrance of the Main Shrine to which it must have belonged.[2]

The style of carving is assignable to the mediæval period and the other capital D (*g*) 6 which supported the lintel of this entrance on the opposite side was also found at the same place.

D (*g*) 6.—Capital of the same dimensions as D (*g*) 5. Both must have been employed together. The scenes depicted on it are:—

(*a*) The enlightenment as in D (*g*) 5, but here the two *stūpas* assume the aspect of temples.

(*b*) Group of three figures apparently witnessing the devouring by a wild animal of another figure lying in front. This scene has been identified with the birth story (*jātaka*) in which Gautama Buddha gave away his body to a hungry tigress.[3]

(*c*) The meaning of this scene is doubtful, but possibly it refers to the miracle of Śrāvastī. The Buddha is seated in the centre in the attitude of preaching. The two figures to his left may be one of the heretical teachers and his disciple. The action of the remaining two figures is uncertain.[4]

(*d*) Presentation of a cup of honey by a monkey in the Pārilēyyaka forest. The Buddha is seated between a pair of pillars with crocodile caps. The bowl which he held in his lap is broken off. To his right, is the monkey presenting the cup of honey with a celestial (*dēva*) figure above. To the Buddha's left we see the monkey disappearing in a masonry well to be re-born as a *dēva*.

It is tempting to refer the eight scenes found on these two capitals to the eight main events of Buddha's life but some of the details militate against such an interpretation. Discovered in 1904-05.[5]

---

[1] *Cf.* Kern, *Manual of Buddhism*, p. 21.

[2] *A. S. R.*, 1904-05, p. 85 and p. 101, No. 464. The face showing the last scene is illustrated in Pl. XXX, *b*.

[3] *Ibid.*, Pl. XXX, *c*.

[4] This scene is illustrated also on C (*a*) 3, *f*.

[5] *A. S. R.*, 1904-05, p. 85, and p. 101, No. 465.

D (*g*) 7.—Capital (ht. 11¼") square in plan with four brackets, similar in style to a capital unearthed in 1907-08 in the Gupta Monastery III and presumably of the Gupta period.[1]

Unearthed in one of the recent diggings.

D (*g*) 8.—Capital (ht. 9"; length 1' 6"; width 1' 2½") similar to D (*g*) 7. It does not seem to have been finished. Found in 1904-05 in the Main Shrine.[2]

D (*g*) 9.—Square abacus (ht. 7"; width 10½") with a grotesque lion's mask (*kīrttimukha*) on each side. Late Gupta style. Chunār standstone. Excavated in 1904-05 in the centre of the Main Shrine.[3]

D (*g*) 10.—Square abacus (ht. 5½"; width 1' 1½") with recessed corners, adorned with foliated scroll work as on the door jambs of the Main Shrine. Mediæval style. Traces of red paint. Chunār sandstone. Excavated in 1904-05.[4]

D (*g*) 11.—Square abacus (ht. 2½"; width 8") of a column similar to D (*g*) 10. Unearthed in 1904-05 north-east of Main Shrine.[5]

D (*g*) 12.—Square abacus of a column identical in size and other respects with D (*g*) 11. Excavated in 1904-05.[6]

D (*g*) 13.—Square abacus (ht. 8"; width 1' 1") similar to D (*g*) 10. Mediæval. Probably excavated in 1904-05.

D (*g*) 14.—Capital (ht. 4"; width 1' 1½") with a bracket on each side, as in D (*g*) 7. Excavated in 1904-05 south-west of Main Shrine.[7]

D (*g*) 15.—Unfinished capital (ht. 3¾"; width 1' ¼") of a column, similar in form to D (*g*) 14. Find-spot not known.

D (*g*) 16.—Fragment (ht. 1' 2"; width 1' 1") of the capital of a column which was afterwards converted into a pedestal for an image. Unearthed in 1906-07 in area north-west of Main Shrine, 4' below the surface.

D (*g*) 17.—Fragment (ht. 1' 4"; width 1' 2") of the capital of a column. Find-spot not known.

D (*g*) 18.—Capital (ht. 10½") of a column of the vase and foliage type. Late Gupta style. Pale buff stone of Chunār. Excavated in 1904-05 north-east of *stūpa* south of *stūpa* No. 7 on south of Main Shrine.[8]

---

[1] *A. S. R.*, 1907-08, Pl. XV, Fig. *a*.
[2] *Ibid.*, 1904-05, p. 100, No. 429.
[3] *Ibid.*, No. 419.
[4] *Ibid.*, No. 420. D (*g*) 10—13 must have been employed in the Main Shrine.
[5] *Ibid.*, No. 404.
[6] *Ibid.*, No. 403.
[7] *Ibid.*, p. 101, No. 444.
[8] *Ibid.*, 1904-05, p. 100, No. 434.

D (*g*) 19.—Two square capitals (ht. 9"; width 1′ 2") of identical form which must have been supported on octagonal columns. Mediæval. Excavated in 1904-05 west of Main Shrine.[1]

D (*g*) 20.—Star-shaped capital (ht. 10½"; width 1′ 3") of mediæval date. Excavated in 1904-05 north-east of Jagat Singh *stūpa*.[2]

D (*g*) 21.—Square abacus (ht. 6"; width 1′ 1½") of a column, quite plain. Excavated in 1907-08 on the approach to the Main Shrine from east.

D (*g*) 22.—Square abacus (ht. 8"; width 1′ 1"). Find-spot not known.

D (*g*) 23.—Capital (ht. 2′ 6"; width 1′ 7") of a column with necking of rope pattern. The style seems to be mediæval and as the stone was found in 1906-07 near the north-east corner of Main Shrine, it may have been employed in that edifice.

D (*g*) 24.—Star-shaped base (ht. 9"; width 1′ 7") of a pilaster of mediæval date. Excavated in 1906-07 in monastery I, 2′ 6" below the surface.

D (*g*) 25.—Vase-shaped capital (ht. 1′ 1") adorned with bead-and-reel and rope patterns. Back half broken off. Mediæval. Unearthed in 1904-05.

D (*g*) 26.—Base (ht. 1′; width 1′ 6") which may have supported a votive *stūpa* or a column. Back half cut away. On front, in a chapel we have Buddha seated in the attitude of expounding the law. Mediæval style. Find-spot not known.

D (*g*) 27.—Base (ht. 1′ 1"; width 1′ 6½") similar to D (*g*) 26. On front, in a chapel, is a figure of Kuvēra, god of wealth, holding a purse in his left hand. To his right is shown a vase upside down. His right hand is damaged. It must have held a lemon (*bījapūraka*). Mediæval. Chunār sandstone. Excavated in 1904-05 south-west of Main Shrine.[3]

D (*g*) 28.—Capital (ht. 11"; width 1′ 5½") of a pilaster which must have been employed in the mediæval monastery I.

D (*g*) 29.—Capital (ht. 7"; width 1′ 7½") square in section ornamented all round with conventionalized petal decoration. Mediæval. Found in 1904-05 in Main Shrine.[4]

D (*g*) 30.—Fragment (ht. 7"; width 1′) of a capital similar to D (*g*) 29. Find-spot not known.

D (*g*) 31 (*a*).—Fragment (ht. 5½"; width 1′ 9½") of the base of a column. Mediæval. Evidently from monastery I.

D (*g*) 31 (*b*).—Another fragment similar to D (*g*) 31 (*a*).

---

[1] *A. S. R.*, 1904-05, No. 426 and p. 101 No. 445.
[2] *Ibid.*, p. 99, No. 393.
[3] *Ibid.*, p. 101, No. 462.
[4] *Ibid.*, p. 101, No. 459.

D (*g*) 32.—Base (ht. 1′ 2″; width 2′ 4½″) of a pilaster similar in design to those *in situ*[1] in the mediæval monastery I, to which edifice no doubt it must have belonged.

D (*g*) 33.—Base identical in all respects with D (*g*) 32. Excavated in 1906-07.

D (*g*) 34.—Fragment (ht. 1′; width 1′ 6½″) of the base of a column from mediæval monastery I. Excavated in 1906-07.

D (*g*) 35.—Abacus (ht. 9½″; width 3″) of a column. From mediæval monastery I. Excavated in 1906-07.

---

[1] *A. S. R.*, 1906-07, p. 82, fig. 6.

D (*h*).—Architraves and Brackets.

D (*h*) 1.—Fragment (ht. 1′ 1½″; width 1′ 4″) from one end of a *tōraṇa* architrave, decorated on each face with a fabulous elephant with a coiled tail and raising a garland with its trunk. The top of the fragment is pierced with a rectangular hole to receive the tenon of a bracket to support an upper lintel. The style seems to be Kushāṇa. This is confirmed by the form of the letter *a* carved on the top of the fragment. This was perhaps followed by a numeral.[1]

The similarity in design which this fragment shows to the architraves of Barahut and Mathurā is to be noted. In the latter two places, diverse monsters are chosen for ornamentation.[2]

Buff-coloured sandstone of Chunār. Unearthed in 1906-07 in the area on the east of the Main Shrine.

D (*h*) 2.—Fragment (ht. 1′ 1½″; width 1′ ½″) which must have belonged to the same *tōraṇa* lintel as D (*h*) 1. The back is broken off; the ornamentation on the front is identical with that on the preceding fragment. It was found in 1906-07 in the stone paving around the Aśōka Column.[3]

D (*h*) 3.—Statue (length 3′ 5″) of a leogryph with a rider. The legs and lower jaw of the monster are broken off. He has curved horns, large eyes and a well-executed mane. The harness consists of an ornamental band decked with bells and circular discs round his body, saddle and reins. The upper part of the rider above the waist is missing. On the head of the monster we notice remains of a tenon which makes it apparent that the sculpture was used as an ornamental bracket probably to support a *tōraṇa* architrave. The style of carving exhibits a marked similarity to the fine mediæval carving of Kōnārak near Puri. Such brackets were abundantly used in *tōraṇas* at Mathurā[4] and other places. Chunār sandstone with traces of red paint. Excavated in 1904-05 north of Jagat Singh *stūpa*.[5]

D (*h*) 4.—Statuette (length 3′ 1″) of a leogryph with rider identical with D (*h*) 3. The head and legs of the beast are missing. The rider is in better preservation for only the head and right foot are wanting. He seems to be nude in the upper body, but wears a *dhōtī* and a short double-edged dagger on the right side.

---

[1] Such mason's marks occur on two columns from Mathurā. *Cf.* Smith, *Jaina Stupa*, Pls. XLIII and XLIV.

[2] *Cf.* Anderson, *Handbook and catalogue of Arch. collections in the Indian Museum*, I, p. 119 and Vogel, *Mathurā Catalogue*, Pl. XXV, No. M-2; also Smith, *Jaina Stupa*, Pls. XXIV and XXV.

[3] *A. S. R.*, 1906-07, p. 68 and p. 94, No. 64. Also photo. on Pl. XIX, 2.

[4] Smith, *Jaina Stupa*, Pl. XXXVII.

[5] *A. S. R.*, 1904-05, p. 98 No. 269.

Unearthed in 1904-05 south-east of shrine near the south-west corner of the Main Shrine.[1]

D (*h*) 5.—Statuette (ht. 2′ 11″; width 1′ 11½″) of a goblin (*yaksha*) in the round, with corpulent belly standing with the legs bent at the knees. Head, feet and fore-arms missing. The lower part of the statuette is clad in a *dhōtī* fastened to the loins by a rope-like girdle. The arms are raised up thus showing that the sculpture must have been used as an atlante or bracket. Such brackets are found in abundance in mediæval temples. One such figure is lying in its original position in the Rājghāṭ fort of Benares and two others are preserved in the Mathurā Museum.[2]

Chunār sandstone. The style is mediæval. The torso was unearthed in 1904-05 north-east of Main Shrine,[3] and the arms in 1906-07 to the east of the Main Shrine.

D (*h*) 6.—Fragment (length 1′) representing part of the trunk of a lion with legs of the rider. The sculpture was evidently of the type of D (*h*) 3 and 4 and served as a bracket under a *tōraṇa* architrave.

Style similar to that of the preceding sculptures. Chunār sandstone. It must have been discovered at Sārnāth.

D (*h*) 7.—Incomplete statuette (length 1′ 10″) of a fabulous lion with two paws and a foliated tail. The head is lost. The carved back and the position of the fore-legs leave no doubt but that it was meant to be an ornamental bracket. Gupta work. Chunār sandstone. Excavated in 1906-07 north of *stūpa* No. 22 in the area west of the Main Shrine, 4′ below the surface.

D (*h*) 8.—Fore-paws (length 6¾″) of a lion finely modelled which may have formed part of one of the preceding sculptures presumably D (*h*) 3 or 4. Unearthed in 1907-08 in the area around the Jagat Singh *stūpa*.[4]

D (*h*) 9.—Fragment (length 6″) of a leg of a rider which must have formed part of a sculpture like D (*h*) 3 or 4. Same style. Chunār sandstone with traces of red colour. Excavated in 1904-05.

D (*h*) 10.—Statuette (ht. 10″) of an atlante supporting with arms and feet which are bent up, a pedestal bearing a claw of a lion. A tenon on the underside shows that the sculpture was used as a bracket. The carving is of the Gupta period. Chunār sandstone. Traces of red paint. Unearthed in 1904-05 north-west of Main Shrine.[5]

D (*h*) 11.—Fragmentary head (length 9″) of a lion bracket, the mane being indicated by shallow incised wavy lines. Mediæval.

---

[1] *A. S. R.*, 1904-05, p. 98, No. 275.
[2] Vogel, *Mathurā Catalogue*, C. 3 and 24.
[3] *A. S. R.*, 1904-05, p. 86, fig. 10 and p. 95, No. 137.
[4] *Ibid.*, 1907-08, p. 66, J. S. 2.
[5] *Ibid.*, 1904-05, p. 97, No. 222.

Chunār sandstone. Excavated in 1906-07 near south-east corner of monastery I, 2′ 10″ below the surface.

D (*h*) 12.—Bracket (length 6″) consisting of a fabulous horse or lion with rider. The beast has no trappings and its head and hind legs are broken off. Gupta style. Chunār sandstone. Excavated in one of the recent diggings.

D (*h*) 13.—Fragment (length 8¼″) which to judge from the position of its fore-paws may have been meant for a bracket. Gupta work. Chunār sandstone of reddish colour. Unearthed in one of the recent excavations.

D (*h*) 14.—Head (ht. 10″) of a lion with curved horns and large eyes. Lower jaw broken off. Crest of feathers on brow. The remains of a tenon between the horns show that this sculpture also did duty as a decorative bracket in a *tōraṇa*. Style similar to D (*h*) 3 or 4 with which it must be contemporaneous.

Chunār sandstone. Faint traces of red paint. Excavated in 1904-05.[1]

D (*h*) 15.—Fragment (length 5¾″) of an animal which must have been meant for a bracket. Chunār sandstone. Presumably excavated in one of the recent diggings.

D (*h*) 16.—Fragment (ht. 5½″) with the fore-legs of a rampant animal, which presumably served the purpose of a bracket. Chunār sandstone. Mediæval. Found in 1906-07 near the stair of monastery I, 5′ below the surface.

D (*h*) 17.—Statuette (length 6½″ ; ht. 3½″) of a horse with legs of a rider sitting astride on a saddle. He has no shoes. The head and the legs of the horse are broken off. The figure may have been used as a bracket. Mediæval. Found in 1906-07 in monastery I.

D (*h*) 18.—Statuette identical with D (*h*) 17 in all respects. Found in 1906-07 near the stair of monastery I, 5′ below the surface.

D (*h*) 19.—Fragment (ht. 8″) adorned with a human head raised on a staff. It was probably meant for a bracket. Gupta period. Chunār sandstone. Traces of red paint. Excavated in 1904-05.[2]

---

[1] *A. S. R.*, 1904-05, p. 97, No. 201.

[2] *Ibid.*, p. 100, No. 414.

D(i).—Pediments and face-stones.

D (i) 1.—Pediment or top of a shrine of triangular shape (ht. 1′ 1″; width 1′ 5″) with a lion's head on paws in a circular sunken niche which is enclosed in an ornamental border. Below, dentil cornice. Gupta style. A comparison of this fragment with a pediment preserved in Mathurā[1], shows that this member may well have been borrowed from that school of art.

Discovered in 1907-08 in area on north of Dhamēkh *stūpa.*[2]

D (i) 2.—Pediment (ht. 1′ ½″; width 1′ 1½″) carved on front with a lion's head and fore-paws in an ornamental sunken niche. Gupta style. Excavated in 1906-07.

D (i) 3.—Pediment of same form (ht. 1′ 6″; width 1′ 7″) with Buddha seated in the earth-touching attitude in a sunken panel. Gupta work. Unearthed in 1904-05 north-east of Jagat Singh *stūpa.*[3]

D(i) 4.—Pediment of different design (ht. 1′ 6½″; width 2′) with a figure of a goddess holding a lotus in her left hand and seated in a sunken niche. Above, foliated decoration. Late Gupta style. Was formerly preserved in the Queen's College, but style very similar to Sārnāth carvings. Buff-coloured sandstone of Chunār.

D (i) 5.—Pediment of triangular form (ht. 1′ 3″; width 1′ 7″). Above, Gautama Buddha seated in the earth-touching attitude and attended by a pair of male attendants in a trefoil sunken niche enclosed in a decorative beaded border. Conch (*śaṅkha*) in each spandrel. Below, sunken niches alternating with pillars with bracket capitals. Late Gupta. Sandstone of Chunār.

Excavated in 1904-05 south-east of Main Shrine.[4]

D (i) 6.—Pediment of triangular form (ht. 1′ 6″; width 2′) with mediæval carving on front. The carving on the back shows that the pediment was made out of an octagonal pillar of the late Gupta period. Unearthed in 1904-05 north-east of Jagat Singh *stūpa.*[5]

D (i) 7.—Carved pediment (ht. 1′ 6″; width 1′ 11½″) similar to D (i) 6 and presumably from the same edifice. No figure sculpture.

D (i) 8.—Fragmentary pediment (ht. 1′ 5½″; width 2′ 4″) of similar design. Find-spot not known.

D (i) 9.—Pediment (ht. 1′ 5″; width 2′) carved in the style of D (i) 6 and 7. This stone may also have been employed in the same building.

D (i) 10.—Building stone (ht. 1′ 2″; width 2′ 1″) which must have been employed for face-work around the basement of a *stūpa* or other

---

[1] Smith, *Jaina Stupa*, Pl. XXXI, Fig. 1.
[2] *A. S. R.*, 1907-08, p. 62, K-1.
[3] *Ibid.*, 1904-05, p. 101, No. 456.
[4] *Ibid.*, 1904-05, p. 96, No. 164.
[5] *Ibid.*, p. 101. No. 456.

monument. It is carved on front, with a four-armed goddess seated in easy attitude in a circular sunken niche with a decorative border. The right lower hand of the goddess is in the gift-bestowing attitude and the upper left holds what appears to be a leaf. Possibly Vasundhārā.

Circa 600 or 700 A.D. The stone was found in 1907-08 built in a temporary viaduct over the nullah to west of the Sārnāth site.

D (*i*) 11.—Face stone (ht. 1′ 2½″; width 3′ 3″) with a figure of Buddha seated in the earth-touching attitude in a circular sunken panel enclosed in an ornamental border. Late Gupta style. Buff-coloured sandstone of Chunār. Must have originated from Sārnāth.

D (*i*) 12.—Face-stone (ht. 1′ 1½″; width 2′ 1″) with a male head in a sunken niche with an elaborate border. Gupta style. Buff-coloured sandstone of Chunār.

D (*i*) 13.—Sculptured stone (ht. 11½″; width 2′ 3″) which must have been used in the face-work of a Buddhist monument. On front in a circular niche of usual form is a male figure seated in easy attitude, with the right hand in gift-bestowing attitude. The object in the left hand is broken off. It may have been a vase, the emblem of Maitrēya.

Late Gupta style. Buff-coloured sandstone of Chunār. Traces of red paint. Probably of the Queen's College collection.

D (*i*) 14.—Architectural stone (ht. 1′ 5½″; width 2′ 5″) carved with a niche containing a corpulent figure seated in easy attitude resting his left arm on a pot. The appearance suggests Kubēra but the hands are damaged. Late Gupta style. Traces of red paint. Brought from Queen's College.

D (*i*) 15.—Corner stone (ht. 1′ 4″; width 1′ 6½″) of a building with an elaborate sunken niche containing female heads on two sides. Late Gupta style. From Queen's College.

D (*i*) 16.—Architectural stone (ht. 1′ 5″; width 2′ 10½″) which may have formed the lower part of a pediment. On front, in a niche of usual form we notice a four-armed male figure, presumably a Bōdhisattva. His upper hands hold a rosary (*akshamālā*) and a wheel (Sanskrit *chakra*) respectively. The lower right hand is in gift-bestowing attitude, the left holds a vase. Is it Maitrēya? But the wheel in the upper left hand is inexplicable. Late Gupta style. Brought from Queen's College.

D (*i*) 17.—Architectural fragment (ht. 1′; width 1′ 5″) with male figure seated in niche of ordinary type, in easy posture. He holds a flower (?) in right hand. Left hand is damaged.

Late Gupta. Sandstone of Chunār. Brought from Queen's College.

D (*i*) 18.—Architectural stone (ht. 10″; width 1′ 10½″) which has been used in the facing of a monument. On front, in elaborate niche,

Buddha seated in earth-touching attitude. Late Gupta. Traces of red paint. Chunār sandstone. From Queen's College.

D (*i*) 19.—Fragment of same size and character as D (*i*) 18.

D (*i*) 20.—Architectural stone (ht. 1′ 1¾″; width 2′ 7½″) carved with the figure of a celestial holding full-blown lotus in left hand. The figure is shown flying to proper right and is enclosed in a circular niche with an ornamental border.

D (*i*) 21.—Stone frieze (ht. 4′ 2″; width 1′ 5″). To proper right, circular niche containing pot-bellied male figure with right hand on knee, left raised against shoulder, probably a goblin (*yaksha*). To left, part of grotesque lion's head (*kīrttimukha*). Part of niche on proper right flank. Gupta style. Buff-coloured sandstone of Chunār.

D (*i*) 22.—Architectural stone (ht. 1′ 2″) carved on two sides. On front, in a niche between pilasters, is a male figure seated in easy attitude, with the left hand holding the end of a cloth which is fastened round the waist and the left knee. Right hand was raised to shoulder. Presumably a Bōdhisattva. Similar carving on other side. Buff-coloured sandstone of Chunār.

D (*i*) 23.—Architectural stone (ht. 1′ 2″; width 2′ 5″). On front in a niche, as in D (*i*) 22, is a Bōdhisattva (?) seated in easy attitude with a flower in right hand. The object in left hand is broken off. On proper left flank, half niche with part of seated figure. Late Gupta style. Buff-coloured sandstone. The fragment is depicted in Major Kittoe's Manuscript Drawings,[1] but the provenance is not stated.

D (*i*) 24.—Architectural stone (ht. 1′ 2″; width 2′ 5½″) carved with richly ornamented figure seated, in a deep circular niche in Indian style, with a writing board (?) on the knees. Gupta style. Traces of red paint.

D (*i*) 25.—Architectural stone (ht. 1′ ½″; width 2′). On front, in sunken niche, male figure seated with right arm reclining on pot filled with something and left hand holding flower-bud. Gupta style. Delineated in Major Kittoe's Manuscript Drawings but without any clue to provenance.[2]

D (*i*) 26.—Stone (ht. 1′ 2½″; width 2′ 3½″) similar to D (*i*) 25. It must have been employed in the same building.

*D (*i*) 27.—Pediment (ht. 11″; width 2′) with figure of Buddha, seated in the attitude of expounding the law in elaborate trefoil niche. Late Gupta work. On proper right flank, inscription in mediæval characters *Vākūkasya* "Of Vākūka."

Brought from Queen's College.

---

[1] Vol. I, No. 127, on Pl. 151.
[2] Vol. I, No. 78, on Pl. 145.

D (*i*) 28.—Face-stone (ht. 11½″; width 2′ 4″) with a figure of Buḍdha seated in the attitude of expounding the law. Late Gupta. Chunār sandstone.

D (*i*) 29.—Face-stone (ht. 1′ 3″; width 2′ 1″). To proper right, half niche with Buddha seated in the attitude of expounding the law. To left, niche with pilaster in middle.

Late Gupta. Chunār sandstone.

D (*i*) 30.—Face-stone (ht. 9″; width 2′ 9″) with Buddha seated in earth-touching attitude and a niche with pilaster on either side. Late Gupta work. From Queen's College.

D (*i*) 31.—Face-stone (ht. 1′ 2½″; width 2′ 11″) with Buddha in the attitude of expounding the law in centre. Late Gupta style.

D (*i*) 32.—Fragment (ht. 1′ 4″; width 1′ 10½″) with richly ornamented figure of male deity with circular halo around head. His hands held objects which are broken.

Late Gupta. Chunār sandstone. From Queen's College.

D (*i*) 33.—Fragment (ht. 11″; width 1′ 9″) with a bust of Buddha in trefoil niche. Late Gupta. Traces of red paint.

D (*i*) 34.—Architectural fragment (ht. 6½″; width 1′ 2½″). On front, in niche, male figure seated with right hand raised against shoulder as in holding a fly-whisk and the left resting on the knee. Late Gupta. From Queen's College where it must have gone from Sārnāth.

D (*i*) 35.—Building stone (ht. 1′ 7½″; width 1′ 7″) for face-work. Above, frieze of lions' heads alternating with geese (*haṁsa*). Below, to proper right, Gautama Buddha at the moment of enlightenment (*bōdhi*). To his right, traces of the Evil One (Māra). To his left, Māra's daughter. Further, in the same direction, figure seated cross-legged with axe (*kuṭhāra*) in right hand, presumably a demon of Māra's army.

Early mediæval. Excavated in 1907-08 in 1st outer court of Monastery I, south of Monastery III.

D (*i*) 36.—Face-stone (ht. 1′; width 2′ 6½″) carved with Buddha in the earth-touching attitude in a circular sunken niche. Traces of red paint. Late Gupta.

From Queen's College. But its similarity to D (*i*) 30, D (*i*) 31, etc., leaves no doubt that it must have been discovered at Sārnāth.

D (*i*) 37.—Architectural stone (ht. 11½″; width 1′ 8″) for face-work. On front, in niche, figure as in D (*i*) 34. From Queen's College.

D (*i*) 38.—Face-stone (ht. 10½″; width 2′ 4″) carved with a figure of a celestial with his legs as in flight. Garland (*mālā*) in left hand. Sword (?) in right. From Queen's College.

D (*i*) 39.—Face-stone (ht. 1′ 1″; width 3′ 10″) with seated male figure in niche. From Queen's College.

D (*i*) 40.—Face-stone (ht. 1′ 1½″; width 1′ 1½″) with male figure reclining on pot filled with gold. *Cf.* D (*i*) 25 and 26. Late Gupta. From Queen's College.

D (*i*) 41.—Middle portion (ht. 2′ 2½″; width 1′ 3″) of a pediment adorned with a figure of Buddha seated in a chapel in the attitude of expounding the law. He has no halo and wears a high three-peaked head-dress. To his right and left, are celestials bringing garlands. Late mediæval style. Pale buff stone of Chunār. Discovered in 1906-07 in the area to the east of the Main Shrine.

D (*i*) 42.—Architectural stone (ht. 1′ 2″; width 2′ 2″) for face-work. Above, representation of temple supported on two pilasters. Below, frieze of four dentils with grotesquely shaped lion heads (*kīrttimukha*). Late Gupta style. Delineated in Major Kittoe's Manuscript Drawings where it is labelled as a Sārnāth sculpture.[1]

D(*i*) 43.—Frieze stone (ht. 1′; width 1′ 2″) for face-work. Above, cornice with ornamental niche; below, two square dentils with carved geese and lion's head. Early mediæval.

Pictured in Major Kittoe's Manuscript Drawings with the remark that it is from Sārnāth.

D (*i*) 44.—Face-stone (ht. 1′ 1″; width 3′ 5″). Above, representation of a room with pilasters inside. Below, frieze of six dentiles with lions' heads. To proper left, chess pattern. Mediæval style. Excavated in 1906-07.

D (*i*) 45-47.—Frieze stones (ht. 1′ 2″, 8″, 10½″; width 2′ 11″, 2′ 11″, 3′ 1″) similar to D (*i*) 44, which must have been discovered at Sārnāth. They were formerly preserved in the Queen's College.

D (*i*) 48.—Architectural stone (ht. 2′ 1½″; width 1′ 5″) which must have been employed for covering the surface of a *stūpa* or other monument. Below, pair of cornices and floral decoration. Above, Gautama Buddha at the moment of enlightenment (*bōdhi*). To his right, the Evil One (Māra) standing with a noose (*pāśa*) in right hand and a demon couching behind him. Above, celestial figure (*dēva*) carrying garland. Late Gupta work. Unearthed in 1906-07 on south of monastery I.

D (*i*) 49.—Fragment of frieze (ht. 1′ 2″; width 2′ 5½″). To right, elaborate niche with grotesquely shaped lion's head (*kīrttimukha*). To left, part of another niche. Late Gupta style. Unearthed in 1904-05.

D (*i*) 50—53.—Frieze stones (ht. 1′ 4½″, 1′, 1′ 2″, 1′ 6″; width 2′ 10½″, 3′ 2″, 1′ 10″, 2′) with lions' heads in niches as in D (*i*) 47. Late Gupta period. From Queen's College. It is obvious from the style that the stones were discovered at Sārnāth.

---

[1] Vol. I, No. 95, Pl. 23-B.

D (*i*) 54.—Frieze stone (ht. 10″; width 3′) with lion's head emitting swags of beads, between circular niches with similar heads. From Queen's College.[1]

D (*i*) 55.—Fragment of frieze (ht. 10″; width 1′). Mediæval. Found at Sārnāth.

D (*i*) 56.—Frieze stone (ht. 1′ 2″; width 2′ 9½″). Above, cornice with ornamental niches alternating with geese. Below, row of five dentils with square rosettes. Belonged to the Queen's College collection.

D (*i*) 57—58.—Two frieze stones (ht. 1′, 1′; width 4′, 3′ 5″) with ornamental niches which must have been used in the same building. Excavated in 1904-05 east of Main Shrine.[2] Mediæval style.

D (*i*) 59—76.—Frieze stones (ht. 1′, 1′ 1½″, 1′, 1′, 1′ 1″, 8½″, 1′, 1′ 1½″, 1′ 1″, 1′ 2″, 1′ ½″, 1′ 2½″, 1′ 2½″, 1′ 1½″, 11½″, 11½″, 1′ 2½″, 1′ ½″; width 1′ 9″, 3′, 2′ 5½″, 2′ 8″, 2′ 1″, 2′ 2½″, 1′ 10″, 1′ 9″, 1′ 11″, 2′ 4″, 3′ 9½″, 3′ 2″, 2′ 9″, 3′ 5″, 3′, 1′ 10″, 1′ 5″) adorned with niches. Probably late Gupta. D (*i*) 63 was found in 1907-08 in area around Jagat Singh *stūpa* and D (*i*) 74 in 1906-07 in monastery I, 4′ below the surface. Other fragments have come from the Queen's College, but obviously originate from Sārnāth.

D (*i*) 77.—Ornamental panel (ht. 2′ 6½″; width 1′) divided up into parallel rows of sunken squares and adorned with rosettes which must have been employed in the facing of the walls of a shrine or other building. Mediæval style. Excavated in one of the recent diggings. Found on east of the Main Shrine.

D (*i*) 78—81.—Four stones (ht. 2′ 6″, 2′ 6″, 2′ 6″, 1′ 2½″; width 11″, 11″, 1′ 1½″, 1′ 10″) similar to D (*i*) 78. They were formerly in the Queen's College but were evidently found at Sārnāth.

D (*i*) 82—83.—Two panels (ht. 2′ 6″, 10½″; width 11½″, 1′ 9″) of the same form as D (*i*) 78—80, but decorated with an intricate pattern composed of mystic crosses. This pattern is evidently copied from the carvings on the Dhamēkh *stūpa*. Late Gupta. Formerly preserved in the Queen's College.

D (*i*) 84—85.—Two stones (ht. 1′ 1″, 1′ 1½″; width 2′ 6″, 2′ 6½″) with finely executed floral work, which were employed in the face-work of the Dhamēkh *stūpa*. They had been taken away by the villagers and built up into a temporary bridge on west of the site of the Deer Park.

D (*i*) 86.—Face-stone (ht. 1′ 2″; width 4′ 2″) showing grotesquely shaped lion's face with protruding eyes, broad nostrils and foliated horns, between pair of geese facing away from it. From the mouth

---

[1] Major Kittoe's Manuscript Drawings, Vol. I, No. 155, Pl. 132. The provenance is not stated, but it may well have been found at Sārnāth.

[2] *A. S. R.*, 1904-05, p. 100, No. 441; and p. 101, No. 453.

of the lion, issued two swags of pearls, the other ends of which were held in the beaks of the birds. The fragment is from a continuous frieze of the basement of a *stūpa* or similar structure. Unearthed in 1904-05 south of Main Shrine.[1]

D (*i*) 87—95.—Nine stones of various lengths with the same decoration, which must have been discovered at Sārnāth and some of them may even have been employed in covering the surface of the same edifice as D (*i*) 86. They belonged to the Queen's College collection.

D (*i*) 96.—Face-stone (ht. 1′; width 3′) with a frieze of geese in flight, carrying garlands. The stone was rescued from the modern aqueduct on road to village of Singhpur on west of the Sārnāth site. The style seems to be of the early mediæval period.

D (*i*) 97.—Fragment of lintel (ht. 1′; width 2′ 6½″). At the proper right end, is a square niche with a pediment, containing a figurine of Avalōkitēśvara with his right hand in gift-bestowing attitude, left holding a full-blown lotus (Sanskrit *padma*). The rest of the surface is occupied by shallow floral decoration similar to that on stones found in monastery I. Late mediæval.

D (*i*) 98.—Face-stone (ht. 1′; width 2′ 8½″) with frieze of lions' masks (*kīrttimukha*) with garlands issuing from their mouths. Mediæval style. From Queen's College.

D (*i*) 99.—Face-stone (ht. 1′ 2½″; width 2′ 2½″) with corpulent male figure seated in circular niche. His left arm reclines on a pot. Probably a goblin (*yaksha*). Gupta style. From Queen's College.

D (*i*) 100.—Frieze stone (ht. 10″; width 3′ 7″) with four dentils carved with busts of a goose, a crocodile, a lion and a man. These figures have well-executed foliated tails. The dentils are separately drawn in Major Kittoe's Manuscript Drawings where we are told that they originate from Sārnāth.[2]

D (*i*) 101.—Face-stone (ht. 1′ 4″; width 1′ 5½″) with interlaced mytic cross (*svastika*) pattern. The fragment is apparently from the facing of the Dhamēkh *stūpa*.

D (*i*) 102.—Face-stone (ht. 9½″; width 3′ 6½″) with four square dentils containing lotus rosettes. Late mediæval. Was discovered in 1904-05.

D (*i*) 103—106.—Four fragments of a large cornice with bold floral moulding. One of them was unearthed in the recent excavations. The other three pieces came from the Queen's College.

D (*i*) 107.—Water-spout or gargoyle (ht. 1′ 1½″; length 2′ 5½″) in the form of a crocodile with crooked horns and foliated tail which are indicated on both sides. The channel is cut through the length of the

---

[1] *A. S. R.* 1904-05 p. 100, No. 440.
[2] Vol. I, No. 146, Pl. 32.

stone, the water was discharged by the mouth. The snout of the animal is partly broken. The carving is particularly vigorous. Late Gupta period. There is a sketch of the sculpture in Major Kittoe's Manuscript Drawings where we are told that the spout must have belonged to an elegant edifice of Sārnāth.[1] The style is identical with that of Dhamēkh carvings. May we not assume that it may have been employed in that structure at the top of the lower portion which is built of stone ? Its size would be in perfect accord with the huge proportions of that tower. D (*i*) 108—109 evidently also belonged to the same edifice.

D (*i*) 108—109.—Two gargoyles of the same dimensions and form as D (*i*) 107 which must have been employed in the same building.

D (*i*) 110.—Part of gargoyle (ht. 11½" ; length 1' 3½") with crocodile head. The snout and back are broken off. The style of technique appears to be mediæval. Unearthed in 1907-08 in 1st outer court of monastery I.

D (*i*) 111.—Part of gargoyle (ht. 1' 2" ; length 1') of the same type as D (*i*) 110. The snout and tusks are preserved. The tail is missing. Late mediæval.

D (*i*) 112.—Gargoyle (ht. 1' 7½" ; length 3' 7") which was merely intended for a decorative purpose. There is no channel or escape for water. Dr. Marshall, who discovered it, describes it as an " Akroterion ornament (?) and Makara gargoyle, unfinished work. The elephant and lion fighting are very vigorous."[2] It was found in the courtyard of monastery I, and must have been employed in that building.

D (*i*) 113.—Decorative gargoyle ornament (ht. 1' 1½" ; length 3' 3½") similar to D (*i*) 112. The crowning figures are broken off. Late mediæval. Excavated in 1st outer court of monastery I.[3]

D (*i*) 114.—Snout (ht. 8¾" ; length 6½") of crocodile head which served the purpose of a gargoyle. Late mediæval. Found in 1906-07 in courtyard of monastery I, 8' below the surface.

D (*i*) 115—116.—Two face-stones (ht. 10", 1' 1"). From Queen's College.

D (*i*) 117.—Slab (length 2' 9½" ; width 1' 10½") with conventional lotus flower cut on it. The stone was found on the floor of the courtyard of monastery I, and must have been employed as a roof slab in it. We may also conclude that the roof was constructed on the trabeated system.

D (*i*) 118.—Face-stone (ht. 13" ; width 1' 10") with two half lotus rosettes and chess decoration. From Queen's College.

---

[1] Vol. I, No. 10, Pl. 33.

[2] *A. S. R.*, 1906-07, p. 94, No. 63 and Pl. XXVI, 2.

[3] *Ibid.*, 1907-08, p. 50, No. η 143.

D (*i*) 119.—Face-stone (ht. 1′ 2″; width 2′ 3″) adorned with chains hanging from lions' heads. Mediæval.

D (*i*) 120.—Face-stone (length 4″; ht. 8½″) ornamented with bold scroll work, flat on the surface. Late Gupta style. Excavated in 1904-05.

D (*i*) 121.—Architectural stone (ht. 2′ 1″) ornamented with a figure of Padmapāṇi in easy attitude, a couchant deer and a dancing figure. Late Gupta style. Excavated in 1904-05 north-east of Jagat Singh *stūpa*.[1]

D (*i*) 122.—Face-stone (length 2′ 4″; ht. 7½″) bearing intricate scroll work with geese ingeniously introduced into it. Late Gupta style. Excavated in 1906-07 in the area on the east of the Main Shrine.[2]

D (*i*) 123.—Face-stone (length 2′ 1¾″; ht. 7½″) with similar scroll work with a goose and a crocodile introduced in it. Excavated in 1906-07.

D (*i*) 124.—Frieze stone (length 2′ 6″; ht. 11½″). Below, panels with chess design separated by pilasters surmounted with bracket capitals. Above, cornice with empty niches, on a row of dentils. Early mediæval. Excavated in 1904-05 south-west of Main Shrine.[3]

D (*i*) 125.—Face-stone (length 1′ 7½″; ht. 1′ 1½″) with a bold torus moulding ornamented with festoons. Late Gupta. Unearthed in 1906-07 in area west of Main Shrine.

*D (*i*) 126.—Face-stone (length 3′ 9″; ht. 1′ 11″) with ornamental niches and cornice. *Cir.* 7th century A.D. On the top of the stone is an inscription of two lines with a list of names below. The inscription is in characters of the 12th century A.D. and states that [the stone] is a gift of a lay-woman (*upāsikā*) whose name is not clear.

Probably unearthed in 1904-05.

D (*i*) 127.—Face-stone (length 1′ 6½″; ht. 1′) similar to D (*i*) 126. Find-spot not known.

D(*i*) 128.—Fragment (length 1′ 9″; ht. 9″) with two half lotus-rosettes. Late Gupta. Find-spot not known.

D (*i*) 129.—Face-stone (ht. 6″; width 2′ 6½″) ornamented with a highly conventionalized lotus pattern. Late mediæval. Excavated in 1904-05.

D (*i*) 130.—Face-stone (ht. 11″; width 1′ 9½″) similar to D (*i*) 129.

D (*i*) 131—132.—Two fragments (width 1′ 8½″, and 1′ 5½″) for facework, carved like D (*i*) 130. Unearthed in 1906-07.

---

[1] *A. S. R.*, 1904-05, p. 109, No. 431.
[2] *Ibid.* 1906-07, Pl. XXIII, 1.
[3] *Ibid.*, 1904-05, p. 100, No. 442.

D (*i*) 133.—Slab (length 5′; ht. 9½″) for face-work, ornamented with a flowing foliated design. Late Gupta. It was excavated in 1904-05 in the neighbourhood of the Main Shrine.

D (*i*) 134.—Slab (ht. 6½″; width 2′ 4″) for facing adorned with geese (Skt. *haṁsa*) with bushy tails in festoons of beads. Late Gupta style. Chunār sandstone. Unearthed in 1904-05 north-east of Jagat Singh *stūpa*.[1]

D (*i*) 135.—Facing stone (ht. 10½″; width 8′ 4″) ornamented with the familiar chess pattern. Unearthed in 1906-07 in mediæval Monastery I, for which it must have been intended.

D (*i*) 136.—Stone (ht. 5½″; width 5′) adorned with the same pattern as D (*i*) 135. Excavated in 1906-07.

D (*i*) 137.—Stone (ht. 9½″; width 2′ 1½″) with traces of two niches. Mediæval. Excavated in 1904-05.

D (*i*) 138.—Fragment (ht. 11″; width 1′ 5½″) of a facing stone of mediæval date. Chunār sandstone.

D (*i*) 139.—Fragment (ht. 11½″; width 3′ 7″) from the superstructure of mediæval Monastery I. Carving flat and stencil like. Excavated in 1906-07.

D (*i*) 140.—Fragment (ht. 10″; width 2′ 6″) with carving identical with that on D (*i*) 139.

D (*i*) 141.—Fragment (ht. 5½″; width 1′ 10″) carved with a corpulent figure dancing and pilasters in relief. Mediæval or late Gupta. Excavated in one of the recent diggings.

D (*i*) 142.—Fragment (ht. 1′ 3½″; width 1′) ornamented with a niche with an elaborate border. Excavated south of 1st outer court of Monastery I, 3′ below the surface.

D (*i*) 143—168.—Twenty-six carved stones from mediæval Monastery I excavated in 1906-07. The carving is, as usual, flat and stencil like.

D (*i*) 169.—Fragment (ht. 7″; width 1′ 1½″) with three panels. In the middle one, a young man is assaulting an old sage with a long beard. Mediæval. Find-spot not known.

D (*i*) 170.—Carved fragment (ht. 5½″; width 1′ 1½″) of late Gupta period. Find-place not known.

D (*i*) 171.—Carved fragment (ht. 10″; width 10½″). Find-spot not known.

D (*i*) 172.—Carved fragment (ht. 1′; width 1′ 4″) with scroll decoration. Mediæval. Find-place not known.

---

[1] *A. S. R.*, 1904-05, p. 100, No. 433.
[2] *Ibid.*, p. 99, No. 397.
[3] *Ibid.*, 1906-07, p. 83, fig. 7.

D (*i*) 173.—Face-stone (ht. 6″; width 2′) with a line of rosettes in late mediæval style. Excavated in 1904-05 north-west of Jagat Singh *stūpa*.[1]

D (*i*) 174.—Face-stone (ht. 2′ 3¼″; width 8″) with *svastika* decoration similar to that on the Dhamēkh *stūpa*. Late Gupta style. Find-spot not known.

D (*i*) 175.—Face-stone (ht. 1′ 5″; width 1′ 1″) with a geometric pattern above and a row of pilasters with bracket capitals below. Late Gupta work. Find-spot not known.

---

[1] *A. S. R.*, 1904-05, p. 100, No. 432.

D (*j*)—Finials.

D (*j*) 1.—Finial (ht. 1′) of a temple. The body is grooved in the form of an *āmalaka* fruit and there is a vase-shaped member in the middle. The lower end has a double flange. Gupta period. Chunār sandstone. Probably unearthed in one of the recent excavations.

D (*j*) 2.—Base of a finial (ht. 7¾″). Body grooved as in D (*j*) 1. Below it, dentil cornice. Above, square mortice for the reception of the tenon of the upper member. Gupta period. Find-spot not known.

D (*j*) 3.—Finial (ht. 1′ 2½″). Lower part has the shape of an *āmalaka* fruit, the upper of a cone. Gupta style. Chunār sandstone. Excavated in 1904-05 in shrine north-east of Jagat Singh *stūpa*.[1]

D (*j*) 4.—Imperfect finial (ht. 7¾″) similar in design to D (*j*) 1 and 2 but inferior in execution. Mediæval. Chunār sandstone. Discovered in one of the recent excavations.

D (*j*) 5.—Base of a finial (ht. 7½″) partly broken, grooved like an *āmalaka* fruit. On underside, tenon. Above, square mortice for upper member. Mediæval. Chunār sandstone. Excavated in 1907-08.

D (*j*) 6.—Base (ht. 3″) of a finial, grooved like D (*j*) 5. Circular mortice in top and flange on underside. Mediæval. Found in 1907-08.

D (*j*) 7.—Finial (ht. 8½″) with conical top. Mediæval. Chunār sandstone. Traces of red paint. Unearthed in the entrance chamber of Monastery I, 3′ 4″ below the surface.

D (*j*) 8.—Finial with conical top and circular base. Mediæval. Chunār stone. Excavated in 1904-05.[2]

D (*j*) 9.—Finial (ht. 8½″) with conical top. Mediæval. Chunār stone. Unearthed in area west of monastery I, 8′ below the surface.

---

[1] *A. S. R.*, 1904-05, p. 100, No. 416.
[2] *Ibid.*, p. 97, No. 256.

D (*k*) —Miscellaneous Architectural Fragments.

D (*k*) 1.—Part (ht. 10″; width 2′ 2½″) of a pediment. Proper left end broken off. In middle, double-storeyed *chaitya* with a figure of Mārīchī in the lower compartment and another goddess in the upper. To proper right, single-storeyed *chaitya* with trefoil niche showing a corpulent figure seated in Indian style. A smaller fragment which fits to this end bears a dancing figure. Mediæval style. Chunār sandstone. Excavated in 1904-05.[1]

D (*k*) 2.—Central part (ht. 1′; width 1′ 1½″) of a pediment. In middle, a niche surmounted with a pediment, and containing a figure of a Buddha seated on a lotus throne in earth-touching attitude. Behind his shoulders, pair of twigs resembling wings. To proper right of the niche, part of an arch with ornamental border with figure of a celestial (*dēva*) playing a flute (*vaṁśī*) above, and a lotus flower below it. To proper left of the niche, headless male figure clutching the snout of a crocodile (*makara*). Late mediæval. A complete pediment of this type is sketched in Major Kittoe's Manuscript Drawings.[2]

Greenish sandstone of Chunār. Excavated in 1904-05 south-west of Main Shrine.[3]

D (*k*) 3.—Fragment (ht. 1′; width 1′) which may have belonged to the same pediment as D (*k*) 1. The niche in the middle contains a figure of Buddha in the attitude of expounding the law. To proper right, part of figure holding snout of crocodile (*makara*). On other side, part of an arch with traces of a celestial (*dēva*) and a flower below it. Greenish stone of Chunār. Excavated in 1904-05 south-west of Main Shrine.[4]

D (*k*) 4.—Two fragments (ht. 10¾″; width 1′ 3½″) of a pediment similar to D (*k*) 2 and 3. In centre, Buddha expounding the law in a niche with a pediment. To proper right, a man curbing a crocodile (*makara*). To proper left, arch with corpulent figure of a celestial (*dēva*) above and a flower below it.

Same material as in D (*k*) 2 and 3. Excavated in 1906-07 in area east of Main Shrine.[5]

D (*k*) 5.—Base (ht. 1′ 1½″) of a column of the type of D (*f*) 3. Vase with palmette and head of atlante in corner. Late Gupta work.

Chunār sandstone. Excavated in one of the recent diggings.

D (*k*) 6.—Fragment (ht. 8½″) from a corner of a column of the same type as D (*k*) 5, showing an atlante. Late Gupta. Chunār

---

[1] *A. S. R.*, 1904-05, p. 100, No. 405.
[2] Vol. I, No. 149, Pl. 19.
[3] *A. S. R.*, 1904-05, p. 100, No. 421.
[4] *Ibid.*, p. 100, No. 420.
[5] *Ibid.*, 1906-07, Pl. XXIII, 8.

sandstone. Found in 1906-07 in monastery west of Dhamēkh *stūpa*, 5′ below the surface.

D (*k*) 7.—Fragment (ht. 1′ 4″) of large octagonal column with band of lions' heads (*kīrttimukha*) with festoons of beads. Gupta work. Chunār sandstone. Probably discovered in one of the recent excavations.

D (*k*) 8.—Fragment (ht. 1′ ½″) of base or capital of a column of the vase-and-foliage type. Late Gupta. Chunār sandstone.

Excavated in one of the recent diggings.

D (*k*) 9.—Fragment (ht. 1′ ½″) similar to D (*k*) 8. Found in one of the recent excavations.

D (*k*) 10.—Fragment (ht. 1′ 7″) of a column bearing an imperfect medallion with foliage. Late Gupta work. Chunār sandstone. Discovered in one of the recent excavations.

D (*k*) 11.—Fragment (ht. 1′) of a column with a goose with foliated tail in a festoon of beads. Late Gupta work. Chunār sandstone. Excavated in the area around the Jagat Singh *stūpa*[1].

D (*k*) 12.—Fragment (ht. 6½″) from the top of a circular column with a band of foliated pattern with jewels and a celestial carrying a garland in the left hand introduced in it. Gupta work. Chunār stone. Discovered in the area east of the Main Shrine.

D (*k*) 13.—Fragment (ht. 1′ 5½″) of a column adorned with a lion's head emitting a line of well-executed foliage. Late Gupta work. Chunār sandstone. Excavated in 1904-05 east of Main Shrine.[2]

D (*k*) 14.—Portion (ht. 6¾″) of an octagonal column with a band of half lotus-rosettes above and geese in festoons below. Late Gupta style. Chunār sandstone of red colour. Excavated in area around the Jagat Singh *stūpa*.[3]

D (*k*) 15.—Fragment (ht. 1′ 2½″) of an octagonal column with half lotus rosettes. Traces of red colour. Late Gupta. Chunār sandstone. Excavated in one of the recent diggings.

D (*k*) 16.—Fragment (ht. 10″) of a column showing a vase with palmettes. Late Gupta. Chunār sandstone of red colour. Discovered in 1906-07 in monastery west of Dhamēkh *stūpa*, 3′ 4″ below the surface.

D (*k*) 17.—Fragment (ht. 1′ 2″) of an octagonal column with a band of lions' heads with foliated horns. Late Gupta style. Chunār sandstone. Excavated in 1906-07, in monastery west of Dhamēkh *stūpa*, 8′ below the surface.

D (*k*) 18.—Fragment (ht. 10″) of an octagonal column with foliated decoration and festoons of beads. Late Gupta work. Chunār sandstone. Excavated in one of the recent diggings.

---

[1] *A. S. R.*, 1907-08, p. 66, J. S. 4.
[2] *Ibid.*, 1904-05, p. 100, No. 427.
[3] *Ibid.*, 1907-08. p. 66, J. S. 3.

D (*k*) 19.—Fragment (ht. 6″) of an octagonal pilaster with a band of foliated pattern. Late Gupta. Discovered in 1906-07 in monastery west of the Dhamēkh *stūpa*, 4′ 6″ below the surface.

D (*k*) 20.—Fragment (ht. 10½″) of a column with vase and foliage decoration. Late Gupta, or mediæval. Chunār sandstone. Excavated in 1906-07 in area to the east of the Main Shrine.

D (*k*) 21.—Fragment (ht. 1′ 3″) similar to D (*k*) 20. Excavated in 1904-05 to the south-east of the Main Shrine.[1]

D (*k*) 22.—Fragment (ht. 1′ 5¼″) of a column with foliated decoration. Late Gupta. Chunār sandstone. Discovered in 1907-08 in 2nd outer court of Monastery I.[2]

D (*k*) 23.—Fragment (ht. 11½″) similar to D (k) 22. Excavated in 1904-05.

D (*k*) 24.—Fragment (ht. 9″) of a column with foliated motives in festoons. Gupta work. Chunār sandstone. Excavated in 1904-05.[3]

D (*k*) 25.—Fragment (ht. 1′ 2½″) of a column with a lion emitting a festoon of beads and other ornamentation. Gupta style. Excavated in 1904-05 to the south-east of the Main Shrine.[4]

D (*k*) 26.—Fragment (ht. 8½″) of a column with a foliated pattern. Gupta style. Chunār sandstone. Discovered in one of the recent excavations.

D (*k*) 27.—Fragment (ht. 8″) of a column with foliated decoration and head of an atlante in one of the corners. Gupta work. Chunār sandstone. Excavated in 1904-05 to the south-east of the Main Shrine.[5]

D (*k*) 28.—Fragment (ht. 8″) of the base of a column with foliated decoration and the left arm of an atlante raised up in a corner. Gupta work. Chunār sandstone. Excavated in 1906-07 in the area to the east of the Main Shrine.

D (*k*) 29.—Bust (ht. 7″) of a male figure with hands holding an uncertain object before the chest. The figure must have been disposed in a corner of the base of a column. Fine Gupta work. Chunār sandstone; traces of red paint. Excavated in 1904-05.[6]

D (*k*) 30.—Fragment (ht. 8″) of a column with a lion's head spitting a festoon of beads. Gupta style. Chunār sandstone. Traces of red paint. Excavated in one of the recent diggings.

D (*k*) 31.—Fragment (ht. 1′) of a column adorned with *kadamba* fruits and leaves. Chunār sandstone. The stone must have been used in the Main Shrine. Traces of red paint.

---

[1] *A. S. R.*, 1904-05, p. 100, No. 402.
[2] *Ibid.*, 1907-08, p. 53, ι 108.
[3] *Ibid.*, 1904-05, p. 96, No. 189.
[4] *Ibid.*, p. 100, No. 410.
[5] *Ibid.*, p. 96, No. 178.
[6] *Ibid.*, No. 188.

D (*k*) 32.—Base (ht. 9") of a pilaster with half-rosettes containing fabulous crocodiles with bushy tails above and a foliated pattern with festoons of beads below. Late Gupta. Chunār sandstone. Unearthed in 1904-05.

D (*k*) 33.—Section (ht. 4") of the octagonal shaft of a column adorned with festoons. Late Gupta style. Chunār sandstone. Discovered in 1st outer court of Monastery I.

D (*k*) 34.—Fragment (ht. 1′ 5½") of a column adorned with a conventional vase with foliage. The stone belonged to monastery I in which it was found in the courtyard, 1′ below the surface.[1]

D (*k*) 35.—Two fragments (ht. 1′ 5½") of a column adorned with scroll work with birds in curves and decorative borders in which dancing figures occur. Mediæval. Chunār sandstone. Discovered in 1907-08 in the 1st outer court of Monastery I.

D (*k*) 36.—Base (ht. 10½") of a pilaster similar to D (*k*) 31. Excavated in 1904-05.[2]

*D (*k*) 37.—Fragment (ht. 8½") of a circular column inscribed with epigraph of eight lines in characters of about the 11th century A.D.

It was first read by Dr. Konow.[3]

l. 1. ....*pautraḥ*[4] *śrī Vra*..................
l. 2. .... *patyaṁ mātā bhuvanāśr*........
l. 3. [*ba*]*bhūva tasya* ‖ *Saumyaḥ śrī* ....
l. 4. [*ma**]*ṇḍitō* S *bhūt sutō* S *sya.*
l. 5. ....*śarvvadāsa-sutō*........
l. 6. ....*sarvvasatvasya hētōḥ svasmi*..................
l. 7. [*Dha**]*rmmachakrē chakāra* ‖ *śrī Saṭṭāda*.............
l. 8. *taḥ. Lōhēśvaradāsaḥ* ‖ *Oṁ.* ‖

A connected translation of the inscription is impossible; but it is obvious that the object of the epigraph was to record the construction of some object at the Dharmmachakra which we know from other inscriptions had become the common name of the Buddhist establishment at Sārnāth in the mediæval period.

Chunār sandstone. Excavated in 1907-08, in the 1st outer court of Monastery I.[5]

D (*k*) 38.—Fragment (ht. 8") of a column with scroll-work in late Gupta style. Chunār sandstone. Excavated in 1907-08 in the long trench to the east of monastery I.

---

[1] *A. S. R.*, 1906-07, Pl. XXVI, 5.
[2] *Ibid.*, 1904-05, p. 99, No. 398.
[3] *Ibid.*, 1907-08, pp. 75-76, Inscription No. XVII.
[4] This word is quite clear.
[5] *A. S. R.*, 1907-08, p. 50, ¶ 149.

D (*k*) 39.—Fragment (ht. 6⅛") similar to D (*k*) 38. Found in 1906-07 in the monastery to the west of the Dhamēkh *stūpa*, 2′ 9″ below the surface.

D (*k*) 40.—Fragment (ht. 5") of a pilaster bearing a lion's head with a long moustache. Gupta style. Chunār sandstone. Found in 1906-07 in Monastery I, 1′ 6″ below the surface.

D (*k*) 41.—Fragment (ht. 5") similar to D (*k*) 40. Excavated in the trench crossing the south boundary wall of Monastery I, 1′ below the surface.

D (*k*) 42.—Fragment (ht. 7½") of the base of a column showing a figure of an atlante with up-raised left arm in the corner. Gupta work. Found in one of the recent excavations.

D (*k*) 43.—Fragment (ht. 7") from the base of a column with a headless atlante wearing a necklace and a band on the belly. Gupta work. Chunār sandstone. Excavated in 1906-07, in the area to the south of Monastery II, 7′ below the surface.

D (*k*) 44.—Fragment (ht. 5") of an atlante similar to D (*k*) 43. Gupta work. Chunār sandstone. Traces of red paint. Excavated in the area to the east of the Main Shrine.

D (*k*) 45.—Fragment (ht. 5") with the hind legs of an animal and scroll-work. Late Gupta. Chunār sandstone. Excavated in the area to the east of the Main Shrine.

D (*k*) 46.—Fragment (ht. 5½") of a column with scroll-work and a festoon of beads. Late Gupta. Excavated in 1904-05 to the north of the Jagat Singh *stūpa*.[1]

D (*k*) 47.—Fragment (ht. 7") with scroll-work. Unearthed in 1904-05.

D (*k*) 48.—Fragment (ht. 10½") of a column with decoration as on D (*k*) 47. Late Gupta. Chunār sandstone. Found in 1907-08 in the trench crossing the south boundary wall of Monastery I, 9′ below the surface.

D (*k*) 49.—Fragment (ht. 9½") of a door-jamb with an incomplete figure of a female. Mediæval. Chunār sandstone. Excavated in the western precinct of Monastery I, 6′ below the surface.[2]

D (*k*) 50.—Fragment (ht. 5") apparently of a column with the face of a lion emitting beads. Late Gupta. Chunār sandstone. Found in Monastery I, 3′ below the surface.

D (*k*) 51.—Fragment (ht. 5½") with the left ear of an elephant. Late Gupta. Chunār sandstone. Found in 1904-05.[3]

---

[1] *A. S. R.*, 1904-05, p. 101, No. 470.
[2] *A. S. R.*, 1907-08, p. 48, a 11.
[3] *Ibid.*, 1904-05, p. 99, No. 352.

D (*k*) 52.—Fragment (ht. 6") of a column with an atlante, blended with scroll work. Late Gupta. Chunār sandstone. Excavated in 1904-05.[1]

D (*k*) 53.—Fragment (ht. 1' 3") from a corner of a column with scroll work and a figure of an atlante with left hand on knee. Gupta style. Excavated in 1904-05 in the trench to the south of the 2nd outer court of Monastery I, 7' 6" below the surface.[2]

D (*k*) 54.—Fragment (ht. 7") of a pilaster with traces of two seated figures on pilasters and a lion on a couchant elephant on border to proper left. Mediæval. Chunār stone. Excavated in the 2nd outer court of Monastery I, 3' below the surface.[3]

D (*k*) 55.—Fragment (ht. 1' 4") of a column. On front, part of a standing figure with a lion (?) at its right side. To proper right, a rat. On proper left flank, a warrior holding a sword in left hand. Mediæval. Chunār sandstone. Excavated in one of the recent diggings.

D (*k*) 56.—Fragment (ht. 1' 1") of a column showing a figure of bull Nandi under the pedestal of an image which must have been Śiva. To proper left, on border we notice a figure holding a water-pot in its left hand probably Brahmā. Mediæval. Chunār sandstone. Excavated in 1904-05.[4]

D (*k*) 57.—Fragment (ht. 9½") of a pilaster with a female figure dancing on front. Mediæval. Chunār sandstone. Excavated in the western precinct of Monastery I, 4' below the surface.[5]

D (*k*) 58.—Fragment (ht. 8") of a door-jamb. On pilaster, a female figure seated on a lotus throne in easy attitude, with its right hand on knee in the gift-bestowing attitude. Object in left hand not certain. Perhaps Tārā. On border on proper left, a leogryph rampant. Mediæval. Chunār sandstone. Excavated in 1906-07 in Monastery I, near the well, 10' 8" below the surface.

D (*k*) 59.—Fragment (ht. 7½") of a jamb stone with a figure of a warrior apparently attacking the beast above him. Below the warrior, head of a lion. Mediæval. Chunār sandstone. Excavated in 1906-07 in Monastery I.

D (*k*) 60.—Fragment (ht. 5¾") with the back part of a lion couchant. Mediæval. Chunār sandstone. Unearthed in 1907-08 in western precinct of Monastery I, 3' below the surface.

D (*k*) 61.—Fragment (ht. 1' 4") of jamb with a female figure looking at a mirror which she holds in her left hand. In front of her, we

---

[1] *A. S. R.*, 1904-05, p. 96, No. 192.
[2] *Ibid.*, 1907-08, p. 53, *i* 12 and Pl. XIII, *d*.
[3] *Ibid.*, p. 52, *i* 11.
[4] *Ibid.*, 1904-05, p. 96, No. 181.
[5] *Ibid.*, 1907-08, p. 48, *a* 4.

observe a figure of an old man with a long beard. To proper right, a male figure standing with a bow in left hand. Below, a figure seated cross-legged holding an uncertain object in left hand. Mediæval. Chunār sandstone. Find-place not known.

D (*k*) 62.—Fragment (ht. 7½″) with Buddha seated on a lotus in the attitude of expounding the law. Chunār sandstone. Late mediæval. Excavated in 1904-05 on the south of the Main Shrine.[1]

D (*k*) 63.—Pediment (ht. 9″ ; width 1′ 8″) with a figure of a celestial flying with a flower in his left hand in a circular niche with an ornamental border. Late Gupta. Excavated in 1907-08 in the area on the north of the Dhamēkh *stūpa*.

D (*k*) 64.—Portion (ht. 7½″ ; width 1′ 7½″) of a pediment with a lion's face in an ornamental niche. Below, a row of dentils. Gupta style. Chunār sandstone. Found in one of the recent diggings.

D (*k*) 65.—Face-stone (ht. 8½″ ; width 1′ 5″) with geese alternating with lions' heads. Below, a dentil cornice. Gupta work. Chunār stone. Excavated in the 1st outer court of Monastery I.[2]

*D (*k*) 66.—Base (ht. 6″) of a square column. On front in niche, Buddha seated in earth-touching attitude. On back, parts of two lines of writing containing the Buddhist creed in mediæval characters :—

l. 1. .... *tēshāṁ tathā* ....

l. 2. .... *ñcha yō* ....

Chunār stone. Excavated in 1906-07, 5′ 4″ below the surface.

D (*k*) 67.—Fragment (ht. 8½″) of a window jamb with a semi-circular pilaster. On latter, bust of Padmapāṇi with right hand in the attitude of granting protection, left holding a lotus flower. Pointed head-dress like Buddha's. Late mediæval. Chunār sandstone. Discovered in one of the recent excavations.

D (*k*) 68-69.—Two fragments (ht. 8½″ and 6½″) of face-stones with lions' heads in circular niches. Mediæval or somewhat earlier. Discovered in 1906-07 in the monastery to the west of the Dhamēkh *stūpa*, 2½′ and 3′ below the surface.

D (*k*) 70.—Fragment (ht. 5½″) with traces of a niche. To proper right, corpulent figure playing on lute. Below, atlante with up-raised arms. Mediæval. Chunār sandstone. Discovered in western precinct of Monastery I, 5′ below the surface.[3]

D (*k*) 71.—Fragment (ht. 4″) of carving. It has certainly been polished like the Lion Capital (A-1) and is undoubtedly Maurya. Discovered in 1906-07 in the area to the north-west of the Main Shrine.

---

[1] *A. S. R.*, 1904-05, p. 97, No. 254.

[2] *Ibid.*, 1907-08, p. 60, η 205.

[3] *Ibid.*, p. 48, ε 6.

D (*k*) 72.—Fragment (ht. 5″) with the headless figure of a goose in flight. The modelling is wonderfully realistic. The fragment dates from the Maurya period.

D (*k*) 73.—Figure (ht. 8½″) of elephant, trunk, legs and tail broken off. On neck, legs of a driver (*mahāwat*) and a rider on back. The harness consists of a band across the body and another round the waist. Probably late Gupta or later. Chunār sandstone. Unearthed in 1907-08 in the 1st outer court of Monastery I.[1]

D (*k*) 74.—Fragment (ht. 6¾″) of a leogryph (?) with the right leg of the rider. Mediæval. Chunār sandstone. Traces of red paint. Found in 1906-07 south of south-east corner of Monastery I, 14′ below the surface.

D (*k*) 75.—Fragment (ht. 2¼″) from the middle of a stone umbrella, representing the mortice for the tenon of the post surrounded by a rim with lotus decoration. Excavated in 1906-07 in the area to the east of the Main Shrine.

D (*k*) 76.—Object (ht. 3½″) resembling a finial with a lotus ornament on the underside. Mediæval. Chunār sandstone. Unearthed in 1904-05 to the west of the Main Shrine.[2]

D (*k*) 77.—Fragment (ht. 11½″) of a halo with a boldly carved lotus flower. Gupta style. Chunār sandstone. Probably excavated in 1904-05.

D (*k*) 78.—Fragment (ht. 11½″) similar to D (*k*) 77. Excavated in 1904-05 to the north-west of the Main Shrine.[3]

D (*k*) 79.—Fragment (ht. 5½″) of a halo with a lotus flower in relief. Gupta work. Chunār sandstone. Discovered in 1906-07 in the area to the east of the Main Shrine.

D (*k*) 80.—Lotus-flower (diam. 5″) probably from the halo of an image. Excavated in 1904-05.[4]

D (*k*) 81.—Lotus-flower (diam. 5″) finely executed. Gupta work. Chunār sandstone. Discovered in 1906-07 to the south of the south-east corner of Monastery I, 6′ below the surface.

D (*k*) 82.—Dentil (width 8¾″) from a face-stone, cut with lotus petals. Mediæval (?). Chunār stone. Discovered in 1906-07 in monastery I, 5′ below the surface.

D (*k*) 83.—Dentil (width 8¼″) similar to D (*k*) 82. Discovered in one of the recent excavations.

D (*k*) 84.—Fragment (ht. 8″) with scroll work. Gupta work. Chunār sandstone. Find-spot not known.

*D (*k*) 85.—Architectural fragment (ht. 9¼″; width 11¼″). Below, line of lotus petals. Above, part of figure resembling a celestial to pro-

---

[1] *A. S. R.*, 1907-08, p. 49, η 32.
[2] *Ibid.*, 1904-05, p. 100, No. 411.
[3] *Ibid.*, p. 97, No. 239.
[4] *Ibid.*, No. 259.

per right and claws of a leogryph to left. At the base, parts of two lines of writing containing the Buddhist creed in characters of about the 11th century A.D.

l. 1. ....*yē dharmā hē*

l. 2. ....*śravaṇa*

Chunār sandstone. Excavated in 1904-05.[1]

D (*k*) 86.—Fragment (ht. 5½") with scroll-work. Gupta work. Excavated in 1904-05.[2]

D (*k*) 87.—Fragment (ht. 5") with vase filled with palmettes. Late mediæval. Pale buff stone. Discovered in 1907-08 on the approach to the Main Shrine from east, 7′ below the surface.

D (*k*) 88.—Fragment (ht. 3½") with scroll work. Late Gupta style. Excavated in 1904-05.[3]

D (*k*) 89.—Fragment (ht. 4") with two lotus petals carved on it. Mediæval. Found in 1907-08 on the approach to the Main Shrine from the east, 7′ 8" below the surface.

D (*k*) 90.—Base (ht. 8½") with a figure of Buddha seated in the earth-touching attitude with a *stūpa* on either side. Traces of attendant on proper right flank. Mediæval. Chunār sandstone. Presumably unearthed in one of the recent excavations.

D (*k*) 91.—Fragment (ht. 8") with a *stūpa* in relief. Mediæval. Excavated in 1904-05 to the north-east of the Jagat Singh *stūpa*.[4]

D (*k*) 92.—Fragment (ht. 7") similar to D (*k*) 91. Excavated in 1907-08 on the approach to the Main Shrine from the east, 7′ below the surface.

D (*k*) 93.—Snout (ht. 8") of a crocodile which may have served the purpose of an ornamental spout. Mediæval. Chunār sandstone. Unearthed in 1907-08 in the western precinct of Monastery I, 4′ 5" below the surface.

D (*k*) 94.—Fragment (ht. 8") of a railing post carved with a lotus flower on two sides. Chunār sandstone. Found in one of the recent excavations.

D (*k*) 95.—Fragment (ht. 6") of a railing pillar adorned with floral rosettes. Kushāṇa (?) period. Chunār stone. Unearthed in one of the recent diggings.

---

[1] *A. S. R.*, 1904-05, p. 92, No. 31.
[2] *Ibid.*, p. 97, No. 236.
[3] *Ibid.*, p. 99, No. 399.
[4] *Ibid.*, p. 97, No. 267.

D(1).—Inscribed slabs.

D(*1*) 1. Fragment (1′ 1½″×7″) of an inscribed slab bearing portions of two lines of an inscription in Kushāṇa characters, which refers itself to the reign of a certain Rājan Aśvaghōsha. Another epigraph dated in the 40th regnal year of this same ruler is inscribed on the lower portion of the Aśōka column which is *in situ* to the west of the Main Shrine.[1] The fragment was found in 1904-05 to the east of the Main Shrine.[2]

D(*1*) 2. Fragment (ht. 6¾″; width 5½″) of an inscribed slab with portions of four lines in Gupta characters. The inscription reads :—

l. 1. *Māgha di 30* svam [vatsarē]............

l. 2. *dharmmō dīp*...................

l. 3. ....

l. 4. *yad*.................

Found in 1904-05.[3]

D(*1*) 3. Fragmentary slab (ht. 11″; width 1′ 2½″) of buff sandstone bearing mutilated remnants of a Sanskrit inscription of the 6th or 7th century A. D. The slab was discovered in 1904-05 in Monastery No. I.[4]

D(*1*) 4. Stone (ht. 6½″; width 8½″) with five lines of writing which contain the Buddhist creed followed by a *stūpa* and the formula *bhrūṁ huṁ*. The characters are of about the 9th century A. D. Found in 1904-05 east of the chapel near the south-east corner of the Main Shrine.[5]

D(*1*) 5. Fragment (ht. 4½″; width 5″) with the beginning of the Buddhist creed, *yē dharmmā hē*......in characters of the 8th or 9th century A. D. Found in 1904-05.[6]

D(*1*) 6. Fragment (ht. 8″; width 10″) showing a part of the Buddhist creed...... *rōdha ēvaṁvādī mahāśramaṇaḥ*, in characters of about the 11th century A. D. Found in 1904-05.[7]

D(*1*) 7. Imperfect stone (ht. 6″; width 10″) inscribed with an epigraph of eight lines in characters of the 8th or 9th century A. D. The writing is too much corroded to yield any useful information. Found in 1906-07 in the area east of the Main Shrine. The material is a kind of black stone which was not quarried at Chunār.

D(*1*) 8. A broken and fragmentary stone inscription in corrupt Sanskrit and Nāgarī characters which was found in 1906-07 in the

---

[1] See page 30 above.
[2] *A. S. R.*, 1904-05, p. 70 and p. 103, VIII.
[3] *Ibid.*, p. 98, No. 279 and p. 103, No. XII and Pl. XXXII.
[4] *Ibid.*, 1904-05, p. 98, No. 277 and p. 104, XXXII.
[5] *Ibid.*, p. 98, No. 276 and p. 104, XXXIII.
[6] *Ibid.*, p. 98, No. 283 and p. 103 XXIX.
[7] *Ibid.*, p. 103, XXVII.

monastery to the east of the Dhamēkh *stūpa.* There are altogether six inscribed fragments. All proper names are missing. The inscription is one of the Kalachuri (Chēdī) Karṇadēva of Tripurī and is dated in the Kalachuri Samvat 810, the 15th day of the bright fortnight of Āśvina, on a Sunday, which corresponds to Sunday the 4th October A. D. 1058. The inscription states that on the date specified above in the big Vihāra called Saddharmachakrapravarttana, certain Sthaviras were caused to give their blessing. We then learn that a certain worshipper Māmakā, a follower of the Mahāyāna who was the wife of Dhanēśvara, a follower of the Mahāyāna, caused a copy of the Ashṭasāhasrikā to be written and presented something, the nature of which cannot be ascertained, to the order of monks. The inscription is important as it shows that the whole Buddhist establishment of Sārnāth was known by the name of Saddharmachakrapravarttanavihāra or "the Convent of the turning of the Wheel of the noble Law" in the 11th century A. D.[1]

D(*l*) 9. Rectangular slab of sandstone inscribed with a Sanskrit epigraph (*praśasti*) in verse in Nāgarī characters of a very ornamental kind which came to light at Dr. Marshall's excavations of 1908 to the north of the Dhamēkh Stūpa. The inscribed surface measures 21"×15½". The record is in an excellent state of preservation and consists of 26 verses.[2] The first two verses contain invocations of Vasundhārā and the Moon. The next eleven verses give the genealogy and dwell on the virtues of Kumaradēvī the Buddhist queen of Gōvindachandra of Kānyakubja, modern Kanauj, whose inscriptions range from A. D. 1114 to 1154. Verse 21 tells us that the queen named above built a *Vihāra*, at Dharmachakra (modern Sārnāth) and in the next two verses we are informed that she caused a copper plate to be prepared in connection with the teaching of the Lord of the Wheel of the Law and that she then restored the image of the Lord of the Wheel of the Law as it existed in the days of Aśōka. The inscription was composed by the poet Śrīkunda and engraved by the mason Vāmana.[3]

---

[1] The inscription was deciphered by Dr. Konow, *A. S. R.* 1906-07. p. 100 f.
[2] *A. S. R.*, 1907-08, p. 76, XXIII and *Ep. Ind.* Vol. IX, pp. 319 ff.
[3] For further remarks on this inscription see above Introduction, p. 7

E.—DOMESTIC OBJECTS OF STONE.

E 1.—Dish (diam. 1′ 8″; ht. 4¼″) with two projecting handles which must have been used for the preparation of flour. Finely finished. Buff-coloured sandstone of Chunār. Unearthed in 1907-08 in the area on the north side of the Dhamēkh *stūpa.*[1]

E 2.—Offertory dish (diam. 4¾″) with four projecting handles, a round rim and a lotus in relief inside. The edges are burnt from which it may be inferred that the dish was used as a lamp during worship (*pūjā*).

Unearthed in 1907-08 in the 2nd outer court of Monastery I, 1′ below the surface.[2]

E 3.—Miniature *liṅga* on *argha* (ht. 3″) which must have done duty for a household deity. Mediæval style. Excavated in1907-08 in the area on the north side of the Dhamēkh *stūpa.*[3]

E 4.—Boat-shaped mortar (ht. 3¼″; length 1′ 3¼″) hollowed out in the middle, such as are used at the present day for the preparation of antimony. Discovered in 1907-08 in the monastery, the so-called "Hospital" to the west of the Dhamēkh *stūpa*, 6′ below the surface.

E 5.—Pestle in the shape of a rolling pin (length 1′ 2″) which was found by the side of E 4 and must have been used with it. It is broken into two pieces and seems to be polished.

E 6.—Fragment (length 8½″; width 8½″) of a mortar (Hindī *sil*) with its surface roughened by incised lines. Such stones are still used for crushing spices upon. Red sandstone which from constant grinding has acquired a shiny surface. Find-spot not known.

E 7.—Rectangular slab (length 1′ 1″; width 10″) with roughened surface for grinding spices upon. Excavated in 1906-07 in the monastery, the so-called "Hospital" to the west of the Dhamēkh *stūpa*, 8′ 4″ below the surfce.

E 8.—Fragment of a mortar (length 6½″; width 8¼″) roughened with incised lines. Unearthed in 1906-07 in the 1st outer court of Monastery I, 5′ below the surface.

E 9.—Fragment of grind-stone (length 7″; width 8¾″) similar to E 8. Find-spot not known.

E 10.—Half of a grind-stone (length 6¼″; width 6½″). Traces of red paint. Excavated in 1906-07 to the north-west of the Main Shrine.

E 11.—Small-sized grind-stone (length 6″; width 4″) pointed at one end and roughened with incised curves. Reddish sandstone. Find-spot not known.

---

[1] *A. S. R.*, 1907-08, p. 61, η 4.
[2] *Ibid.*, p. 53, ι 28.
[3] *Ibid.*, p. 61, η 178.

E 12.—Grinding stone (length 7" ; width 5") similar to E 11. Provenance not known.

E 13.—Stone pestle (length 1' 1¼") in the shape of a cylindrical rolling pin with a round handle at each end. Unearthed in 1907-08 to the east of the 2nd gateway of Monastery I.[1]

E 14.—Unfinished pestle (length 11") square in section. Excavated in 1906-07 in the monastery to the west of the Dhamēkh *stūpa*, 5' 6" below the surface.

E 15.—Pestle (length 10½") in an unfinished condition. Found in 1906-07 in the area to the west of the Main Shrine.

E 16.—Upper stone (diam. 1' 5¼") of a hand flour-mill with a circular projection at the top pierced with a hole through which grain is poured. The handle was attached to a horizontal wooden bar let into the groove cut across the projection. Excavated in 1907-08 in the 2nd outer court of Monastery I, 11' below the surface.

E 17.—Lower stone (diam. 1' 5½" ; ht. 6") of a hand flour-mill. Projection on underside. Circular hole in centre meant to receive the vertical rod by which the mill was fixed into the ground. Unearthed in 1906-07 in the 1st outer court of monastery I, 4' below the surface.

E 18.—Lower stone of a hand flour-mill (diam. 1' 6" ; ht 2") with a circular hole in the centre for the reception of the pin by which the mill was fixed in the ground. Buff-coloured sandstone. Find-spot not known.

E 19.—Upper stone (diam. 1' 3" ; ht. 2¼") of a hand flour-mill with a circular socket near the edge for the handle. The hole in the centre is for the vertical pin by which the mill was fixed into the ground and the large hole near it to hold grain. Excavated in 1904-05 to the north-east of the Main Shrine.

E 20.—Upper member of a hand flour-mill (diam. 1' 4" ; ht. 2½"). Unearthed in 1907-08 in the western precinct of monastery I, 4' 3" below the surface.

E 21.—Lower stone (diam. 11" ; ht. 2¾") of a hand flour-mill with a hole in the centre for the pin by which the mill was fixed into the ground. This may be identical with "a nether hand mill-stone, diameter 11 inches, sandstone," excavated by Professor Hall.[2]

E 22.—Upper member of a hand flour-mill (diam. 10½" ; ht. 2¾") of the type of E 16. Discovered in one of the recent excavations.

E 23.—Lower member of a hand flour grinding mill (diam. 1' ; ht. 2¾"). Found in one of the recent diggings.

E 24.—Nether hand mill-stone (diam. 1' 1" ; ht. 4½"). Probably excavated in 1907-08.

---

[1] *A. S. R.*, 1907-08, p. 54, ¶ 88.

[2] *J. A. S. B.*, Vol. XXV, 1856, p. 399, No. 2.

E 25.—Unusually heavy upper hand millstone (diam. 11″; ht. 8¼″) of the form of a cylinder. The handle was attached to a horizontal rod fixed in the groove cut across the top. Sandstone of Chunār. Provenance not known.

E 26.—Upper member of a hand mill (diam. 10½″; ht. 6½″). Found in the entrance chamber of Monastery I, 2′ 6″ below the surface.

E 27.—Upper stone of a hand flour-mill (diam. 9¾″; ht. 4¾″) with the projection at the top broken. Found in one of the recent diggings.

E 28.—Half of upper hand mill-stone (diam. 1′ 6″; ht. 2¾″). Professor Hall excavated at Sārnāth a similar stone broken into two pieces.[3] This may be one of them.

E 29.—Two pieces of a stone stool (diam. 1′; ht. 2¼″) supported on low legs, resembling the *chaklū* on which bread (*chapātī*) is made. Mediæval. Excavated in 1906-07 to the east of the entrance of Monastery I, 2½′ below the surface.

E 30.—Stone finial (ht. 5″) of the shape of a bead. Unearthed in the same year in the entrance chamber of Monastery I, 3′ below the surface.

E 31.—Finial (ht. 4″) similar to E 30. Find-spot not known.

E 32.—Cubical stone (ht. 4¾″) pierced with a hole in the middle, which presumably belonged to a floor rammer, or it may have been used for thrashing paddy seeds. Found in 1906-07 in the monastery to the west of the Dhamēkh *stūpa*, 3′ 5″ below the surface.

E 33.—Similar to E 32, ht. 4½″. Found in the same building, 4′ below the surface.

---

[1] *J. A. B. S.*, Vol. XXV, 1856, p. 399, No. 3.

F.—TERRA-COTTAS.

F (a).—*Terra-cotta and concrete figures.*

F (a) 1.—Head (ht. 14") of a colossal Buddha statue made of pounded brick with a coating of fine *kankar* lime. The right half of the face is broken off. The hair is, as in stone images, arranged in schematic curls and the ear-lobes are elongated. The style is characteristic of the early Gupta period. The statue to which this head belonged must have been built into some building. Found in 1904-05.

F (a) 2.—Terra-cotta plaque (ht. 11¾"; width 9") showing the great miracle displayed by Gautama Buddha at Śrāvastī. The Buddha is seated cross-legged, preaching the sermon which he delivered to the people in the presence of king Prasēnajit and the six heretical teachers (*tīrthikas*), on a lotus the stem of which is supported on either side by a serpent deity (*nāga*). At the proper right lower corner of the plaque we notice a male figure seated on a low stool and facing towards the lotus throne of the Buddha. He is attended by a parasol-bearer and an elephant standing to front and must evidently be Prasēnajit, king of Śrāvastī. Of the three miniature figures in the other corner of the plaque the first one sitting on a stool with his right hand raised to his head and his left hand on the knee is one of the six heretics whom the great Teacher confounded by his superhuman powers on this occasion. The other two figures, one of which holds a fly-whisk, are obviously the disciples of the Tīrthika.

The same scene is also illustrated on the sculptures C(*a*) 3, C(*a*) 6, C(*a*) 7, D(*g*) 6 and F(*a*) 3, as well as on a sculptured stele from Sārnāth now preserved in the Indian Museum, Calcutta.[1]

The style of technique is of the Gupta period.

The sculpture was discovered in 1906-07 in the area west of the Main Shrine.

F (*a*) 3.—Terra-cotta plaque (ht. 1′ 5¾"; width 11") representing apparently the same event as F (*a*) 2. The Buddha is seated in the centre in the attitude of expounding the law. The stem of the lotus on which the Buddha sits is effaced, but the figures on either side of it remain. They are in the same attitude as in C (*a*) 6 and 7. To the right and left of the Buddha is an attendant holding a fly-whisk in right hand, possibly Śāriputra and Maudgalyāyana or perhaps the Bōdhisattvas Maitrēya and Avalōkitēśvara though their emblems are absent. On either side of the halo of the Buddha are miniature Buddha figures seated in meditation on lotuses. The style of technique is of about the late

---

[1] Burgess, *The ancient monuments, temples and sculptures of India*, Part I, Pl. 68, 1.

Gupta period, *i.e.*, nearly contemporaneous with C (*a*) 6 and 7. Found in one of the recent excavations in a *stūpa* north of Main Shrine.

F (*a*) 4.—Terra-cotta plaque (ht. 1′ 4″ ; width 11″) showing Gautama Buddha's enlightenment (Sanskrit *bōdhi*). The Buddha is, as usual, seated on a throne in the attitude of touching the earth. The proper right side of the sculpture is broken off and the figure of Buddha defaced. Beneath his throne, we notice the half-bodied earth-goddess rising from the earth immediately below the right hand of the Buddha, with the treasure vase on her hands. On the other side of the base is a daughter of the Evil One in flight. The omission of her lower part below the waist suggests that she is being drowned or devoured by the earth.

Of the army of the Evil One, two demons remain to the proper left of the Buddha's head. One of the demons has a double-edged axe (*kuṭhāra*) in his left hand. The head and hands of the other are missing. The style of carving is of the late Gupta period.

This sculpture was found built in the same mediæval *stūpa* as F (*a*) 3.

F (*a*) 5.—Fragment (ht. 10″ ; width 8″) of a terra-cotta sculpture showing the Buddha in the attitude of expounding the law. His right half and lower part below the waist are missing. The features are also damaged. Circular halo around head. To the proper left of the Buddha is Avalōkitēśvara holding a lotus in his left hand. Probably Gupta. Unearthed in one of the recent excavations.

F (*a*) 6.—Terra-cotta figure (ht. 6½″ ; width 6″) of Buddha seated in meditation (*dhyānamudrā*). His head is missing. Probably Gupta. Found in 1904-05.

F (*a*) 7.—Terra-cotta figure (ht. 9¼″ ; width 7″) of Buddha seated cross-legged in the attitude of expounding the law. Both hands and head wanting. The relief on base is broken off *in toto*. The sculpture bears traces of red colouring and was found in 1904 05.

F (*a*) 8.—Terra-cotta plaque (ht. 7⅜″ ; width 6½″) with traces of a figure. Probably excavated in 1906-07.

F (*a*) 9.—Fragment (ht. 4½″ ; width 6″) of a terra-cotta sculpture with the legs below knees of a standing Buddha. The attitude must have been that of bestowing a gift or of granting protection. Edges of garments above ankles. Typical Gupta style. Found in 1907-08 in the trench crossing the south boundary wall of Monastery I, 9′ below the surface.

F (*a*) 10.—Fragment (ht. 9″ ; width 7½″) of a terra-cotta plaque with the crossed legs and left arm of a seated figure, presumably Buddha in meditation or earth-touching posture. Too much defaced to allow of dating. Found in 1907-08 in the long trench east of Monastery I.

F (*a*) 11.—Fragment (ht. 7″) of the head of a Buddha with the hair treated in formal curls. It is made of the same material as F (*a*) 1. The right half of the face and the back of the head are broken off. Gupta or perhaps earlier. Found in 1906-07 in the area west of the Main Shrine.

F (*a*) 12.—Head (ht. 3¼") of a miniature statuette of Buddha made of pounded brick covered with lime plaster. Gupta period. Found in the area around Jagat Singh *stūpa* in 1907-08.

F (*a*) 13-15.—Three fragments (hts. 5", 4", 3") of Buddha heads with the hair arranged in usual curls. They are made of the same materials as F (*a*) 12 and are finished off in lime in excellent Gupta style. Found in 1907-08 in the area south of Monastery II, 6′ below the surface.

F (*a*) 16.—Hand (length 3¾") probably right, which has apparently held a flower stalk. Made of concrete covered with fine lime. Probably Gupta. Found at the same spot as F(*a*) 13-15.

F (*a*) 17.—Portions of two hands (length 4¼") resting one over the other as in the attitude of meditation and may have belonged to a Buddha image. Made of the same material as F (*a*) 16 and found at the same spot.

F (*a*) 18.—Portion of a human face (ht. 4½") with the nose, eyes and forehead remaining. Probably Gupta. Made of lime mixed with *kankar*. Found in 1906-07 in the area west of the Main Shrine.

F (*a*) 19.—" Head (ht. 6") with cap. The long nose, high cheek bones, full lips and small chin proclaim it of the Gupta period. It is made of coarse concrete covered with plaster."[1] Found in 1907-08 among the group of *stūpas* to the north of the Dhamēkh *stūpa*.

F (*a*) 20.—Head (ht. 6") with the hair parted in the middle and falling in twisted curls on both sides. The features are well modelled and the teeth are visible between the lips. Traces of large ear-rings. Gupta style. Made of concrete covered with plaster and lime. Unearthed in one of the recent excavations.

F (*a*) 21.—Portion of a head (ht. 5½") with an open mouth and a wrinkled brow which may have belonged to a demoniacal figure. Made of the same material as F(*a*) 20. Probably Gupta. Found in 1906-07 in the area to the north-west of the Main Shrine, 9′ below the surface.

F (*a*) 22.—Fragment (ht. 3½") of a female head with the nose, lips, cheeks and chin remaining. Gupta style. Made of coarse concrete covered with plaster. Unearthed in one of the recent excavations.

F (*a*) 23.—Fragment (ht. 3½") of a head similar to F (*a*) 22 and of the same period.

F (*a*) 24.—Fragment (ht. 3¾") of a head with the back and the left eye broken off. Gupta. Made of the same materials as F (*a*) 23.

F (*a*) 25.—Fragment (ht. 4¼") of a concrete figurine which may have been meant for the head, the features being indicated by mere dots. Found in 1906-07 in the area north-west of the Main Shrine.

---

[1] *A. S. R.*, 1907-08, p. 61, *n* -122, Pl. XIX, *b*.

F (*a*) 26.—Fragment (ht. 3") showing the proper right side of a male face. The style is of the Gupta period. Made of concrete covered with plaster and lime. Found in the monastery area in 1906-07.

F (*a*) 27.—Fragment (ht. 4½") showing the right ear and eye of an animal, perhaps a boar. Made of concrete, plaster and lime. Excavated in 1906-07.

F (*a*) 28.—Fragment (ht. 3¾") of a hand holding a roundish object. Probably Gupta. Made of concrete covered with plaster and lime. Found in 1906-07 in the area north-west of the Main Shrine.

F (*a*) 29.—Fragment (length 2¾") showing three toes of the left foot. Gupta style. Made of plaster covered with lime. Found in 1907-08 in the area north of the Main Shrine, 4′ below the surface.

F (*a*) 30.—Fragment (diam. 3") with a lotus flower in relief. Made of concrete with plaster. Found in 1906-07 in the area north-west of the Main Shrine.

F (*a*) 31.—Fragment (length 2½") bearing an ear in relief. Made of plaster and lime. Found in one of the recent excavations.

F (*a*) 32.—Terra-cotta figurine (ht. 7¾") of a celestial (*dēva*). The garland which it held in front of the chest is extant in part. The legs are broken off but they seem to have been raised. On the chest we notice a mark resembling *śrīvatsa*. Late Gupta. Excavated in 1906-07 in the Monastery I, 3′ below the surface.[1]

F (*a*) 33.—Fragment (ht. 8½" ; width 6") of a panel with a garland border. Inside, a male figure with three-peaked coronet standing in the position of an archer. The right hand and left arm are missing. The right arm is stretched out and there are traces of an arrow or bow-string on the chest. The legs below the thighs are missing. The style appears to be of the Gupta period. Excavated in 1904-05.

F (*a*) 34.—Fragment (ht. 8¼" ; width 5") of a terra-cotta sculpture. Above, lower part of a figure seated cross-legged in the attitude of meditation. Below, head and joined hands of a worshipper and front part of a bull, the emblem of Vṛishabhanātha. The main figure may therefore have been the *tīrthaṅkara* of that name. Probably late Gupta. Found in 1906-07 in the area north-west of the Main Shrine.

F (*a*) 35.—Bust (ht. 5½") of a female figure with the right arm broken off, ornamented with ear-rings, a necklace and an armlet. Found in area north of the Main Shrine, 6′ below the surface.

F (*a*) 36.—Fragment (width 5¾") with the legs of a seated figure. Mediæval. Found in 1907-08 in the 2nd outer court of Monastery I, 5′ below the surface.

---

[1] *A. S. R.*, 1906-07, Pl. XXVI, 1.

F (*a*) 37.—Terra-cotta figure (length 8¾") of a tortoise with the tongue jutting out. Mediæval. Found in the western precinct of Monastery I, 13′ below the surface.

F (*a*) 38.—Fragment (ht. 1′ 2″; width 7¼") of a panel with part of an elephant standing in profile in relief. The style seems to be of the early Gupta or Kushāṇa period. Traces of red paint. Unearthed in one of the recent excavations.

F (*a*) 39.—Head (ht. 3¼") from eyes upwards. The hair is combed back and there is a snail-like projection on the crown similar to that in Kaṭrā image of Buddha.[1] The fragment would therefore have belonged to a Buddha or Bōdhisattva head. Made of concrete, finished in lime. Gupta style. Excavated in 1906-07 in the area to the east of the Main Shrine.

F (*a*) 40.—Terra-cotta head (ht. 3¼") of Buddha with the usual curls. Gupta period. Found in 1906-07 in monastery I.

F (*a*) 41.—Terra-cotta figure (ht. 3") of Gaṇēśa with four arms. He is seated in easy attitude. He has his usual attributes but they are effaced. His elephantine trunk rests, as usual, on a bowl of sweets which he holds in his lower left hand. Mediæval.

F (*a*) 42.—Figure of Gaṇēśa identical with F (*a*) 41 in all respects and found at the same spot.

F (*a*) 43.—Miniature terra-cotta figure (ht. 2¼") with corpulent belly. Head, left arm and leg missing. Probably a goblin (*yaksha*). Mediæval. Found in 1907-08, in western precinct of Monastery I, 8′ below the surface.

F (*a*) 44.—Imperfect figure of a horse with a rider (ht. 3¼"). The rider has a round headdress. The object was evidently meant for a child's toy. Mediæval. It is hollow and was cast in a mould. Found in 1907-08 in the area north-west of the Main Shrine, 4′ 6″ below the surface.

F (*a*) 45-48.—Busts (ht. 1½" to 2½") of human figurines which must have belonged to toys of the type of F (*a*) 44. The exact find-spot of F(*a*) 45 is not known. The other three were found in Monastery I, the monastery west of the Dhamēkh *stūpa* and the area south of Monastery II, 4′, 4′ and 2′ 9″ below the surface respectively.

F (*a*) 49.—Head (ht. 3") with a pointed projection on the crown and a broad band over the forehead. Late mediæval. It must have belonged to a toy. Found in Monastery I in 1906-07.

F (*a*) 50.—Bust (ht. 2") of a female figurine with a child in her left arm. Probably Gupta. Found in 1907-08 in western precinct of Monastery I, 6′ 4″ below the surface.

---

[1] Vogel, *Catalogue of the Archæological Museum at Mathurā*, Pl. VII.

F (*a*) 51.—Hand (length 3¼″) wearing a bracelet and holding a round object. Probably Gupta. Excavated in 1906-07 in the area to the west of the Main Shrine.

F (*a*) 52-54.—Three birds (ht. 1½″, 2⅛″, 1⅞″) which must have been used as toys. Mediæval. F(*a*) 52 was found in 1906-07 in Monastery I, 14′ 4″ below the surface.

F (*a*) 55.—Front (ht. 3⅜″) of a figurine of a horse, with reins, but the rider is broken off. Evidently a toy. Mediæval. Found in 1907-08 in the trench crossing the south boundary wall of Monastery I, 6′ below the surface.

F (*a*) 56.—Front part (length 3¼″) of a tortoise. It is hollow on the underside. Late mediæval. Found in trench near the Old Sculpture Shed.

F (*a*) 57.—Figurine (length 2″) of a mouse. Late mediæval. Found in Monastery I in 1906-07.

F (*a*) 58.—Snout (length 3⅜″) of a crocodile. Found in 1906-07 in Monastery I, 7′ below the surface.

F (*a*) 59.—Fragment (length 2½″) similar to F (*a*) 58. Found in Monastery I in 1906-07.

F (*a*) 60.—Head (ht. 1¾″) of a mouse. Mediæval. Found in area north-west of the Main Shrine, 3′ below the surface.

F (*a*) 61.—Torso (length 3¼″) of an animal. The head is broken off. The legs are not indicated but a pair of holes pierced across the body clearly show that the figure was meant for a child's toy-cart. The wheels must also have been of clay. Dr. Marshall unearthed a large number of such carts at Bhīṭā near Allahabad in 1909-10. Late mediæval. It must have been excavated in one of the recent excavations.

F (*a*) 62-77.—Sixteen figurines of horses very roughly modelled but well-baked. Some of them have saddles but no riders. They may have been presented as offerings at shrines or been meant for children's toys. They are of a very late date. Found in 1906-07 and 1907-08 all over the site.

F (*a*) 78.—Front part (ht. 5¼″) of a bull. The head is ornamented with strings of beads. Late mediæval. Found in 1907-08 in the trench crossing the south boundary wall of Monastery I, 2′ below the surface.

F (*a*) 79.—Hind part (ht. 6¼″) of a horse with trappings and traces of a saddle. Hollow inside. Late mediæval. Found in 1907-08 in the long trench east of Monastery I.

F (*a*) 80.—Terra-cotta fragment (7″×5½″) with scroll-work. Gupta style. Found in 1906-07 in the area west of the Main Shrine.

F (*a*) 81.—Conical-shaped terra-cotta ear-ornament (length 2¼″). Late mediæval. Found in 1906-07 in Monastery I.

F (*a*) 82.—Top (length 1¼″) of a child's rattle similar to those found complete at Sahēṭh-Mahēṭh. Found in 1906-07 in the area to the east of the Main Shrine.

F (*a*) 83.—Ear-ornament (ht. 1⅛″) of the shape of a *rahlī*, with incised lines on front. Late mediæval. Found in 1907-08.

F (*a*) 84-85.—Ear-ornaments of the same type. Made of grey clay. Found in Monastery I.

F (*a*) 86.—Terra-cotta finial (ht. 2¾″) of the shape of an *āmalaka* with tenons at both ends. Found in 1907-08 in the area north of the Main Shrine, 3′ below the surface.

F (*a*) 87.—Terra-cotta plaque (2″ square) with a flower cut in relief. Found in 1906-07 in the area north-west of the Main Shrine.

F (*a*) 88.—Terra-cotta solid cone (ht. 2¾″) with incised lines. Object unknown. Found in the monastery west of the Dhamēkh *stūpa*, 5′ 2″ below the surface.

F (*a*) 89-192.—Conical objects with spiral ornament on the outside. The diameter at base varies from ¾″ to 1⅞″. The purpose of these objects is not known. They may have been presented as offerings at shrines. They are found in abundance on all Buddhist sites. Found all over the site.

F (*a*) 193.—Ten objects of the same type.

F (*a*) 194.—Statuette of elephant (length 2¼″) couchant. Traces of red paint. Gupta or earlier. Found in 1906-07 in the area west of the Main Shrine.

F (*a*) 195-96.—Two large terra-cotta beads (length 1¾″ and 1⅝″). Found in 1906-07 in Monastery I, 10′ 5″ below the surface.

F (*a*) 197-235.—Spindle whorls of usual type. The height varies from ½″ to ⅞″. Found all over the site.

F (*a*) 236.—Two terra-cotta wheels (diam. 1⅝″ and 1⅜″) of a toy-cart marked with spokes on one face.

F (*a*) 237-240.—Circular discs (diam. 1¼″ to 1½″) which must have been some sort of toys. Found in recent excavations.

F (*a*) 241.—Bull (length 1′ 7″ ; ht. 9½″) couchant on a pedestal. Its head is broken off. Found in 1906-07 in Monastery I. west of the Dhamēkh *stūpa*, 5′ 6″ below the surface.

F(*b*)—Pottery.

The bulk of the pottery exhibited in the northern room of the museum was unearthed by Dr. Marshall in 1906-07 and 1907-08. An interesting feature of this collection are three big *chāṭīs* which came to light in 1907-08 in 2nd outer court of Monastery I, two of which are displayed on stone tables in the middle of the room. Two other jars of the same size were found in the same area but they are broken to pieces and cannot be exhibited. These jars must have been employed for the storage of corn and water.

F (*b*) 1.—Large-sized jar or *chāṭī* (ht. 2′ 10″; inner diam. at aperture 10½″) with low rim, round bottom and convex sides. Must have been used for the storage of corn or water. It is made of a fine clay with a slip of the same colour. There is no decoration of any kind on the exterior. Probably late Gupta. Discovered in 1907-08 in the 2nd outer court of Monastery I, 7′ below the surface.

F (*b*) 2.—Large-sized jar (ht. 3′ 2″; inner diam. at aperture 11½″) similar to F (*b*) 1. It is made of a coarse buff clay burnt grey with traces of a dark red wash. Cracked all over. Unearthed in 1907-08 in the 2nd outer court of Monastery I, 8′ below the surface.

F (*b*) 3.—Large-sized jar (ht. 2′ 5″) with the mouth and a part of the body broken off. Made of coarse clay with traces of a dark red wash. Discovered in 1907-08 in the 2nd outer court of Monastery I, 7′ below the surface.

F (*b*) 4.—Jar (ht. 1′ 4½″; inner diam. at aperture 9½″) gracefully shaped. It has a low rim flat at the top and adorned with a chain pattern. The bottom is round. Incised lines around the neck. Made of a fine buff clay with red slip. Found in 1907-08 in the long trench east of Monastery I.

F (*b*) 5.—Jar (ht. 1′ 5″; inner diam. at aperture 7″) of the type of a *chāṭī* for the storage of corn or water. Made of a fine buff clay with slip. No colour around the bottom. Found in the area north of the Main Shrine, 2′ below the surface.

F (*b*) 6.—Jar (ht. 11″; inner diam. at aperture 7″) of the shape of a *chāṭī* with a low rim, and round bottom and decorated with incised lines in the upper part of the body. It is made of a buff clay with a red slip. Discovered in 1906-07 in Monastery I, 10′ below the surface.

F (*b*) 7.—Jar (ht. 1′ 2″; inner diam. at aperture 6½″) of the form of a *chāṭī* adorned around the neck with incised lines and dots. Made of buff clay with red slip. Found in the same place as F (*b*) 6.

F (*b*) 8.—Jar (ht. 6¾″; inner diam. at aperture 9½″) resembling a *chāṭī* in form. Ornamented below the neck with an incised zigzag pattern and a series of crescents. Made of coarse buff clay with a red slip which has mostly worn away. Discovered in 1906-07 at the same spot as F (*b*) 6 and 7.[1]

F (*b*) 9.—Jar (ht. 11″ ; inner diam. at aperture 6¼″) of the form of a *gharā* made of buff clay with a red slip. The bottom is burnt and the jar must have been used for heating water. Unearthed in 1906-07 or 1907-08.

F (*b*) 10.—Jar (ht. 11″ ; inner diam. at aperture 6¼″) similar to F (*b*) 9. Coarse buff clay with red slip. Discovered in 1906-07 in Monastery I, 19′ below the surface.

F (*b*) 11.—Jar (ht. 11″) or *gharā* made of fine buff clay with a red slip in the upper half. The rim is partly broken. Discovered in 1906-07 in Monastery I, 6′ below the surface.

F (*b*) 12.—Jar (ht. 8½″) with a concave rim and decorated with the same patterns as F (*b*) 8. Fine buff clay with dark red slip. Found in 1906-07 in Monastery I, 11′ 7″ below the surface.

F (*b*) 13.—Jar (ht. 10″; inner diam. at aperture 3½″) of the type of a goblet ornamented with incised lines. Buff clay with red slip. Discovered in 1907-08 in the western precinct of Monastery I, 5′ 5″ below the surface.

F (*b*) 14.—Jar (ht. 10½″) or *gharā* with the neck broken off. Modern. Buff clay with a red slip. Excavated in 1907-08 in the long trench east of Monastery I.

F (*b*) 15.—Jug (ht. 7¾″ ; inner diam. at aperture 5½″) with over-burnt bottom. It must have been used for heating milk. Fine buff clay with a red slip. Found in 1907-08 in the long trench east of Monastery I.

F (*b*) 16.—Jug (ht. 8¼″ ; inner diam. at aperture 4″) with a narrow neck. Buff clay with a red slip. Found in the long trench east of Monastery I.

F (*b*) 17.—Jug (ht. 8¼″) similar in form to F (*b*) 16 but adorned below the neck with a zigzag pattern and incised lines. Found in 1906-07 at the same spot as F (*b*) 6 and 7.

F (*b*) 18.—Jug (ht. 8¾″ ; inner diam. at aperture 5″) with a high curved rim and depressed bottom. Buff clay with a red slip. Discovered in 1907-08 in the western precinct of Monastery I, 15′ 6″ below the surface.[2]

F (*b*) 19.—Jug. (ht. 7¼″ ; inner diam. at aperture 3¼″) similar in shape to F (*b*) 13. Buff clay with a red slip. Straight rim slightly curved inwards. Found in 1906-07 in the area north-west of the Main Shrine.

---

[1] *A. S. R.*, 1906-07, Pl. XXVII, 13.

[2] *Ibid.*, 1907-08, p. 48, fig. 4, *c*.

F (*b*) 20.—Jug (ht. 4¾″; inner diam. at aperture 2¾″) of the type of a modern *lōṭā*, with a high straight rim. Buff clay with a red slip. Found in 1906-07 near the north-west corner of structure No. 23, 4′ below the surface.

F (*b*) 21.—Jug (ht. 5¾″; inner diam. at aperture 3½″) of the form of a *lōṭā*. Coarse buff clay with a red slip. Found in the area east of Main Shrine in 1906-07.

F (*b*) 22.—Jug (ht. 4¾″) with the neck broken off. Coarse buff clay with a red slip. Mediæval. Unearthed in 1907-08 in the 2nd outer court of Monastery I, 1½′ below the surface.

F (*b*) 23.—Jug (ht. 5½″) or *lōṭā* with a flat bottom. The neck is partly broken. Coarse buff clay with a thin red slip. Mediæval or modern. Found in 1906-07 in Monastery I, 10′ below the surface.

F (*b*) 24.—Jug (ht. 4¾″; inner diam. at aperture 3¼″) for milk, of modern type. Buff clay over-burnt. Unearthed in the trench south of Monastery II, 8′ below the surface.

F (*b*) 25.—Small-sized jug (ht. 4¼″) with the neck damaged. Mediæval or later. Coarse buff clay with a red slip. Found in 1906-07 or 1907-08.

F (*b*) 26.—Jug (ht. 5″) which may have been meant for holding oil. It was evidently never used for that purpose. Mediæval or later. Coarse buff clay with a red slip. Unearthed in 1907-08 in the second outer court of Monastery I, 4′ below the surface.

F (*b*) 27.—Jar (ht. 6¾″) with the neck broken off. It seems to have been used in the whitewashing of houses. Coarse buff-clay. The slip has worn away. Mediæval or later. Found in 1906-07 in Monastery I, 12′ below the surface.

F (*b*) 28.—Jug (ht. 6½″; inner diam. at aperture 4¾″) with a small piece broken away from one side. Buff clay with a red slip. Mediæval or later. Unearthed in 1906-07 at the same spot as F (*b*) 6 and 7.

F(*b*) 29.—Jug (ht. 7″; inner diam. at aperture 4¾″) with the rim turned outwards. Coarse grey clay with slip. Mediæval or later. Excavated in 1906-07 in Monastery I, 4′ 6″ below the surface.[1]

F (*b*) 30.—Jug (ht. 5¾″; inner diam. at aperture 3¾″) or *lōṭā* with the rim partly damaged. Mediæval or later. Coarse red clay without slip. Discovered in 1907-08 in the western precinct of Monastery I, 5′ below the surface.

F (*b*) 31.—Jug (ht. 6⅛″; inner diam. at aperture 3⅝″) of the form of a *lōṭā*. Buff clay with a red slip which has mostly disappeared. Found in 1907-08 in the long trench east of Monastery I.

F (*b*) 32.—Jug (ht. 6¼″; inner diam. at aperture 4¼″) of the shape of a *lōṭā* of buff clay with a red slip.

---

[1] *A. S. R.*, 1906-07, Pl. XXVII, 9.

F (*b*) 33.—Jug (ht. 5¼″; inner diam. at aperture 3½″) with thick solid sides and a low flat rim, decorated around the neck with deep incised lines. Pots of this type are used at the present day for holding clarified butter. Buff clay with a red slip. Found in 1906-07 south of structure No. 23, 1½′ below the surface.

F (*b*) 34.—Pot (ht. 6¾″; inner diam. at aperture 5¼″) similar to F (*b*) 15. Rim partly broken. Coarse buff clay with traces of a red slip. Mediæval or later. Find-spot same as of F (*b*) 29.[1]

F (*b*) 35.—Jug (ht. 6½″) with sides rising straight to the middle. Such vessels are at the present time tied to the stems of palm trees to receive their juice (*tāṛī*). Mediæval or later. Coarse buff clay with traces of a red slip. Found in 1907-08 in the area north of Main Shrine, 3′ below the surface.

F (*b*) 36.—Water-jug (ht. 7″; inner diam. at aperture 4″) with a short spout at one side, similar to the present day *kūzah* of the Muhammadans. Vessels of this type are also occasionally met with in Hindu households. Buff clay with a deep red slip. Found in 1907-08 in the long trench east of Monastery I.

F (*b*) 37.—Water-jug (ht. 6½″; inner diam. at aperture 3¾″) with a spout. Fine pink clay with a slip of the same colour. Found in 1907-08 in the 2nd outer court of Monastery I, 4′ below the surface.

F (*b*) 38.—Water-jug with a spout (ht. 6″; inner diam. at aperture 3¾″). Buff clay mixed with mica or sand. Found in 1907-08 in the long trench east of Monastery I.

F (*b*) 39.—Water-jug (ht. 6¾″; inner diam. at aperture 4¼″) with four spouts at equal distances. The spouts themselves are broken. Buff clay without slip. Found in 1907-08 in the western precinct of Monastery I, 9′ below the surface.

F (*b*) 40.—Water-jug (ht. 6¼″; inner diam. at aperture 4″) of the same shape as F (*b*) 39. Buff clay with a red slip. Found in 1907-08 in the long trench east of Monastery I.

F (*b*) 41. Water-jug (ht. 7″; inner diam. at top 4″) with spout. Coarse clay mixed with sand but no slip. Found in 1907-08 in the long trench east of Monastery I.

F (*b*) 42.—Jug (ht. 6″; inner diam. at top 2¾″) or *lōṭā*. Coarse buff clay without slip. Mediæval. Found at the same spot as F (*b*) 6 and 7.

F (*b*) 43.—Jug (ht. 6½″; inner diam. at top 3¾″). The spout is broken off. The bottom is flat and ornamented with a zigzag pattern while there are incised lines around the body. Fine buff clay with a red slip. Found in 1906-07 in Monastery I, 20′ below the surface.

F (*b*) 44.—Jug (ht. 6½″; inner diam. at top 3½″) with a hole for a spout which itself is missing. Coarse reddish clay with a red slip.

---

[1] *A. S. R.*, 1906-07, Pl. XXVII, 5.

Found in 1907-08 in the trench south of the 1st outer court of Monastery I.

F (*b*) 45.—Jug (ht. 6¾"; inner diam. at aperture 2⅝") resembling a *martabān* of the present day with a spout at one side. Buff clay with a red slip. Found in western precinct of Monastery I, 4′ 6" below the surface.

F (*b*) 46.—Jug (ht. 6") with the top broken off. The spout is also missing. The body of the pot is decorated with bands of horses and cowries stamped in relief. Buff clay mixed with sand, with a coating of a red slip. Discovered in 1907-08 in the western precinct of Monastery I, 7′ below the surface.[1]

F (*b*) 47.—Jug (ht. 7¾"; inner diam. at aperture 3⅞") with one spout. Buff clay strewn with pounded mica before exposure to fire. Excavated in 1906-07 probably in Monastery I.

F (*b*) 48.—Goblet (ht. 7¾") with the neck partly broken. The bottom is flat. Around the body is a broad band of dots, and vertical lines stamped in relief and strewn over with pounded mica before firing. Buff clay with a deep red slip. Mediæval. Unearthed in 1907-08 in the western precinct of Monastery I, 6′ below the surface.[2]

F (*b*) 49.—Jug (ht. 7⅜"; inner diam. at top 4") with a spout. Buff clay with a sprinkling of mica but no slip. Mediæval. Discovered in 1906-07 in Monastery I, 10′ below the surface.[3]

F (*b*) 50.—Jug. (ht. 6⅛"; inner diam. at top 4") with a spout. Mediæval. Buff clay without slip. Unearthed in 1906-07 or 1907-08.

F (*b*) 51.—Jug (ht. 7"; inner diam. at top 3¼") with a hole for a spout. Fine pink clay with slip of the same colour which is still bright and uninjured. Found in 1907-08 in the trench crossing the south boundary wall of Monastery I, 12′ below the surface.

F (*b*) 52.—Jug (ht. 3¾"; inner diam. at top 6½") with a spout. Buff clay with traces of a red slip. Mediæval. Unearthed in 1906-07 or 1907-08.

F (*b*) 53.—Jug (ht. 7"; inner diam. at top 4") with a spout. Buff clay with a red slip and sprinkling of pounded mica. Excavated in 1907-08 in the area south of Monastery II, 4′ below the surface.

F (*b*) 54.—Small-sized goblet (ht. 5½"; inner diam. at top 2⅝") with a narrow flat bottom and a high rim. Buff clay strewn with mica. No slip. Mediæval. Excavated in one of the recent diggings.

F (*b*) 55.—Small jug (ht. 4¾") with the rim partly broken. Flat bottom. Mediæval or later. Pink clay with a thin red slip. Excavated in 1906-07 north of *stūpa* No. 45, 3′ below the surface.

---

[1] *A. S. R.*, 1907-08, p. 48, *a* 16 and fig. 4 *a*
[2] *Ibid.*, *a* 28, fig. 4 *b*.
[3] *Ibid.*, 1906-07, Pl. XXVII, 8.

F (*b*) 56.—Small jug (ht. 4¼″) with the rim broken. Spout at side. Coarse clay with traces of a slip. Found in the principal courtyard of Monastery I, 4′ 6″ below the surface.

F (*b*) 57.—Small-sized jug (ht. 4″) with a spout. Rim broken in part. Late mediæval. Coarse clay without slip. Excavated in one of the recent diggings.

F (*b*) 58.—Cooking pot or *hāṇḍī* (ht. 5¾″; inner diam. at top 6⅞″) of comparatively late date. Discovered in 1906-07 in Monastery I, 2′ below the surface.

F (*b*) 59.—Pot (ht. 5″) with the rim broken off. Such pots are now used in the United Provinces for the preparation of curds. Mediæval or later. Found in one of the recent excavations.

F (*b*) 60.—Pot (ht. 5″) with the rim broken off, similar to F (*b*) 59 but the sides are somewhat higher. Mediæval or later. Found in 1906-07 on the south of Monastery III, 10′ below the surface.

F (*b*) 61.—Pot (ht. 5¼″; inner diam. at top 8½″) with straight sides and rim turned outwards. Mediæval. Coarse clay with a red slip. Found in 1907-08 in the 2nd outer court of Monastery I, 10′ below the surface.

F (*b*) 62.—Pot (ht. 5¾″; inner diam. at top 9½″) similar to F (*b*) 61. Must have been used for cooking purposes. Mediæval. Coarse clay. The slip has disappeared. Found in 1907-08 in the 2nd outer court of Monastery I, 9′ below the surface.

F (*b*) 63.—Cooking pot (ht. 6½″; inner diam. at top 7¾″) similar to F (*b*) 62. Mediæval. Coarse clay. No slip. Found in 1906-07 in the area north-west of the Main Shrine.

F (*b*) 64.—Cooking pot (ht. 5½″; inner diam. at top 6½″) with curved sides. Mediæval. Coarse clay with red slip. Found at the same spot as F (*b*) 63.

F (*b*) 65.—Cooking pot (ht. 4½″; inner diam. at top 6″) with straight sides. Mediæval. Coarse clay. Found in one of the recent diggings.

F (*b*) 66.—Cooking pot (ht. 6″; inner diam. at top 6¼″) with high sides. Mediæval. Coarse buff clay without slip. Found in 1907-08 in the long trench east of Monastery I.

F (*b*) 67.—Cooking pot (ht. 2¾″; inner diam. at top 5¾″) of coarse buff clay without slip. Mediæval or later. Found in 1906-07 north of *stūpa* No. 44, 19′ below the surface.

F (*b*) 68.—Cooking pot of same size and style as F (*b*) 67. Found in 1907-08 in the trench to the south of Monastery II, 5′4″ below the surface.

F (*b*) 69.—Cooking pot (ht. 5½″; inner diam. at top 6″) of buff clay with a thin red slip. It does not seem to have been used. Probably late Gupta. Excavated in the western precinct of Monastery I, 10½′ below the surface.

F (*b*) 70.—Cooking pot (ht. 3¾″; inner diam. at top 5½″) of coarse clay without slip. Excavated in 1907-08 in the western precinct of Monastery I, 4′ 6″ below the surface.

F (*b*) 71.—Cooking pot (ht. 4¼″; inner diam. at top 5¼″). Buff clay with a deep red slip. Found in 1907-08 in the western precinct of Monastery I, 10′ 5″ below the surface.

F (*b*) 72.—Cooking pot (ht. 4¼″) with the top broken. Buff clay with a red slip. Found in 1907-08 in the long trench east of Monastery I.

F (*b*) 73.—Pot (ht. 3½″; inner diam. at top 4½″) which must have been used for the preparation of curds. Fine clay with a red slip. Found in 1907-08 in the 2nd outer court of Monastery I, 8′ below the surface.

F (*b*) 74.—Pot (ht. 3¼″; inner diam. at top 4¼″) of the shape of a bowl. Coarse clay with traces of slip. Found in 1907-08 in the 2nd outer court of Monastery I, 2′ below the surface.

F (*b*) 75.—Pot (ht. 3¾″; inner diam. at top 4¾″) not bigger than a bowl of ordinary size. Coarse clay with a thin slip. Mediæval or later. Excavated in 1907-08 in the 2nd outer court of Monastery I, 3′ below the surface.

F (*b*) 76.—Pot (ht. 3¼″; inner diam. at top 3¾″) with straight sides and a flat rim. Mediæval. Coarse clay without slip. Found in 1907-08 in the long trench east of Monastery I.

F (*b*) 77.—Pot or *hāṇḍī* (ht. 5″; inner diam. at top 3¾″) with round body and low flat rim. Ornamented with concentric incised lines. Coarse buff clay with traces of a red slip. Found in 1907-08 in the 2nd outer court of Monastery I, 10′ 6″ below the surface.

F (*b*) 78.—Pot (ht. 4¼″; inner diam. at top 6″) with a portion broken off. The rim is similar to that of F (*b*) 77 but the sides rise straight up. Coarse clay with traces of a slip. Found in one of the recent excavations.

F (*b*) 79-90.—Twelve cooking pots or *hāṇḍīs* of varying sizes. In form they resemble those now used for the preparation of curds in the United Provinces and are made of coarse buff clay, the slip having disappeared owing to constant exposure to fire. They must be mediæval or even much later and seem to have been excavated in 1906-07 and 1907-08.

F (*b*) 91.—Pot or *hāṇḍī* (ht. 6½″; inner diam. at top 5¾″) of the ordinary type which was found filled with shells. Mediæval or later. Coarse clay without slip. Unearthed in 1907-08 in the 2nd outer court of Monastery I, 7′ below the surface.

F (*b*) 92.—Monk's bowl (*bhikshāpātra*, ht. 5¼″; inner diam. at top 6⅝″), nearly hemispherical in shape, with the sides slightly turned inwards. There is no incised or other decoration but the cup is skilfully made of exceedingly fine clay and washed with a red slip which is quite intact to the present day. A small piece is knocked off one side. The close similarity of its style to an inscribed bowl of the Kushāṇa period unearthed in a *stūpa* at Sahēṭh-Mahēṭh in 1908-09 is unmistakable evidence of its being of the same date. Found in 1906-07 near the north-west corner of the Main Shrine.

F (*b*) 93.—Monk's alms bowl (ht. 5¼″; inner diam. at top 7¾″) of the same form as F (*b*) 92, but made of fine grey clay with a black slip or paint. Two pieces broken off from the opposite sides. Probably Maurya. Found in 1906-07 near the Aśōka Column.

F (*b*) 94.—Two fragments (ht. 5¼″) of a monk's alms-bowl identical in all respects with F (*b*) 93 and found at the same spot with it.

F (*b*) 95.—Fragment (ht. 5½″) of a monk's bowl made of the same sort of clay as F (*b*) 93 and 94. The slip has worn away on the exterior. Found in 1906-07 in the area west of the Main Shrine.

F (*b*) 96.—Cup (ht. 2¼″; inner diam. at top 4¼″) with nearly straight sides and roundish bottom, made of "fine pink clay, not baked through, with a slip of the same colour and a thin wash of darker red paint which has mostly worn off." It was discovered in 1906-07 on the level of Monastery III and is to be assigned to the Gupta period.[1] Found in 1906-07 near the south-east corner of the Monastery I, 13′ 6″ below the surface.

F (*b*) 97.—Cup (ht. 2⅛″; inner diam. at top 3⅞″) of which a portion equal to half of it is broken off. It is made of the same kind of clay as F (*b*) 96, and is adorned on the exterior with a series of lotus rosettes, dots and plain lines stamped in relief.[2] Unearthed in 1906-07 in the same place as F (*b*) 96 with which it is contemporaneous.

F (*b*) 98.—Bowl (ht. 1¾″; inner diam. at top $4\frac{7}{16}$″) with sloping sides, ornamented on the outside with the same pattern as F (*b*) 97. Coarse buff clay without slip. Found at the same place as F (*b*) 96-97.

F (*b*) 99.—Bowl or dish (ht. 2½″; inner diam. at top 8½″) with round bottom and sloping sides. A lip-like depression in the rim on one side indicates that it must have been used for doling out liquid curries. Coarse buff clay with sprinkling of mica but no slip. Construction very solid. Mediæval or later. Excavated in one of the recent diggings.

F (*b*) 100.—Bowl or *hāṇḍī* (ht. 3¼″; inner diam. at top 5¼″) with projecting rim. Made of buff clay with a red slip. Mediæval. Discovered in 1906-07 in Monastery I.

F (*b*) 101.—Bowl (ht. 2¾″; inner diam. at top 5¼″) similar to F (*b*) 100, broken on one side. Mediæval. Unearthed in the 2nd outer court of Monastery I, 8′ below the surface.

---

[1] *A.S.R.*, 1906-07, p. 86, and Pl. XXVII, 2.
[2] *Ibid.*, Pl. XXVII, 1.

F (*b*) 102.—Jug (ht. 4″; inner diam. at aperture 2½″) with roundish bottom, straight walls and a high neck with a projecting rim. Buff clay with a red slip. Found in 1907-08 in the long trench east of Monastery I.

F (*b*) 103.—Jug or *lōṭā* (ht. 5″). The sides are straight up to the middle and then slope towards the neck. Buff clay with a red slip. Found in the long trench east of Monastery I.

F (*b*) 104.—Jug (ht. 5″; inner diam. at top 3⅛″) of which the sides are nearly straight. Such vessels are used at the present day for collecting the juice of palm-trees. Mediæval or later. Excavated in 1907-08 in the 2nd outer court of Monastery I, 10′ below the surface.

F (*b*) 105.—Cup (ht. 3⅞″; inner diam. at top 3⅛″) of the form of a crucible. Coarse clay without slip. Mediæval or later. Found in one of the recent excavations.

F (*b*) 106-107.—Two jugs (ht. 3⅛″ and 4⅛″) which must have had spouts. Coarse clay. Mediæval or later. Found in 1907-08 in the trench around the south-west angle of Monastery I, some 6′ below the surface.

F (*b*) 108-113.—Six small vessels of various sizes which must have been used for holding salt, chillies, turmeric and spices. Made of buff clay with or without slip. They were all found in Monastery I in 1906-07.

F (*b*) 114-118.—Five small vessels (ht. 2½″ to 2¾″) of about the same size, which must have served the same purpose as F (*b*) 108-113. They are all made of a coarse clay and a few of them are coloured with a red slip. They seem to be mediæval in date. Excavated in the area around the south-west corner of Monastery I.

F (*b*) 119-131.—Thirteen small vessels (varying in ht. from 2″ to 4¼″) which must have been used for holding spices. They appear to be all mediæval or later and are made of very coarse clay. Unearthed during the recent excavations.

F (*b*) 132.—Jug (ht. 4″; inner diam. at aperture 2½″) with a spout. Buff clay with a red slip. Broken on one side. Found in 1907-08 in the trench north of Monastery IV.

F (*b*) 133.—Jug (ht. 3½″) with a spout. The neck is broken off. Fine grey clay with a bluish slip and some incised decoration. Presumably Gupta. Exact find-spot not known.

F (*b*) 134-140.—Seven small vessels (ht. 1⅞″ to 4″) which must have been used for the same purpose as F (*b*) 119-131. Buff clay with or without slip. Most of them must be mediæval or even much later. They were all found in 1907-08 in the 2nd outer court of Monastery I, at depths of 1′ to 11′ below the surface.

F (*b*) 141-147.—Seven small vessels (ht. 1¾″ to 3⅛″) similar to F (*b*) 134-140. Most of these have not been coloured with a slip. Excavated in 1907-08 in the long trench east of Monastery I.

F (*b*) 148-149.—Two small vessels (ht. 2½″ and 1¾″) one of which has a spout. Made of buff clay with a red slip. Mediæval. Found in the trench to the west of the Old Sculpture Shed.

F (*b*) 150.—Small vessel (ht. 2½″) of the form of a *lōṭā* made of grey clay with a black slip. Found in 1907-08 in the trench to the north of Monastery IV.

F (*b*) 151.—Small vessel (ht. 1¾″; inner diam. at aperture 1½″) of the form of a *lōṭā*. Buff clay with a thin red slip. Presumably late Gupta to judge from the depth of 13′ at which it was found in Monastery IV.

F (*b*) 152.—Lower part (ht. 2¾″) of a jug or *lōṭā*. Coarse buff clay. Exact find-spot not known.

F (*b*) 153.—Bowl (ht. 2¼″; inner diam. at top 3″) similar in shape to F (*b*) 100. The slip has mostly worn away. The vessel may have served the purpose of a lid for a water pot. Probably Gupta. Discovered in 1907-08 in the long trench east of Monastery I.

F (*b*) 154.—Bowl (ht. 1½″; inner diam. at top 2″) similar in shape to F (*b*) 153. Coarse buff clay. Found in 1907-08 in the 2nd outer court of Monastery I, 2′ below the surface.

F (*b*) 155.—Small vessel (ht. 3″) with a spout. Buff clay with a red slip. Mediæval. Find-spot not known.

F (*b*) 156.—Small jug (ht. 3¼″) similar to F (*b*) 155. Traces of a red slip. Found in 1906-07 in the area to the west of the Main Shrine.

F (*b*) 157-163.—Seven small vessels (ht. 1″ to 3¾″) found all over the site. Coarse clay. Presumably mediæval or later. Found in the recent excavations.

F (*b*) 164.—Hollow cone (ht. 4½″) of clay closed at base by a flat piece. Objects of this type are offered at the shrines of Gaṇēśa and other village and forest deities in the United Provinces as models of shrines or *kalaśas* as they are called in this province. Made of buff clay with a red slip. Excavated in 1907-08 in the 1st outer court of Monastery I.

F (*b*) 165.—Cone or *kalaśa* (ht. 5½″) similar to F (*b*) 164, broken into several fragments which have been re-fixed. Found in the same area as F(*b*) 164.

F (*b*) 166.—Earthen cone (ht. 5½″) open at base. This must also have been apparently offered as a model of a shrine to a forest deity. The style and material are coarse. Mediæval or much later. Found in 1907-08 in the 2nd outer court of Monastery I.

F (*b*) 167.—Top (ht. 6″) of a conical earthen finial of a shrine or other dwelling. Mediæval. Buff clay with a thin coating of a slip. Found in 1907-08 in the 1st outer court of Monastery I.

F (*b*) 168-170.—Three finial tops of coarse buff clay without slip. Mediæval or later. Discovered in 1907-08.

F (*b*) 171.—Crucible (ht. 4½″; inner diam. at top 6″) broad at top and round and narrow at base. Seems to be modern. Exact find-spot not known.

F (*b*) 172.—Pot (ht. 2″) with three perforated projections on the sides. This is evidently an old-fashioned ink-pot used by infants who are taught at Pāṭhaśālās to write with white clay or chalk on blackened wooden tables. The holes in the sides are meant for the string on which the pot is suspended by children when going to school. Buff clay with a red slip. Found in 1907-08 in the 1st outer court of Monastery I.

F (*b*) 173.—Lid (ht. 4½″) of a large *chāṭī* with sloping sides and a cylindrical vertical handle in the middle. The edges are broken. Buff clay without slip. Excavated in 1906-07 in the area north-west of the Main Shrine.

F (*b*) 174.—Handle of a similar lid. Buff clay with traces of a red slip. Found in one of the recent excavations.

F (*b*) 175.—Finial (ht. 7″) which seems to have been meant for presentation at a shrine. Found in one of the recent excavations.

F (*b*) 176.—Top of a finial (ht. 2¾″) of fine clay with a red slip. Found in 1906-07 near the north-east corner of the principal court of Monastery I, 13′ 8″ below the surface.

F (*b*) 177-178.—Two lids (inner diam. 3¾″ and 4″) of pots. Low solid handle in the middle. Found in one of the recent excavations.

F (*b*) 179.—Fragment (ht. 1½″) of a lid with a vase-shaped hollow handle in the middle. Found in 1907-08 in the long trench on east of Monastery I.

F (*b*) 180.—Cup (ht. 2″) broken on one side. Coarse clay without slip. Found in 1906-07 in the area to the west of the Main Shrine.

F (*b*) 181.—Mouth (ht. 4½″) of a big *chāṭī*, of buff clay. Excavated in 1907-08 in the 2nd outer court of Monastery I, 2′ below the surface.

F (*b*) 182-185.—Four lids (inner diam. 5¾″ to 7″) with sloping sides, without handles. The interior is ornamented with incised lines. Coarse clay. Evidently mediæval. Discovered in 1907-08 in the area east of Monastery I.

F (*b*) 186.—Small pot (ht. 1½″) for oil. Buff clay with a black slip. Found in 1906-07 in the monastery to the west of the Dhamēkh *stūpa*, 3′6″ below the surface.

F (*b*) 187.—Incense-burner (*dhūpadāna*, ht. 2¼″) with hollow base. No handle. Coarse buff clay with slip. Mediæval or later. Excavated in 1907-08 in the 2nd outer court of Monastery I, 10′ below the surface.

F (*b*) 188.—Incense-burner (ht. 3½″) with the base broken off. Found in 1906-07 near the north flanking wall of the eastern stair to the principal court of Monastery I, 9′ below the surface.

F (*b*) 189.—Earthen lamp (ht. 2″) with a solid flat base. The lip still retains the black marks of burning. No slip. Unearthed in 1906-07.

F (*b*) 190.—Earthen bell (ht. 2½″) with a ring handle at the top. The tongue which must also have been of clay is missing but the holes for strings by which it was suspended remain in the top. Buff clay with a red slip. Unearthed in one of the recent excavations.

F (*b*) 191.—Cylindrical block (ht. 2½″) of baked clay concave at the top which must have done duty as a stand for a pot or a lamp. Buff clay without slip. Mediæval or later. Found in 1907-08 in the trench around the south-west corner of Monastery I.

F (*b*) 192-194.—Three dabbers (Hindī *thāpī*, ht. 2¼″ and 2″) of a potter. They are of the common shape of the present day. The top is modelled into a handle. Made of buff clay. One of them was found in 1906-07 in the principal court of Monastery I, 4′ below the surface.

F (*b*) 195.—Lower part (ht. 3″) of a potter's dabber with incised lines. Coarse buff clay. Find-spot not known.

F (*b*) 196.—Lid (ht. 2¼″) of a primitive type consisting of an imperfectly baked conical lump of clay with four depressions for finger-ends. Found in one of the recent excavations.

F (*b*) 197.—Long cylindrical top (ht. 7″) of a monk's water-bottle with a very fine hole. Such fragments are found in abundance on all Buddhist sites. One complete specimen of this vessel was unearthed at Bhīṭā near Allahabad by Dr. Marshall in 1909-10. Fine buff clay with a red slip. Excavated in 1906-07 near the south-east corner of *stūpa* No. 22.

F (*b*) 198-208.—Eleven fragments of various lengths similar to F (*b*) 197. Some of them have been very highly glazed with some vitreous substance. They belong to various dates the earliest might well be assigned to the Kushāṇa and even earlier periods.

F (*b*) 209.—Rectangular baked brick (3″×2¾″×1¼″ in thickness) which must have done duty for a weight. Found in 1906-07 a few feet to the north of *stūpa* No. 43, 5′6″ below the surface.

F (*b*) 210.—Earthen ladle (Skr. *darvī*, length 3″). The handle is broken at one end. It may have been used at a Brahmanical sacrifice (*yajña* or *hōma*) or may only be a child's toy. Buff clay with traces of a slip. Mediæval or later. Excavated in the area to the east of the Main Shrine.

F (*b*) 211-222.—Twelve melting pots or crucibles of different sizes, in which metals of all sorts must have been fused and melted. They were found all over the site.

F (*b*) 223-266.—Bowls with sloping sides which must have been used by monks for eating their food from. They were found in all parts of the site, at various depths.

F (*b*) 267-410.—Bowls of smaller size which must have been used to hold curries or as lids. Found all over the site.

F (*b*) 411-449.—Earthen lamps similar in shape to F (*b*) 267-410 but smaller. Found all over the site.

F (*b*) 450.—Crucible (ht. 2") of mediæval date. Found in 1907-08.

F(*c*)—Bricks.

The bricks described below mainly reproduce decorative patterns taken from architectural stones. The commonest devices among these are variations of lotus petals and the well-known vase and palmette design which form ubiquitous elements in the ornamentation of the columns of the Gupta period.

F (*c*) 1-4.—Four bricks (average dimensons 18″ to 19″×9″ to 10″ ×3½″ to 4″) without any carving or decoration. They are made of a porous clay which exhibits a small admixture of some sort of husk. This fact coupled with their enormous size affords proof of their being very ancient, perhaps Maurya. They were probably unearthed in 1906-07.

F (*c*) 5.—Brick (17½″×11″×3″) of the same kind of clay as F (*c*) 1-4 and presumably of the same period. Excavated in one of the recent excavations.

F (*c*) 6.—Brick (18¼″×10¼″×3″) probably Maurya.

F (*c*) 7.—Brick (16¼″×11″×2¼″) with sharp edges. The material is grey clay. Probably Kushāṇa or earlier.

F (*c*) 8-18.—Eleven bricks (14½″ to 16″×7½″ to 10½″×2½″ to 3″) of porous pink clay. Probably Kushāṇa or early Gupta.

F (*c*) 19.—Fragment of a brick (length 8½″; width 10″) adorned with a lion's head spitting out foliage. This motif was apparently copied from the stone columns of the Gupta period. Unearthed in 1907-08, in the trench crossing the south boundary wall of Monastery I, 5′ below the surface.

F (*c*) 20.—Brick capital (ht. 5½″; depth 7½″) of a brick pilaster ornamented on the front with a finely executed lion's head with a moustache and a foliated crest over the forehead. Gupta period. Coloured with a red slip. Excavated in 1906-07 near the south-west corner of building No. 23 near the surface.

F (*c*) 21.—Large-sized brick or tile (length 1′ 4¾″; width 10½″) ornamented with lotus petals arranged in squares.[1] Probably Gupta. Excavated in one of the recent excavations.

F (*c*) 22.—Brick or tile (length 1′ 3″; width 9″) with decoration as in F (*c*) 21. Presumably Gupta. Unearthed in one of the recent diggings.

F (*c*) 23-29.—Seven brick-bats of varying sizes ornamented with floral decoration similar to F (*c*) 22. Gupta work. One of the bricks was found in 1906-07 in the area west of the Main Shrine, and one other near the south-east corner of the principal court of Monastery I, 7′ below the surface.

---

[1] *Cf.* Kittoo's Manuscript Drawings, Vol. I, Pl. 164, *c*.

F (c) 30.—Fragment (length 6½"; width 11") of tile with scroll-work in fine Gupta style. Discovered in one of the recent excavations.

F (c) 31.—Square tile (width 7") decorated with a well-executed lotus in relief. Gupta work. Excavated in the 2nd outer court of monastery I, 2' below the surface.

F (c) 32.—Tile (length 1'; width 9½") decorated with a half lotus in relief enclosed in a raised garland pattern. We have noticed the latter motif in connection with the Kushāṇa and Gupta stone images. Found in 1906-07 a few feet south of *stūpa* No. 22, 3' 6" below the surface.

F (c) 33-34.—Two fragments of a similar tile. The first fragment was found in 1906-07 in Monastery I, 3' below the surface; the other between *stūpas* Nos. 3 and 4.

F (c) 35.—Brick-bat (5½"×9") adorned with a garland pattern enclosing a miniature tower. Gupta style. Excavated in 1906-07 in the area on the east of the Main Shrine.

F (c) 36.—Fragment (length 8"; width 6") of a facing brick with bold scroll-pattern. Gupta work. Found in 1906-07 near the north-west corner of structure No. 23, 5' below the surface.

F (c) 37.—Tile (length 1' 2½"; width 6") ornamented with palmettes disposed in triangular fields. Gupta style. Unearthed in one of the recent excavations.

F (c) 38.—Fragment (5½"×4½") of a similar tile. Gupta style

F (c) 39.—Fragment (6½"×5") of a tile or brick with a wavy line, the intervals or curves being filled with palmettes.[1] Good Gupta work. Unearthed in one of the recent excavations.

F (c) 40.—Fragment (7¾"×5¾") of a brick or tile decorated with rows of ornamental crosses. Presumably Gupta. Unearthed in one of the recent excavations.

F (c) 41-43.—Three tiles (5"×4½") ornamented with a palm leaf pattern. Probably Gupta. The first tile was excavated in 1906-07 in the first outer court of Monastery I, 7' 5" below the surface and the third in the area north of the Main Shrine, 6' below the surface.

F (c) 44.—Corner (8"×6") of tile decorated with a lotus rosette in relief. Gupta style. Unearthed in one of the recent excavations.

F (c) 45.—Brick-bat (10"×6") with a pattern resembling that on F (c) 44. Gupta style. Find-spot not known.

F (c) 46.—Fragment (6"×4") with a cross-like pattern.[2] Found in 1906-07 in the area north-west of the Main Shrine, 2' below the surface.

---

[1] Kittoe's Manuscript Drawings, Vol. I, Pl. 164, *d*.
[2] Kittoe's Manuscript Drawings, Vol. I, Pl. 162, *g*.

F (*c*) 47.—Brick-bat (5¾″ × 4″) with palmettes and dots. Presumably Gupta. Excavated in 1906-07 between *stūpas* Nos. 3 and 4.

F (*c*) 48-50.—Three brick-bats with parallel rows of ornamental crosses. F (*c*) 50 was found in 1906-07 some 32′ north of *stūpa* No. 45, 8′ below the surface.

F (*c*) 51-56.—Six brick-bats with floral patterns similar to F (*c*) 21-22. The first fragment was found in 1906-07 to the south of the structure No. 23, 13′ below the surface and F(*c*) 54 and 56 in the area east of the Main Shrine.

F (*c*) 57.—Fragment of a circular panel with floral decoration surrounded by a border of a zigzag pattern.

F (*c*) 58.—Fragment (8″ × 6″) with a border of rosettes and other patterns. Probably late Gupta. Excavated in one of the recent diggings.

F (*c*) 59.—Fragment (7″ × 7″) similar to F (*c*) 58 in all respects. Excavated in one of the recent diggings.

F (*c*) 60.—Brick-bat with floral decoration. Excavated in 1906-07 near the south-east corner of *stūpa* No. 22.

F (*c*) 61.—Brick-bat (8½″ × 6″) with floral decoration. Probably mediæval. Found in 1907-08 in the 2nd outer court of Monastery I, 7′ below the surface.

F (*c*) 62.—Brick capital (length 1′ 2″; width 11″) of a brick pilaster broken on proper left side. It is ornamented on the front with the familiar vase and palmette[1] design in fine Gupta style. We may compare the same motive on Gupta stone columns.

Unearthed in one of the recent excavations.

F (*c*) 63-82.—Twenty brick capitals of pilasters adorned with the same ornament as on F (*c*) 62. A few of them are broken. They are all of the Gupta period. Found in 1906-07 and 1907-08 in various parts of the site.

F (*c*) 83.—Abacus (1′ ½″ square) of a pilaster ornamented on the front with a lion's head and with palmettes in the corners. Gupta style. Presumably excavated in 1904-05.

F (*c*) 84.—Brick capital (1′ 5″ × 1′ 1″) of a pilaster ornamented with a lotus pattern with a wavy line round the middle.[2] Probably Gupta. Discovered in one of the recent excavations.

F (*c*) 85-94.—Ten brick capitals of the same size bearing the same decoration as F (*c*) 84. Probably Gupta. Unearthed in different parts of the site.

F (*c*) 95.—Brick capital (ht. 5″) cut in the form of a vase ornamented with lotus petals below, and a zigzag pattern above. Probably Gupta. Discovered in one of the recent excavations.

---

[1] *Cf.* Kittoe, Drawings, Vol. I, Pl. 163, *a*, *b* and *c*.
[2] *Cf. ibid.*, Pl. 163, *i*.

F (*c*) 96-100.—Five capitals of the same kind as F (*c*) 95. Found in different parts of the site.

F (*c*) 101-107.—Seven brick capitals of different sizes ornamented on front with a lotus pattern below, and a frieze of dentils above. The upper edges are cut away. Probably Gupta work. Found all over the site.

F (*c*) 108-115.—Eight brick caps of pilasters adorned with a lotus pattern below, and a frieze of dots above. The upper edges are cut away. Probably Gupta. F(*c*) 110 was found in 1906-07 near the stair of the principal court of Monastery I, 6′ below the surface ; F(*c*) 115 in the area west of the Main Shrine and F(*c*) 111 near the north-east corner of the principal court of Monastery I, 4′ 7″ below the surface.

F (*c*) 116.—Brick capital (8″ × 7½″) ornamented on three sides with a lotus pattern and a projecting cornice above. Probably Gupta. Excavated in one of the recent diggings.

F (*c*) 117-118.—Two brick caps similar to F (*c*) 116. The second fragment was found in 1906-07 in the area north-west of the Main Shrine, 2′ 6″ below the surface.

F (*c*) 119-132.—Fourteen brick caps of different sizes, ornamented on the front with a lotus pattern below and a plain line at the top. Found all over the site.

F (*c*) 133.—Brick cap (9½″ × 9″) of a pilaster ornamented with palm leaf decoration. Upper edges cut away. Gupta or earlier. Found in one of the recent excavations.

F (*c*) 134.—Brick cap (1′ square) with identical ornamentation. Found in 1906-07 in the area west of the Main Shrine.

F (*c*) 135.—Brick cap (8½″ × 8″) similar to F (*c*) 119-132.

F (*c*) 136.—Brick cap (1′ square) of a pilaster with palm leaf decoration below, and chequer pattern above. Found in one of the recent diggings.

F (*c*) 137.—Brick cap (10¼″ × 6½″) similar to F (*c*) 136. Found in 1906-07 north of *stūpa* No. 15, 4′ below the surface.

F (*c*) 138.—Brick cap (1′ × 11½″) ornamented with lotus decoration. The upper edges are cut off. Found in one of the recent excavations.

F (*c*) 139.—Brick (9½″ × 7½″) ornamented with floral and other ornamentation.

F (*c*) 140.—Brick (1′ × 9″) with a garland pattern below, lotus decoration above. Found in one of the recent excavations.

F (*c*) 141-142.—Two fragments of caps ornamented with a floral pattern.

F (*c*) 143.—Brick cap (9″ × 5½″) of a pilaster with the projecting portion in front ornamented with a palm leaf pattern. Its upper edges are bevelled.

F (*c*) 144.—Brick cap (10″×10″) with floral decoration below, and a wavy line above.

F (*c*) 145.—Brick cap (7¾″×2¾″) of a pilaster with a floral pattern below, and a zigzag design above.

F (*c*) 146.—Brick cap (ht. 2½″) with the same kind of ornamentation as on F (*c*) 144. Unearthed in 1906-07 in the area to the west of the Main Shrine.

F (*c*) 147-185.—Bricks and brick-bats with a lotus pattern on one edge. Probably Gupta. Found all over the site.

F (*c*) 186-193.—Brick caps (ht. 3¾″ to 7½″) of pilasters with a lotus pattern.[1] Probably Gupta.

F (*c*) 194.—Brick cap (ht. 8⅜″) with the middle portions of sides cut off. Found in 1906-07 in the area to the east of the Main Shrine.

F (*c*) 195-196.—Two brick caps (ht. 5¼″ and 6″) with bevelled sides. Unearthed in recent excavations.

F (*c*) 197.—Brick cap (ht. 5½″) similar to F (*c*) 195-196 but ornamented with a chequer pattern at the top. Excavated in 1906-07 in the monastery to the west of the Dhamēkh *stūpa*, 6′ 6″ below the surface.

F (*c*) 198.—Brick cap (ht. 8½″) with floral patterns. Probably Gupta. Found in 1906-07 near *stūpa* No. 20, 1′ or 2′ below the surface.

F (*c*) 199.—Brick cap (ht. 7⅜″) with a pattern resembling the pediment of a shrine. Gupta work. Found in 1906-07 in the principal court of Monastery I, 7′ below the surface.

F (*c*) 200.—Brick cap (ht. 9¼″) adorned with an *āmalaka* and a lotus pattern. Found in 1906-07 to the south of *stūpa* No. 22.

F (*c*) 201.—Brick (length 9″; width 2¼″) with a lion's head on the front. The brick must have been employed in a frieze. Excavated in 1907-08 in the long trench east of Monastery I.

F (*c*) 202.—Brick cap (length 7″; width 6¼″) with decoration as on F (*c*) 117.

F (*c*) 203.—Fragmentary brick cap (ht. 4½″) with lotus and other patterns. Found in 1906-07 between *stūpas* Nos. 12 and 22.

F (*c*) 204.—Brick cap (ht. 4⅜″) similar to F (*c*) 89.

F (*c*) 205-211.—Brick-bats of sizes with chequer pattern.

F (*c*) 212-241.—Bricks of sizes with a pattern resembling an inverted pyramid. Found all over the site.

F (*c*) 242-243.—Two brick-bats with rows of triangular incisions disposed diagonally.

F (*c*) 244.—Two brick caps (ht. 5¾″) of octagonal pilasters.

F (*c*) 245.—Brick cap (ht. 5¾″) with a lotus rosette in a square diagram.

[1] Kittoe's Manuscript Drawings, Pl. 156, *l*.

F (c) 246.—Brick cap (ht. 5¾") with palm leaf or lotus pattern. Probably Gupta. Excavated in 1906-07 in the area south of Monastery II, 1′ or 2′ below the surface.

F (c) 247.—Brick bracket (ht. 7¾") which must have supported the ornamental cornice of a basement of some sort. It is ornamented on the front with an atlante with arms and legs bent up as in stone columns, etc. Gupta work. Excavated in 1907-08 in the long trench east of Monastery I.

F (c) 248-249.—Two brick-bats with floral pattern. Found in 1906-07 in the area west of the Main Shrine.

F (c) 250.—Brick-bat (6"×4¾") with a T-shaped device and cornices of dots above and below.

F (c) 251-253.—Three brick-bats with dog-tooth cornice.

F (c) 254.—Brick-bat (10"×8¾") with a beaded edge.

F (c) 255.—Brick (9¼"×7") with a jagged edge. Discovered in 1906-07 presumably in the area to the west of the Main Shrine.

F (c) 256.—Brick-bat (8"×3⅜") with a crenelated edge.

F (c) 257-262.—Bricks of sizes cut after the fashion of an *āmalaka*. The first fragment was found in 1906-07 in the area east of the Main Shrine and F (c) 259 and 262 near *stūpa* No. 20, 1′ to 2′ below the surface.

F (c) 263-270.—Circular bricks of sizes which may have been employed as abacuses on pilasters of basements. But the pilasters must have stood free of the wall. F (c) 270 is covered with lime. F (c) 263 and 266 were found in 1906-07 a few feet to the east of *stūpa* No. 22, 2′ to 3′ below the surface ; F (c) 265 and 270 north of the *stūpa* situated to the north of *stūpa* No. 15, 5′ below the surface and F (c) 267 near the south-east corner of structure No. 23, 12′ below the surface.

F (c) 271.—Circular brick (diam. 6¼") with a hole in the centre which may have been employed to receive the tenon of a finial.

F (c) 272-273.—Two brick-bats of similar type. Excavated in 1906-07 between *stūpas* Nos. 16 and 17, 3′ below the surface.

F (c) 274-277.—Circular bricks with bevelled edges, evidently abacuses or bases of finials. F (c) 276 was excavated in 1906-07 near the north-west corner of *stūpa* No. 17, 9′ below the surface.

F (c) 278.—Brick (10"×7") with the front edge cut off. It must have surmounted a pilaster in a basement.

F (c) 279-284.—Finials of sizes, conical in shape. All carved with a chisel. F (c) 279 was discovered in 1906-07 at the same spot as F (c) 265 and F (c) 284 in structure No. 23, 5′ 6" below the surface.

F (c) 285.—Brickbat (6"×4¾") with nicely cut floral decoration.

F (c) 286.—Fragment (ht. 5¼") of a terra-cotta column with floral decoration.

F (c) 287 —Brick abacus (height 2") similar to F (c) 278.

F (*c*) 288.—Final (ht. 9¼″) of the form of a cone. It was covered with plaster, which still adheres to it. Mortice hole on underside to receive the tenon of a lower member or base.

F (*c*) 289-291.—Three terra-cotta finials with a lotus pattern cut in plaster on them. They are conical in shape and to judge from style of Gupta date. Discovered in 1906-07 in the area west of the Main Shrine.

F (*c*) 292.—Piece of plaster (diam. 7″) carved with a floral pattern. Gupta. Excavated in 1904-05.

F (*c*) 293-311.—Fragments of plaster decoration with floral and other patterns. Found in 1904-05 and 1906-07 in the area around the Main Shrine.

* F (*c*) 312.—Brick (6¾″ square) carved on one face with a lotus pattern. On upper face, in Gupta characters the word *śaraṇa*. Discovered in 1906-07 a few feet to the east of *stūpa* No. 22.

F (*c*) 313.—Terra-cotta finial (ht. 4¾″) shaped like an *āmalaka* fruit in the middle. In the upper portion there was a floral pattern. Gupta. Found in 1907-08 in the trench crossing the south boundary wall of Monastery I, 9′ below the surface.

F (*c*) 314.—Brick cap (ht. 5″) of the vase and palmette type. Gupta style. Found in 1906-07 in the area north-west of the Main Shrine, 4′ below the surface.

* F (*c*) 315.—Brick (1′ 3″×6″) incised with one line of writing in the eastern variety of the northern Gupta script which reads *Prakulasya*. Found in 1907-08 to the south of the Main Shrine.

F (*c*) 316.—Face-brick (ht. 5½″ ; width 10½″) adorned with a couchant lion with its head turned backward and spitting pearls. Good Gupta style. It must have been cast in a mould. Unearthed in one of the recent excavations.

F(*d*)—Inscribed terra-cotta objects.

Seal-dies.

*F(*d*) 1.—Seal die of baked clay of circular shape 1⅜″ in diameter and surrounded by a deeply incised circular line. The upper portion of the face, which is separated from the lower by a double horizontal line, shows a row of three *stūpas*, the central one being larger than the others and adorned with streamers. The lower portion contains the Buddhist creed, *yē dharmā, etc.*, in four lines in characters of the Gupta period.

The die was furnished at the back with a handle which is broken off. It must have been used for the production of mementos for pilgrims visiting Sārnāth, but no impressions made with it have apparently so far been found.

Found in 1906-07 in the monastery area ; the exact find-spot is not known.

*F(*d*) 2.—Fragment of a circular die, ⅞″ in diameter, in sun-dried clay, containing the Buddhist creed in six lines in reversed characters of about the 8th century A. D.

Found in 1906-07 in the area east of the Main Shrine.

*F(*d*) 3.—Tablet of sun-dried clay, ¾″ in diameter, containing the greater part of the Buddhist creed in three lines in countersunk reversed characters of about the 7th century A. D. We may suppose that the tablet was intended to be baked.

Found at the same spot as F(*d*) 32-33.

Seals of the principal Gandhakuṭī.

*F(*d*) 4.—Unbaked clay sealing. The inscribed surface was circular, 1½″ in diameter. More than half the sealing is missing. The surface was divided into two halves by a straight line across the middle. The upper half was occupied by a wheel with a deer couchant on either side, which as we noticed above in connection with the sculptures is the symbol of the first sermon of Gautama Buddha at the Deer-park. The deer on the proper right side is missing and that on the other side faces away from the wheel and not towards it as is generally the case.

The lower half of the face contained a legend of two lines in characters of the Gupta period. The first line is obliterated ; the extant portion of the 2nd line reads [*saṁ*] *ghasya*. It is difficult to guess what the complete reading was. If the sealing belonged to the Sārnāth monastery or the Deer-park, the legend might have been [*Śrī-saddharmma-chakkrē bhikshu*]*saṁghasya*,[1] " of the community of friars of the illustrious Dharmmachakkra " by which name we know the Sārnāth

[1] *Cf.* Seals found at Kasiā, *A. S. R.*, 1906-07, pp. 62-63.

monastery was known down to the time of king Gōvindachandra of Kanauj. The back of the sealing shows two impressions of a tape or cord of a very rough fabric. It is thus evident that the sealing must have been attached to a letter or a parcel.

The sealing was discovered in 1906-07 in the area to the north-west of the Main Shrine.

*F(*d*) 5.—Tablet of baked clay. The inscribed surface is nearly circular, ⅞" in diameter. The upper half, which is separated from the lower by a double horizontal line, shows a wheel between a pair of deer couchant, symbolizing the Buddha's first sermon at the Deer-park. The legend which occurs in the lower half reads [*Śrī*] *saddharmma*. The sealing belonged to the principal gandhakuṭī of Gautama Buddha at the monastery of Sārnāth. This is evidenced by the fact that the other sealings of this type bear the legend

l. 1. *Śrī saddharmmachakkrē=mū-*

l. 2. *la-gandhakuṭyāṁ Bhaga-*

l. 3. *vata*[*ḥ*] which means "In the principal Gandhakuṭī of the Exalted One in the illustrious Saddharmmachakkra".[1] Unfortunately all these sealings have disappeared. A similar sealing was found by General Cunningham.[2] The characters of the inscription belong to the 6th or 7th century A. D. In this legend Saddharmmachakkra is the name of the whole Sārnāth monastery by which name it continued to be known down to the time of king Gōvindachandra of Kanauj. The *mūlagandhakuṭī* [3] has not yet been identified. But lamp posts bearing the name of and belonging to this shrine have already been found.

The tablet has no string marks on the back and is one of the class of tokens which pilgrims to Sārnāth would take away to their houses as mementos of their visits to this sacred site. It is for this reason that the tablet is baked and not merely dried. It was found in 1906-07 in the area to the west of the Main Shrine.

*F (*d*) 6.—Tablet of baked clay, the inscribed surface being 1" in diameter, similar to F (*d*) 5; but the legend is rubbed off.

Found in 1906-07, in the long room south of the entrance chamber of Monastery I, 4′ 6″ below the surface.

*F (*d*) 7.—Tablet of baked clay, ¾" in diameter, of the same type as F (*d*) 5. The wheel-and-deer symbol is partly preserved in the upper half; but the legend is rubbed off. Discovered in 1906-07. The exact find-spot is not known.

*F (*d*) 8.—Tablet of baked clay. The inscribed surface is rectangular measuring ¾"×½". The upper half contains a pair of feet (*pādukā*);

---

[1] *A. S. R.*, 1906-07, pp. 75 and 97

[2] *Ibid.*, Vol. I, pl. XXXIV, 6.

[3] *Ibid.*, 1906-07, p. 95, II; and p. 97, V.

the lower half the legend °*ghasya*. The first syllable is obliterated. The tablet is of the class of votive sealings meant for pilgrims' mementos.

Found in 1906-07 at the foot of *stūpa* No. 37 in the area east of the Main Shrine.

Votive Stūpas and Tablets.

*F (*d*) 9.—Miniature *stūpa* of baked clay, 2¼" high, with a flat circular bottom. The base has the shape of a bowl. The drum is of the usual cylindrical form and the *hti* or finial is broken off. Inside the *stūpa* near the bottom is inserted a little tablet with the Buddhist creed as is proved by other *stūpas* of this type which were found in a broken condition. The *stūpa* dates from about the 10th century A. D. Such *stūpas* were made in India in abundance in the time of Hiuen Thsang, and were called *dharma-śarīra*.[1] That such *stūpas* were frequently built into larger ones is shown by the fact that the core of *stūpa* No. 40 to the north-east of the Main Shrine at Sārnāth was, in the main, constructed of *stūpas* of unbaked clay.[2] Similar *stūpas* were also unearthed by Dr. Marshall in 1905-06 at Rājagṛiha.[3]

Found in 1904-05. The exact find-spot is not known.

*F (*d*) 10.—Miniature *stūpa* of baked clay, 1½" high, similar to F (*d*) 9. The finial is missing and the bottom is also broken off thus revealing the little tablet bearing the Buddhist creed, which is inserted in it. The inscription on this tablet consists of five lines, the letters being very small. The characters of the inscription belong to *Cir.* 10th century A. D. The *stūpa* was found in 1904-05 in the area around the Main Shrine.

*F (*d*) 11.—Miniature *stūpa* of baked clay, 1⅜" high, similar to F (*d*) 9-10. The finial is missing and as the base is also broken off, the inscribed tablet let into it is exposed to view. The inscription on it contains as usual the Buddhist creed in five lines in extremely minute reversed (?) characters of the same date as those in F (*d*) 9 and 10.

Discovered in 1904-05 in the area around the Main Shrine.

*F (*d*) 12.—Miniature *stūpa* identical with F (*d*) 11.

*F (*d*) 12 (*a*).—Oval-shaped tablet in baked clay which must have been originally let into the bottom of a diminutive *stūpa* similar to those described above. The inscribed surface is oval, measuring ⅝" along the major axis. The inscription which comprises five lines of minute writing consists of the Buddhist creed. The characters are attributable to *Cir.* 10th century A. D.

Found in 1904-05 in the area around the Main Shrine and the Jagat Singh *stūpa*.

---

1 Beal, *Buddhist Records of the Western World*, Vol. II, p. 146

2 *A. S. R.*, 1906-07, p. 80 seq.

3 *Ibid.*, 1905-06, p. 97.

*F (*d*) 13.—Diminutive *stūpa* or *dharma-śarīra* of sun-dried clay, 1¼″ high. The plinth is square, 1½″ along each side. The *hti* is broken off. The tablet bearing the creed which is let into the bottom is, of course, not visible. The *stūpa* dates from the mediæval period.

Found in 1907-08 in the trench crossing the south boundary wall of Monastery I, 6′ below the surface.

*F (*d*) 14.—Diminutive *stūpa* of sun-dried clay similar to F (*d*) 13 in all respects. The bottom is damaged thus making the creed tablet inside partly visible.

Found at the same spot as F (*d*) 13.

F (*d*) 15-18.—Four diminutive *stūpas* in sun-dried clay in fragmentary condition. Their heights vary from 1″ to 1¾″. They have all lost the creed tablets, but are evidently of the same date as F (*d*) 13 and 14, and were also found at the same spot.

*F (*d*) 19.—Elliptical tablet of sun-dried clay measuring 2¾″ × 2¼″ convex on the back. A small piece is missing at the proper left upper corner and the rest is broken into four pieces. The die-surface is surrounded by an elliptical raised line. In the centre of the composition we notice Gautama Buddha seated cross-leged on a conventional lotus flower in the attitute of expounding the law (*dharmmachakkramudrā*). He has, as usual, long ear-lobes and a prominent protuberance (*ushṇīsha*) of the skull. To the right of the Buddha is a Bōdhisattva standing on a lotus flower with his right hand hanging down at the side. This figure is partly defaced, but the one to the left of the Buddha is well preserved and shows the Bōdhisattva Padmapāṇi standing on a lotus flower with his right hand hanging down in the gift-bestowing attitude (*varadamudrā*) and his left holding the stalk of a lotus. We may assume that the figure on the other side of the Buddha must be one of Maitrēya. Each of these figures is surrounded by an elliptical line which may represent the halo, or a chapel. The lower portion of the tablet contains the Buddhist creed in two lines. The forms of the letters are not clear but the style of the figures in the upper portion of the tablet is probably of the late Gupta period. Below the inscription is a pair of indistinct symbols which judged from the analogy of a similar figure [F (*d*) 20] must have been two pitchers (*ghaṭas*).

Found in 1907-08 in the trench crossing the south boundary wall of Monastery I, 6′ below the surface.

*F (*d*) 20.—Two fragments of an oval-shaped sun-dried clay tablet measuring about 3″ along the major axis, and convex at the back. The upper part of the surface is taken up by a figure of Buddha seated cross-legged in the attitude of expounding the law, with remnants of Bōdhisattvas standing on both sides. Of the inscription beneath the three figures, only a few syllables remain. The tablet belongs to the same period as F (*d*) 19 and was found at the same spot.

F (*d*) 21.—Fragment ($1\frac{3}{4}'' \times 1\frac{1}{8}''$) of a tablet of sun-dried clay. The subject depicted was, apparently, Gautama Buddha's enlightenment at Gayā, which in sculpture is represented by the temptation of the Sage by the Evil One. The extant portion of the tablet only shows the head of the Buddha under the arch of a shrine (*chaitya*) surmounted with a tapering spire (*śikhara*), on the front of which we notice a miniature *stūpa*. On grounds of technique, the tablet may be assigned to the mediæval period. Found in 1906-07 in the entrance chamber of Monastery I, 4′ below the surface.

*F (*d*) 22.—Oval tablet of well-baked clay with a raised rim $\frac{1}{4}''$ high. The inscribed surface which is also oval measures $1\frac{1}{2}'' \times 1\frac{1}{4}''$, and contains eighteen lines of closely executed writing in very minute characters. The 10th and 11th lines are divided in the middle by a very small *stūpa*. From the four lines in the beginning and the last four lines which I have read I am led to think that the legend consists entirely of salutations to Gautama Buddha under some of his principal appellations followed by the Buddhist creed which begins at the end of the 15th line. The characters belong to about the 9th century A. D. The die with which this tablet was stamped has not been found but the excavations brought to light three other fragmentary impressions [F (*d*) 23-25] of the same die.

Found in 1907-08 in Monastery IV.

*F (*d*) 23-25.—Three fragmentary tablets of sun-burnt clay which were produced with the same die as F (*d*) 22. One of these was found in the area west of the Main Shrine and the other two in spoil earth.

*F (*d*) 26.—Oval tablet of half-burnt clay. The die-surface measures $\frac{3}{4}'' \times \frac{5}{8}''$ and contains the Buddhist creed in 6 lines. The characters belong to about the 8th century A. D.

Found in 1906-07 in the area west of the Main Shrine.

*F (*d*) 27.—Circular tablet of half-burnt clay. The die-surface is $\frac{3}{4}''$ in diameter and contains the Buddhist creed in five lines. The characters belong to about the 9th century A. D. Found in 1907-08 in the western precinct of Monastery I, 6′ below the surface.

*F (*d*) 28.—Circular tablet of half-burnt clay. The die-surface is elliptical measuring $\frac{7}{8}'' \times \frac{3}{4}''$, and contains the Buddhist creed in five lines. The characters belong to about the 8th century A. D. Found in 1906-07 in the area to the north-west of Monastery I.

*F (*d*) 29.—Circular tablet of well-burnt clay, $\frac{3}{4}''$ in diameter, containing the Buddhist creed in five lines in characters of the 9th or 10th century A. D.

Found in 1907-08 in the area between the Main Shrine and Monastery I, 3′ 6″ below the surface.

*F (*d*) 30.—Fragment of a sun-dried clay tablet, $\frac{7}{8}''$ in diameter, stamped with the Buddhist creed in characters of *Cir.* 7th century A. D. Find-spot not known.

*F (*d*) 31.—Circular tablet of slightly burnt clay. The die-surface, which is $\frac{5}{8}''$ in diameter, contains the Buddhist creed in five lines in characters of the 7th or 8th century A. D.

Found in 1906-07 in the narrow chamber south of the entrance chamber of Monastery I, 4′ 6″ below the surface.

*F (*d*) 32-33.—Two impressions of sun-dried clay produced with the same die. The die-surface is circular, 1″ in diameter, and shows a row of three *stūpas* above and traces of the Buddhist creed (?) in the exergue. Mediæval period. Found in the trench crossing the south boundary wall of Monastery I, 9′ below the surface.

*F (*d*) 34.—Sun-dried clay tablet, die-surface $\frac{3}{8}''$ in diameter, containing the Buddhist creed in four lines. The tablet must have been let into the bottom of a diminutive *stūpa* (*dharmaśarīra*). Found at the same spot as F (*d*) 32-33.

*F (*d*) 35.—Sun-dried clay tablet of the same kind as F (*d*) 34. Found at the same spot as F (*d*) 32-33.

*F (*d*) 36.—Sun-dried clay tablet with oval face, measuring $\frac{1}{2}'' \times \frac{3}{8}''$ and stamped with the Buddhist creed in four lines. The characters seem to be of about the 8th century A. D. Found in one of the recent excavations.

*F (*d*) 37.—Fragment of a sun-dried clay tablet, $\frac{1}{2}'' \times \frac{3}{8}''$, containing the latter portion of the Buddhist creed, in characters of about the 9th century A. D. Found near the south wall of the stair of Monastery I, 4′ 4″ below the surface.

*F (*d*) 38.—Terra-cotta tablet, circular in shape, $\frac{3}{4}''$ in diameter, stamped with the Buddhist creed in four lines. The characters are small and attributable to the 8th or 9th century A. D.

Found in 1906-07 in Monastery I.

*F (*d*) 39-50.—Thirteen tablets of sun-dried clay produced with the same die. Only three specimens are complete. The die-surface is oval, measuring $1\frac{1}{4}''$ by $1\frac{1}{8}''$. The upper portion contains a row of three *stūpas*, the middle one slightly larger than the others. The lower portion contains the Buddhist creed in five lines in characters of *Cir.* 7th century A. D.

Found in the trench crossing the south boundary wall of Monastery I, 9′ below the surface.

*F (*d*) 51.—Circular tablet of half-burnt clay, 1″ in diameter. It is stamped with an inscription of seven lines containing the Buddhist creed followed by some writing which cannot be made out. The characters belong to about the 9th century A. D.

Found in 1906-07 in the area east of the Main Shrine.

***F (*d*) 52.—Oval-shaped tablet of sun-dried clay, measuring ¾″ × ⅝″, containing an impression of die No. F (*d*) 3. Found in one of the recent excavations.**

***F (*d*) 53.—Tablet of baked clay. The stamped surface is circular, ½″ in diameter, and contains traces of six syllables which cannot be deciphered. Find-spot not known.**

Personal Seals.

*F (*d*) 54.—Irregularly shaped mass of clay, 1¼″ high. The upper surface is stamped with three impressions of the same die. The inscribed surface is circular, ⅝″ in diameter, and shows a rosette above and the legend *Apramāda* below. The characters of the legend are of the 6th or 7th century A. D. The same legend also occurs on a seal [1] found at Kasiā.

Apramāda is probably a proper name. In its general sense the word means 'diligence' which in the Besnagar pillar inscription is enumerated among the three paths to immortality (*amata-padāni*).

The underside of the mass bears string marks thus showing that it was attached to a parcel. The clay is not burnt, but it has been evidently exposed to fire.

Found in 1904-05 somewhere in the area around the Main Shrine and the Jagat Singh *stūpa*.

*F (*d*) 55.—Circular tablet of slightly burnt clay, the die-surface being ¾″ in diameter. The legend which is stamped across the face in characters of the 8th or 9th century A. D. reads *Śīladēvaḥ*. The back of the tablet is, as usual, convex. Found in 1906-07 in Monastery I.

Non-inscribed Seals.

F (*d*) 56.—Circular tablet made of sun-dried clay. The die-surface is ⅝″ in diameter and is surrounded by a single line. There is no legend but in the lower portion we have possibly a figure of a deer (?) couchant facing to proper left.

Found in 1906-07 in Monastery I.

F (*d*) 57-60.—Four tablets of baked clay, ⅞″ to 1⅜″ in diameter. They are stamped with a wheel without any legend. The wheel possibly represents "the wheel of the law."

Find-spot is not known.

---

[1] *A. S. R.*, 1906-07, p. 63, No. 13.

G.—OLD SCULPTURE SHED.

The sculptures exhibited in the Old Sculpture Shed, which was erected in 1905, do not originate from Sārnāth. They were formerly reserved in the Queens' College, Benares, and were removed to Sārnāth at the instance of His Excellency Lord Curzon, then Viceroy of India. The provenance of most of these sculptures has been ascertained from a volume of manuscript drawings prepared by Major Kittoe about 60 years ago.

G 1.—Slab (ht. 3′ 1″; width 1′ 7″) representing the Hindu triad of Brahmā, Vishṇu and Mahēśa in a single image, with three faces and six arms. All hands which must have held the different attributes of these deities are lost. The figure is profusely decorated with ornaments, and has a male attendant at either side. The bull Nandi, the vehicle of Śiva, appears on the top of the base at the proper right side, while the goose who carries Brahmā, the creator, is portrayed at the other end. The vehicle of Vishṇu is depicted on the front of the base. It seems to be three horses, perhaps in allusion to the Vaidika character of this deity.

On grounds of style the sculpture is assignable to the late mediæval period. Provenance is not known. It is not portrayed in Major Kittoe's Manuscript Drawings. The material is Chunār sandstone.

G 2.—Fragmentary sculpture (ht. 3′ 7½″; width 3′ 7½″). To the proper left we see the goddess Yamunā standing facing on her vehicle, the tortoise. The face of the goddess is broken off. She wears an undergarment which reaches down to her ankles. Her upper body is bare, but she wears circular ear-ornaments, a necklace, armlets and other trinkets. Between her hands is a garland (?). To her left is shown a kneeling worshipper; to her right, a female holding a fly-whisk (Sanskrit *chāmara*) in her right hand. Further to the right is a larger female figure holding an umbrella over Yamunā's head. The top of the umbrella is missing. In the back-ground of the sculpture, we notice a headless female, carrying a basket (?) at her right side.

To the proper right of the sculpture are the feet of a male figure with those of a smaller female figure. On the front of the base, behind the tortoise, is a little cupid with a long tail running along the entire width of the slab. Chunār sandstone.

The carving is particularly vigorous and I have no doubt that it dates from the Gupta period. Dr. Vogel is of opinion that this sculpture came from Bhītargāon.

G 3.—Sculpture (ht. 2′ 8″; width 1′ 10″) representing Śiva seated in easy attitude on a high cushion with his consort Pārvatī sitting on his left thigh. The heads of both and the right leg of the god are wanting. They are both profusely ornamented. Śiva has four arms, the goddess only two, one of which is thrown round Śiva's neck. To right and left, we notice an attendant; the one on the proper left holds a trident (the attribute of Śiva), the other has presumably a fly-whisk. The smaller figures in front of these attendants must be the donor and his wife. The bull and the lion, the vehicles of Śiva and his wife respectively are delineated on the top of the base. The dancing figure between them cannot be identified. Pale buff stone of Chunār. The sculpture is mediæval in style. Its find-place is not known.

G 4.—Slab (ht. 2′ 10½″; width 2′) representing Śiva and Pārvatī standing side by side with their arms thrown round each other. Śiva has a high head-dress and four arms, two of which are visible. One of these, *i.e.*, the upper right one, holds the trident (*triśūla*) and the other, the upper left, a three-hooded snake. Mediæval. Chunār sandstone. Sketched in Major Kittoe's Manuscript Drawings where it is labelled as "Śiva Pārvatī, fragment of a Śaiva temple Kuntil."[1] Perhaps Kuntil is the name of the place from which the sculpture was obtained.

G 5.—Slab (ht. 2′ 2″; width 1′ 7″) showing a male and a female figure standing after the fashion of G 4, probably Śiva and Pārvatī. The sculpture is much chipped. To the proper right of the group is a male attendant and to the left a female.

Chunār sandstone. Mediæval. Find-place not known.

G 6.—Slab (ht. 2′ 5″; width 1′ 10″). To proper left we notice Śiva standing facing. He has four arms. The upper right arm is broken off, while the lower right holds the staff of the trident. The upper left hand has a snake; the fourth hand is damaged. To the proper right of Śiva is a female standing, apparently Pārvatī. The miniature figure between her and her husband cannot be recognised. The faces of both the deities are broken.

Mediæval style. Chunār sandstone. Provenance not known.

G 7.—Slab (ht. 3′ 3″; width 1′ 6½″) with a four-armed figure of Śiva standing to front. His upper right hand and face are broken off, while the lower right hand holds the staff of his trident. The upper right hand holds a snake while the lower hand rests on the hip. The left leg of the image is missing. At its right side, we notice the bull Nandi couchant.

Mediæval. Buff-coloured sandstone of Chunār. Provenance unknown.

G 8.—Slab (ht. 3′ 3″; width 1′ 8″) with a four-armed figure of Śiva standing. His face, three hands and left leg are broken off. Around his head is a circular halo. The upper right hand seems to hold

---

[1] Vol I, pl. 60, No. 34.

a flower (?). The god is profusely decorated with ornaments. His vehicle, the bull Nandi, is crouching at his right side. Mediæval. Buff-coloured sandstone of Chunār. Provenance not known.

G 9.—Slab (ht. 2′ 8″; width 9½″) showing a four-armed figure of Mahādēva standing facing. His three hands are broken off. The fourth, or upper left one, holds a snake. The right leg of the image between the knee and the foot is missing. The bull is crouching at the proper left side. Mediæval. Chunār sandstone. Provenance not known.[1]

G 10.—Fragmentary sculpture (ht. 1′ 5½″; width 1′ 3½″) with the legs of a standing figure of Śiva. To his right, the bull Nandi, couching. To left, part of a kneeling human figure. Mediæval. Chunār sandstone. Find-place not known.

G 11.—Slab (ht. 2′ 5½″; width 1′ 7½″) with a group of three headless figures standing side by side. The two figures at the proper right end, a female and a male embracing each other must be Śiva and Pārvatī. The third figure is persumably an attendant. Mediæval. Chunār sandstone. The sculpture is from a Śiva temple in the old fort of Benares.[2]

G 12.—Lower part (ht. 2′ 6½″; width 1′ 8½″) of a column with rectangular niches on three sides. One of the niches contains a combined figure of Śiva and Pārvatī (Ardhanārīśvara) in which the proper right half is male, the other half female (*vāmāngī*). The head is broken in part. Of the four hands, the lower left rests on the head of a tiny figure.[3]

In the middle niche, we notice Śiva sitting to front on his vehicle, the bull Nandi. The staff in his left hand is probably of the trident. The third niche contains a Śiva-linga placed on a moulded pedestal.

The style of the sculpture is of the late Gupta period. Chunār sandstone. Major Kittoe informs us that this sculpture was found in Benares.[4]

G 13.—Lower part (ht. 2′ 3″; width 1′ 7″) of a door-jamb. On one side, is carved a four-armed male figure standing to front. Its head and hands are missing. At the proper left side of the sculpture is the head of a crocodile (*makara*).

On other face, four-armed Śiva standing. His face is cut off and all hands missing. His vehicle, Nandi, crouches at his proper left side.

Mediæval. Chunār sandstone. Provenance not known.

---

[1] Sketched in Kittoe's Manuscript Drawings, Vol. I, Pl. 96, No. 23.
[2] Kittoe's Manuscript Drawings, Vol. I, Pl. 48-A, No. 30.
[3] For this figure see Kittoe's Manuscript Drawings, Vol. I, Pl. 125, No. 22.
[4] Manuscript Drawings, Vol. I, Pl. 45 *d*, No. 42.

G 14.—Lower part (ht. 2′ 1″; width 1′ 7½″) of a door-jamb or pilaster. One of the two carved faces presents Śiva standing to front with his vehicle, the bull Nandi, at his proper left side.

The male figure on the other face has four hands all of which are broken off. It appears to be quite nude. The face which is damaged seems to have been of a boar. Is the figure to be identified as the Boar incarnation of Vishṇu (?) The figure lying behind his feet may then be the earth goddess whom he rescued from the ocean.

Mediæval. Chunār sandstone. Provenance not known.

G 15.—Lower part (ht. 3′ 3″; width 1′ 9″) of a door jamb or pilaster. On the front, in a niche, is a goddess standing, giving an uncertain object to a tiny figure, at her right side. Her left hand holds a flower (?) To the proper right of the goddess, we notice a male figure (Śiva ?) holding a skull-mace in its left hand. The female figure to the proper left of the goddess cannot be identified.

On the proper left flank of the column is carved another female figure. Mediæval. Chunār sandstone. Provenance not known.

G 16.—Two fragments (ht. 1′ 3″; width 1′ 5½″) showing a bust of Śiva in his terrific aspect. He has two tushes, a third eye on his forehead and a halo of flames around his head, and wears a garland of skulls (*muṇḍamālā*) over his head. Mediæval. Chunār sandstone. Find-place not known.

G 17.—Lower part (ht. 3′ 3″; width 1′ 3″) of a pilaster or door-jamb. At the base is a group of two figures. The four-armed male figure to the proper left holds a trident and a snake and must be Śiva. His bull we see crouching behind him. The other figure, I take to be Pārvatī. The carving in the upper part of the column follows the style of the carvings of the mediæval Monastery I at Sārnāth.

Chunār sandstone. Sketched in Major Kittoe's Manuscript Drawings.[1]

G 18.—Slab (ht. 2′ 2″; width 1′ 5″) with a figure of Gaṇēśa, characterised by elephantine trunk and ears, seated in easy style. He has four hands; the upper right holds an axe (?); upper left a flower (?); lower hands are damaged. On either side of the deity is an attendant. The much-defaced figure under the deity's right leg may have been meant for his vehicle, a rat.

The sculpture seems to be of mediæval date. Chunār sandstone of reddish colour. Find-place not known.

G 19.—Pedestal with a bull couchant (ht. 1′ 5½″; width 1′ 2″). Head lost. Necklace around the neck. Traces of human figure on back. The bull may have done duty as Nandi in a Śaiva sanctuary. Chunār sandstone. Find-place not known.

---

[1] Vol. I, Pl. 140 *b*, No. 24. The find-place is not indicated.

G 20.—Pedestal with a couchant bull (ht. 10½"; width same) similar to H 19. Traces of human figure on back; another figure in the act of climbing its proper right side.

Chunār sandstone. Provenance not known.

G 20 (*a*).—Fragmentary pedestal with a bull couchant (height 1' 3"). The bull's head is missing. Between its feet we notice a headless male figure seated cross-legged facing to the front and with hands folded before the chest. Mediæval period. Chunār sandstone of buff colour. Provenance not known.

G 21.—Slab (ht. 10¾"; width 1' 4") with a figure of Gaṇēśa standing. Legs from thighs downwards wanting. He has four arms, the upper left holds a flower, while the lower left hand rests on the hip. The objects in the right hands cannot be distinguished. Probably mediæval. Chunār sandstone. Find-place not known.

G 22.—Lower part (ht. 3' 6"; width 1' 9½") of a pilaster. On the front, in a niche, is a two-armed figure of a goddess, perhaps Pārvatī. To her right we notice a standing figure, much defaced. The proper left flank of the column shows a female standing holding a water-pot in her left hand, presumably a river goddess.

G 23.—Fragment (ht. 1' 8¾"; width 1' 3") of a pilaster. On one face, a male corpulent figure seated in Indian style. He has a goat's head and four hands. Upper right hand holds a staff or other object, lower right, a rosary (?) In upper left hand, we notice a manuscript (*pustaka*) and in lower left a water-pot (*kamaṇḍalu*). There is a similar figure in the Indian Museum. I identify it as Daksha whose head was cut off by Mahādēva and was afterwards replaced by that of a he-goat. Another figure of the same kind is carved on the adjoining face of the pilaster.

Mediæval. Chunār sandstone. Provenance not known.

G 24.—Upper part (ht. 2' 10"; width 11½") of a pillar, square at base and top and octagonal in the middle. The octagonal portion has a niche with a trefoil arch on each face. These niches contain standing figures of deities. I can identify the following five :—

(*a*) Brahmā, wearing a *dhōtī* and a conical headdress recognised by a water-pot (*kamaṇḍalu*) in his left hand.

(*b*) Varuṇa similarly dressed. His attribute is a noose (Sanskrit *pāśa*) which he holds in his right hand.

(*c*) Kuvēra (?) holding a purse in his left hand. We also notice a vase at his left side.

(*d*) Vishṇu holding a conch (*śaṁkha*) in his left hand.

(*e*) Śakra who holds his emblem thunderbolt (Sanskrit *vajra*) in his right hand.

The sculpture seems to date from the early mediæval period. The material is Chunār sandstone. Provenance not known.

G 25.—Pilaster (height 2′ 1″). The projecting pilaster has three figures. The lowest one which is shown as flying has the hair treated in curls and has the protuberance of the skull (*ushṇīsha*). The middle figure represents a four-armed goddess, whose upper left hand holds an arrow while the lower left rests on the abdomen. The other two hands hold uncertain objects. The uppermost figure has lost the upper half. The panels in the proper left portion of the stone contain four-armed figures of a boar-headed goddess. Mediæval period. Reddish sandstone from Chunār. Provenance not known.

G 26.—Lower part (ht. 1′ 10½″) of a column, bearing a four-armed figure of a goddess seated with the right leg hanging down. Her arms are broken off. To her proper left stands a river-goddess recognized by a water-pot in her right hand. Mediæval period. Buff-coloured sandstone of Chunār. Provenance not known.

G 27.—Slab (ht. 1′ 6″; width 10¾″) representing a much damaged four-armed goddess seated on a human figure which lies on the pedestal. Mediæval period. Buff-coloured sandstone of Chunār. Provenance not known.

Vaishṇava images.

G 28.—Four-armed image (ht. 2′ 8″; width 1′ 2″) of Vishṇu standing facing. His head and feet are broken off. The deity wears a lower garment, a necklace and bracelets and a long flower-garland reaching down to a little below the knees. The upper arms are broken off. Vishṇu's left hand rests on the head of a male deity with an oval halo, while to his right stands a female figure. On grounds of style the sculpture may be assigned to the Gupta period.

The material is buff-coloured sandstone of Chunār. Provenance unknown.

G 29.—Slab (ht. 1′ 9¼″; width 1′ 2¼″). On the front side we have in a sunken panel a four-armed figure of Vishṇu. His head and upper hands are broken off. His lower right hand holds a lotus (?) flower and lower left a conch (*śaṅkha*). The deity is adorned with a necklace, a long garland, armlets and bracelets. To his right, we notice a standing female and to his left, a standing male figure. The back of the slab shows a two-armed headless deity standing facing and wearing ornaments, and a short sword at his left side. On each side of the central figure stands a male figure. The style of carving is of the late Gupta period.

The material is Chunār sandstone. Provenance unknown.

G 30.—Slab (ht. 1′ 8″; width 1′ 1½″) representing Vishṇu riding his vehicle Garuḍa. His consort Śrī is seated on his left thigh. The head and arms of Vishṇu are missing with the exception of one of his left hands which holds the wheel (*chakra*).

The sculpture dates from the mediæval period and is made of reddish sandstone of Chunār. Provenance not known.

G 31.—Fragment (ht. 1′ 7″ ; width 2′ 2½″) of a sculpture showing the head and halo of an image of Vishṇu (?) The headdress consists of a high diadem decked with jewels. At either end of the halo is carved a male figure seated on a crocodile and above the one on the proper left side a pair of Gandharvas in flight. The sculpture dates from about the 6th century A. D.

The material is buff-coloured sandstone of Chunār. The provenance is not known.

G. 32.—Torso (ht. 2′ 1½″) of an image of Kuvēra or Vishṇu. The head, arms and feet are missing. The deity is decked with a necklace, a garland and an armlet. The style of the sculpture is of the late Gupta period.

The material is buff sandstone of Chunār. Provenance unknown.

G. 33.—Slab (ht. 2′ 2″ ; width 1′ 11″) representing a scene from the Rāmāyaṇa. In the upper part of the composition we notice a headless figure of Rāma seated on a rock or throne holding a bow in his left hand and a crossed band on his breast. He is attended by a male figure standing behind him which must be identified as Lakshmaṇa. In front of Rāma is a seated male figure behind which is evidently the monkey warrior Hanumant. The lower part of the sculpture is occupied by a party of monkey musicians. The scene probably represents the installation of Bibhīshaṇa by Rāma, as king of Laṅkā after the death of Rāvaṇa.

The sculpture presumably dates from the late Gupta period.

The material is buff-coloured sandstone. Provenance unkown.

G. 34.—An obelisk (ht. 2′ 9¾″ ; width 11½″) carved on all four faces with representations of some of the events of the Kṛishṇa legend. The top of the sculpture which was pyramidal is broken off so that only four complete panels remain on each face.

The scenes represented are as follows :—

Face 1.—From top downwards—

(*a*) A large figure holding a smaller one close to the trunk (?) of a tree. The interpretation is doubtful

(*b*) Male figure slaying a bull which he has overthrown. One of the hind legs of the animal is held in the left hand of the figure, while his right foot rests on the belly of the animal. This scene probably represents the destruction of the demon Dhēnuka by Kṛishṇa.

(c) This scene consists of an elephant standing to right with up-raised trunk while a male figure whose right foot rests on the animal's back is striking a blow with the up-raised right hand. This scene is doubtful.

(d) A cow standing to left under a tree.

Face 2.—

(a) Male figure with a long beard holding a child in the right arm. The child must be Krishṇa, but who the old man is is not certain. Is it Vasudēva ?

(b) The next lower scene on this side shows a female with a child sucking her left breast while the hands of the female are thrown up in anguish. This scene obviously represents the destruction of the demoness Pūtanā who wished to poison the child Krishṇa, but was herself destroyed by the deity.

(c) A male figure standing facing and holding what appears to be a large garland in each hand.

(d) Same scene as in the lowest panel of the 1st side.

Face 3.—From the top—

(a) Male figure sitting astride on a serpent. This scene evidently shows the destruction of the serpent Kāliya by the child Krishṇa.

(b) Male trampling with right foot a circular object which he seems to be splitting with a weapon in his left hand. His right hand is thrown up towards the head. This incident cannot be identified.

(c) Male figure trampling on a square object in the same way as in (b).

(d) A cow under a tree.

Face 4.—

(a) Similar to (a) on Face 1.

(b) Female clinging to what seems to be the trunk of a tree (?)

(c) Male figure standing facing with a snake-hood over his head. If the figure is Baladēva, the long object which it holds in its right hand, must be a plough (*hala*).

(d) A cow under a tree.

What purpose the sculpture served is not apparent. The Sārnāth Museum contains another fragment of a similar sculpture and there are two others in the Provincial Museum at Lucknow.

The sculpture dates from the mediæval period. It is made of buff-coloured sandstone. The provenance is unknown.

G. 35.—Upper portion (ht. 1′ 7″; width 6½″) of an obelisk similar to G. 34. The top is pyramidal. Three panels remain on each side, and they contain—

Face 1.—

(a) A pile of three balls.
(b) A female seated facing.
(c) A cart (?)

Face 2.—

(a) A pile of three balls as in (a) above.
(b) A female figure sleeping on her right side on a couch (?)
(c) Portion of a river (?)

Face 3.—

(a) As on the two faces described above.
(b) A fish disposed diagonally.
(c) Male figure standing holding a long garland or staff in each hand.

Face 4.—

(a) As on the other sides.
(b) A tortoise.
(c) Portion of a river (?)

The sculpture dates from the mediæval period and is made of red Chunār sandstone. Provenance unknown.

G. 36.—Image (ht. 3′ 9½″; width 2′) of the sun-god (Sūrya) seated cross-legged on a cushion. His head and four arms are broken off, but the position of the lotus flowers which the deity held in hands is clearly marked. Of the seven horses which draw his car, only three horses are represented on the pedestal. In the upper corners of the sculpture are Gandharvas carrying garlands. The sculpture dates from the mediæval period.

The material is buff-coloured sandstone. Provenance unknown.

G. 37.—Slab (ht. 1′ 11½″; width 1′ 9½″) showing a figure of the sun-god (Sūrya) seated cross-legged in a sunken panel. The deity holds, as usual, a full-blown lotus flower in each hand. The style points to the late mediæval period as the date of the sculpture.

The material is buff-coloured sandstone of Chunār. Provenance unknown.

G. 38.—Lintel (ht. 1′ 10¾″; width 8′ 3″) of a doorway. It is relieved by three projecting blocks, one in the middle and one at each end. The central projection represents the goddess Śrī seated cross-legged on a thick cushion. She has four arms. The lower left hand holds a water-pot (*kamaṇḍalu*), while the corresponding right hand is held down in the attitude of bestowing a gift (*varadamudrā*). Her upper hands grasp lotus flowers on which stand elephants pouring water over the goddess's head. The block at the proper right end contains a four-armed figure of the elephant-headed deity Gaṇēśa. He holds a battle-axe in his lower right hand and a bowl of sweets in the lower left. The upper hands hold flowers. In the third projection, we notice a four-armed figure of Sarasvatī, goddess of learning, standing, playing on a lute (*vīṇā*) which she holds between the lower right and upper left hands. The upper right hand has a closed bud and the lower left a manuscript (*pustaka*). The goddess's vehicle, the goose (*haṁsa*), is carved in the proper left lower corner.

The sunken panels between the projections just described contain the nine planets (*navagraha*) which are frequently portrayed on lintels of temples.[1] The symmetry of arrangement has been secured by the mason by placing the demon Kētu above Rāhu at the end of the proper left panel. Kētu, as the fable has it, has the coiled tail of the dragon while Rāhu is represented by the head and two arms of the monster, namely the portion which became immortal by the swallowing of nectar before the fact was detected by the sun and the moon when Vishṇu severed it from the trunk of the demon. The sun is the first figure in the proper right panel. He has only two arms and holds a full-blown lotus in each hand. His consort Chhāyā is seated between his feet with a water-pot in her left hand. The remaining six planets stand facing to the front, with water-pots in the left hands while their right hands are raised in the attitude of imparting security.

As the central projection contains a Vaishṇava deity, the lintel must have belonged to a temple of that denomination.

The sculpture is carved in mediæval style and is made of buff-coloured sandstone. Provenance unknown.

G. 39.—Fragment (ht. 1′ 5½″; width 2′ 11″) of a lintel which contained the nine planets (*navagraha*). Four figures now remain, of which the three from the proper right end must be identified as Vṛihaspati or Jupiter, Śukra or Venus and Śani or Saturn. The fourth figure, which consists of a head and two arms, is Rāhu.

We may suppose that the other demon Kētu, was represented at the other end of the lintel, which is missing.

The sculpture seems to be coeval with G. 38. It is made of buff-coloured sandstone, but it is not known where it was found.

G. 40.—Fragment (ht. 1′ 10¼″; width 1′ 1¼″) with rectangular niches surmounted with pyramidal roofs on two adjoining faces. In

[1] One such example is the beautiful lintel of the Black Pagoda at Kōnārak near Purī.

each of them is a four-armed male deity seated in Indian style on a cushion. His lower right hand rests on the knee in the attitude of imparting security, while the lower left holds a water-pot. The upper hands hold flower buds.

The sculpture dates from the mediæval period. The material is Chunār sandstone, and the find-place of the sculpture is unknown.

G. 41.—Slab (ht. 1′ 10½″; width 1′ 6½″) showing a figure standing in a devotional attitude in a niche surmounted with a spire. Mediæval. Chunār sandstone. Provenance unknown.

G. 42.—Slab (ht. 1′ 10″; width 1′ 4½″) showing a four-armed bearded figure seated cross-legged. The objects which he holds in his hands cannot be recognised. Mediæval. The sculpture was found in Benares.

G. 43.—Face-stone (ht. 8½″; width 1′ 6½″) from a mediæval Brahmanical shrine. There are four figures, of which the two in the proper left portion are seated. These are apparently Vishṇu and Śrī. Of the remaining two the one attended by a bull is Mahādêva while the one with a pointed beard must be Brahmā.

The sculpture is made of Chunār sandstone, but its provenance is not known.

G. 44.—Frieze (ht. 8¾″; width 1′ 6″) from a mediæval Brahmanical shrine. The sculpture shows three warriors. Two of them marching to the proper left have a sword and a shield and they are preceded by a fourth warrior who is riding on an elephant.

The material of the sculpture is Chunār sandstone of red colour. Provenance unknown.

G. 45.—Corner stone showing three monkeys, two of which are engaged in conversation, on one side and three mutilated ones on the adjoining face. Mediæval. Provenance unknown.

G. 46.—Pediment (ht. 1′ 8¼″; width 2′ 8½″) of a shrine, showing in an elaborate niche a Gandharva flying with a garland between his hands. The ends of the niche meet in a lion's head (*kīrttimukha*) and on each side of it is a crocodile with a long flowery tail. To judge from the style of execution we may assign the sculpture to the late Gupta period.

The material is buff-coloured sandstone. Provenance unknown.

G. 47.—Face-stone (ht. 1′ 10″) showing a mutilated four-armed deity seated in a niche capped with a pediment. Mediæval style. Provenance unknown.

G. 48.—Large slab (ht. 3′ 9″; width 3′ 5½″) bearing an image which is too much defaced to be identified. The stone must have been discovered at the Sārnāth site. On occasions of marriages in the neighbouring villages, the stone is worshipped by the bridegroom and the bride. The stone has hitherto stood to the north of the monastery excavated by Major Kittoe. It has now been transferred into the compound of the old sculpture shed.

G. 49.—Model[1] (ht. 4′ 4″; width 1′ 7½″) of a spire temple (*śikhara*) with a hollow niche at the bottom, cut out of a single block of sandstone. In a niche over the open side which represents the doorway, is carved a miniature seated figure of Śrī holding a full-blown lotus in her left hand. The shrine must therefore be a Vaishṇava one. On the remaining three sides, keeping the shrine to our right we have:

Face 1.—Standing figure of the sun-god (*Sūrya*) holding a full-blown lotus in each hand.

Face 2.—A four-armed standing figure of Gaṇēśa holding a goad (?) and a flower in the upper hands. His right elbow rests on an inverted battle-axe while the fourth hand holds a bowl of sweets. To the proper right of the deity is a standing figure of Chāmuṇḍā holding a skull-mace in her left hand, while her vehicle (which cannot be recognized) crouches near her left foot. On the other side of Gaṇapati we notice a standing figure of Bhairava with his vehicle, the dog, at his right side.

Face 3.—In the niche in the centre is a four-armed goddess standing. Her emblems are broken off. To the proper left of the goddess is a male standing figure with another figure represented as rising from the ground.

The shrine dates from the mediæval period. It was formerly deposited in the Queen's College, Benares, and must have been found somewhere in the city.

G. 50.[2]—Model (ht. 4′ 9″; width 1′ 6¼″) of a Brahmanical shrine similar to G. 49. The figure in the niche over the doorway which would have supplied a clue to the sect to which the shrine belonged, is broken. On the outside of the shrine, keeping it to our right, we have:

Face 1.—A standing figure of Gaṇēśa.

Face 2.—A standing figure of the sun-god (*Sūrya*) holding a lotus flower in each hand.

Face 3.—A four-armed standing goddess, holding a flower (?) in each upper hand, and a water-pot in the lower left hand, while the fourth is stretched down in the gift-bestowing attitude. The shrine was formerly preserved in the Queen's College at Benares.

---

[1] This shrine is standing outside the compound wall of the shed at the south-east corner.

[2] This shrine is placed outside the south-west corner of the compound wall of the old sculpture shed.

G. 51.—Model [1] (ht. 4′ 2″; width 2′ 2″) of a Brahmanical spire temple. The finial is missing. Over the open side is a frieze consisting of the eight divine mothers (*ashṭa-mātaraḥ*) and a dancing figure of Gaṇapati. Of the goddesses, the one at the proper right end is Sarasvatī, the goddess of learning, playing on a lute. The sixth goddess from this end is Vārāhī, recognized by her boar's head and the eighth Chāmuṇḍā who grasps a skull-mace in her left arm and a skull bowl in the right. The emblems of the remaining goddesses are worn. Above this frieze is a seated male figure holding a mace-like object on the knees. On the other sides, keeping the shrine to his right, the spectator has:

Face 1.—A figure of Gaṇēśa engaged in a dance. He holds a flower in his upper right hand and a mace (*gadā*) in the corresponding left hand. In the lower right hand he has a battle-axe and in the lower left a bowl of sweets.

Face 2.—In the niche in the centre, we notice a four-armed standing figure of Durgā, with her vehicle, the lion, crouching near her left foot. Her upper right hand holds a flower on which is placed a *liṅga* and *yōni*. The flower in her upper left hand bears a figure of Gaṇēśa. The figures on the proper right and left of the niche are presumably Śiva and Vishṇu respectively.

Face 3.—The niche in the centre contains a standing figure of the sun-god who holds a lotus in each hand. The figure to the proper right of the deity is Brahmā if we may judge from his long beard; the figure on the other side may have been Vishṇu. On the proper right side of the niche we notice a figure of Indra with a thunderbolt (*vajra*) in his left hand and his elephant (Airāvata) near his left foot. The figure on the other side of the niche shows Mahādēva standing holding a trident (*triśūla*) in his right hand with his vehicle, the bull, at his right side.

The shrine was formerly deposited in the Queen's College, Benares.

G. 52.—Model [2] (ht. 4′ 11″; width 1′ 10″) of a Brahmanical spire temple. The figure in the niche over the doorway resembles the one on the corresponding side of G. 51. On the remaining three sides are represented, Gaṇēśa, the sun-god (Sūrya) and a third deity which cannot be identified.

The shrine came from the Queen's College at Benares.

---

[1] This shrine stands outside the north-west corner of the compound wall.

[2] This shrine is placed outside the north-east corner of the compound wall of the old sculpture shed.

*G. 53.—Model (ht. 1′ 11″; width 1′ 2″) of a Brahmanical shrine. The lintel of the doorway has the inscription *Oṁ Balēśvaraḥ* in Nāgarī characters. On each jamb is a door-keeper. On the remaining three sides we have, keeping the shrine to the right:

Face 1.—A four-armed figure of Gaṇēśa seated, holding a flower and an axe in the upper hands. The lower right hand is laid in the gift-bestowing attitude, while the lower left holds a bowl of sweets.

Face 2.—A four-armed goddess seated cross-legged on a throne supported on a pair of lions.

Face 3.—A four-armed goddess seated in Indian style on a human corpse. The figure must therefore be one of Chāmuṇḍā.

The shrine came from the Queen's College at Benares.

G. 54.—Model (ht. 1′ 11″; width 1′ 1″) of a Brahmanical shrine somewhat later than G. 53. There is no figure sculpture on the exterior. The sculpture was formerly preserved in the Queen's College at Benares.

G. 55.—Model (ht. 3′ 2″; width 1′ 1½″) of a Brahmanical shrine. The lintel of the doorway has a miniature figure of Gaṇēśa. On the other three sides the spectator sees:

Face 1.—Śiva seated on a couch with Pārvatī on his left thigh.

Face 2.—A standing figure of the sun-god (Sūrya) holding a lotus in each hand, with attendants.

Face 3.—Four-armed Vishṇu standing holding his usual emblems.

The shrine was formerly preserved in the Queen's College at Benares.

G. 56.—Model (ht. 2′ 11½″; width 11½″) of a Brahmanical shrine. Only two of the faces have figures of deities which are, however, so much worn that they cannot be identified.

The sculpture was formerly preserved in the Queen's College at Benares.

G. 57-59.—Three slabs, averaging 3′ 2″ to 3′ 4″ in height; carved each with a figure of an elephant running grasping a male human figure with his trunk.

They date from the late mediæval period. The sculptures came from the Queen's College at Benares.

G. 60.—Unfinished sculpture (ht. 1′ 7″; width 1′) showing Vishṇu and Śrī standing side by side. The sculpture is of modern date. Provenance unknown.

Jaina sculptures.

G. 61.—A *sarvatōbhadrikā* stone (ht. 2′ 10¼″; width 1′ 1″) bearing:

Face 1.—A standing headless nude figure of the Jaina patriarch Mahāvīra, with another *jina* seated in meditation on either side. His cognisance, the lion, is carved on the pedestal.

Face 2.—A standing nude figure of Ādinātha recognized by his cognisance, the bull, on the pedestal.

Face 3.—A standing nude image of Śāntinātha with his emblem, the antelope (*Mṛiga*), on the pedestal.

Face 4.—A standing nude Jaina saint. On the pedestal we notice a wheel between a pair of elephants. The saint may be Ajitanātha.

The sculpture was formerly deposited in the Queen's College at Benares.

G. 62.—Image (ht. 1′ 3¼″ ; width 1′ 1″) of the Jaina saint Śrī Aṁśanātha standing naked, with an attendant on either side. The head of the saint is broken off. There is a *śrīvatsa* mark on his breast. The cognisance, the rhinoceros (*khaḍgin*), is indicated on the pedestal. The sculpture dates from the Gupta period.

It was formerly preserved in the Queen's College at Benares.

G. 63.—Image (ht. 4′ 8½″ ; width 2′ 1½″) of a Jaina saint seated in meditation. On either side of the sage we notice a female fly-whisk-bearer and on either side of his halo a celestial (*dēva*) in flight. The base has carved on it a wheel with a lion couchant on either side, and exterior to them Jaina saints in meditation. Late Gupta style. The material is buff-coloured sandstone of Chunār. The provenance is not known. The sculpture was formerly preserved in the Queen's College, Benares. It is now exhibited in the large room in the east wing of the new Museum building.

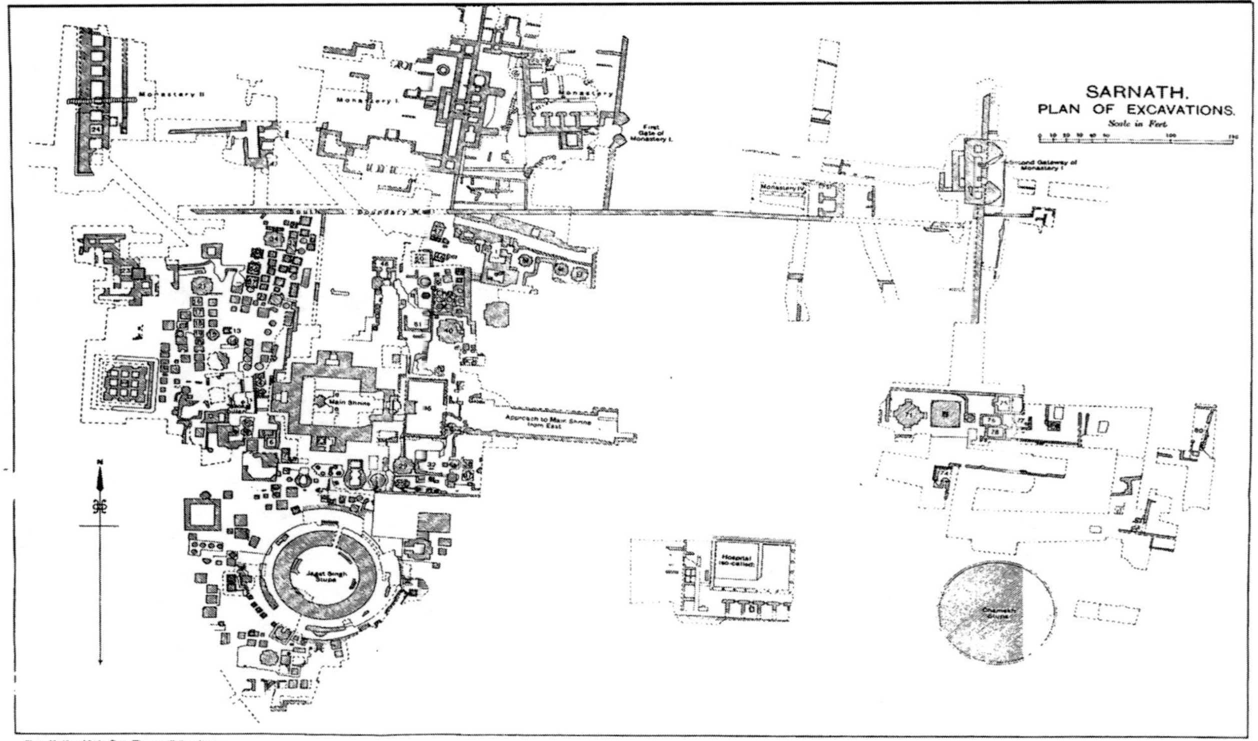

Photo.-Mechl. and Litho. Dept., Thomason College, Roorkee.

Zinco, September, 1913.—No. 884,1000

PLATE II.

Photo,-Mechl Dept., Thomason College, Roorkee.

THE SARNATH MUSEUM.

PLATE III.

Photo.-Mechl Dept., Thomason College, Roorkee.

VIEW OF EXCAVATIONS, 1907.

Photo.-Mechl Dept., Thomason College, Roorkee.

No. A-1 ; ht. 7'.

LION CAPITAL OF ASOKA.

(c. 250 B. C.)

PLATE V.

Photo,-Mechl. Deps., Thomason College, Roorkee.

No. D (*g*) 4 ; ht. 1′ 1½″.

CAPITAL.

Photo.-Mechl. Dept., Thomason College, Roorkee.

Nos. D. (*a*) 1, 6, 7, 11 ; ht. 4′2″ to 4′5″.

RAILING PILLARS.

Photo.-Mechl. Dept., Thomason College, Roorkee.

No. B (a) 1 ; ht. 9'6".
BODHISATTVA STATUE OF THE REIGN OF KANISHKA.

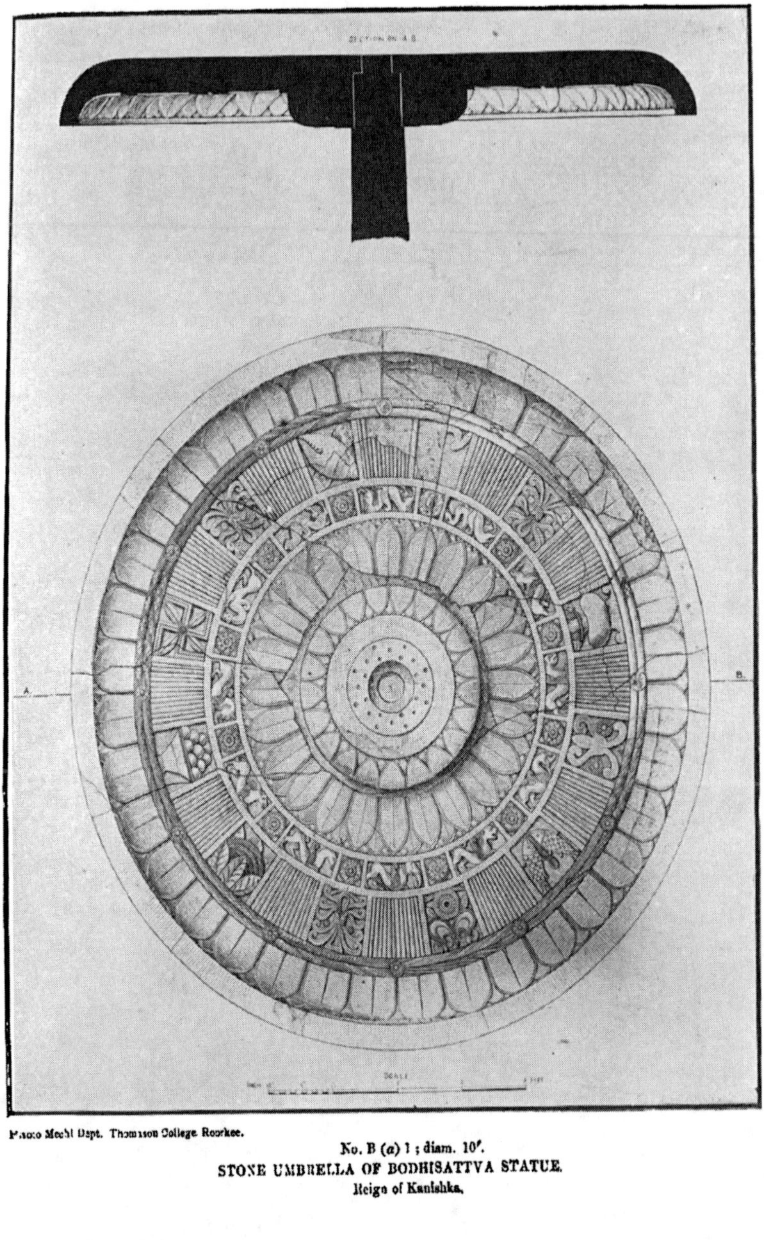

Photo Mechl Dept. Thomason College Roorkee.

No. B (*a*) 1 ; diam. 10′.

STONE UMBRELLA OF BODHISATTVA STATUE.

Reign of Kanishka.

Photo.-Mechl. Depts., Thomason College, Roorkee.

No. B (*b*) 175 ; ht. 5'1".

BUDDHA CALLING THE EARTH TO WITNESS.

Photo.-Mechl. Dept., Thomason College, Roorkee.

No. B (b) 181 ; ht. 5'3".

BUDDHA PREACHING HIS FIRST SERMON.

Gupta period.

Photo.-Mechl. Depts., Thomason College, Roorkee.

No. B (c) 1 ; ht. 1′7¼″.

PEDESTAL WITH SANSKRIT INSCRIPTION RECORDING RESTORATION OF BUILDINGS IN A. D. 1026.

Photo.-Mechl. Dept., Thomason College, Roorkee.

(a) No. B (c) 2 ; ht. 3'8".

BUDDHA CALLING THE EARTH TO WITNESS.

Early mediæval period.

(b) No. B (d) 8 ; ht. 3'11½".

THE BODHISATTVA AVALOKITESVARA.

Early mediæval period.

Photo.-Mechl. Dept., Thomason College, Roorkee

(a) No. B (*f*) 2 ; ht. 4'9".
THE GODDESS TARA.
Late mediæval period.

(b) No. B (*d*) 1 ; ht. 4'6".
AVALOKITESVARA.
Gupta period

(c) No. B (*d*) 6 ; ht. 4'.
MANJUSRI (?).
(c. 7th century A. D.)

Photo.-Mechl. Dept., Thomason College, Roorkee.

(a) No. B (d) 3 ; ht. 3′10½″.
AVALOKITESVARA (?).
Gupta period.

(b) No. B (e) 6 ; ht. 1′6″.
UNIDENTIFIED GROUP.
Late mediæval period.

Photo.-Mechl. Dept., Thomason College, Roorkee.

(a) No. B (*e*) 1 ; ht. 2′2½″.

AMBHALA THE GOD OF RICHES AND VASUDHARA THE GODDESS OF PLENTY.

(11th century A.D.)

(b) No. B (*f*) 19 ; ht. 2′1″.

VASUDHARA THE GODDESS OF PLENTY.

Late mediæval period.

PLATE XVI.

Photo.-Mechl. Deps., Thomason College, Roorkee.

No. B (*f*) 4 ; ht. 2′ 7½″.

UNIDENTIFIED FEMALE FIGURE.

Late mediæval period.

Photo.-Mechl. Dept., Thomason College, Roorkee.

(a) No. B (*f*) 7 ; ht. 1′10″.
TARA.
Late mediæval period

(b) No. B (*f*) 23 ; ht 1′10″
MARICHI.
Late mediæval period.

Photo.-Mechl. Dept., Thomason College, Roorkee.

No. B (A) 1; ht. 12' 1¼".
SIVA DESTROYING A DEMON.
Late mediæval period.

PLATE XIX.

Photo.-Mechl. Depe., Thomason College, Roorkee.

(a) No. C (a) 1 ; ht. 4′5″.
THE FOUR GREAT SCENES :
(a). NATIVITY ; (b). ENLIGHTENMENT ;
(c). FIRST SERMON ; (d). NIRVANA.
Gupta period.

(b) No. C (a) 3 ; ht. 3′1″.
THE EIGHT GREAT SCENES :
(a). NATIVITY ; (b). ENLIGHTENMENT ; (c). OFFERING OF THE MONKEY ;
(d). SUBMISSION OF THE ELEPHANT ; (e). DESCENT FROM HEAVEN ;
(f). GREAT MIRACLE ; (g). FIRST SERMON ; (h). NIRVANA.
Gupta period.

Photo.-Mechl. Dept., Thomason College, Roorkee.

No. C (a) 2 ; ht. 3′2″.

SCENES OF BUDDHA'S LIFE: (a). CONCEPTION AND NATIVITY; (b). GREAT RENUNCIATION; (c). ENLIGHTENMENT; (d). FIRST SERMON.

Gupta period.

Photo.-Mechl. Deps., Thomason College, Roorkee.

No. C (a) 6 ; ht. 3′2¼″.
THE GREAT MIRACLE OF SRAVASTI.
Gupta period.

Photo.-Mechl. Dept., Thomason College, Roorkee.

Nos. C (*b*) 2 (ht. 2′11″) and C (*b*) 1 (ht. 2′11″).
LEOGRYPHS WITH SWORDSMEN.
Gupta period.

PLATE XXIII.

(a) No. D (*d*) 1 ; length 16′.

LINTEL WITH SCENES OF THE KSHANTIVADI-JATAKA.

Gupta period

Photo.-Mechl. Dept., Thomason College, Roorkee.

(b) No. C (*b*) 9 ; ht. 1′6″.

FRAGMENT OF LINTEL WITH BAS-RELIEF REPRESENTING THE STUPA OF RAMAGRAMA.

Photo.-Mechl. Dept., Thomason College, Roorkee.

No. D (*d*) 1 ; detail of panel 1.

JAMBHALA THE GOD OF RICHES.

Photo.-Mechl. Dept., Thomason College, Roorkee.

No. D (*d*) 1 ; detail of panel 2.

APOTHEOSIS OF THE BODHISATTVA KSHANTIVADIN.

Photo.-Mechl. Dept., Thomason College, Roorkee.

No, D (*d*) 1 ; detail of panel 3.

THE DANCING GIRLS OF THE KING OF BENARES.

Photo.-Mechl. Dept., Thomason College, Roorkee.

No. D (*d*) 1 ; detail of panel 4.
THE DANCING GIRLS OF THE KING OF BENARES.

PLATE XXVIII.

Photo-Mechl. Dept., Thomason College, Roorkee.

No. D (*d*) 1 ; detail of panel 5.

KSHANTIVADIN MUTILATED BY THE KING OF BENARES.

PLATE XXIX.

Photo.-Mechl. Dept., Thomason College, Roorkee.

No. D (*d*) 1 ; detail of panel 6.

JAMBHALA THE GOD OF RICHES.